MW01136795

THE SAUCERIAN

THE SAUCERIAN

**UFOs, Men in Black, and the
Unbelievable Life of Gray Barker**

GABRIEL MCKEE

The MIT Press
Cambridge, Massachusetts
London, England

The MIT Press
Massachusetts Institute of Technology
77 Massachusetts Avenue, Cambridge, MA 02139
mitpress.mit.edu

The MIT Press would like to thank the anonymous peer reviewers who provided comments on drafts of this book. The generous work of academic experts is essential for establishing the authority and quality of our publications. We acknowledge with gratitude the contributions of these otherwise uncredited readers.

This book was set in Adobe Garamond Pro by Jen Jackowitz. Printed and bound in the United States of America.

Library of Congress Cataloging-in-Publication Data

Names: Mckee, Gabriel, 1979- author.
Title: The Saucerian : UFOs, men in black, and the the unbelievable life of Gray Barker /
    Gabriel Mckee.
Description: Cambridge, Massachusetts ; London, England : The MIT Press,
    [2025] | Includes bibliographical references and index.
Identifiers: LCCN 2024020067 (print) | LCCN 2024020068 (ebook) | ISBN
    9780262049542 (hardcover) | ISBN 9780262382007 (epub) | ISBN
    9780262382014 (pdf)
Subjects: LCSH: Barker, Gray. | Ufologists—United States—Biography. |
    Unidentified flying objects—Research—United States.
Classification: LCC TL789.85.B34 M44 2025 (print) | LCC TL789.85.B34
    (ebook) | DDC 001.942092 [B]—dc23/eng/20241216
LC record available at https://lccn.loc.gov/2024020067
LC ebook record available at https://lccn.loc.gov/2024020068

10 9 8 7 6 5 4 3 2 1

EU product safety and compliance information contact is: mitp-eu-gpsr@mit.edu

Dedicated
to all of Earth's people
Adonai vasu borragus

In sponsoring a book like this, Mr. Barker, you tend to make a side show act or a cheap movie script out of UFO research, performing a distinct disservice to serious and competent investigators of the subject. . . . No one with a mental age over 15 could swallow such guff as fact.
—George Massinger, in *Bender Mystery Confirmed*

CONTENTS

INTRODUCTION: THE UNIDENTIFIED

Against a grainy, green-gray background the oblong, silvery object seems to hang motionless. The hands of the man recording its silent passage shake, causing it to shudder up and down in the frame. He sputters with confusion: "What the hell is that?" Further from his camera's microphone, we hear two onlookers comment. "It's almost, like, transparent," one remarks. Another replies, in a tone that sounds almost bored by the event that has flabbergasted her companions, "Yeah, that's definitely a UFO."[1]

This offhand comment, captured in a grainy clip recorded in San Diego, California, in December 2015, demonstrates the central paradox of unidentified flying objects (UFOs) in American culture. The nature of an unidentified object is, by definition, unknown to the speaker. The term *UFO* means to create a semantic space for discussing things that are not understood. Their unidentified nature, in fact, is the most important thing about them.

And this is what makes *That's definitely a UFO* such a curious statement. The term *UFO* was created to point to a receding referent, but the culture surrounding that term has imbued it with omnipresence. Unidentified flying objects may be incomprehensible, but UFOs have become mundane. The phrase "That's definitely a UFO" in the San Diego video is a positive identification, establishing that the speaker *knows what that is*. A corollary is the phrase, commonly uttered by a witness of an unusual object responding to a debunker's explanation that seems too simple, too obvious, so believable as to be unbelievable: "I know what I saw."[2] The unidentified nature of an unidentified flying object means that, tautologically, the percipient *doesn't* know what they saw. The UFO comes to exist in the space between perception and understanding. Author Michael Daley wonders: "What causes a flash of light in the sky to become a flying saucer? Our fear made hallucination? Visionary longing or the random spasms of neurons that retain the residue of a late-night movie? Or is the flying saucer just a flying saucer, a hunk of metal, interstellar bicarbonate, whipping through the sky, its designs unknown to us below? What, in fact, has more sprawling implications?"[3] An object in the sky may be unidentified, but the process of identification is an interior one, akin to a mystical experience, and nonfalsifiable as such.[4] The implied meaning of "I know what I saw" is that I saw something inexplicable, ineffable, undebunkable. But "That's definitely a UFO" goes even further. Combined with the speaker's jaded tone of voice, it makes the perceived object seem familiar, even passé. As individuals, we may see things in the sky that we can't identify, comprehend, or explain. But as a culture, we know a UFO when we see it.[5]

This is a book about some of the ways in which we got to the paradoxical point where the referent of the term *UFO* has become commonplace. Its central character is a man who simultaneously strove to preserve the mystery surrounding this ungraspable subject and to package and commodify it for an audience that he cultivated and nurtured. Ultimately, its subject is not the unidentified objects themselves, but the traces they leave behind, in patterns of ink upon paper. It is a story about stories—or, more importantly, the ways in which stories are recorded, shared, distributed, and preserved.

At its center is Gray Barker, the editor and publisher of one of the first saucerzines—*The Saucerian*, launched in 1952. Following this, Barker authored his best-known work, *They Knew Too Much about Flying Saucers*, and published numerous books under the Saucerian Books imprint for decades thereafter. Over a thirty-year career, he was central in the development of ufological mysteries like the Men in Black, the Philadelphia Experiment, and the Mothman, and his publishing firm established itself as the home for the most outré saucer and paranormal narratives of the postwar era. Science fiction author Jack Womack described him as "a complex figure with wild talents for both hoaxing and propagandizing."[6] Barker inhabited the fringes of the ufological world—a world in which the fringe has a stubborn habit of migrating to the center. The works he wrote, published, and marketed played a key part in the development of the UFO macronarrative. And his own life—including his origins in rural West Virginia, his work in motion-picture promotion, and his homosexuality—impacted his writing and publishing in ways that reverberated throughout the subculture he made his home.

HOW DOES A UFO BECOME A NARRATIVE?

For the purposes of this work, the term "UFO" does not refer to things seen in the sky, be they physical or paraphysical objects, alien or interdimensional beings, experimental aircraft, misperceived natural phenomena, or hallucinations. The subjects of perception, the *experiential* UFOs, are beyond the scope of this book. Numerous individuals have seen something inexplicable in the sky, have undergone a mysterious experience, or believe that they have communicated with beings they do not understand, but we do not have direct access to that experience. Even if we have had individual, mysterious experiences of our own, we have no direct access to the comparable experiences of others. For the vast majority of us, flying saucers exist, first and foremost, as stories. Even in cases of photographic or video evidence of an unusual object, the images must be contextualized by a narrative. This mass of narratives constitutes the true UFO phenomenon. Barring a UFO experience of our own, all we have are individual narratives—the brief and the epic, the vague and the distinct, the extraordinary and the banal. This means that the flying saucer mystery, like all paranormal phenomena, is a *literary* phenomenon.[7]

Once experienced, the UFO encounter becomes a narrative—first an internal one for the witness, then an external one once communicated.[8] From here, the narrative is subject to a series of transformations that can be conceived in biological terms as ongoing processes of mutation, symbiotic fusion, and evolution.[9] But in using these metaphors, it is important to remember that these narratives do not develop via natural selection. At every stage, conscious agents with their own agendas—experiencers, investigators, authors, and skeptics—shape and engineer these mutations. These stories are disseminated as folklore, their impact multiplied through print and electronic media.[10]

In his book *Knowledge and the Production of Nonknowledge*, Mark Featherstone explores the process of narrative change in writing about UFOs. According to Featherstone, UFO narratives exist in a state of dialectical tension between fact and fiction, and "when this undecidability is lost, the mythology implodes."[11] The UFO community holds certain narratives to be authentic, but as the available facts and attitudes toward them shift, the reigning narratives periodically fall out of legitimacy. In Featherstone's conception, this moment of implosion disrupts the equilibrium in the dialectical tension between "fact" and "fiction," tilting a narrative toward fictionality. Key events, like the definitive debunking of a widely discussed close encounter or the release of a major government report casting doubt on the reality of UFO experiences, can function—to apply a biological metaphor—like mass extinction events. Individual narratives about UFOs, unmoored from their place in a sustaining story, seek a new narrative structure, encouraging mutation and ultimately the rise of a new dominant framing.

In this book I will use the following functional terminology of narrative, intended for the interdisciplinary study of UFOs as a cultural phenomenon:

Micronarrative: An individual witness's report of an event, often vague or fragmentary; analogous to the folkloristic terms *memorate* and *fabulate*.[12]

Narrative: A micronarrative that has been shaped by an interpreter (who may or may not be the percipient or experiencer) and that is more likely to include theorization about the causes or meanings of the experience; analogous to the folkloristic term *legend* or *tale*, and to the work Thomas Bullard ascribes to the UFO field investigator.[13]

Metanarrative: An interpretive layer that combines multiple paranormal narratives, typically with a proposed explanation or an emphasized mystery; analogous to Featherstone's "submyth." The key feature of a metanarrative is its linking together of different narratives in an imposed interpretive framework.[14]

Macronarrative: The overall universe of ufological and paranormal metanarratives constitutes a realm of experience, interpretation, and expression that may be termed a *macronarrative.*

This narrative typology, though novel, seeks to encompass the process through which individual experiences become parts of larger stories about the relationships between the realms of earth and heaven, individual and state, matter and spirit.[15] Key analyses of UFO stories can be considered using this terminology—for example, Charles Ziegler, Benson Saler, and Charles Moore's *UFO Crash at Roswell* analyzes the eponymous UFO case, examining in depth a progression that may be put in terms of micronarrative (the initial, fragmentary report of unusual debris found on a ranch in New Mexico) to narrative (brief news reports of a captured flying saucer) to metanarrative (the various stages of the "crashed saucer" legend that developed decades after the initial event).[16] This typology of UFO stories facilitates an understanding of the spread, variation, and reinterpretation of paranormal narrative.

BIBLIOGRAPHY, BOOK HISTORY, AND THE UFO

In the period that is the focus of the present work (1947–1984), UFO narratives were chiefly propagated through print media.[17] For many students of the UFO macronarrative, books are the primary means through which they experience and learn about their subject of study, and even for those who have experienced a sighting, reading facilitates interpretation and reinforcement of that experience. Thus UFOs, in addition to being a literary phenomenon, are also *bibliographically mediated.*[18] A reader arrives at an understanding of the nature of the UFO through a process of reading about it, whether that be on a website or in a hardcover book, a cheap paperback, or a mimeographed zine.[19] These stories are then shared again, both orally and in print, changing and reentering the printed record in what Ziegler calls "punctuated transmission."[20] Folklorist William Dewan notes that "an examination of how [UFO] narratives are performed, retold, disseminated, and circulated within the community is essential."[21] This ultimately means that the study of UFOs as a cultural phenomenon must encompass the study of books and their reception, and the tools most appropriate to this task are bibliography and book history.[22] To understand how the UFO macronarrative has grown and influenced our culture, we should first examine the only physical evidence that we have of UFO experiences: the books that describe, contextualize, and speculate about those experiences.

Both book history and bibliography have largely concerned themselves with the late Renaissance and early modern periods, eras in which the new technology of printing wrought enormous cultural change.[23] But the tools developed to explore the nascent period of print are just as applicable to later periods and further innovations in print technology. The same processes initiated by early printing presses are recapitulated by later developments. But compared to the revolutionary changes catalyzed by the first printing presses of the fifteenth century, the cultural impact of office copying technology in the twentieth century is remarkably understudied.[24] The series of technological developments, beginning with hectographic stencil printing in the late nineteenth century and culminating with electrostatic photocopying in the postwar period and inkjet printing in the 1980s, represent an increasing democratization of print culture.

These print technologies did not merely facilitate new modes of expression; they guided and shaped those forms and opened new avenues for subcultural communication and connection. The flying saucer subculture that emerged in the early 1950s, which centered on small-circulation newsletters issued by groups like the Aerial Phenomena Research Organization (APRO) and the International Flying Saucer Bureau (IFSB), is a prime example of this. Ufological bibliographer Tom Lind calls these periodicals "the backbone of UFO literature," the primary source for information about sightings, theories, and analysis.[25] The overwhelming majority of UFO periodicals from the first twenty years of flying saucer history could have been produced only using the copying technology developed in the early and mid-twentieth century.

In looking at these publications, it is important to pay close attention not only to the texts themselves but also to the various elements relating to their physical embodiment, marketing, and reception. Gérard Genette names these features *paratexts*: "that which enables a text to become a book and to be offered as such to its readers."[26] Paratext includes both the *peritext*—the external presentation of a book, including its front matter, title page, cover blurbs, and so on—and the *epitext*, or material outside the physical book that relates to its publication, including catalog listings, advertising leaflets, reviews, and author interviews. This paratextual information, particularly the text used to advertise material to its audience, is paramount in occult-knowledge distribution.[27] Alongside these paratextual elements it is essential to consider the related but distinct category of elements that Jerome McGann calls the "bibliographic code": the physical aspects of a text's embodiment, including typeface, paper stock, binding, and other aspects that inform the reader about the nature of the work as much as linguistic paratext does.[28] A work published as a jacketed hardcover will have a different impact than the same text issued as an unbound, smudgy tabloid. This book will explore paratexts and bibliographical information as much, and in some cases even more than, texts themselves, in the interest of exploring their readers' experience.

In his 2020 book *Intimate Alien*, David Halperin notes that, though Barker has been the subject of two documentary films (Ralph Coon's *Whispers from Space* and Bob Wilkinson's *Shades of Gray*), "no one has attempted a biography" of him.[29] This work seeks to redress that absence, though it cannot pretend to be comprehensive. I have approached Barker and his press primarily through the avenues of analytical bibliography (the physical details of books he wrote and published), published material by and about him, and archival records, particularly those in the Gray Barker UFO Collection at the Clarksburg-Harrison Public Library. I have included many of the details of Barker's personal life that these sources have illuminated, but my focus on Barker's publishing career necessitates overlooking many aspects of his personal life that a traditional biography might explore more exhaustively. I encourage readers to keep in mind the primary focus of the work at hand—exploring Barker's role in and impact on the production, distribution, and consumption of the stigmatized knowledge associated with UFOs and the paranormal—and forgive the relatively short shrift that other areas of his life may receive in what follows.[30]

I have striven to provide detailed citations wherever possible, particularly given the tendency of popular works on the paranormal to fail to cite the sources they discuss, or to cite only other secondary works in what Michael Barkun calls a system of "reciprocal citation."[31] Throughout the text, I have made an effort to avoid anachronistic terminology—for example, I use the term *flying saucer* when discussing time periods when this term was dominant, and introduce the term "UFO" later. This bibliographical and historicizing approach is essential to understanding how stories and ideas about unusual occurrences have influenced culture.

1 "HECKLING THE PERFORMER IN DERISION": GRAY BARKER BEFORE FLYING SAUCERS

The Blue Ridge Mountains form a natural barrier between eastern Virginia and the mountainous territory beyond. Though European colonists moved rapidly westward following the foundation of Jamestown in 1607, the land between the Blue Ridge Mountains and the Ohio River remained a frontier well into the eighteenth century, which saw periodic bloody conflict between colonizers and Indigenous people. This period culminated in Lord Dunmore's War, in which John Murry, Earl of Dunmore, ordered the destruction of Shawnee towns in the Ohio Valley; the Shawnee chief Cornstalk fought against Dunmore's colonists at the Battle of Point Pleasant in 1774. Three years later, while Cornstalk was on a diplomatic visit to Fort Randolph at Point Pleasant, American soldiers lynched him. In the following decades, settlers from the east continued to push out and massacre the Shawnee and Delaware peoples, a process finalized by the Indian Removal Act of 1830.[1]

Among the settlers claiming territory in western Virginia in the late eighteenth and early nineteenth century was Joseph Barker, Jr., born in Massachusetts in 1744. By the 1840s some of Barker's descendants had settled in Braxton County, in the geographic center of the region that would become, in the middle of the Civil War, the state of West Virginia.[2] In Braxton, like in much of rural West Virginia, narrow mountain roads follow the twisting pathways of shallow creek beds, running in narrow valleys between sharp hilltops covered with thick trees. Sutton, the county seat, sits on the Elk River, which flows into the Kanawaha River at Charleston. But most of the creeks that form in the hills north of the town flow the opposite direction, forming the headwaters of the Little Kanawaha, which joins the Ohio River some ninety miles to the northwest at Parkersburg. Though West Virginia is known for coal mining, coal is scarce in the hills of Braxton County, the economy of which relies primarily on agriculture. Small houses and the occasional larger barn dot the edges of creeks, and the hillside "hollers" host patches of corn, chicken coops, and small cow pastures. One such creek, starting five miles due north of Sutton, is Perkins Fork, which winds through a narrow valley before passing the cluster of a dozen or so houses that constitute the unincorporated town of Riffle.

Among the residents of Riffle in the 1920s were George E. and Rosa L. Barker. Rosa was a member of the Frame family, which lent its name to Frametown, a few miles down the Elk River from Sutton.[3] George's father, Isaac Barker, and Rosa's, Lemuel Morgan Frame, had both fought for the Confederacy in the Civil War. George and Rosa married in 1897, and by 1920 lived on a small farm in Riffle with their seven children: Lela (born 1900), Walter (1903), Blanche (1908), Herman (1911), Marie (1913), Henry (1918), and Edyth (1920).[4] A double tragedy struck the family in 1922: first Marie's appendix ruptured, and she succumbed to the resulting peritonitis on September 12, at the age of nine.[5] Less than two months later, on November 8, the second-youngest Barker child, Henry Graceland Barker, died of croup.[6] He was four years old. Three years later, on May 2, 1925, one more child was born to George and Rosa Barker. Perhaps in honor of Henry—whose middle name is listed as Grayson in some sources—they named their eighth and final child Gray Roscoe Barker.[7]

The farms in the vicinity of Riffle were primarily dairy and chicken farms, and Barker described his family's home there as isolated and remote.[8] Sometime in the 1930s the Barkers relocated a few miles north to the town of Exchange, to a farmhouse about a mile from the general store and post office, where the Elk River Railroad train arrived daily to deliver mail and pick up cans of cream from area farms.[9] Barker later described himself as a fearful child: "Afraid to climb hills particularly. Afraid to ride horses (and lived on a farm); afraid of railroad trains; afraid of explosions like firecrackers and gunshots . . . So you can see I led a very frustrated childhood."[10] Despite Barker's fearfulness, hints of his early love of the outdoors appear in a short

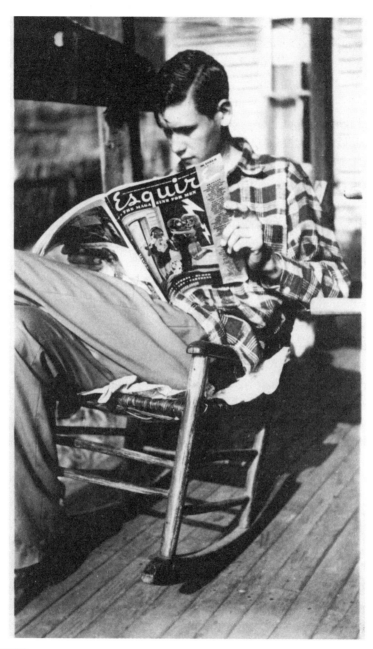

Figure 1.1
Gray Barker reading *Esquire*, ca. August 1943. Gray Barker UFO Collection, Clarksburg-Harrison Public Library/Courtesy of the Gray Barker Estate.

1954 prose piece in which he relates sentimentally to an experience of the Mountain State: "A smell of the wood fire, a feel of the hill-locked mountaineer. You cautiously tread across a frozen brook, on the way to church, or walk, as a child, along the roads of spring; and though the mud may squash between your toes, you recapture a half-remembered thrill."[11] He attended Perkins Fork School, a one-room schoolhouse near Riffle, where he was the only child in his grade.[12] On his second-grade report card, issued in spring 1933, teacher Marmel Brown notes that the school is allowing him to skip directly to the fourth grade, but adds a word of caution: "Does splendid work but absent too much."[13]

Barker later recounted that his strongest memories of childhood involved ghost stories and superstitions: "I remember an Edison Phonograph record that had a ghost at the end of it which always scared me when they played it. I remember crying about something one night and the Devil coming up to the door and knocking—somebody dressed up like the Devil, I suppose, but to me at that time it was Old Billy Bit the Scissors himself."[14] His family members also reported unusual experiences, including a time when his aunt saw the devil: "When she was in pasturefield at lonely place, suddenly a big spotted Devil rose right up out of the ground. She was, of course, quite frightened, but decided to pray. Whereupon the Devil sank back into the ground and she walked right over the place where he'd been standing, shouting ecstatically."[15] Prior to Barker's birth, an even stranger event had occurred in the family home: "A woman working at the house for the people who owned the farm heard a growling and carrying on, and a big black wooly thing like a bear started rolling across the floor, then into the bedroom, and under the bed. I don't know exactly, having forgotten, how the story ends, but I think that she got frightened and ran about that time without investigating the bedroom."[16] Barker's mother told him a story of a ghostly apparition—a black-haired woman dressed in white—that she encountered in their home a few days after the birth of his older brother Walter: "The figure spoke in a soothing voice. 'Don't be frightened. It isn't you I'm after, nor do I want your baby. I want the one who was born at three o'clock. But I'm not ready for her now.'"[17] Two weeks later, according to Rosa's story, her sister Florence, who had been born at three o'clock, died of typhoid fever. Barker's childhood was steeped in these stories of the unusual.

Barker graduated from Sutton High School at the age of seventeen in 1942, and that fall entered Glenville State College, a teacher-training school in Gilmer County about thirty miles north of Sutton and Riffle.[18] Barker majored in English, with a minor in Social Science Education.[19] Glenville was already a small school, but the Second World War diminished it significantly. In Barker's first semester, only 180 students were enrolled—90 fewer than the previous fall—and men made up only a third of the student body.[20] In 1944, Barker's junior year, the total number of enrolled students dropped to 86, with only 9 men among the class of incoming freshmen.[21] In this environment, Barker's active avoidance of dating was noticeable, drawing comment in the *Glenville Mercury*'s gossip column: "What would happen if . . . Gray Barker dated a campus gal?"[22] Barker registered for the draft on his eighteenth birthday in 1943, but was rejected by the draft board as "psycho-neurotic"—possibly a euphemism for his homosexuality.[23]

Among the clubs Barker joined in his first year were the Braxton County Club, a social group for residents of his home county, which he helped revive after several moribund years; the Canterbury Club, a storytelling group; and the drama club, the Ohnimgohow Players.[24] He also wrote for the school newspaper, the *Glenville Mercury*, receiving his first byline in the issue for November 17, 1942, with a profile of student David Tewell, a visually impaired sophomore.[25] Barker and Tewell became friends and soon collaborated on what may have been Barker's first publishing venture. In February 1943 the two issued the *Glenville Prognosticator*, given out to residents of their dormitory. The parody newspaper carried "all the news not fit to print."[26] Barker was involved in other student groups, including the school's YMCA chapter, but he devoted a significant amount of time to the *Mercury* and by his senior year was the newspaper's editor.[27]

Humor is a hallmark of many of Barker's activities at Glenville. Throughout his time there, the *Mercury*'s columns on campus life frequently quoted stories of his jokes and humorous performances. For his initiation performance into the Ohnimgohow Players, at which other pledges recited poetry or Shakespearean soliloquies, Barker participated in a three-part performance of "She'll Be Coming 'Round the Mountain."[28] In his sophomore year he served as master of ceremonies at an April Fools' Dance, and may have been involved in the mimeographed humor publication issued at the event, the *Glenville Smirkury*.[29] The culmination of both his humor and his drama came in a variety show his senior year, in which he wrote, directed, and appeared in the short play *Croak Not, Black Angel*, described as a "mock horror melodrama."[30]

Barker's college years were also characterized by a growing love for the cinema. He wrote a weekly movie column, "Off the Reel," giving brief reviews of attractions at Glenville's two movie theaters, the Pictureland Theater and the Lyric Cinema. By October 1945 he was working part-time as a projectionist at the Pictureland.[31] He took this work seriously, viewing the projection of film as an art, and was deeply critical of technically inept presentations.[32]

According to a story he told in the early 1950s, Barker became a reader of science fiction (SF) during his time at Glenville State: one night a roommate lent him a science fiction magazine, and he became instantly hooked.[33] In another, later telling, Barker inverted the story: now it was he who was the fanatic introducing his roommate to the genre, and not with just any issue, but specifically the February 1945 issue of *Amazing Stories*, containing Richard Shaver's debut novella, *I Remember Lemuria!*[34] But even more apparent than his interest in science fiction was his love of horror. At a 1944 Halloween party he was in charge of a "Chamber of Horrors" that included "a corpse upon which blue fire played from a Tesla Coil, communication with the spirit world in which an icy hand gripped the hands of visitors, a lantern slide made from a film clip showing Frankenstein's monster and a 'witches brew' consisting of colored water being distilled over a Bunsen burner."[35] A mimeographed publication, *The Horrible Gazette*, was issued at this event, and Barker may have been involved in its writing and production. He also had a small role in a performance of "Durso's Spook Show" at the Pictureland, in which he and another part-time Pictureland employee were to remove an actor pretending to be drunk; two Glenville students did not realize the disruptive patron was part of the act and joined in his removal.[36] Barker's participation in the "spook show," which combined elements of stage magic, seances, horror film, and comedy, is telling, as the same blend of entertainment and the occult would become a hallmark of his publishing career.[37]

But it was not just fictional horror that intrigued Barker. A column in early 1945 foreshadowed his later fascination with the paranormal, recounting the story of a mysterious occurrence in the girls' dormitory: "[Peggy] Sweeney, it seems, retired late Monday night, carefully locking her room door. Came the dawn and she happened to look at the rings on her hands. During the night a friendship ring that was on one hand had been transferred to the opposite hand! And the previously locked door was all of two feet ajar!"[38]

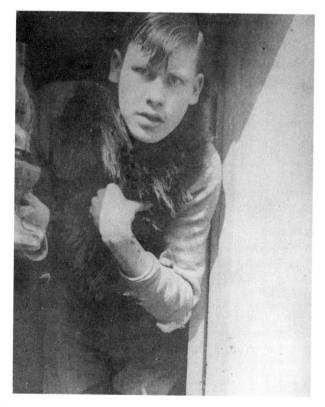

Figure 1.2
Gray Barker's author portrait from the poetry collection *Who Knows*, 1946. West Virginia and Regional History Center, West Virginia University Libraries/Courtesy of the Gray Barker Estate.

Barker's creative writing of the period also previews some of his future work. A short prose poem in the *Mercury* describes a nighttime stroll across Glenville's campus. Written in first-person plural, the piece describes several of the school's buildings in metaphors drawn from the fantastic: the chimney of Louis Bennett Hall is compared to a genie, and the library's columns to ghosts. The piece concludes with a description of the bell pealing in the library's cupola: "Then the clock, striking in a pedantic monotone, adds a finale to our night's walk, and the echoes from the science building add a like note to each of its peals, as if being jealous of its place in the campus stage, is heckling the performer in derision."[39] Though brief, "The Campus at Night"—particularly the final image of the heckling echo—is powerful. Its narration involves the reader in the narrative and can be seen as an important step toward the second-person narration that became a key part of Barker's work.

Barker also wrote poetry during this period, and in his senior year compiled a collection of his work under the title *Who Knows*.[40] The book contains fifty poems, the overwhelming majority of which are very brief—some a single line long. Barker's dark sense of humor is present throughout, as in "Anticlimax":

The Christmas tree fell,
    Crashing the candles
Many were maimed and injured.[41]

Intimations of the appeal of the uncanny are clear in "Behold the Behemouth":

Behold the Behemouth !
His form looms large.
And we say over and over again,
"Behold the Behemouth !"

Because things like this
Sound like they do strange things
to people when they say them.[42]

The collection's eponymous poem consists of the phrase "Who knows," repeated several times over three lines; notably, in neither the title nor the poem itself is there a question mark, indicating that it may be a statement rather than a query. Overall, the brief poems in *Who Knows* seem almost like jokes, setting up the reader for an unexpected conclusion. The collection is preceded by two brief essays attributed to Hunter Whiting, an instructor in English and French with whom Barker took several classes—but the content suggests that they are in fact by Barker parodying Whiting's grandiloquent teaching style. The pompous introduction jokingly gets the author's name wrong: "There has just appeared a fresh volume of verses, slender in form but not tenuous in content, from the dactylograph of Mr. H. Barker Grey, an inveterate litterateur of West Virginia—autochthonous in all verity."[43]

In April 1946, shortly before his graduation, Barker was hired as an English teacher by the Howard County Public School System.[44] He most likely taught at Howard High School in Ellicott City, Maryland, about fourteen miles west of Baltimore. The school drew on his literary skills, asking him to write a responsive reading for a Thanksgiving assembly. He later called the resulting prayer "a bit of religious hack writing"—though he also said it was "*good*, for the purpose it evidently serves."[45] But Barker's career as a teacher was brief: he left the position in December 1946 after less than a semester. He later explained his departure: "Did not like teaching."[46] After returning to West Virginia, Barker never again lived outside of the state. Though he would make occasional trips out of state (and, in one instance, overseas), he was a homebody, and his friend James Moseley later recalled that he hated to travel: "He really didn't like the idea of leaving West Virginia or the difficulty of travel . . . and he would start to drink excessively, even for him, during these trips."[47]

After leaving his teaching job in Maryland, Barker returned to Glenville. He worked again at the Pictureland Theater—not as a projectionist this time, but as the manager of both the Pictureland and the Lyric, for thirty dollars per week.[48] On May 7, 1947, during a screening of the MGM film *Two Smart People*, a fire broke out in the Pictureland's projection booth.[49] The *Mercury* recorded Barker's wry response to the disaster at his workplace:

"Gray Barker, impresario at the local cinema place, said with a smile on his smoke-smudged face, 'Here's something for your column: Comment from the crowd followed the line, "Wonder how the picture ended?" or "I didn't even get my money back."'"[50] No one was injured in the fire, but the theater was in urgent need of new projection equipment, and Barker hired Lovett & Co., a small cinematic equipment company based in Clarksburg, to provide it.[51] Barker seems to have impressed the technician sent to handle the installation, who recommended him to proprietor Delbert "Doc" Lovett. On August 27, 1947, Lovett's secretary, Virginia Howell, contacted Barker to offer him a sales position.[52]

Shortly thereafter, Barker began work for Lovett & Co, selling projectors and other equipment to schools. Before long, though, he had added a second specialty, owing to a new type of movie theater that was beginning a boom that would last well into the 1950s: drive-in theaters. Drive-ins had surged in popularity beginning in the late 1940s, and proliferated in the 1950s, with over three thousand theaters opening nationwide between 1948 and 1958.[53] In West Virginia, the number of theaters expanded from eighteen in 1948 to seventy-six in 1954, and most survived into the 1970s.[54] Lovett & Co. equipped many of these theaters, and at the height of the construction boom, Barker was well-positioned to benefit from this expansion. It was in connection with drive-ins that Barker first encountered alcohol. He later recounted the first time he got drunk, at an opening party for a drive-in owned by Alex Silay in Philippi, West Virginia, for which Lovett had provided the projector and other equipment: "They had all sorts of different alcoholic beverages on hand, and being rather young and inexperienced I decided to sample all of them. . . . I got so drunk I couldn't see the screen."[55]

Barker also continued writing. Throughout 1948 he was a regular contributor to *Boxoffice*, providing pieces for the Modern Theatre section, which concerned mechanical maintenance and theatrical equipment. His first contribution was a series of humor articles entitled "Atomic Projection Made Easy in Ten Simple Lessons" that provided a projectionists' wry take on operating a movie theater. The first installment instructs the aspiring projectionist on how to find the projection booth:

Let's now imagine a period of time has elapsed and you are standing there by the door of the booth, elated; but nervous in speculating upon your new career. But don't open the door immediately as would the unversed. This is important!

After all, are you sure this is the door to the projection room? Is there a sign, "Projection Booth," above the door? Does it also read, "No Admittance?" The new operator should proceed with caution through all new projection room doors; for in some booths not even the projectionist is admitted. And, too, often wags on the theatre staff tax the new man by transferring the traditional booth sign to the ladies rest room entrance. Beware![56]

In addition to these humorous pieces, he continued writing technical essays on projector operation for the Cine'clinic column. One notable piece concerns projection booth fires.[57] These essays, though drier than the boisterous "Atomic Projection" series, make it clear that Barker was dedicated to the art and science of film presentation and hoped to provide the best possible experience for a motion-picture audience.

Barker's work for Lovett & Co. put him in touch with theater managers in West Virginia, Maryland, Pennsylvania, and Ohio. Realizing that many of them had little experience with the practical aspects of managing a theater or marketing films, he began offering them his services as a freelance booker, buyer, and promoter.[58] He described his area of expertise in a 1953 letter to a new theater owner: "I provide complete services which include 'buying' or arriving at prices for films and their selection, 'booking' them in at the best possible times, and most any other service desired by the theatre owner."[59] By June 1949 this work had become steady enough that he was able to leave his sales position with Lovett & Co. and open his own business—though he did not travel far, operating out of Lovett's office in the Ritz Theatre and staying in close contact with his former coworkers.[60]

After George Barker died on April 1, 1950, Lovett became a father figure for his former employee.[61] He later recalled, "Doc Lovett practically raised me."[62] Their closeness is reflected in the title of a compilation of jokes Barker privately printed for his coworkers as a Christmas gift sometime between 1948 and 1950: *Mr. Lovett and Mr. Barker*.[63] Though this book does not seem to have survived, a similar work from the following year entitled *The Trip to the Moon* gives a sense of its tone: a collection of jokes involving Lovett, Barker, their coworkers, and others involved in the film distribution and exhibition business:

> "I'll get right to my two points, declared Ed, stroking his abdomen lovingly. "First of all, will you lend me five hundred dollars?"
>
> "I'm a little deaf," replied Mr. Lovett; "step around to the other ear."
>
> Ed stepped around to the other ear. "Will you lend me a thousand dollars?"
>
> "Go back around to the five hundred dollar ear," answered Mr. Lovett.[64]

These jokes are embedded in a loose science fiction narrative, displaying Barker's love of both humor and the otherworldly.

Barker's business grew quickly, and by June 1952 his client list included twenty drive-in theaters, including Lovett's own, which opened in 1950.[65] In mid-1953, Barker described his personal life as that of a bachelor with few attachments: "I am still single myself, though I'm only 28. I don't think any woman would put up with the schedule I keep. I am generally out until around 12 midnite, loafing at some drive-in theatre or other, and then I am out of town a great deal. I must make calls on exhibitors for which I book film, go to Cincinnati, Pittsburgh, and Washington, where the film exchanges are located."[66] In another letter, he described his living arrangements as spartan: "I just rent a room and eat out all of the time. Later I may obtain an apartment where I'll have more room and can get my own breakfast."[67]

Barker exercised growing skill as a promoter. He sent news of humorous events at his theaters to *Boxoffice*, including a May 1949 description of cattle from a farm adjoining one drive-in becoming excited during a stampede scene in a western and rushing into the lot.[68] Barker devised innovative promotions for the theaters on his client list, and his marketing was mentioned several times in *Boxoffice*'s Showmandiser section. In 1950, he introduced midnight double features of horror movies at Snyder's Drive-In in Clarksburg, and received a "Boxoffice Bonus" award for his promotions of it.[69] Showmanship was necessary to hold onto a steadily shrinking audience. When Barker launched his film booking business in 1949, over 40 percent of the American population attended a movie theater at least once per week; by 1960, fewer than 20 percent did.[70]

By the fall of 1952, Barker had become an experienced showman, salesman, and humorist. He was soon to turn these skills toward the bizarre series of occurrences that had been unfolding across the country for the past five years and begin marketing the mysteries of the skies.

2 FLYING SAUCERS BEFORE GRAY BARKER

The beginning of the space age is generally dated to the Soviet Union's launch of the first Sputnik probe in 1957. But that event was ten years behind a space age of the imagination that had begun on June 24, 1947. On that date, while searching for a downed plane between Chehalis and Yakima, Washington, private pilot Kenneth Arnold saw a group of nine disklike objects flying in the vicinity of Mount Rainier.[1] He estimated their speed to be approximately 1,700 miles per hour, twice the air speed record for a jet plane at the time. Arnold compared their shape to that of a pie plate, but newspapers picked up a different term for their headlines, from Arnold's comment that they moved "like a saucer would if you skipped it across the water."[2] The Associated Press picked up the story, which appeared in newspapers across the country. Other mysterious sightings preceded Arnold's, but this was the moment when "flying saucers" became an American cultural phenomenon. Dozens of reported sightings followed throughout the summer of 1947.

Many witnesses reported these sightings to the Army Air Force, in addition to the local and national news, in hope that the government might be able to identify the objects. But one notable event was reported instead to Raymond Palmer, editor of the science fiction magazine *Amazing Stories*. Fred Lee Crisman and Howard Dahl told Palmer that, three days before Arnold's sighting, they had witnessed a group of donut-shaped craft over the Puget Sound near Maury Island. One of the objects ejected hot metal debris into the water, damaging their boat, injuring Dahl's son, and killing their dog. To investigate the incident, Palmer hired someone he knew who was both local to the area and interested in strange aerial sightings: Kenneth Arnold himself. Arnold detailed his investigation in *The Coming of the Saucers*, a 1952 book coauthored with Palmer. The story is filled with strange occurrences, including mysterious black-clad strangers, abandoned buildings, and disappearing samples of saucer debris, and ends with the plane crash that killed two army intelligence officers sent to investigate the Maury Island event.[3] The Army Air Force ultimately determined that the sighting was a hoax, but the narrative of the events and their investigation set a template that has echoed throughout UFO history.

Crisman and Dahl chose Palmer as the recipient of their report for good reason: he had been deliberately blurring the line between science fiction and outrageous fact for years. Palmer saw these mysterious aerial objects as a natural sequel to the phenomenon to which he had devoted many pages of *Amazing Stories* during the mid-1940s. Branded by Palmer as "the Shaver Mystery," the subject was inaugurated in the February 1945 issue, which carried the novella *I Remember Lemuria!* by a new author, Richard Shaver.[4] This story—and dozens more by Shaver that followed—concerned the distant past of planet Earth that the author claimed were true, having been communicated to him as "thought records" through his contact with mysterious subterranean creatures. Shaver believed that there exists below Earth's surface a complex world of caverns, altogether larger than the surface world above, inhabited by a malevolent race of beings he called "dero" (short for "detrimental robots") and their benign but powerless counterparts, the "tero" (for "integrative robots"). The dero could affect events in the world above through the use of ancient ray weapons, which they used to torment surface dwellers. Through communications with these beings, Shaver had recovered an ancient language he called Mantong, a sort of substitution cypher he used for interpreting the occult meaning of words in any language. Palmer backed up Shaver's claims and opened up the reader letter section to those who claimed similar experiences. Among the correspondents reporting encounters with dero was Fred Crisman, who provided Palmer with dramatic accounts of a subterranean firefight with a group of dero beneath the Karakoram Mountains during the Second World War and a later deadly expedition to an Alaskan cavern.[5] The sensationalistic Shaver Mystery dominated the pages of *Amazing Stories* for four years, massively increasing circulation but also leading to a harsh backlash in the small but vocal world of science fiction fandom, perhaps in part because, as Andrew May notes, the Shaver stories attracted an educationally and socioeconomically diverse group of readers who threatened fandom's self-conception as an intellectual elite.[6] In late 1947, under pressure from both his publishers and fandom, Palmer left *Amazing Stories*. Made a pariah in the world of science fiction, he quickly branched out into a parallel field: stories of the paranormal.

SIGNS AND GRUDGES

By the end of 1947, the United States Air Force—as of September, an independent branch of the armed forces—had received enough reports of flying saucers to devote resources to their investigation. Major General L. C. Craigie, director of research and development, approved a study group under the classified code name Project Sign; the group began its work in January 1948. The same month saw the next major saucer incident, when Kentucky Air National Guardsman Thomas F. Mantell, Jr., perished in a plane crash while pursuing an unidentified object in the skies near Franklin, Kentucky. The object was later determined to have been a Skyhook balloon—a classified high-altitude reconnaissance device.[7] But the official Air Force statement, designed to protect the top-secret balloon project, was that Mantell had mistaken the planet Venus for a flying saucer. This explanation proved difficult for the public to accept. Some trusted that the Air Force was investigating these sightings seriously and would soon issue a definitive public statement on the matter. Others were not so sure.

Into the information void surrounding the saucers stepped Ray Palmer. In spring 1948, the Clark Publishing Company issued the first issue of his new venture, *Fate Magazine*. *Fate* had tantalizing covers of supposedly real but inexplicable events—the "damned facts" or "data that Science has excluded" that Charles Hay Fort explored in his 1919 work *Book of the Damned*.[8] The cover story of the premiere issue was Kenneth Arnold's firsthand account of his sighting the year before, under the title "I *Did* See the Flying Disks!"[9] Nearly a third of the first issue concerns flying saucers.

There is a long narrative of the Maury Island incident alongside reports of other strange occurrences and mystical ideas, including automatic writing, radio signals from Mars, and prehistoric giants. In light of the new wave of mysterious sightings, saucer investigators reinterpreted older phenomena, including the "foo fighters" reported by some World War II pilots and a series of mysterious airships that appeared in newspaper reports in the late nineteenth century.[10]

Project Sign members were unable to come to a consensus on an explanation for the sightings they reviewed, but believed that continued investigation would be valuable. In February 1949 Sign was replaced by Project Grudge. Though Air Force project names are generally assigned at random, the classified name of the new project suggests a change in philosophy. Where Sign had sought to collect data on sightings of unidentified objects, Grudge's goal was to explain them away.[11] To this end, Grudge cooperated in the production of a two-part article by Sidney Shalett, published in the April 30 and May 7 issues of the *Saturday Evening Post*, which sought to offer terrestrial explanations for the objects that saucer witnesses had seen and to dismiss the rest as hoaxes or the reports of crackpots.[12] Instead of diminishing the number of reported sightings, the *Post* article was followed by a large spike in new saucer reports.

Shortly after Shalett's article, journalist and former pilot Donald Keyhoe was hired to write an article for *True Magazine*, which believed the Air Force was hiding something about flying saucers. His article, "Flying Saucers Are Real," appeared in the January 1950 issue, and he expanded it into a paperback that spring—the first book-length treatment of flying saucers.[13] Keyhoe quickly became the most prominent proponent of an increasingly popular theory about the origins of flying saucers: that they originate on another world. Later ufologists called this the "extraterrestrial hypothesis," or ETH, and it quickly emerged as the dominant metanarrative of the early 1950s.[14] Keyhoe also argued that the government was covering up what it knew about the saucers and their origin, and thus the second major metanarrative, conspiracism, went hand in hand with the first. The second flying saucer book, Frank Scully's *Behind the Flying Saucers*, was based in large part on the story of the crash of a flying saucer near Aztec, New Mexico, and the retrieval of the bodies of several extraterrestrials from the wreckage.[15] The book became a bestseller, but the story was soon revealed as a hoax perpetrated upon Scully by two con men named Silas Newton and Leo GeBauer (the book's anonymized witness, "Dr. Gee") as part of an oil prospecting scam.[16] Crashed saucers would nonetheless emerge decades later as another major metanarrative.

The Air Force ended Project Grudge, replacing it in early 1952 with a new project that would last longer than the previous two saucer projects combined: Project Blue Book. The extraterrestrial hypothesis was proving influential—a *Life* magazine article in April asked, "Have We Visitors from Space?"—and a new series of sightings in June and July constituted a major flap.[17] A well-publicized evening of visual and radar sightings in Washington, DC, made front-page news across the country. The Air Force's explanations of these events were beginning to backfire, leaving many members of the public to speculate that the government was covering up what it knew.[18] Meanwhile, the narratives surrounding sightings were becoming more elaborate, as in the August 1952 case of scoutmaster "Sonny" Desvergers, who claimed not only to have seen a saucer, but to have climbed aboard it and scuffled with its humanoid pilots.[19]

The period from 1947 to 1952 shows the Air Force repeatedly attempting and failing to control the flying saucer macronarrative. The cumulative result of its efforts to provide rational explanations for sightings, its obligation to provide dishonest explanations where classified aircraft had been witnessed, and its policy of maintaining silence where a rational explanation could not be given was an erosion of public confidence in the government's ability or willingness to provide information about the mysterious sightings. Moreover, attempts to quiet the growing saucer hysteria in the press, as in the 1949 *Saturday Evening Post* articles, had failed, instead increasing public awareness not only of flying saucers in general, but of the fact that some sightings remained unexplained. If there had ever been hope of the Air Force gaining control over the plot of the flying saucer story, it was gone by 1952.

One sign of this eroding confidence was the formation of civilian saucer research clubs. The first of these was Civilian Saucer Investigation, founded in December 1951 by Los Angeles–based aviation writer Ed Sullivan.[20]

The Aerial Phenomena Research Organization (APRO), begun by Jim and Coral Lorenzen of Sturgeon Bay, Wisconsin, followed in January 1952.[21] The third—and the one with which Barker was to become the most closely involved—was the International Flying Saucer Bureau (IFSB), launched by Bridgeport, Connecticut, resident Albert Bender in April, 1952.[22] Occult groups got involved as well, most notably the Borderland Sciences Research Associates (BSRA), which claimed psychic contact with the saucers.[23] These occult information sources provided something that few other saucer witnesses could: firsthand knowledge of the nature of the unearthly apparitions. Project Blue Book's approach—commenting in vague and limited ways on individual sightings, often long after the media had moved on—created an information void, and an increasing number of groups and publications were on hand to provide speculative explanations, particularly for the strangest saucer narratives.

THE PHANTOM OF FLATWOODS

This was the atmosphere in September 1952, when Gray Barker first turned his attention toward flying saucers. He had certainly heard of the subject, from headlines as well as the 1951 films *The Day the Earth Stood Still* and *The Thing from Another World*, two early successes in what would grow into a science fiction film boom throughout the 1950s. In the summer of 1952 he latched on to the growing craze over the unidentified discs, advertising drive-in showings of *When Worlds Collide* by printing hundreds of flying saucer–shaped leaflets.[24] But there's no indication that he had thus far felt any personal connection to the subject.

As he later reported in the *Saucerian*, Barker was eating at a restaurant in Clarksburg on the morning of September 15 when he noticed an Associated Press newspaper article reporting a strange occurrence in his home state. The story reported that on Friday, September 12, seven residents of the town of Flatwoods, West Virginia, had seen a glowing fireball descend to a nearby hilltop. The group—Kathleen May, two of her sons, and four other boys between the ages of ten and seventeen—went to investigate. While looking at the glowing saucer, the group was approached by a "fire-breathing monster, 10 feet tall with a bright green body and a blood-red face."[25] The story's Sutton dateline no doubt grabbed Barker's attention as much as the headline did. Flatwoods, a small town of about three hundred people northeast of Sutton, was just a few miles from the communities of Riffle and Exchange where Barker had grown up. Barker saw an opportunity and sent a telegram to Robert Webster, the pseudonym under which Ray Palmer edited *Fate Magazine*, to see if the magazine was interested in an article on the monster sighting. Palmer soon responded, hiring Barker to submit a three-thousand-word article on the subject, with a September 22 deadline.

Barker traveled to Flatwoods on Friday, September 19, a full week after the sighting, to find that most of the key witnesses were out of town. Biologist and journalist Ivan Sanderson, a far more experienced researcher than Barker, had arrived earlier the same day, and local officials gave him priority.[26] Late on Sunday Barker was able to meet with Kathleen May, but she was unwilling to share much information. According to Barker's report, "Someone from the government had asked her to give out no information to anybody, and a lawyer had told her the story might be worth considerable money if she found the right market. Her father warned me I shouldn't write up anything about it."[27]

After returning to Clarksburg on the evening of Sunday, September 21, Barker sent *Fate* the text of "The Monster and the Saucer," which appeared in the January 1953 issue.[28] In its brevity, "The Monster and the Saucer" misrepresents several aspects of Barker's short investigation. Barker says he spent three days in the Flatwoods area, when in fact it was much closer to two, and intimates that he spoke to all seven witnesses, when his later, more detailed account in the *Saucerian* makes it clear the only witness interviews of any depth that he conducted were with May and teenage witness Neil Nunley. Most of his investigation concerned secondhand witnesses and those who had seen different aerial lights on the night of the monster sighting.

With the appearance of "The Monster and the Saucer," Barker began contacting organizations that he thought might be interested in more of his saucer writing, finding their contact information from advertisements and notices in science fiction magazines. On November 20, 1952, he wrote to the IFSB, about which he had learned from a letter in the December 1952 issue of Palmer's science fiction magazine *Other Worlds*.[29]

The IFSB's presence in *Other Worlds* indicates its origins in SF fandom. SF author and historian Jack Womack has described saucer and science fiction fandoms as nonoverlapping categories, "each group being far too embarrassed to be lumped in with the other."[30] But according to fanzine writer Gary Hubbard, "a lot of the original saucer fans were SF fans, Shaverites for whom saucers held more possibilities than stim-rays did."[31] Moreover, as William Sims Bainbridge notes, SF "is a highly effective cultural redoubt for deviant knowledge," a place where ideas rejected by mainstream scientists can live on.[32] Hubbard argues that the early flying saucer publications were created as an imitation—or even a subcategory—of SF fanzines, a suggestion borne out by the inclusion of SF reviews in both the IFSB's *Space Review* and the early issues of Barker's own *Saucerian*.[33] Barker made the comparison himself in a 1955 letter to Dean Grennell, editor of the SF fanzine *Grue*:

> Though a great deal different in many respects saucers amounts to a fandom pure and simple. It is wild-eyed, all right, in a different way than is sfandom, but the petty jealousies and NNF's [no-name fans] are right there in saucerdom too. . . . Although I believe there is something up there all right I can't explain, my biggest kick comes from corresponding with and knowing other folks interested in the same thing, with whom I can kick around wild theories.[34]

Barker's emphasis on camaraderie is telling: while he may have begun his saucer career intending to uncover some kind of truth about the phenomena he reported, his motivation very quickly changed to building and maintaining relationships. The IFSB's membership, which included active science fiction fans like Wilson "Bob" Tucker, demonstrates that at least some inhabitants of the saucer world of 1953 saw themselves as being closely intertwined with science fiction fandom, unaware of the rift to come.[35]

Bender named Barker the IFSB's West Virginia representative in the second issue of the organization's newsletter, *Space Review*, issued on January 3, 1953.[36] Around this time Barker gave up on offering his full report on the Flatwoods incident to other venues. Perhaps inspired by the notices of science fiction fanzines in Bender's *Space Review*, he decided to publish his report himself.

3 "THE SKIES SEETHE WITH MYSTERY": THE SAUCERIAN

After his appearance in *Fate*, Barker wasted little time in beginning to prepare a publication of his own, but his first effort had nothing to do with flying saucers. In November 1952 he sent out copies of a small-run publication entitled *Hoaxoffice* to several of his associates in the movie exhibition trade. Printed on a spirit duplicator in blue and purple ink, *Hoaxoffice* was a spoof of movie trends in the early 1950s, modeled on the trade magazine *Boxoffice*, for which Barker had written a few years earlier.[1] Articles on "Feel-a-vision," "elastofilm" (which allows exhibitors to stretch the running time of features), and "televised popcorn" mock the dubious technical innovations introduced by movie theaters in the 1940s and '50s, while the article "New Action Cycle Launched by Majors" pokes fun at the bandwagoning prevalent in motion-picture production:

> Major studios launched production on twenty-seven films featuring the new cycle that came to great popularity with the release of "The Man Who Jumped Over Niagara Falls."
>
> Exhibitors are clamoring for films in which the main characters jump off of or fall from high locations.
>
> Expected for release early next month is "Ma and Pa Skillet Fall Off the Empire State Building," and "The Man Who Jumped Off the Flatiron Building." The latter is being completed in actual locales in New York. Production was momentarily halted when the stunt man, employed to play the lead, was unable to continue in the production, after the leap described in the title was made.[2]

The cover features an illustration of Mr. Magoo, representing theater owner "J. W. Fattbubs." The tagline above the title is borrowed from Barker's college prank journal, the *Glenville Prognosticator*: "All of the news unfit to print." Though the use of the term *hoax* in the title is suggestive, there is little evidence of Barker's growing interest in flying saucers in the publication. The sole exception is a joke review of a film entitled *Destination Earth*, in which a group of Martians fly to Earth on a mission of exploration. The review encourages promotors to "advertise a flying saucer in your lobby and have someone there to throw china around."[3]

Apart from some borderline-risqué jokes in the "Feel-a-vision" article and in a review of a film of the Kinsey Report, the humor throughout *Hoaxoffice* is relatively innocuous. Nevertheless, not everyone on the small list of people to whom Barker sent the publication was amused. Though he received kind responses from projector manufacturer W. C. DeVry and *Boxoffice* staffer Morris Schlozman, Chester Friedman, editor of *Boxoffice*'s Showmandiser section, sent Barker a telegram threatening legal action if the publication were distributed.[4] Friedman followed up with a letter hyperbolically arguing that *Hoaxoffice* targeted *Boxoffice* specifically rather than industry publications as a whole and threatening dire legal consequences if the limited-run publication should somehow harm *Boxoffice*'s circulation.[5]

Barker was traveling when these messages were sent and was unable to respond until nearly two weeks after he had sent *Hoaxoffice*. He wrote long, apologetic letters to both Friedman and *Boxoffice* editor Ben Shylen, assuring them that, though the publication was intended in fun, he would not distribute it. He reminded them of his past relationship with *Boxoffice*, both as a writer and as the recipient of an award from Friedman.[6] The *Boxoffice* editors' responses to Barker, if any were sent, have not survived, but it appears that *Hoaxoffice* was effectively suppressed, with only a handful of copies sent to Barker's colleagues.

Around the same time that *Hoaxoffice* was released, Barker contributed to the local poetry journal *Echoes of West Virginia*, edited by Doris Miller. Barker's contribution, which appears in neither *Who Knows* nor his later privately circulated compilation *The Early Poems of Gray Barker*, is a piece of blank verse entitled "Mountain Poet," which gives a glimpse of Barker's emerging role as an outsider and skeptical mystic. The narrator contrasts himself with the wise men of an earlier age, who climbed to high places to exhort the muses to fill their pens with the blood of angels. The narrator, too, climbs to high places for inspiration, but encounters no divine beings there: "It may be I hear many echoes from / A multitude of beings of the Earth."[7] It is not the inhabitants of heaven that provide Barker with his source material, but the earthbound beings below.

THE DEPARTMENT OF INVESTIGATION

Despite the negative experience of *Hoaxoffice*, Barker had high hopes for his second publishing project, undertaken immediately after: a saucer zine of his own. By the beginning of February he had determined to issue his own publication and chosen the title *The Saucerian*.[8] Throughout the spring Barker expanded his network of contacts through the IFSB. Among the first saucer enthusiasts he contacted was the Reverend S. L. Daw, a member of Bender's organization based in Washington, DC, who had been in West Virginia on the night of the monster sighting in Flatwoods and had witnessed and attempted to photograph an aerial fireball.[9] Around the same time that Daw and Barker's correspondence began, Bender named Barker the chief investigator of the IFSB's Department of Investigation.[10]

The Department of Investigation began its work in June 1953, when Bender sent three sighting reports, marked with official-looking stamps, to the committee's members. In addition to Barker and Daw, these were August Roberts, a socially awkward New Jersey man who specialized in saucer photographs; Dominick Lucchesi, a brash and mischievous mechanical engineer from Jersey City; and Lonzo Dove, an amateur astronomer based in Washington, DC.[11] The department's work primarily consisted of sending official-sounding letters to witnesses requesting more details on their sightings and similarly formal letters to one another commenting on the sightings. Dove's note to Barker about "Case #3" is representative of the general tone of the committee's internal communications: "In a recent letter to Mr. Bender, I made the suggestion that inquiries to reporting individuals be done by just one of us investigators, preferably by you the Chief, to whom we can send pointers which you can embrace into your single inquiry. This will avoid repeated inquiries, and not bother the person beyond what is necessary. Writing is a burden to some people, and repeated inquiries about the same event might scare some into silence."[12] Daw's suggestion about witnesses being scared into silence would prove prescient.

Bender appears to have sent only a handful of cases to the investigation committee, and little came of its work. But camaraderie grew among the group, and their overly formal correspondence provided the basis for lasting friendships. Still, the self-serious tone of the committee's communications also appeared to Barker as an invitation. To a committed jokester, the pretentious language in which his new friends wrote to one another was a setup in need of a punchline.

LAUNCHING *THE SAUCERIAN*

Barker's work on the *Saucerian* continued slowly. He had hoped to have the first issue printed by April 1953, but drive-in business took precedence over his new saucer hobby.[13] He finally completed the edition of three hundred copies of the thirty-one-page debut issue on August 5, printing it on "a rather decrepit ditto machine which would ball up the paper every now and then."[14] Barker priced the periodical at twenty-five cents per copy, with six-issue subscriptions priced at a dollar. These prices immediately sent Barker's publishing venture into a deficit: the printing alone cost sixty dollars, meaning that he would lose money on subscriptions.[15]

Aesthetically, the *Saucerian* inhabits a different universe than other saucer zines of the early 1950s. Bender's *Space Review* was very plain in design, professionally typeset and printed using offset lithography; subject matter aside, it resembled a no-frills trade publication. Coral and Jim Lorenzen's *APRO Bulletin*, though printed on an office duplicator similar to Barker's, featured a simple but formal two-column design that implied the information it contained was reliable and trustworthy. Max Miller's *Saucers* took a different approach, seeking to attract attention with photographic covers. Bender describes the impulse behind his design decision, which applied to

Figure 3.1

The dittographic Flatwoods Monster, from *The Saucerian* 1, no. 1, 1953. Courtesy of the Archives for the Unexplained/Public domain.

these other fringe publications as well: "We desired a publication of dignified appearance, one that would make a favorable impression upon anybody picking it up, yet a booklet which could be produced economically."[16] Barker's visual approach, on the other hand, seems to draw more from the world of science fiction fandom, with little need to appear dignified. Science fiction fanzine creators had developed a coherent aesthetic around the limitations and opportunities of mimeograph and dittographic printing processes—and a general attitude of one-upmanship. On the front cover of the *Saucerian*, a full-page, three-color stencil of the Flatwoods Monster glowers at the reader, green beams shooting from its eyes. From the title lettering, which descends vertically on the left side of the cover, stick figures wave and dangle. Though amateurish, the image is striking, showing that Barker saw the spirit duplicating process not as an artistic limitation but as an opportunity for a raw and playful creativity.

Beneath a cartoonishly hand-lettered masthead and the motto "keep your head in the stars—and your feet on the ground," Barker's opening editorial is fustily and bombastically poetic, perhaps betraying the influence of the loquacious Hunter Whiting as well as another aesthetic forerunner: the self-consciously grandiloquent prose commonly used in science fiction fanzines. Following a quotation from *Hamlet*, the editorial begins, "The saucers are upon us, and the skies seethe with mystery."[17] That mystery is the central theme of the editorial, setting the stage for a parade of strange questions but few answers. Barker speaks of flying saucers as "our aerial protagonists," a telling phrase suggesting that they are more than physical objects or spiritual apparitions; they are elements in a narrative, a tale that Barker was only beginning to spin.[18]

But the editorial also states that humor—and perhaps even hoaxing—would have its place in the zine: "Since this is not a prozine, we have few taboos. We may even try to have some harmless fun now and then. But you will know when we are serious and when we are trying for a laugh. For a guy of that ancient and respected age of 28, you may even think the editor downright juvenile now and then. We have never quite grown up, and may never do so—at least we hope not."[19] As Barker's saucerological career progressed, he made good on his promise to have "harmless fun"—but not on his promise that his audience would always know when he was joking.

The centerpiece of the issue is an expanded twenty-four-page report on the Flatwoods Monster. There is very little overlap between this report of Barker's investigation and that published by *Fate* the previous fall. Barker updates his earlier report with information from more-recent interviews and witness drawings.[20] He is also careful to establish his own credentials as a primary "investigator," despite the rather secondhand nature of his investigation. "I have carefully investigated the hilltop where seven people may have seen something out of space, and I have taken measurements," he proclaims.[21] But he is also aware of the fun value of the monster report, and he includes the lyrics to a parody folk song played on the radio station WPDX called "The Phantom of Flatwoods."

Most of the text of this article, along with several other of Barker's substantive pieces from the first two years of his fanzine, were later adapted into his book *They Knew Too Much about Flying Saucers*, including the opening portion, written in the second-person narration that is a hallmark of Barker's prose style. The introductory section makes the reader a witness to the Flatwoods saucer and monster: "When you look over the top of the hill several things happen all at once. You see a fiery something totally outside your experience and as you puzzle for a moment, your eyes fixed upon the unknown, you do not see the horror approaching from your left."[22] Barker's use of the second person strives to give the reader a part in the ineffable experience of seeing something that they cannot explain; to make the audience a participant in a singular, unrepeatable experience; to make the act of reading into an act of witnessing. In this, the *Saucerian* seeks to make its readers not just followers of the "flying saucer mystery" but actors within it.

Just a few weeks after the issue's release, Barker and his associate editor Roger Parris traveled to Philadelphia to attend Philcon II, the eleventh World Science Fiction Convention. They were the sole members of a delegation of IFSB members that Bender had attempted to organize.[23] Barker used the occasion to publicize the *Saucerian* and to collect the autographs of author E. E. "Doc" Smith and fan-turned-author Harlan Ellison.[24] Both the *Saucerian* and the IFSB positioned themselves on the outskirts of science fiction fandom, but Parris and Bender seemed more committed to the genre than Barker.

WHAT HAPPENED TO AL BENDER?

The month in which the first issue of the *Saucerian* appeared proved eventful for Barker and his friends in the IFSB. One notable event took place not far from Bender's home in New Haven, Connecticut, on August 20. On that night, a red fireball rapidly descended from the sky, crashing through a steel billboard. A local saucer fan named Joseph Barbieri collected samples of material from the signboard, sending some to Coral Lorenzen of APRO for analysis. According to Barker's account of the event in *They Knew Too Much*, navy investigators were also on the scene.[25] A few days later, Roberts and a recent arrival to saucer investigation, James Moseley, obtained a similar sample from a nearby wooden support beam; Bender acquired a sample as well, either firsthand or through Roberts.[26] Moseley later speculated that this fireball—which may have been "an American missile of some sort"—was "the proximate cause" of events that would befall Bender within a few weeks.[27]

Around the same time, three members of the investigation committee came into contact with the authorities. Each was contacted under different circumstances, for different reasons, but the combination of events fed into a growing sense of persecution in the IFSB that would have long-lasting consequences. First, sometime in late August, Dominick Lucchesi dropped one of the IFSB's "secret documents" on the street.[28] The document, related to the investigation committee's evaluation of a possible saucer photograph, was turned in to the police in Jersey City, possibly because of its official-sounding language.[29] The police then contacted IFSB member August Roberts, whose contact information was included in the document, asking him to come to pick it up.[30]

In addition, on August 22, Barker picked up a hitchhiking soldier in Clarksburg and gave him one of his IFSB business cards.[31] Sometime that week, the unnamed man had an epileptic seizure in Clarksburg. He was taken to the hospital, and though he had no identification, the authorities found Barker's card in his pocket. Someone investigating the case contacted Barker to see if he could identify the man. In both *They Knew Too Much* and later correspondence, Barker claimed it was an FBI agent that spoke to him, but there is no evidence for this beyond Barker's own claim, and it seems far more likely that the local police rather than the FBI would be the ones to investigate the identity of a hospitalized John Doe.[32] A few months after the alleged interview, Barker dismissed its importance, referring to it as "a routine checkup on another matter" from "this local man"—not, in this telling, an FBI agent, though he discusses the FBI specifically elsewhere in the document.[33] David Houchin, curator of the Gray Barker collection, speculates that the hitchhiker may have been someone with whom Barker had had a sexual encounter.[34] In that case Barker would have had reason to obfuscate, both to the local authorities and to his IFSB associates.

The night after his interview, Barker called his fellow IFSB investigator S. L. Daw to inform him that he, too, "was liable to have visitors."[35] Very shortly afterward, three FBI agents knocked on Daw's door. The trio questioned him at length about his saucer research, leaving him with the impression that their goal was to discourage any kind of civilian saucer investigation.[36] In a conversation with Barker a few months later, Daw said that he did not know why the FBI would want to visit him, but later in the conversation he indicated that he had taken photographs at a gun emplacement in Washington where photography was not permitted, and that he had shown some of his photographs to "a government party."[37] It seems likely that it was his sharing of photographs of military sites, rather than saucer investigation per se, that concerned the government.

Bender had been growing increasingly distrustful throughout 1953. In the summer, he charged Barker, in his role as chief investigator, with investigating Max Miller, founder of the West Coast organization Flying Saucers International, to determine if he had been copying from or criticizing the IFSB and thus generate grounds for expelling him from the organization.[38] On September 9, Bender returned from a short vacation to find letters from Barker and Daw describing their recent experiences, in particular the IFSB report submitted to the New Jersey police.[39] He was furious over Lucchesi's carelessness in misplacing an IFSB document. Moreover, he seemed to conflate the events reported to him separately by Barker and Daw, representing their separate experiences as being related to a single FBI investigation of the IFSB.[40] Bender notes that the authorities had not yet contacted him, but that he was preparing himself for that eventuality.[41] In a letter to Daw the same day, Bender went even further, stating that if he was not contacted within a few days he would visit the FBI's local office himself to inquire about the supposed investigation.[42]

Within a few days of writing these letters, something happened to Albert Bender. Between Bender's secrecy about the events and Barker's mythologizing of them, the true nature of the events is unknowable. There is no version that reaches us without first passing through Barker's typewriter, and in that passage what happened to Bender ceases to be a historical event subject to scrutiny and becomes a mystery. Indeed, by 1956 Barker was framing the events as "The Bender Mystery" in an explicit attempt to capture the same sense of the inexpressible to which Ray Palmer had appealed in his framing of both the "Shaver Mystery" and the "Flying Saucer Mystery." Speaking of Palmer's use of the word, David Halperin notes: "'Mystery' isn't a riddle to be answered or a crossword puzzle to be solved. It's a metaphysical state wherein lies the salvation of the human mind and soul."[43] In describing the story of what happened to Bender as a *mystery*, Barker appealed to Palmer's terminology specifically, placing the events beyond the realms of truth and fiction in the domain of myth. Moreover, this sort of mystery invites collaborative narrative construction, the distributed effort to respond to the unexplained. This turned what could have been a mundane and soon-forgotten event— the demise of a small and only briefly active fan club—into an event that reverberated through the field of UFO research for decades.

In the absence of documentary evidence, we must turn to the story as it has been received, which is as Barker framed it. In September 1953 Bender wrote up a theory about the origin of the flying saucers and mailed it to one of his correspondents. Shortly thereafter—possibly on the morning of Saturday, September 12—three men dressed in black suits knocked on Bender's door, holding the paper he had mailed out. In a lengthy conversation, they somehow—through threats, persuasion, or something more *mysterious*— convinced him to end his saucer research. In the weeks to come, Bender refused to discuss the subject with his friends and correspondents, including Barker, Lucchesi, and Roberts. Barker later mythologized the encounter in the opening of his 1956 book *They Knew Too Much about Flying Saucers*, using second-person narration to maximize audience identification with the shocking events he describes:

> Three men in black suits with threatening expressions on their faces. Three men who walk in on you and make certain demands.
>
> Three men who know that *you* know what the saucers really are!
>
> They don't want you to tell anyone else what you know.
>
> The answer had hit you like a flash, one night when you had gone to bed after running all the theories through the hopper of your brain. You had sat up in bed, snapped your fingers, and said, 'This is IT! I KNOW I have the ANSWER! . . . You wrote this down and sent it to someone. When the three men came into your house one of them had that very same piece of paper in his hand.
>
> They said that you, among the thousands working on the same thing, had hit pay dirt. *You* had the *answer!* Then they filled you in with the details.
>
> After they got through with you, you wished you'd have never heard of the word, "saucer."[44]

Barker's dramatic picture of what came to be known as the "Men in Black" proved to be a lasting one, but he arrived at this carefully constructed framing only after several years of effort and consideration. In the fall of 1953, he had much less clarity around the subject.

The first hint Bender's associates had of these events were letters he sent on Monday, September 14, in which he advised them not to sign up any new IFSB members until after the release of the October issue of *Space Review*.[45] On October 4, Lucchesi and Roberts visited Bender, who was evasive about the subject of his visit and about flying saucers in general; he answered most of their questions by flatly stating, "I can't answer that."[46] Ultimately Bender forbade his friends to even mention the topic to him, writing to Roberts: "If you are coming up to see me—please do not expect to discuss 'Saucers' in any way, shape, or form. I do not care to talk about this subject to anyone anymore."[47] Barker, Roberts, and Lucchesi corresponded throughout the fall of 1953, attempting to discern what had happened to Bender (whom they privately called "daddy" or "Z1") and what the mysterious theory he had stumbled upon might have been.

The October issue of *Space Review* made it clear that something had changed. The first page contained a brief report on the New Haven fireball and then a pair of cryptic notices. The first, under the heading "Late Bulletin," read: "A source, which the IFSB considers very reliable, has informed us that the investigation of the flying saucer mystery and solution is approaching its final stages. This same source to whom we had referred data, which had come into our possession, suggested that it was not the proper method and time to publish this data in Space Review."[48] Below, under the headline "Statement of Importance," was this note:

> "The mystery of the flying saucers is no longer a mystery. The source is already known, but any information about this is being withheld by orders from a higher source. We would like to print the full story in Space Review, but because of the nature of the information we are sorry that we have been advised in the negative."
>
> We advise those engaged in saucer work to please be very cautious.[49]

Though the following pages contain the usual saucer sighting reports and articles, the issue closes with a "Special Announcement" that the International Flying Saucer Bureau will no longer focus on flying saucers and a new organization exploring "matters pertaining to the universe in general" will take its place.[50] The final page contains a form for those who wish to receive refunds for their IFSB membership dues. After less than eighteen months of operation, the International Flying Saucer Bureau was finished.

Barker didn't know what had happened to Bender, but he quickly latched on to the strange circumstances in service of his own self-promotion. In a letter to CBS radio presenter Arthur Godfrey, who had mentioned the *Saucerian* on his radio show, Barker hinted at "recent developments" and "reliable information" about the answer to the saucer mystery, clearly hinting at Bender's experiences.[51] But he was hesitant to say too much, either to protect Bender's privacy or to intrigue Godfrey with the promise of more information to be revealed. He made similarly suggestive comments to Laimon Mitris, a Canadian saucer investigator who initiated a subscription in mid-October: "Either something completely fantastic is about to break wide open or I'm being made a terrific fool of. I hope it's the latter."[52]

In the midst of the unfolding situation surrounding the IFSB, Barker completed the second issue of the *Saucerian* in mid-October.[53] The cover art, drawn by Bender, shows a scene of an elevated flying saucer landing pad emerging from a moon crater; Barker later speculated that the secret of what Bender had discovered might have been related to this image. But Bender had requested that Barker remain silent on his predicament, and so this issue of the *Saucerian* contains no mention of his experiences. The news would be broken elsewhere: an article in the November 22 issue of the Bridgeport *Sunday Herald* made public, in broad outline, the story of the "mystery visitors" whose appearance had led Bender to shut down the organization.[54]

Privately, Barker expressed frustration with the newspaper article. Bender had sworn him to secrecy, and he felt betrayed by Bender's release of the story through another channel.[55] But after the newspaper article, the cat was out of the bag. Barker reprinted the complete text in a special bulletin released around December 1, 1953, and followed it with his first substantial piece of writing on the topic in a ten-page editorial for the third issue of the *Saucerian*. This text is a sensationalistic affair, but clumsier in its phrasing than what Barker would later develop. He uses capital letters to drive home the sinister nature of the events: "THREE MEN, IN DARK CLOTH-ING, CAME TO HIS HOME UNANNOUNCED AND ENTERED HIS ROOM WHERE HE HAPPENED TO BE AT THE TIME IN A RATHER DISCOURTEOUS MANNER."[56] Barker then speculates on the nature of Bender's secret information, conjecturing that the visitors were government agents, that the saucers were a threat to humankind, and that an official announcement of a solution to the saucer mystery was imminent. There is an underhanded aspect to portions of the editorial: Barker publishes Bender's home address and details about his workplace, revealing the personal information of a man he knew was already subject to harassment from saucer enthusiasts eager to uncover his secrets. He also entertains several gossipy rumors about the IFSB, including Lorenzen's theory about a "well-known science fiction publisher" backing the organization.[57] "To me friendships are far more important that flying saucers," Barker comments, "however, there is no obligation to refrain from considering every angle."[58]

Barker spent the winter of 1953–1954 chasing down leads that he hoped might help him uncover the secret that Bender claimed to have learned. He picked apart their correspondence; reviewed accounts of conversations between Bender, Roberts, and Lucchesi; and pored over issues of *Space Review* for clues. He wrote to anyone he thought might be able to provide a clue as to what Bender knew, including Richard Shaver, Meade Layne of the Borderland Sciences Research Associates, and Harold Fulton, IFSB's Australian representative, with whom Bender had corresponded about the possibility of an Antarctic origin for the saucers.[59] By the year's end, following a visit to Connecticut to speak with Bender in person on December 13, Barker was entertaining the possibility that the entire affair was a hoax.[60] Roberts and Lucchesi may have contributed to this conclusion: in November 1953, just two months after Bender's experience, they released a trial issue of a hectograph fanzine entitled *Nexus*.[61] The issue is peppered with obvious hoax articles, but also with hints that the editors, like Bender, know the solution to the saucer mystery but will not divulge it.[62] The apparent parody of Bender's predicament shows that pranksterism was present from the earliest days of the Bender Mystery—and Roberts and Lucchesi, whom Barker presents as serious investigators of Bender's experiences, may have actually considered them a joke.

But Barker's tone in the first editorial on the Bender affair is deadly serious. He argues that he was able to confirm Bender's story with details from another narrative, paralleling his discussion of Bender with the story of the Australian Flying Saucer Bureau (AFSB), headed by Edgar H. Jarrold. He again uses dramatic capital letters to imply that this vague information has shocking implications: "JARROLD WAS VISITED BY A MAN, WHO SAID HE WOULD DISCLOSE CERTAIN INFORMATION ABOUT SAUCERS IF JARROLD WOULD GIVE HIM HIS WORD NOT TO REVEAL IT TO ANYBODY."[63] There's little similarity between the two stories, but the general themes of secrecy and silence are enough for Barker to suggest that they represent the same phenomenon. Combining the two narratives, he abandons the idea that Bender's visitors could have been government agents, not least of all because the actions of the three men "resulted in exactly the reverse of the supposed motives, in that the matter is gaining nationwide importance."[64]

In the years to come, other saucer researchers would further pursue "every angle" of Bender's experiences. Some concluded that the three men were FBI agents—a conclusion that Halperin, with several decades of hindsight, endorses.[65] Though Halperin makes a plausible case for this conclusion, there is scant evidence for it outside of Barker's own writings, which must be viewed with a high degree of skepticism. The FBI's publicly released UFO files do contain references to Barker and Bender—but only in the context of saucer enthusiasts who wrote to the agency later in the 1950s to find out what they knew about the "Three Men."[66]

In the saucerological realm, others filled in the blanks in Barker's account with their own devils: H. P. Beasley and A. V. Sampsel suggested the three men were demons, while psychic contactee George Hunt Williamson related them to the antisemitic trope of "International Bankers."[67] In later years, others drew Bender's account into broader metanarratives of postwar conspiracism; ufologist Brian Burden suggests that Bender was part of a government mind-control experiment.[68] Others laid the blame on the IFSB itself: rival saucer researcher Lonzo Dove speculated that Barker himself was behind Bender's visitors, and ufological historian Loren Gross concluded that the visitors were "just the product of Bender's confused mind."[69]

Barker's initial account of the events makes it clear he suspected Bender's visitors were government agents and his primary concern was with the legality of the government shutting down a civilian organization. Privately, however, he hinted at the more extraordinary possibilities that he would later explore, writing to Jacqueline Sanders, "As far as I know, Bender's visitors were from the government; although that does not say they had to be humans necessarily."[70] Perhaps, he suggests, they came from somewhere else—somewhere seething with mystery.

4 "TOMORROW WE SHALL AGAIN HAVE OUR HEAD IN THE STARS": 1954–1955

On November 20, 1952, an amateur astronomer named George Adamski was driving with some associates near Desert Center, California. Adamski, who operated a food stand not far from Mount Palomar Observatory, had been a saucer enthusiast for several years, photographing mysterious lights in the sky through his telescope and claiming a sighting that preceded Kenneth Arnold's by nearly a year.[1] But he had a background in spiritual entrepreneurship as well: in the 1930s, he operated an organization called the Royal Order of Tibet, which promulgated a "Universal Law."[2] Around noon on November 20, Adamski and several associates were on a saucer expedition, hoping to see and photograph flying discs. Before long the group spotted several spacecraft, and Adamski went off on his own, warning the others not to follow him. Shortly thereafter a saucer appeared, flying to where Adamski had walked. Accounts vary as to exactly what the other members of the group witnessed, but shortly afterwards Adamski returned to the group, telling them that a saucer had landed and he had met its pilot. The blond-haired, silver-jumpsuited Venusian—given the name Orthon in Adamski's later works—telepathically communicated an antinuclear message, then departed, leaving behind footprints in the desert sand bearing mysterious hieroglyphic designs. Adamski's firsthand account was published in the 1953 book *Flying Saucers Have Landed*. His encounter in the desert opened a new chapter in the story of the flying saucers: stories of personal contact with extraterrestrials.[3]

The flying saucer contactees illuminate the scale of the shift that had occurred in the six years since Kenneth Arnold's initial sighting. While no physical evidence of a spacecraft was found, there was no such shortage of narrative evidence produced to support the extraterrestrial origin of the saucers. For many, the existence of the space people, their advanced abilities, and their superior morality were foregone conclusions. The contactees inhabited a world in which the presence of superior space beings was not a theory but a basic assumption. As saucer historian Aaron Gulyas notes, this view is a fundamentally optimistic alternative in stark contrast to the Cold War era's pervasive anxiety of atomic annihilation.[4] This was a story worth telling.

Adamski has been remembered as the first flying saucer contactee, but by the time the impact of *Flying Saucers Have Landed* was apparent, Barker's circle had already been discussing several other contact narratives.[5] The story of Orfeo Angelucci was published in the first issue of Ray Palmer's *Mystic*, released several weeks before Adamski's book in fall 1953.[6] Angelucci, a resident of Burbank, California, claimed to have ridden in a flying saucer that picked him up in Los Angeles. Another Californian, a freeway construction worker named Truman Bethurum, published an account of his contact with the beautiful spacewoman Aura Rhanes of the planet Clarion in the second issue of Max Miller's *Saucers* zine, issued in August 1953.

In the Mojave Desert, airstrip operator George van Tassel had been engaged in a very different—and arguably more influential—form of flying saucer contact since the beginning of 1952, receiving telepathic messages from spacemen like Ashtar at weekly gatherings in a subterranean room beneath a large boulder known as Giant Rock.[7] Barker's California correspondent Jacqueline Sanders, a married woman in her late thirties living in the San Gabriel Valley, was an occasional attendee at these meetings and frequently sent Barker news of the California saucer scene, contributing to the *Saucerian* under her own byline and later as an anonymous "West Coast Correspondent."[8] Van Tassel's mental contacts were in continuity with nineteenth-century spiritualism and Theosophy.[9] He was not the only psychic contactee: the BSRA's own mental contacts had been ongoing for half a decade, and two members of the group that accompanied Adamski to the desert on November 20—Alfred Bailey and dubiously credentialed anthropologist George Hunt Williamson—had begun receiving their own communications from space three months before accompanying Adamski on his encounter.[10] But Van Tassel proved influential, largely because he organized a spacecraft convention (held more or less annually at the small airport Van Tassel operated at Giant Rock) that became a major nexus of contactee narratives.[11]

Barker's first direct contact with one of the flying saucer contactees came in November 1953, when he sent Adamski a copy of the second *Saucerian*. Barker's initial letter has not survived, but Adamski's response discouraged Barker from publicizing the ideas of psychic and mystical groups like the BSRA, hinting that a rivalry was already emerging between the physical contactee and his psychic counterparts.[12] Barker reviewed *Flying Saucers Have Landed* for the third issue of the *Saucerian*, concluding that both Adamski's account and Leslie's speculations about ancient astronauts fall outside the realm of the modern flying saucer phenomenon: "As far as picking Adamski's story apart, we believe that . . . is quite impossible, for it seems to border the fields of religion and philosophy, precarious grounds on which we refuse to roam."[13] Barker concludes by emphasizing Adamski's apparent honesty, but he suggests a disconnect between different approaches to flying saucers: a conservative wing that believed that the truth about the flying saucers was out there, and contactees who had already found their answers within.

Privately, Barker expressed skepticism toward physical contactees: he referred to Max Miller's organization, Flying Saucers International, as "inclined toward the crackpot" for its coverage of Bethurum.[14] But he showed more willingness to entertain psychic approaches. Regarding the BSRA, he commented: "Their theory on the saucers is quite fantastic, but if it [is] correct, it could explain most of the mystery. Layne doesn't seem to be a wild-eyed mystic, and seems to have his feet on the ground as much as possible under the circumstances. If I ever accept any occult theory, it probably would lean towards Layne's explanation."[15] In print during this early phase, he presented himself as neutral, ostensibly willing to consider any position.

But by the time Bethurum's *Aboard a Flying Saucer* was released in mid-1954, Barker's attitude toward contact narratives was shifting. Never comfortable with empiricism, he began expressing a more aesthetic approach. Barker's review of the fifty-seven-year-old construction worker's account of his meetings with the beautiful Clarionite Aura Rhanes at first suggests doubt. But the conclusion of the review considers the book, and other contactee accounts, in a more romantic light:

> Ourselves, we believe every word of it. It is as real as the gods and demons that beset us on a dark and lonely road; as the golden phaeton, seen between waking and dreaming on a lazy day, unfolding jeweled wings across purple skies.
>
> There are those who would put demons in bottles for display, actually demand proof of the gold where rainbows touch, or throw radar at dream castles in the air. They are the kind that looks for pixies only in congressional committees.
>
> But those who have bridled the winged horse never worry of oats; they are those close to that wonderful and mysterious land we come from, that world half-remembered in childhood and oft visited in dreams. Some may say it's over the rainbow, and some may say that it is what Heaven is.
>
> Some may call it Clarion.[16]

Barker's poetic appeal to the psychic reality of the contact experience suggests something harder to pin down than simple belief or disbelief. The reality of an experience like Bethurum's, Barker suggests, is not subject to empirical testing, but as a story, a desire, a dream, it is as real as anything.

"A SWELL AND SMART GUY": JAMES W. MOSELEY

James Moseley, conducting research for a proposed book on flying saucers, came to Clarksburg in January 1954 for the sole purpose of meeting Barker.[17] Moseley was five years younger than Barker. His father was retired army general George Van Horn Moseley, an outspoken white supremacist and anti-Semite, against whom much of the younger Moseley's life and career seems to have been a protest. James Moseley dropped out of Princeton University following his mother's death in 1950 and used his inheritance to fund travel rather than education. In Miami he met pulp writer Ken Krippene, who had contributed "true adventure" stories to magazines like *Argosy*.[18] Following a failed arrangement for a joint expedition to Peru, Krippene and Moseley came to an agreement in October 1953: Moseley would travel the country conducting research on the flying saucer mystery, and Krippene would use the assembled notes and research materials to write and publish a book on the topic. Thus, throughout late 1953 and early 1954, Moseley crisscrossed the country, meeting and interviewing as many figures from the burgeoning field of flying saucers as he could locate. Among the first people that Moseley contacted on this mission were August Roberts and Dominick Lucchesi, then at the height of their perplexity over Bender and the IFSB.

Barker was suspicious of Moseley from the start, suggesting before their first meeting that he might have been "a Hoover man"—an FBI agent.[19] After meeting Moseley, Barker sent Lucchesi an initial assessment:

> At first he impresses you as a real seedy kid (wh[y] doesn't the guy shine his shoes and put on a clean shirt), but after you talk with him for a while he's such a swell and smart guy you don't notice all thos[e] things. One thing I admire about him is his objectivity—he hasn't yet got the imagination bug on saucers and tends to play the fantastic down instead of letting it run away from him.[20]

For his part, Moseley noted that Barker regarded him with some suspicion in that first meeting, particularly regarding the events surrounding the IFSB's closure, which he had apparently already given the appellation "the Bender Mystery": "I had the sense he was holding back, wanting to hang onto the story for his own future writings rather than handing it to me for my book. I was right."[21]

Barker was, in fact, already at work on a lengthy exploration of Bender's experiences for the third issue of the *Saucerian*, published toward the end of January.[22] The florid conclusion of Barker's editorial in this issue suggests that the Bender Mystery had pushed Barker's journal to the breaking point of its motto:

> We also predict that tomorrow we shall again have our head in the stars, and our feet slightly off the ground. Tomorrow we shall believe the three men story implicitly. Tomorrow we shall imagine that at any moment some dark agency of some secret society will come into our office; or that some green man will abduct us in a saucer. And we shall thus shudder with an excited and ecstatic expectancy, while the everyday problems of the business world vanish and we again tread golden streets of the Planet Pie, which is there only if you

look for it, right there in the sky. We shall send out green bulletins with dire warnings. We may even tell you we have the ANSWER.

And this joyful state will continue until some other dark day when we again may touch earth, and sit down and write something else like this.[23]

This conclusion shows a shift from the assertion of a fact-based exploration of the saucer mystery expounded in prior issues of the *Saucerian*. Further evidence for this comes in the form of a new column, Wild Rumors, illustrated with a bug-eyed monster named "R. Monger."[24] This column, which quickly became a staple of the *Saucerian*, carries a blend of unsubstantiated rumors, anonymously submitted stories (many provided by Sanders), wild theories, and outright fiction.

Following the release of the third *Saucerian*, there is a decided tonal shift in some of Barker's correspondence. This is particularly noticeable in his letters to Lucchesi, who, in contrast to the self-seriousness of the IFSB's other high-ranking members, shared Barker's mischievous outlook. Though Barker still seems interested in serious theories about the saucers' origin, he also shows an increased mockery toward certain witnesses, as well as indications that he was hoaxing some of his correspondents. In one letter, he comments that the proliferation of "hoaxsters and lunatic fringe inhabitants in this saucer business" have him "almost completely disillusioned with most anyone who has any kind of 'saucerian' experience."[25] In the years to come, several of Barker's letters to his closest correspondents refer to an "inner circle"—those with whom he would share his more cynical views of the saucer world.[26]

With Lucchesi, Barker began devising hoaxes, one of which saw print in the fourth issue of the *Saucerian* under the title "They Saw a Saucer Woman." This story describes an encounter between a Mr. Forster of Peekskill, New York, with a glowing-eyed space woman and her saucer, complete with Lucchesi's full-page illustration.[27] Barker and Lucchesi corresponded extensively about the saucer woman story throughout the summer, making joking references to it as the "space girl hoax."[28] A comment on the story makes the story's fictional nature even clearer:

> The sex angle is the most important thing here (in the first installment the horror angle overshadowed the sex but the combination I believe will sell it)[.]

Forster'll have to get her name; it should be a good one. Here's a new angle which might be worked if not too fantastic. Why not let Forster lay this girl, in a nice way of course, and written up in good taste—he could have been under a spell when he did it, etc. etc. Bring in the old parallel down through the ages of a god mating with a human to bear an offspring which would become a great leader. The Second Coming and all that you know, kid. This sounds like a corker if it could be pulled, but of course I want you to make sure that Mr. Forster isn't hoaxing you, for if he is and it ever comes out, we could never kill the story—that's the hell of it, eh?[29]

In print, Barker made much of the high regard he held for his saucerological friends. But there is a growing sense that he was purposefully taking advantage of some of his correspondents and their experiences. Roberts was increasingly agitated over his own saucer experiences and theories. Both Lucchesi and Moseley believed that Roberts's obsession with saucers—and in particular his fear that his friends were keeping secrets from him—was causing his mental health to deteriorate.[30] But rather than set Roberts at ease, Barker needled him, warning him that he was due to receive a visit from the three men.[31]

AT THE *NEXUS:* THE *SAUCERIAN* IN 1954

In early July, James Moseley, August Roberts, and Dominick Lucchesi launched a magazine that would remain intertwined with Barker's own publishing for three decades. The first ten issues of the saucerzine reused the title *Nexus* from Roberts and Lucchesi's earlier, privately circulated zine, but the zine is better-known by the title it adopted in mid-1955: *Saucer News.* The publication billed itself as the official organ of S.A.U.C.E.R.S.—the Saucer and Unexplained Celestial Events Research Society. Its initial issues were printed by mimeograph in an edition of about one hundred copies, distributed at no charge to a mailing list of Moseley, Roberts, and Lucchesi's friends and acquaintances in the saucer world.[32] In a letter to Ted Bloecher after his first issue, Moseley stated that his goal was to gain a reputation for his publication quickly and that offending major names in the saucer community was a means to that end.[33] *Nexus* quickly developed a reputation as a place for gossip and feuds within the saucer research community—a reputation that Barker and Moseley fed for years, hiding their growing friendship behind an apparently vicious public rivalry. At the beginning, however, their public interactions were friendly. In the pages of *Nexus*, Moseley helped stoke interest in Barker's activities during the summer of 1954, spinning the gap in issues of the *Saucerian* as a potential conspiracy: "Can this be another 'hush-up,' we wonder????"[34] Moseley told Bloecher this was a ploy to encourage Barker to hurry up his schedule.[35]

Barker took advantage of the slow fall season in film booking to move out of Doc Lovett's office and set up his booking business in a private office in the same building (the Ritz Theatre in downtown Clarksburg).[36] At the same time, he kept up the momentum on his saucer-related activities. He struck up a correspondence with a new author named Morris Jessup, whose book on the subject of flying saucers was about to be published; revived correspondence with researchers on the West Coast and abroad; and spent more than a week in New York, during which he met Ted Bloecher and attended a séance at Moseley's apartment with Lucchesi, Roberts, and others.[37] Barker made an effort to make the next issue of the *Saucerian*, released in December, more visually striking than the last, explaining to Moseley, "You probably know you can make a dull article look interesting if you stick some pictures through it."[38] The issue is profusely illustrated, with portraits of saucer research personalities, photographs of skyborne disks, clipped newspaper cartoons, and reproductions from science fiction movie posters appearing on all but a handful of spreads. Perhaps the most notable piece in the issue is Moseley's contribution: "Who's Lying? The Wright Field Story" provides the outlines of a narrative concerning a crashed flying saucer held at Wright-Patterson Air Force Base.[39] Variations on this narrative would recur in ufology for decades to come; it is perhaps better known by the later metanarrative label "Hangar 18."

Barker also revived his interest in Bender's experiences the prior year. In November, he wrote to Australian saucerer Harold Fulton, expressing skepticism about the subject:

My own private and confidential opinion of the Bender Mystery is that there is little mystery connected with it other than the mystery of Al's own mind and imagination. I think that it was part persecution complex, developed, perhaps, out of being unable to cope with the administrative details of his large organization, his inability to solve the saucer mystery, and possibly some deep-seated psychoses.[40]

But even as he expressed these doubts, his receipt of several new narratives from international correspondents revived his interest. First, Latvian-born Canadian researcher Laimon Mitris told Barker that he had received a strange visitor who discouraged him from continuing his saucer research.[41] Then John Stuart and Doreen Wilkinson of New Zealand informed Barker that they had received threatening phone calls, encountered a self-identified spaceman, and heard an invisible creature shuffling and breathing.[42] Barker's doubts arose because Bender's experience seemed thoroughly unique: no one else had been "silenced." Now, however, he wasn't so sure. (Never mind that Mitris received only a single visitor, that Stuart and Wilkinson's threatener was invisible, or indeed that none was silenced but all continued their saucer correspondence afterward.) There was enough similarity between what he called "shush-up" cases, in which strange figures attempted to stop select individuals' saucer research, to constitute, with the right editorial framing, a self-sustaining mystery.[43]

On December 19, 1954, Barker's mother, Rosa, died after a long illness. Her passing cast a pall on the Barkers' Christmas festivities.[44] Perhaps to cheer himself, perhaps out of nostalgia, Barker returned to writing poetry, jokingly planning "an immense work, probably stretching into seven green volumes, called, SEVEN SAGAS."[45] One surviving fragment of this work, "The Symphony of the Horns," is an almost Dadaist piece, consisting of a musical score for a bombastic musical piece written out entirely as comic-book sound effects: "(Brass Horns in D Minor) Grung! Gru-n-n-n-ng-g-g-g-g-g Grun-n-ng-g!"[46] This amusing but impenetrable poem would recur in Barker's work, appearing in unexpected places and ultimately becoming a sort of emblem for his publications—suggesting that they, too, are intended more to entertain than to inform.

By January 1955, Barker's financial health was improving: he bought a new car (an Oldsmobile 98) and an IBM electric typewriter, and he hired a secretary, Carolyn Freeland, to assist with the details of his business.[47] (He still referred to the *Saucerian* as "the world's most bankrupt saucerzine.")[48] He poured himself back into work on the saucerzine, leaving the shortest gap yet between issues. At sixty-four pages, the sixth issue was the longest as well as the most richly illustrated. The cover reproduces a striking image of an enormous hand grasping the earth, taken from promotional materials from the 1951 film *The Day the Earth Stood Still*. The issue includes contributions by popular radio host Frank Edwards and bestselling contactee George Adamski, indicating the increasing status of Barker's publication in the burgeoning flying saucer subculture.

The opening editorial, illustrated with a still from the film *When Worlds Collide*, concerns Dorothy Martin and Charles Laughead's prediction of worldwide calamities and the rescue of a select few by flying saucers in December 1954. Martin's group became well-known shortly after these events due to its infiltration by a team of sociologists from the University of Minnesota who published a poorly anonymized analysis of the group's activities in 1956 under the title *When Prophecy Fails*.[49] Martin had corresponded with Barker earlier in 1954, informing him that she was in contact with "the pilot of an active space craft in the vicinity of Flatwoods" and prophesying that Barker would soon meet with a space person, whom he would be able to identify by a scar on his cheek.[50] Barker jokingly commented at the time in a letter to Sanders: "There's a young kid here who keeps wanting me to take him to Pittsburgh with me some time, but the last time he was around I noticed he has a scar on his left cheek . . . so I think I'll watch the little scamp."[51] The *Saucerian* reproduces Martin's prediction, along with a version of the prosaic reality, but the tone differs drastically from Barker's private comments, giving the details as an example of Martin's prophetic powers.[52]

Barker's main concern, however, is with the constitutional rights of those with eccentric beliefs. The editorial emphasizes Laughead's forced resignation from his position at Michigan State College Hospital; a court petition filed by Laughead's sister, Margaret Laughead ("who is hereby added to the SAUCERIAN's villain list"), attempting to have Laughead and his wife committed to a mental institution; and a threat by the local police to charge Martin with "inciting a riot and possibly with contributing to the delinquency of minors" if her husband did not have her committed.[53] As a publisher of similarly eccentric material, Barker takes these threats against Martin and Laughead seriously, on behalf of both himself and his readers. In another instance of second-person narration, Barker places his readers in the position of the Seekers of Oak Park:

> You are interested in flying saucers, or you wouldn't be reading this publication. Your friends likely know you are interested in flying saucers. Your friends have likely told their friends you are interested in flying saucers.
>
> Look toward the door—can you not see them even now, in your mind's eye, seeking out the first object upon which to vent their fright?[54]

The editorial concludes with a strident defense of the rights of flying saucer fans:

> We believe everyone should have the right to predict the end of the world. There is always something dramatic and entertaining about predicting the world will end, or hearing such a prediction. . . . We do not believe your predictions, Dr. Laughead and Mrs. Martin; We seriously doubt either the reliability of your communications or the intelligence of the space men you have talked to. But we believe WE WOULD TAKE UP ARMS TO PROTECT YOUR RIGHT TO TALK WITH SPACEMEN AND TO PREDICT THE END OF THE WORLD.[55]

The role of the *Saucerian* was to provide sympathetic support to contactees and others with unusual beliefs.

Moseley's zine, by contrast, sought to provide a venue for feuds among figures in the field. Throughout 1955 battles raged in *Nexus* (which changed its name in June to *Saucer News*): Moseley attacked Adamski, prompting Desmond Leslie to respond; Frank Scully and Harold Wilkins traded barbs; and both Adamski's *Inside the Space Ships* and Leonard Cramp's pro-Adamski book *Space, Gravity and the Flying Saucer* were given vicious reviews.[56]

Barker's emerging public persona was that of someone who would give the benefit of the doubt to any narrative; Moseley's, on the other hand, was that he wasn't afraid to lend a page to an attack on any figure, no matter how respected.

Barker planned to begin work on a seventh issue of the *Saucerian* in the spring, with an eye to releasing it in June 1955 and thus producing, for the first time, a full year's worth of quarterly issues.[57] However, it was not to be. Barker turned his attention toward a larger project: a full-length book exploring what had happened to Albert Bender.

5 KNOWING TOO MUCH: 1956–1957

In the mid-1950s, Barker's film booking work began to impact his publishing schedule. The seasonal nature of drive-in theaters meant he had a significant busy season from late winter through August, making arrangements for films to be shown during the spring and summer. By mid-September theatrical work slowed, leaving more time to work on correspondence, writing, and publishing. This often meant delays of several months in responding to letters. He explained his system of mail storage to Sanders in an October 1955 letter:

> Your 12/28/4 letter came up while I was going through an old brief case here at the theatre. You see I'm trying to answer my winter mail, and it is collected in old brief cases, in unused corners of file cases, and most anywhere. Some of it is outside in the trunk of my car in my laundry (that is a long story). I hope you do not feel I'm consigning your work to just on OLD brief case, and that I could have, at least, put it in a NEW one—but it happens I have no new one. The old brief case is still in good condition, but I always have trouble wi[t]h brief cases. First of all, I'm not exactly BRIEF, and then when I get a brief case I throw my unanswered mail into it, and then can't use it until I can answer the mail. Since I never answer the mail, that amounts to a lot of old brief cases lying around.[1]

In addition to catching up on mail, in early years, Barker used fall and winter to produce the *Saucerian*, issuing the first three editions between August 1953 and January 1954 and the second three from September 1954 to February 1955.

Though Barker's business was growing enough to justify hiring a secretary, 1955 was a particularly difficult year for his agency. There was a downward trend in the film exhibition business in the mid-1950s, usually attributed to increasing competition from television. Weekly film attendance dropped from a peak of sixty million in 1950 to lower than forty million by 1958.[2] New drive-ins were still being built, but at greater construction cost and with lower return.[3] Barker had increased his client list to thirty theaters, but this meant significantly more work, especially since his services included promotions.[4] Beyond simply feeling overworked, Barker felt his finances were not as healthy as he hoped, as he wrote to Sanders: "It doesn't seem that I, myself, can ever get ahead and have a buck to put away somewhere."[5] On top of this, he suffered from "nerves," possibly indicating depression:

> After going through all this for a certain length of time I take off half a day (it takes that long to get through the waiting room) and see my doctor, and he gives me a shot of B-something for my nerves and tells me I should have my tonsils taken out. That usually straightens me right out. This time he gave me a prescription for some really exciting tablets: Thoro(sumpthing). I don't know what they are but they're terribly exciting and probably real dangerous too.[6]

It's unclear from the context of this playful letter if Barker was serious about this prescription, apparently a reference to the antipsychotic medication Thorazine. Thorazine was a newly developed medication, and though in 1955 it was chiefly being marketed to psychiatric hospitals for the treatment of schizophrenia and bipolar disorder, its brand name was not yet widely known.[7] But it is not out of the question that Barker, who referred occasionally to having a recurring "persecution complex," would have been prescribed it.

Finding overlap between his business and his hobby, Barker wrote a vigorous defense of saucer sightings to the motion-picture trade magazine the *Exhibitor* in response to a drive-in operator who claimed that a rash of sightings in Cincinnati were caused by reflections from his drive-in screen. In addition to providing additional details about the sightings in question that cast the light-reflection explanation into doubt, he brings his understanding of drive-in design and technology to bear: "Getting back to Mr. Kaplan and his screen, we were always under the impression that drive-in screens if tilted, were tilted DOWNWARD, to reflect the maximum light toward the audience. Perhaps his screen is remarkably different from most."[8]

"CLOAKED IN DRAMATIC LANGUAGE": AUTHORING CONSPIRACIES

Though Barker's saucer-related activities slowed, news related to the topic did not. A major development occurred on October 25, with the Air Force's release of *Special Report 14*, a 316-page account of its investigations into unidentified flying objects. According to Jacobs, the Air Force's hope was that the report "would quiet the UFO controversy once and for all, especially because the report was a scientific study that found no evidence for UFOs being interplanetary objects. But instead of laying the controversy to rest, *Special Report 14* created a new battlefront."[9] The report included detailed, illustrated descriptions of the twelve sightings classified as "unknown" that "were described with sufficient detail that they could be used in an attempt to derive a model of a 'flying saucer.'"[10] The twelve sightings were vastly different from each other, describing a wide range of sizes and shapes. The purpose of including so much detail on these sightings was to show that there was no identifiable pattern to the variety of unidentified objects people had seen in the sky: "Having culled the cream of the crop, it is still impossible to develop a picture of what a 'flying saucer' is."[11] Despite the intent of this section—to suggest that there was no unified phenomenon behind what saucer witnesses described—saucer enthusiasts disregarded the Air Force's intentions and analysis and focused on its selections alone. These entered the saucer lore instead as the "twelve best unknown sightings"—proof that the government's debunkers couldn't account for everything.[12] This is the attitude expressed in a short bulletin that Barker issued regarding the report, arguing that the report and the press coverage surrounding it were "an obvi-ous 'cover up' of the UFO mystery."[13] In a letter to Adamski, Barker argued that the report had a much narrower public relations goal: "to try and squelch the new Keyhoe book"—a belief apparently shared by Keyhoe.[14]

The book in question was Keyhoe's third work on the topic, *The Flying Saucer Conspiracy*, released on November 28 by Henry Holt.[15] While Keyhoe's bestselling second book, *Flying Saucers from Outer Space*, had focused on accounts of individual sightings, particularly those made by pilots and military personnel, *The Flying Saucer Conspiracy* digs deep into the content of statements and news releases issued by the Air Force and the rules and regulations governing the release of information to the public.[16] With chapter titles like "The Silence Group Strikes" and "Cover-Up at Quantico," the book calls the Air Force to task for hiding what it knows from the public. The timing of *Special Report 14* could not have been better for Keyhoe: What better time to market a book about the government's efforts to cover up secrets about saucer sightings than immediately on the heels of a government report intended to put the matter to rest once and for all? UFO historian Curtis Peebles notes that government conspiracy, rather than saucers themselves, was now "the central theme" of Keyhoe's work, and "for the next two decades Keyhoe's beliefs about this would dominate the flying saucer myth."[17]

Barker used the release of Keyhoe's book to further his ambitions as a book distributor, accepting preorders for it in the fall. (He later referred to the preorder solicitation as a "sucker letter.")[18] Because he had not done business with the publisher before, his shipment was delayed, and "as a result everyone else had Keyhoe books to sell before I did."[19] Privately, Barker described *Flying Saucer Conspiracy* as "a MASTERPIECE of the clever rewrite. Just read it carefully, and see how exciting and apocalyptic quite ordinary data becomes when it is cloaked in dramatic language."[20]

Barker paid particularly close attention to the rhetorical aspects of Keyhoe's book because at the time of its release he was hard at work on a manuscript of his own. In late October he had hinted to Harold Fulton that he might wright a book the following year, but quickly decided not to put the project off any further.[21] On November 5, 1955, little more than a week after hinting about his authorial ambitions to Fulton, he started working on a manuscript, completing it by the second week of December.[22]

On the weekend of December 9, Barker traveled to New York to visit Moseley, Roberts, and Lucchesi, and to attend a lecture by Donald Keyhoe hosted by the New York saucer club Civilian Saucer Intelligence. On this trip, he brought the manuscript to the office of left-wing political organizer–turned–publisher Felix Morrow.[23] Morrow had arranged the British Book Centre's US publication of Adamski's *Flying Saucers Have Landed,* and thereafter became interested in the occult more broadly, reading *Fate* and launching his own Mystic Arts Book Society. According to literary historian Alan Wald, "Since he only halfheartedly believed in the occult, he invented a persona, John C. Wilson, for his occultist literary endeavors and never wrote under his own name."[24] Barker met Morrow as he was in the process of launching his new publishing house, University Books. The press would issue a number of works of occultism and orientalism in the early 1960s; counterculture historian Gary Lachman has called it "one of the main suppliers for literature for the sixties occult revival."[25]

Barker described the circumstances of his publishing arrangement in a letter to Sanders. He had assumed that Morrow would have his manuscript rewritten by the ghostwriter of Adamski's second book:

> As you know, Charlotte Blodgett re-wrote [*Inside the Space Ships*]. This isn't a fake name—she's an old lady Morrow employs to do his re-write jobs and editing. When I first brought the manuscript in to him he cleared his throat several times and hesitantly told me that probably they would rewrite the book from cover to cover. He was quite surprised, I think, when I immediately agreed that would be a great idea. After reading the thing, however, he had the opinion that it could be published as is—with minor editing, of course.[26]

Just over a month after he began work on the manuscript, Barker's book was accepted for publication, with a projected publishing date just four months away. In January Morrow came up with a title: *They Knew Too Much about Flying Saucers.*[27]

With his book manuscript complete and accepted for publication, Barker turned his attention back to the *Saucerian.* After a gap of nearly a year between issues, the material he had begun assembling months earlier could no longer be considered news. Moreover, with the imminent publication of a widely distributed book, he could expect many more subscriptions. Both to reduce the strain of producing the full-scale *Saucerian* and to meet increased demand, Barker replaced the zine he had launched in 1953 with the *Saucerian Bulletin*, a smaller-scale publication that could be released with less preparation. Subscriptions to the *Saucerian* would be continued with this new title, which would come out irregularly, "as soon as hot news comes in."[28] To provide a venue for the other material from the *Saucerian*, including more in-depth reporting, humor, and longer book reviews, Barker planned a second publication: a book-length annual entitled the *Saucerian Review*.

The first issue of the *Saucerian Bulletin*, released in early 1956, is indeed a far less elaborate production than the *Saucerian* had become. It featured only a single illustration, poorly reproduced from a newspaper clipping. Carolyn Freeland is credited as "Circulation Director," showing that her duties encompassed both Barker's film booking business and his increasingly professional saucer-related work. The California-based Jacqueline Sanders is jokingly credited as the "Eastern Editor."[29] The dense text consists primarily of brief accounts of sightings and related news, along with an editorial that serves primarily as a plug for the *Saucerian Review* and Barker's forthcoming book. There is a more sales-focused spin to the text of the *Saucerian Bulletin* than its predecessor zine had shown: a list of books on the last page shows Barker's growing book distribution business, listing the major hardcover books by Keyhoe, Edward Ruppelt, and Harold Wilkins, as well more mystical works by Franklin Thomas and Daniel Fry. Barker's apparent goal was to find a way to at least break even on his saucer correspondence, as he explained in a letter to Jessup: "If these people expect you to write back to them, why don't you get some various saucer books to sell and at least get back your postage thru mail orders? I think this is what I will do."[30] Barker had another aim as well: using news reports from Sanders, he sought to incite a feud between psychic contactee Dick Miller and George Hunt Williamson's Telonic Research Center. This sort of internal saucerian conflict could ensure having news to report. To help stir the pot in California without blowing her cover, Sanders asked Barker to remove her name from the publication's masthead.[31]

The *Saucerian Review* followed about a month after the first issue of the *Saucerian Bulletin*. The stated goal of the publication was to provide "a report on the entire year of 1955"—an aim shared by Jessup's *UFO Annual*, announced the previous fall but not released until a few months after Barker's

(Editor's Note: Out of Hopkinsville, a small Kentucky town, came a frightening story. A saucer had landed and discharged a dozen little men which attacked a family living in a farmhouse. Knowing that newspaper reports are often garbled, THE SAUCERIAN sent Jacqueline Sanders, Eastern Editor, to that area to investigate. Her report of the amazing incident follows. -- G.B.)

PANIC IN KENTUCKY

-- By Jacqueline Sanders --

"Here we go again," I told myself.
A spaceship landing and little men.

Figure 5.1

Barker used promotional materials from science fiction films to imbue his publications with a strong visual element. Here, he illustrates Jacqueline Sanders's coverage of the "Hopkinsville Goblins" story with an image from the poster for *Target Earth*. From the *Saucerian Review*, 1956. Author's collection/Public domain.

publication.[32] The trim size and general format is the same as the final issue of the *Saucerian*, but the printing is lower quality, and the lower ratio of images to text gives the book a more cramped feeling. The photo cover is a still from the 1955 film *This Island Earth*, showing a flying saucer in orbit around a model of Earth. In this publication Barker continues to act as a foil to the apparently more levelheaded James Moseley, even printing a brief article by Adamski insinuating that Moseley was a member of the "Silence Group"—implicitly connected here with not only the Air Force but also the three men in black who had visited Bender.[33]

Sanders provides two long features to the *Review*, both re-edited by Barker. The first, appearing under the attention-grabbing title "Panic in Kentucky," is an account of the "Hopkinsville goblins" and their night-long siege of a farmhouse. As Sanders notes, her "investigation" was not able to provide much more detail than the news clippings about the event, though the write-up aims for a more entertaining style than a typical newspaper article would provide. The article is illustrated with images of robots and monsters from pressbooks for the science fiction movies *Target Earth* and *Them*. Sanders's second contribution, entitled "'Twas Brillig, or, A Feminine Viewpoint on Project Bluebook Special Report," is a summary and critique of the Air Force's UFO report, to which Barker added a completely fictitious framing story about Sanders visiting the Pentagon to view the document. Barker later explained the rationale behind this sequence: "A thing like this could turn out to be grossly dull, an unforgivable sin in any of SIN [Saucerian] publications."[34] Sanders reviews the methodology by which Project Blue Book reduced the four thousand sightings it analyzed to a mere twelve "good unknowns." She concludes by wondering: "Why had the report been written in such a complicated manner and avoided clear, simple terms? . . . WAS IT DELIBERATELY WRITTEN IN A MANNER THAT COULD BE INTERPRETED IN A NUMBER OF DIFFERENT WAYS?"[35] The article is followed by photographic reprints of illustrations of the "best" sightings, taken from a microfilm copy of the report obtained by Civilian Saucer Intelligence. In addition to these longer pieces, many of the briefer news reports originate with Sanders, including coverage of the Fortean phenomenon of spontaneously burrowing garden hoses in California (an occurrence Sanders witnessed firsthand).

"YOU JUST MIGHT BE SCARED": *THEY KNEW TOO MUCH ABOUT FLYING SAUCERS*

With the *Saucerian Review* off the press, Barker turned his attention to preparing for the release of *They Knew Too Much*. Morrow wanted a "Name Author" to provide an introduction for the book, but few names in the flying saucer field would be recognizable to the general public.[36] He had hoped to get Donald Keyhoe, a bestselling author and surely the most widely known believer in flying saucers, but the arrangement did not work out. Morrow then suggested that Barker "get my banker or some 'very square' person in town to do a writeup on me attesting I am a Successful Businessman, etc. I just go next door to newspaper publisher, write up a letter and have him sign. It is a real 'square' letter."[37] This letter, signed by H. G. Rhawn of the *Clarksburg News*, is the sole introductory matter in the final version of *They Knew Too Much*.

The book was also coming up shorter than Morrow had hoped: he intended to market the book at $3.50, but needed it to be at least 256 pages to justify that price. To fill out the page count, Barker sent the publisher a brief appendix on the Shaver Mystery and an index.[38] Morrow made up much of the page count through a spacious page design: the first edition of *They Knew Too Much* has the same trim size as Keyhoe's *Flying Saucer Conspiracy*, but significantly larger margins, and thirty lines of text per page compared to Keyhoe's thirty-six. After reviewing galley proofs, Barker was pleased to learn that the text was largely unchanged from his manuscript, with the only deletion of note being a passage referencing George Adamski: "Evidently they want to keep Adamski out of the book for fear it will hurt the truthful impression the book gives."[39]

University Books officially released *They Knew Too Much about Flying Saucers* on May 17, 1956, delayed slightly from the original release date of April 20 by the scramble to increase the book's page count.[40] The book features a striking jacket, designed by Morry Gropper: three shadowy figures stand against a blue background with white stipple suggesting stars; superimposed over them, five yellow saucers rush toward the horizon.

Barker's text opens with a passage of second-person narration headed by a shocking statement:

> There are no such things as flying saucers.
>
> The government has told you that. President Eisenhower himself stated to a saucer-conscious public that to his knowledge no one was coming here from another planet to pay us a visit.
>
> If you believe in Donald H. Menzel, President Eisenhower, and Government announcements you need have no fear of being frightened by this story.

Figure 5.2

University Books' *New York Times* advertisement for *They Knew Too Much about Flying Saucers*, 1956. Public domain.

Read it on a stormy night, or in the middle of a graveyard if you wish. Your equanimity will not be challenged.

Unless you don't believe in Donald H. Menzel, President Eisenhower, and government announcements.

In that case you just might be scared.[41]

This opening sets the stage for strange events to come while giving the audience an off-ramp in the form of passing references to official government statements and the work of arch-debunker Menzel. Fanzine reviewer John Hitchcock noted the difference between typical flying saucer books and Barker's entertainment-focused work, commenting that *They Knew Too Much* "is not a flying-saucer book. It should be classified as an unsolved mystery."[42]

They Knew Too Much reproduces edited versions of the Flatwoods and Brush Creek reports from the first two issues of the *Saucerian*, followed by a brief account of the Shaver Mystery; these three sections account for a quarter of the book's chapters and page count. The story of Bender and the IFSB begins in the fifth chapter and is interspersed with brief, dramatic accounts of several of the major saucer sightings of the early 1950s. Barker gives an insider's account of the IFSB's activities during its brief existence, scrutinizing in particular the events of the spring and summer of 1953. After examining Bender's "silencing," Barker presents similar—and, in some cases, not-so-similar—cases collected from around the world. He cleverly frames the stories of Australia's Edgar Jarrold, California's Meade Layne, New Zealand's John Stuart and Doreen Wilkinson, and Canada's Laimon Mitris (poorly anonymized as Gordon Smallwood), implying that there was a worldwide conspiracy at play. In all cases, Barker points to indications that someone had contacted these individuals in an effort to "shush them up" about saucers—even if, as in the case of Meade Layne, there is little evidence such an event ever occurred. Barker pulls Moseley into the mystery as well, painting him as a shadowy figure in the pay of mysterious forces and presenting at face value Moseley's repeated statement—a transparent parody of the Bender case—that the *next* issue of his *Saucer News* would finally contain the true secret of the saucers, promising yet perpetually postponing the final revelation.[43] Barker ultimately declares that Moseley's saucer research and Peruvian treks must be funded by the Silence Group.

Barker spends a significant portion of the book attempting to iden-tify exactly what theory had led to Bender's "shush-up." The book presents a variety of alternatives to the extraterrestrial hypothesis: that saucers are experimental US aircraft; that they originate beneath the surface of the earth and are piloted by Shaver's dero; that they are controlled by Meade Layne's etherians; that they have something to do with Hugh Brown's theory that the accumulation of ice at the poles would cause the world to flip on its axis. Lex Mebane of Civilian Saucer Intelligence wrote to Barker within a few weeks of the book's release with a positive comment about the book's emphasis on theories other than the extraterrestrial hypothesis.[44] But he was critical of several of the specific "crank" theories that Barker explored, as well as of Barker's overblown style, which he compared to Keyhoe's.[45]

The mystery of the three men, as presented in *They Knew Too Much*, is a puzzle without a solution: every piece of evidence, from articles published in *Space Review* to the matter of Barker's misplaced business card, is presented as possibly holding the key. And yet Barker's book is distinctly different in tone from the increasingly conspiratorial works of Keyhoe. A conspiracist worldview, according to Michael Barkun, is based on a trio of core assump-tions: "*Nothing happens by accident . . . Nothing is as it seems . . . Everything is connected.*"[46] These assumptions run through Barker's book, but what's missing is any reliable theory about who might be behind the sinister events described. It is, in a sense, conspiracism without conspirators. Keyhoe was plain in pointing his finger at the Air Force, but by keeping his subject vague Barker produces a sense of almost cosmic horror. The book concludes not with an answer to its questions but with an extension of the mystery:

I am not alarmed about bug-eyed monsters, little green men, or dero who may or may not be shooting at us with rays from far underground.

Something else disturbs me far more.

There exist forces or agencies which would prevent us from finding out whether or not there are such green men, or bug-eyed monsters, or saucers with things in them.

I have a feeling that some day there will come a slow knocking at my own door.

They will be at your door, too, unless we all get wise and find out who the three men really are.[47]

This closing resembles the cliffhanger at the end of a movie serial. Read with the proper dramatic rise, the final sentence could be the ending of a campfire tale.

Morrow was concerned about some of the private information potentially revealed in *They Knew Too Much*, requesting (after the book had been printed and bound) that Barker obtain signed releases from Lucchesi, Roberts, Moseley, and Bender.[48] Barker doubted that Bender would be willing to grant a release, so he concocted a plan to send Bender a copy of the book with a gushing inscription in an attempt to flatter him into sending a letter in response that could be construed as a legal release. It's unclear if Bender sent such a letter, but Barker explained to Sanders, "Bender doesn't seem angry about anything in the book . . . and won't give us trouble."[49]

But Bender was not the only person who might take issue with the material in the book. On the eve of the book's release, Barker received a letter from Mitris that must have made his blood run cold. Mitris, who at that point had heard only the title of Barker's book, expressed his initial fear that the text would divulge his own narrative—but reminded Barker, with heavy irony, of his promise to keep Mitris's confidence.[50] Barker sent a hedging response to Mitris, who had not yet read the book: "I assure you that your name is not mentioned in it"—technically accurate, since Barker presented Mitris's story under the pseudonym Gordon Smallwood.[51] But the book contained enough information to make the person behind the pseudonym easily identifiable to anyone in the saucer research community. After reading the book, Mitris wrote a distraught letter to Barker. He felt that Barker had manipulated him, conning him into revealing more about his experiences than he otherwise would have, and was shocked to learn from the book that Barker had shared his letters with other saucer investigators.[52] In a letter to Sanders, Barker mentioned Mitris's reaction: "He really made me feel like a heel when he reminded me I sorta broke my word . . . to keep his story secret. . . . Another thing that upset him was that in the book I mentioned sending data on him to another researcher. That WAS a slip—he never was supposed to know I told anyone else."[53] Barker's phrasing makes it clear that he felt guilty not about sharing Mitris's private correspondence, but rather about revealing in the book that he had done so.

On May 22 Barker traveled to New York for a week of promotional events arranged by University Books publicist Mary Greene, who booked radio interviews for Bill Slater's program *Luncheon at Sardi's* and a German-language program hosted by Peter Lindt.[54] University Books scheduled Barker to appear on *Wonderama*, a children's television program hosted by Herb Sheldon, with one odd requirement: he had to appear wearing a space suit.[55] Barker was nervous about appearing on television, confessing to Sanders, "I'm rather shy and timid underneath it all and I'll be scared to death when I get up there before those people and those cameras."[56] Within a few weeks, however, his attitude had changed: "I'm at the point where I rather LIKE hamming it up in front of the TV camera."[57]

Barker delivered two lectures on this trip: first to the North Jersey UFO Group in Jersey City on May 24, and then for a large crowd at the Roosevelt Auditorium, under the auspices of Civilian Saucer Intelligence. CSI, which had previously been able to draw audiences of about 200, turned over the event organization to Morrow, who believed he could attract a thousand people or more and told CSI that "they didn't know how to sponsor a lecture."[58] Morrow spent $400 to advertise the talk, but was unable to advertise it to his entire mailing list in time, and only 312 people attended.[59] Still, this made it CSI's second-most-successful event to date; only Keyhoe had drawn a bigger crowd.[60]

Moseley drove Barker to the auditorium, but Morrow had warned them not to be seen together, lest the audience conclude (correctly) that the section of the book concerning Moseley was a joke.[61] Barker's lecture was followed by a long Q&A session, and he characterized most of the questions as being "of the crackpot type"—but one audience member wanted to know why high-profile saucer researchers like Keyhoe and Barker himself had not been silenced.[62] The event ended when a question from audience member Alex McNeill turned into a lengthy discourse about his own contacts with space people.[63] Mebane and his CSI colleague Ted Bloecher attempted to cut McNeill off, but the audience demanded he be allowed to speak, eventually calling him up to the stage, where he began "talking, in a sing-song trance-like state, about seeing the saucer that came to Flatwoods, WV, BEFORE it came to Flatwoods, and either SENDING it there or being told it was there."[64] After this speech, the event staggered to its conclusion.

Barker's promotional tour continued in Ohio with appearances in Dayton, Columbus, and Cincinnati in mid-June, and a weeklong trip to Chicago with publicist Eleanor Langdon at the end of the month. He visited with contactee John Otto and teenage ufologist Frank Reid, conducted several interviews for radio shows and newspapers, and appeared on the *Bob & Kay Show*.[65] In July, book promotions took him to Cleveland, where he lectured at the WHK Studio and was interviewed for several radio programs.[66] In a phone call to Sanders, Barker worried that he was "entertaining instead of informing" and had become distanced from the ideals that had originally driven his saucer work.[67]

These misgivings were to prove short-lived. Barker quickly embraced "entertaining," particularly regarding contactees, whom the more serious side of the flying saucer community viewed as an undesirable sideshow.[68] Bloecher questioned why Barker gave valuable newsletter space to stories related to them, contending that such publicity would only help their narratives spread even further.[69] Barker responded that his goal was "helping to laugh the crackpots out of existence. It's toungue-in-cheek you know."[70] But this was dissembling: Barker was beginning to make contactees a primary subject of his publishing, devoting most of his final two issues of 1956 to Mon-Ka, a Martian channeled by Dick Miller, who promised to present himself for a live interview on a local radio station.[71] Rather than seeking to "laugh them out of existence," he viewed these narratives as an "inevitable" part of the phenomena that he was documenting in the pages of the *Saucerian Bulletin*.[72]

THE BEGINNINGS OF A SAUCER BUSINESS

In August 1956 Barker moved out of his rented room and into his own apartment at 631 Mulberry Avenue.[73] He found that he drank less after the move: "I used to take drink every night when I went home. That was because I had only one room and couldn't do anything around the place late at night.

Now I can clean house, watch TV, or do most anything."[74] The relative privacy of the apartment also granted Barker greater freedom to seek out sexual partners. The earliest concrete evidence of Barker's sexuality is a 1954 letter written when he rented a new post office box for the *Saucerian*. Among those he notified of his new address was *ONE Magazine*, an early promoter of gay rights founded as an activist offshoot of Los Angeles's Mattachine Society.[75] The magazine launched in 1953, making Barker an early subscriber, and his letter to the periodical is a compelling piece of evidence not only for his sexuality, but also for a conscious sense of identity connected to it.

Some night in the mid-1950s, Barker met a man named Don McCulty at the Clarksburg post office.[76] McCulty was five years younger than Barker, and photographs of him from 1957 show him with an ostentatious elephant-trunk hairstyle. Moses Naedele, whose mother met and became close friends with McCulty in 1959, recalls McCulty as a kind and eccentric character with effeminate mannerisms and a flamboyant fashion sense; his sexuality, Naedele notes, was readily apparent.[77] McCulty was Barker's roommate in his new apartment, and their relationship was an intimate and likely sexual one.[78] In a long letter included in a Christmas publication Barker assembled in 1957, he discusses McCulty with a certain caginess, as if he is not sure what words to use with the group of friends who would be receiving the letter: "Recently I gave Don, my room mate, or I should say, my *apartment* mate, a job doing advertising layouts."[79] McCulty was the sports and entertainment editor at the *Clarksburg Exponent*, but his true passion was the movies, in particular *Gone with the Wind* star Vivien Leigh, in whose honor he altered the spelling of his middle name from Lee to Leigh. McCulty eventually founded her official fan club, the Vivien Leigh Society. In addition to his relationship with Barker, McCulty was in a heterosexual relationship with Alma Corder, society editor at the *Exponent*.[80] The relationship between Barker and McCulty would last several years, and McCulty's name occasionally appears on Barker's saucer-themed writings.

Barker relocated his office in addition to his home, moving out of the Ritz Theatre to a two-room office at 158 West Main Street, across the street from Clarksburg's post office.[81] The Ritz had proven an unsatisfactory and even dangerous office: in a letter to the building's manager in October 1956,

Barker requested the cancellation of his lease and a refund of over nine months of rent, claiming that he had essentially abandoned the office in mid-1955 because "the roof of said office did leak, forcing me, the tenant, to conduct business elsewhere, at considerable expense, loss of good will, and mental anguish."[82] (The landlord declined his request.) Canadian saucer researcher Gene Duplantier, who visited Barker not long after he moved to Main Street, later described the new office: "It was a double store situation—the left store was his business with printing press, books, papers, magazines piled on shelves and tables. . . . Gray had his office in the back, a big desk and chair, surrounded by more floor to ceiling bookshelves."[83] A commonly reprinted image of Barker, seated beside a large bookshelf and speaking on the phone with a businesslike expression, was likely taken in this office.[84]

By October 1956 *They Knew Too Much* had sold ten thousand copies of a total print run of fifteen thousand—numbers that Morrow considered disappointing, though he was hopeful that sales would pick up in the coming months.[85] In November Barker received a royalty payment of about $520 from Morrow. He used the bulk of the money to pay off a $500 debt to Doc Lovett, then "took the twenty some dollars, went down to the liquor store and bought all the booze I could carry. Am waiting to throw party when someone comes around who can cry with me when drunk."[86] Despite the immediate consumption of these royalties, he seems to have been making some money, as he also bought his second new car in as many years: a Continental Mark II. As much as he liked this car, within a year he was referring to it as a "heap of junk" and traded it in for an even flashier Mark III.[87] He hid his new signs of success from others in the saucer world. Barker facetiously reported his response in a letter to Sanders: "They should realize that I am JUST LOSING MONEY HAND OVER FIST EVERY DAY IN SAUCERS AND THAT I HAVE TO TAKE MONEY OUT OF MY OTHER BUSINESS, ETC. What's the penalty for lying, in the Next World?"[88]

Throughout the fall of 1956, Barker corresponded with Jessup on the business of publishing and selling books. Both were frustrated at the low royalty rates they were earning for their publications. Jessup was especially irritated at Citadel Press for how they had handled his *UFO Annual*, which was selling poorly. Jessup did not believe that the mainstream publishers understood the flying saucer audience. In October he told Barker that the only path to a sustainable income from UFO books was to self-publish.[89] He suggested that, if Barker could get the mailing list that Morrow had assembled for marketing *They Knew Too Much*—which combined the list that Citadel had used for *The Case for the UFO* with the distribution list for Civilian Saucer Intelligence—they would have a strong basis for starting their own campaign of direct marketing.[90] By marketing directly to the core of those already interested in saucers and cutting out many the expenses incurred in mainstream publishing, there would be more income for the authors.

Barker knew how to market to his audience, presenting himself as the sole information source unafraid to distribute occult knowledge that mysterious unnamed forces wanted to suppress. When Roger Pierce and Howard Neuberger, Ohio-based editors of the saucer publication *Cosmic News*, recalled an issue, Barker related the suppression to an article about a Mr. Von Mobile—who may have been a hoax character Barker invented as a prank.[91] Barker plays up the story for maximum mystery before pivoting to salesmanship: "They tried to buy back our shipment, but no dice. WE'RE DISTRIBUTING THEM. We have a dozen at 50¢ per copy."[92] At that price, who wouldn't want to know too much?

Barker wasn't alone in looking for ways to turn saucer writing into something more lucrative. In September Ray Palmer had contacted Barker about putting together a professional flying saucer magazine. He needed startup money but was hoping to involve all of the major figures in flying saucer research: "If we don't do it, he says, some opportunist in NYC will do it on a 'sensational' basis and ruin the whole thing."[93] While the arrangement with Jessup never came to fruition, Barker would combine Jessup's basic idea with Palmer's sense of showmanship to launch the next phase of his saucer journey.

6 CHASING THE FLYING SAUCERS: 1957–1959

In the spring of 1957 Palmer launched his saucer periodical, changing the title of his SF magazine *Other Worlds* to *Flying Saucers from Other Worlds*. For several months the magazine alternated between the two titles before fully eschewing science fiction for ostensible nonfiction toward the end of 1957. Barker was credited as the magazine's "Eastern Editor" and contributed a regular column, Chasing the Flying Saucers, beginning with the first issue under the new title. Barker wasn't paid for the column but provided it in exchange for a free ad in each issue—a value of about a hundred dollars per column.[1] It may not have brought any direct income, but the publicity was valuable, even if some in the more serious side of saucer study viewed Palmer as a dishonest huckster. CSI's Lex Mebane wrote to Barker to chastise him for his cooperation in Palmer's endeavor, warning him that it would prove harmful to Barker's own reputation.[2] But to Barker, a larger audience was always more important than any semblance of scientific objectivity: he told Mebane flatly that "the mass market of saucer enthusiasts . . . consists of those who like the contact type of article."[3] Privately, he laughed with Moseley over Mebane's dramatic letter.[4] The same audience-pleasing coverage of unreliable but entertaining stories informed Barker's increasingly frequent call-in appearances on Long John Nebel's all-night WNYC radio program, where he provided commentary on the strangest saucer tales.[5]

Barker's column consists primarily of brief, disconnected accounts of saucer sightings, developments in the world of saucer fandom, and Fortean occurrences, often with a short introductory section offering more dramatic

Figure 6.1

Gene Duplantier's column header for Barker's Chasing the Flying Saucers column, 1958. Internet Archive/Public domain.

flavor. What is perhaps most surprising about the column is its length: at about six thousand words, each column in the bimonthly magazine generally exceeded the length of the six-page *Saucerian Bulletin*, which was particularly impressive considering the fact that much of the material in the *Saucerian Bulletin* was retyped from letters, zines, and news clippings rather than written by Barker himself. To invest this much effort, on a stricter schedule than he had been following for the *Saucerian Bulletin*, indicates the increasing importance of Barker's book distribution business. The income produced from mail-order sales through Palmer's nationally distributed magazine likely justified taking time away from theatrical work to produce the column. To pick up some of the resulting slack, Barker expanded his staff, hiring McCulty to lay out newspaper ads and a second assistant for general duties on both the saucer and movie sides of his business.

Alongside a smattering of sighting reports, Barker's first Chasing the Flying Saucers column discusses the biggest saucerological story of the season: the founding of the National Investigations Committee on Aerial Phenomena (NICAP). Though it would go on to become a dominant force in the UFO realm throughout the 1960s, NICAP's origins were inauspicious, and it nearly imploded within months of its founding.[6] NICAP began in

October 1956, under the directorship of inventor and antigravity researcher T. Townsend Brown. At its first meeting the group's governing board voted to give themselves substantial salaries totaling some $85,000.[7] The organization planned to cover these expenses by charging an annual membership fee of fifteen dollars, but with little to show for this hefty fee, the organization failed to attract many paying members. Only three months after NICAP's founding, its entire staff had either quit or were fired, with the sole exception of Brown's secretary, Rose Hackett.

Donald Keyhoe was angered by what he saw as Brown's mismanagement of the fledgling group, and after a tense January 1957 meeting NICAP's board of governors ousted Brown and appointed Keyhoe in his place. Though initially appointed as interim director, Keyhoe stayed on for more than a decade.[8] In that time he successfully used the organization to shape the public discourse around UFOs, focusing for the first several years of his tenure on fighting against the veil of secrecy at the Air Force that had been the subject of his books. The concrete goal Keyhoe sought was congressional hearings on the UFO subject in which Air Force officials could be questioned under oath. Jacobs comments that Keyhoe's strategy meant that NICAP "was inextricably connected with Air Force policies and whims."[9]

Keyhoe wrote to Barker in early March 1957, announcing that he was reaching out to saucer clubs and independent publications to communicate his emerging plans for the organization, but the information went unmentioned in the *Saucerian Bulletin*.[10] The lack of any notice of NICAP's existence in the *Saucerian Bulletin* indicates just how far these conservative aims were from those of Barker's publication, which was moving further and further away from the "feet on the ground" approach indicated by the motto of the original *Saucerian*.

Barker's role as a columnist for a regularly published magazine led to an increase in the frequency of his japes in 1957. The *Saucerian Bulletin* was not released on a set schedule, but for Palmer's magazine Barker need to generate several thousand words of saucer news every two months, regardless of whether there had been notable sightings or other events. The saucers were out of Barker's control, but if he could manipulate researchers into reporting on other, more earthbound happenings—odd letters, phone calls in the middle of the night, and so on—he increased his chances of having something to write about.

Moseley's *Saucer News*, published on a regular bimonthly schedule, faced similar hurdles, and Moseley became both a collaborator in and a target of several of Barker's pranks. Chief among these was a supposed feud between the two saucerzine publishers, who frequently sniped at one another in print despite their growing friendship. In early 1957 Pierce and Neuberger received an anonymous letter falsely claiming that Moseley was in the employ of the United States Air Force, insinuating that his mission was to poison the saucerological discourse.[11] The letter continues with a request that all but guaranteed its publication: "It is high time that someone spoke out against this farce. However, please realize that I am giving you the information in this letter in *absolute confidence*, and for your own information only. Under no circumstances would it be wise for you to publish this information in your UFO magazine."[12] Pierce and Neuberger acceded to this demand to the letter: instead of publishing the missive in *Cosmic News*, they passed it on to Barker—its likely author—who reproduced it in full in the *Saucerian Bulletin*.

In private, however, Barker and Moseley were becoming increasingly close friends. Moseley visited Barker in Clarksburg several times a year, and during these visits the pair would typically drink heavily and engage in pranks. During one visit in early 1957, they made several prank calls to UFO personalities Laura Mundo and Coral Lorenzen. To Mundo, they pretended to be members of the Silence Group; to Lorenzen, Air Force officials with a tantalizing offer of secret information. Barker and Moseley's efforts to bait these researchers was successful. Mundo printed a full account of the call she received in the Interplanetary Foundation's *Newsletter*: "'THIS IS THE SILENCE GROUP. WE HAVE BEEN INFORMED TO TELL YOU TO GET OUT OF THE FLYING SAUCER RESEARCH AT ONCE!'"[13] In her 1982 book *The Mundo UFO Report* Mundo referred again to this phone call, still believing it to be from the "Silence Group, the three men in black (MIB)," but adding an identification of the voice on the other end as "a young man whom I had met at [a] convention planning meeting that afternoon in Grand Rapids."[14] Lorenzen also published an account of the phone call she received, albeit a more skeptical one, in the *APRO Bulletin*.[15] Barker, in turn, reprinted the accounts of both calls in his second Chasing the Flying Saucers column, as evidence of further "shush-ups."[16]

WHY HOAXES?

According to Moseley, one of his and Barker's chief contributions to "the ufoological side of The Field" was "to stir the ufological pot when things got dull."[17] But it wasn't only during slow periods in UFO news that Barker and Moseley engaged in hoaxes: the duo created one notable forgery, the Lost Creek Saucer film, in the summer of 1966, when public interest in UFOs was at its zenith.[18] The film wasn't intended to spice up a slow period but to generate debate at a time of high interest, to produce the "sounding of contrary opinions" that folklorist Linda Dégh identifies as the genesis point of a new legend.[19] Creating a false saucer narrative, photograph, or film; forging a document; or making a prank shush-up call could provide evidence that Barker could use intertextually in support of other narratives. These narratives then entered the broader macronarrative discourse as evidence for UFO enthusiasts to debate and analyze.

A pattern in Barker's hoaxing practices suggests a motivating factor beyond producing weird narratives on which he could report. In many of Barker's hoaxes, he used the shared secrecy over a prank as a means of establishing intimacy. This pattern originated with peers like Lucchesi and Moseley, but in his pranks in the years to come, Barker would often enlist a young, intelligent saucer enthusiast as a partner. This nonsexual intimacy provided an essential pathway for interpersonal connection and platonic pleasure.

Christopher Miller argues that hoaxes devalue their targets and obscure their self-narratives, and from this perspective, Barker's pranks on the likes of Adamski, Mundo, and John Keel appear malicious.[20] But Barker seems to have felt honest affection for his targets. In the introduction to his humorous publication *UFO 96* he writes: "There is no intent to harm or ridicule anybody. . . . I suspect that I like and look up to most everybody who has been satirized or burlesqued broadly in this strange book."[21] In Barker's view, his targets weren't merely interested in alien visitors and sinister silencers; they desired to live in a world where these things were real. In explaining his decision to title John Sherwood's 1967 book *Flying Saucers Are Watching You*, he commented that, for saucer enthusiasts, the idea of "something watching them is most appealing."[22] In Barker's view, if these things were not real, then reality could only disappoint his targets. In providing them with images of a "real" UFO, an experience of being targeted by men in black suits, or a letter communicating secret governmental support, Barker was giving his marks an experience of the reality *that they wanted*.[23] If his goal had been to show his targets up, he would have revealed his pranks publicly and reveled in laughing at them. But his pranks were private affairs between himself and his targets: manifestations of an otherworldly experience.

THE FORGOTTEN SHUSH-UP: DR. REICH

Barker sought out shush-up cases, but he let an important one go unmentioned in his public writings. In March 1957 he received a phone call from Dr. Eva Reich, daughter of the eccentric psychoanalyst Wilhelm Reich—though at the time of the call Barker does not seem to have been aware of who the elder Dr. Reich was. A student of Sigmund Freud, Reich had fled Europe in 1939 and resettled in the United States. After his relocation he developed a theory that the universe was suffused and directed by a force he called *orgone energy*, derived from and named after the orgasm.[24] Reich believed that orgone energy could be used to, among other things, control the weather and heal illness, and he founded the Orgone Institute to study it.

After reading Keyhoe's *Flying Saucers from Outer Space* in 1953, Reich had become fascinated by the subject.[25] He theorized that the saucers were spaceships powered by orgone energy, and speculations about their motive force and potential hostile activity fueled much of his speculative writing in the mid-1950s.[26] In 1954 the Food and Drug Administration challenged Reich in court over his manufacture of orgone accumulators—devices patients could sit in to receive the positive benefits of orgone energy. Reich, believing "that the court had no jurisdiction over fundamental research," refused to appear in his own defense.[27] The court issued an injunction forbidding the sale and distribution of orgone accumulators, as well as the distribution of any of Reich's publications mentioning orgone—including newer editions of his influential early works, like *The Mass Psychology of*

Fascism, which contains only brief references to the theory. After an associate sent accumulator components through the mail in 1956, Reich was found in contempt of court for violating the injunction. He was met with a severe punishment: not only was he imprisoned, but the court ordered the destruction of his orgone accumulators and the incineration of "promotional materials" concerning them, defined so broadly as to include virtually all of Reich's published work. The ACLU issued a press release protesting the destruction, but the story received little press coverage. Biographer Robert Corrington notes the bleak irony of Reich's position: "He had written a brilliant deconstruction of the entire Nazi psychological and mythic structure, only to have his book banned and burned."[28]

Eva Reich contacted Barker on March 13, the day after Wilhelm Reich was imprisoned, because "she remembered, she said, Bender's statement of how he could go to jail if he talked too much."[29] She hoped to enlist Barker's participation in senatorial hearings on her father's case—hearings that had little possibility of ever occurring. Her call to Barker indicated that she shared some of the elder Reich's quixotic, grandiose attitude: "She had brought, she said, a charge of treason against certain officials of the State of Maine.... She said she could force a government investigation, because she could 'flood the whole United States' if they didn't listen to her."[30]

Barker, unaware of Reich's work or his legal troubles, seems to have considered this a crackpot call. The younger Dr. Reich's discussion of a "first battle of the universe" against invading saucers had enough in common with the sorts of calls and letters Barker regularly received that he seems to have doubted the Reichs' very real legal crisis.[31] Barker declined to get involved directly, instead suggesting that Eva Reich enlist Bender's assistance— "seeing, in the back of my mind, a wonderful publicity gimmick."[32] Ultimately, nothing came of Reich's attempts to organize an investigation into her father's persecution, and the elder Reich died in prison in November. The phone call failed to spark interest from Barker beyond a brief summary sent to friends and colleagues several months later in which he asked, "Anyone know any thing about this Dr. Reich?"[33]

It's clear that the Reichs were following saucer culture enough to be aware of the concept of shush-ups and sinister silencers. But it appears that saucer culture was not so aware of the very real silencing of Dr. Reich. Later ufologists would cite Reich's persecution in connection to Barker's "three men in black suits," but Barker himself, faced with a direct report of government suppression of a flying saucer believer, failed to make the connection.[34] Barker's indifference is especially surprising given the parallels between Wilhelm Reich and Charles Laughead, whose right to eccentricity without fear of prosecution Barker had defended in the *Saucerian*. Referring to the call years later, he wrote, "I will always regret not having heard [Eva Reich] out more completely and not being more sympathetic to the daughter of a man who was either mad, a genius, or both."[35]

ALIEN AMONG US: THE LONDON CONVENTION

Several SF magazines made overtures to the flying saucer subculture in 1957. *Fantastic Universe* made its February 1957 edition a special saucer issue (including an essay by Barker), and invited Civilian Saucer Intelligence to provide a regular column to the magazine, which they provided for the next two years.[36] *Amazing Stories* followed with its own flying saucer issue in October 1957, with contributions by Barker, Ray Palmer, Kenneth Arnold, and Richard Shaver, among others. Bill Meyers excoriated the issue in a review for the fanzine *Cry of the Nameless*, singling out Barker's contribution, which he argued "shows how absurd and idiotic the imaginative (but mainly publicity seeking) American public can get."[37]

Around the time that this issue of *Amazing Stories* was released, Barker made his first international trip, traveling to London to attend the 1957 World Science Fiction Convention, or Loncon. To ensure a significant American presence, a group of fans chartered a plane from New York to the event, and Barker and McCulty joined the flight.[38] Barker attempted to rouse interest from others in the saucer world and invited Jacqueline Sanders to travel from California to join them. By this point he was aware of the growing division between SF fandom and the saucer world, cautioning Sanders: "never never NEVER mention saucers. Science Fiction fans HATE saucers. My idea is to take over the plane with saucer fans and turn the whole convention into a saucer convention—Oh, devilish me!!!!!"[39] Ultimately, however, the only other saucer personalities who joined the charter flight were Roger Pierce and Howard Neuberger.

Figure 6.2
Don Leigh McCulty and Gray Barker in London for the World Science Fiction Convention, September 1957. Gray Barker UFO Collection, Clarksburg-Harrison Public Library/Courtesy of the Gray Barker Estate.

Though the convention provided the rationale for Barker's trip to London, he gives surprisingly little account of it. He attended the masquerade ball, wearing a spaceman costume, which he claimed won him second prize.[40] He spends far more effort describing the squalid conditions at the King's Court Hotel, which was under renovation during the convention, and his group's search for other accommodations.[41] Barker and McCulty spent much of the trip exploring London independently. Barker visited London's movie studios, stopped in at a meeting of the contactee organization the Aetherius Society, and went to the offices of publisher Werner Laurie to make arrangements for the publication of a British edition of *They Knew Too Much*.[42]

Barker's interactions with SF fandom largely concluded with Loncon: the tight-knit community of SF fans had little room for someone who was readily identifiable as "the flying saucer man."[43] But his brief period of engagement with fandom gave him an apprenticeship in nurturing a subculture. In the pages of *Amazing Stories*, Ray Palmer had sought to foster a community by encouraging interaction between reader and publisher. When organized science fiction fandom excommunicated Palmer and Shaver, it drove those interested in the paranormal to produce a parallel fandom, which struggled along anemically in a handful of Shaver fanzines before finding an anchoring place in the explosion of flying saucer zines that began in the early 1950s. Barker was a key figure in the early stage of this community, and he expanded the saucer macronarrative along lines drawn from science fiction fandom, specifically "fannish" zines that focused the activities of fans themselves (contrasted with "serious and constructive," or "sercon," writing that focused on criticism of science fiction itself).[44] In turning his attention to Bender and the closure of the IFSB, Barker represents "fannish" flying saucer writing in the *Saucerian* and *They Knew Too Much*, in contrast with the "sercon" writing of investigative organizations like APRO and NICAP.

"MAN SHUDDERS JOYFULLY": A GIFT FOR THE INNER CIRCLE

While NICAP struggled to find its footing, an event in the fall of 1957 had a substantial impact on attitudes about space: the October 4 launch of the

Soviet Union's Sputnik satellite. A wave of saucer sightings followed: The Air Force's Air Technical Intelligence Center received over five hundred reports of unidentified objects in the sky in November 1957, up from fewer than forty per month during the first half of the year.[45] Saucer debunker Donald Menzel declared, "The current rash of flying saucers is tied in with the sensitization of people to the Sputniks."[46] Surely the news from the Soviet Union would have prompted more people to look into the night sky, and a corresponding increase in sightings of unusual phenomena is only natural. The huge spike dropped off rapidly, and 1958 had fewer sighting reports than 1956.[47] But the November wave of sightings, in particular a widely reported series in the area of Levelland, Texas, briefly put saucers back in the headlines.

Barker responded with humor to these relatively serious events unfolding. As 1957 drew to a close, Barker began work on a Christmas present for his friends (including, but probably not limited to, the "inner circle"), which he described as an "a special *private* edition of SIN [the *Saucerian*]."[48] According to the introduction of this spirit-duplicated publication, sent out around Christmastime, it "will be called by a number of names . . . since covers will be different for different addressees."[49] The total edition size, according to a letter to Sanders, was fifteen copies; recipients included Moseley, Sanders, and Frank Scully.[50] The two copies of the publication retained in Barker's archive—at least one of which was sent to Jim Moseley—bear the title *Youranus*, with a cover design parodying the British saucer zine *Uranus*. The back cover—which may have been the front cover of some copies—bears the title *Other Tongues, Other Cash* (a parody of George Hunt Williamson's *Other Tongues, Other Flesh*). Gene Duplantier's copy was titled *The Books of Charles Fart*.[51]

Youranus contains a wide array of jabs at all corners of the saucer world, but especially his friend and rival Moseley and contactees like Adamski, Williamson, and Angelucci. Interspersed throughout are long-form jokes—often bawdy—with no connection to saucers, letters from fans and crackpots, poems, and cartoons. The text is printed on a number of different paper stocks, including booking forms from Barker's film business, pages with tipped-in cartoons, and sheets of toilet paper. A statement in the introduction suggests the possibility of significant variation between copies:

> As you read this issue over you will realize it is not a publication that can be generally distributed. In fact I fear I will have to choose carefully each addressee. Then I will find it necessary to go over his or her issue and carefully tear out the pages that may upset that particular reader, possibly because I may say something terrible about that person. In those issues I will insert blank sheets of paper so that the bulk will not be cut down.[52]

The copy sent to Moseley does contain blank sheets, indicating the possibility of redacted material. But it's just as likely that Barker inserted blank pages into *every* copy of the publication, hoping to convince recipients that he had said something terrible about each of them.

In his opening introduction (signed in jest with the name Orfeo Angelucci), Barker responds to a charge by Moseley that he had abandoned his early ideals in pursuit of money from gullible saucer followers. He quotes in full a poem Moseley wrote about him: "Oh, he sold his soul to the Great Green God, / Now he worships at the Shrine of Green . . . But somewhere there along the way / The Green God beckoned him aside; / And on that saddened, mournful day / The message he had carried died."[53] Barker's response to the poem reveals the more ironic approach he took to saucer activities: "We never did have, to my knowledge, a Message, and as for Truth, that is also debatable."[54] Barker grants that something has changed since his earliest publications, but notes that it has nothing to do with monetary gain: "It is true that the sheer joy of putting out saucer fanzines never quite shows up any more. Issues are never a labor of love as they once were. . . . But I think that I have returned to the sublimity of issuing publications with this effort."[55] The attempt to recover a lost joy extends even to the layout and printing of the publication, which is chiefly done on a spirit duplicator— Barker's first use of this printing method for a full publication since the third issue of the *Saucerian*, nearly four years before. Barker does add a new tool: some of the correspondence in *Youranus* is reproduced using a Verifax machine, a photographic duplicator that produced a copy of a letter-sized document in about a minute, but could make only a handful of copies before the quality degraded.[56]

Barker includes facsimiles of several strange and eccentric letters he had received, presented with little or no comment but implying mockery of their crackpottery. A two-page comic strip entitled "They Knew Too Little about Flying Saucers" is illustrated by Gene Duplantier, who would go on to become a frequent collaborator on Barker's publications.[57] The strip is a burlesque of the Bender story that uses the broad and biting parodic style of EC Comics' *Mad*, of which Barker was a fan; it concludes with the three men in black revealing themselves as doctors from a psychiatric hospital.[58]

Youranus also features hoaxes and confessions of hoaxes, including a long letter from "Clerk 209" of the "International Bankers" to Neuberger and Pierce. Barker introduces the text with sarcasm: "Doesn't this put a cold chill over you, or does it affect you, as it does some more blasé people, by inciting peals of laughter?"[59] Barker would later reprint this letter—without the satirical introduction—as a genuine document in a 1962 issue of the *Saucerian Bulletin*.[60] Here, Barker follows it with another prankish letter to Neuberger signed by Edgar Smith that pushes the "International Bankers" narrative to absurd lengths, pulling in "Otto Von Mobile," a mysterious character with whom Barker had teased Neuberger and Pierce several years before.[61] Smith explains: "Prince Otto [Von Mobile] is the President of the Earth and Venus Interstellar Bankers Association, which is only a small part of the entire Interstellar Bankers Association. . . . The International Bankers Association of the Planet Earth is composed of fallen angels disguised as reputable men going about the work of hushing up serious UFO investigators while taking orders from His Supreme Highness Otto Von Mobile."[62] Barker concludes with a prediction that this absurdist take on the International Bankers would likely recur, in time, and that "their mayhem will be of an intangible, almost pleasant type, as man shudders joyfully."[63] Throughout *Youranus*, but particularly in this section, Barker's glee at hoaxes—whether successful or fizzled, perpetrated by himself or by others—is palpable.

THE STRAITH LETTER

A few days after returning from Loncon in 1957, Barker received a threatening letter from the "International Bankers" advising him to cease mentioning their activities in his publications.[64] Shortly thereafter Barker received a confession from the young saucer enthusiast who had sent the threat.[65] Barker took inspiration from this prank and soon printed up engraved International Bankers stationery to use for future prank letters to saucer researchers.[66] In response the correspondent, whose father worked for the federal government, made an offer of several different kinds of government stationery, including letterhead from the State Department and the US Information Agency. Barker gleefully accepted: "Send me ALL that stationery you mention, and I promise you I won't get in trouble over it—just shut up a few people, that's all."[67]

When Moseley visited Clarksburg in mid-December, the two put this windfall to use. During an evening of drinking, they composed seven hoax letters. According to Moseley: "There was no advance planning of any kind. We made the things up as we went along, emboldened by the evil of alcohol and fully enjoying the chance to throw long-term confusion into ufology."[68] The first six documents—addressed to Laura Mundo, Lex Mebane, Coral Lorenzen, California saucer fan Manon Darlaine, an unidentified saucer researcher, and Moseley's own father—had little impact.[69] But the seventh became, in Moseley's words, "the most successful hoax in ufological history."[70]

Addressed to George Adamski from "R. E. Straith, Cultural Exchange Committee" and written on State Department letterhead, the letter is present in Barker's files as both a contemporary Verifax printed by Barker and a photostat later sent to him by Adamski's organization. It reads in full:

My Dear Professor:

For the time being, let us consider this a personal letter and not to be construed as an official communication of the Department. I speak on behalf of only a part of our people here in regard to the controversial matter of the UFO, but I might add that my group has been outspoken in its criticism of official policy.

We have also criticized the self-assumed role of our Air Force in usurping the role of chief investigating agency on the UFO. Your own experiences will lead you to know already that the Department has done its own research and has been able to arrive at a number of sound conclusions. It will no doubt please you to know that the Department has on file a great deal of confirmatory evidence bearing out your own claims, which, as both of us must realize, are controversial, and have been disputed generally.

While certainly the Department cannot publicly confirm your experiences, it can, I believe, with propriety, encourage your work and your communication of what you sincerely believe should be told to our American public.

In the event you are in Washington, I do hope that you will stop by for an informal talk. I expect to be away from Washington during the most of February, but should return by the last week in that month.

Sincerely,

R. E. Straith
Cultural Exchange Committee
RES/me[71]

The odd name signed to the letter hints at its status as a hoax: "Straith" suggests both *straight*, ironically overstating the document's authenticity, and *wraith*, indicating the character's intangible nature. The first initial—revealed in a later document to stand for Reynold—suggests Reynard the Fox, a trickster figure from medieval folklore.[72] Despite not having been planned in advance, the letter is carefully calculated to appeal to Adamski, who had previously sought to play up even the most minor indications of official support for his claims. The Straith letter targets Adamski's yearning for official recognition, promising that, despite appearances, his efforts had support at the highest levels. But it so fully represented the reality in which Adamski wanted to believe that the hoax became far more successful, and more dangerous, than Barker and Moseley had ever intended.

Within days of receiving their hoax letter, CSI members had correctly deduced that the letter was the work of Barker and Moseley, and they shared this conclusion with Lorenzen and Keyhoe.[73] Deciding that this was a distraction from the subject of UFOs and that publicizing it would reward the behavior, they agreed to remain silent about it. But Adamski took his own approach and made his letter public by the middle of February, sending photostats of it to saucer publishers, including Barker himself. The first published notice of the Straith letter was in an issue of the British saucer zine *Flying Saucer Review* released in late February, which ran quotations from the text; Adamski reprinted the letter in full in his second *Questions and Answers* booklet, published in or around March of 1958.[74] The existence of the Straith letter was now public knowledge in the saucer world, and several amateur investigators immediately set to work tracing its origin.

Barker was hesitant to publish the letter himself, however. The May 1, 1958, issue of the *Saucerian Bulletin* reproduced Adamski's commentary but not the forgery itself. Barker hints that he would rather Adamski had not made it public: "Maybe some official went out on a personal limb, not feeling that Adamski would publicize the letter (which he evidently intends to do through the booklet he mentions). We thoroughly suspect that such an individual is in very hot water."[75] He concludes by asking his correspondents not to write to him about the subject, encouraging them to contact Adamski directly instead.[76] Barker's first published reference to the Straith letter betrays signs of regret that his hoax was beginning to go further than he had intended.

Barker launched his disinformation campaign in earnest in the June issue of the *Saucerian Bulletin*, devoting four pages—nearly a quarter of the issue—to the Straith letter. He at last reproduces the text of the letter itself, followed by several paragraphs of speculation. He concludes by arguing that the Straith hoaxer's goal was to discredit all saucer research, "TO MAKE THE ENTIRE FIELD OF CIVILIAN SAUCER RESEARCH A THING TO BE TAKEN AS A BIG JOKE."[77] Ultimately, he connects the Straith letter to the three men in black:

> The three men, however spooky in their dramatic black garb, are, after all, much easier to deal with than the less-tangible but even more diabolical techniques, such as the Straith letter may well represent. For those intangible demons can be dealt with only by the careful exercise of human logic and the human heart. In facing such a combatant bear in mind that you are facing logic that does not always follow a logical pattern—almost as if you were dealing with some alien intelligence that does not think in terrestrial terms (though we are certainly not suggesting that a space man wrote the Straith letter).[78]

In the context of Barker's perpetration of the hoax, this article hints at his purposes: to sow confusion, to expand the sense of strangeness and menace surrounding saucer investigations, and to delight in adopting the role of a folk devil.

Despite this, there remains a sense that Barker had had his fun and now wants the Straith story to come to an end. Barker makes a passing reference to the hoax letter in his column for the December issue of Palmer's magazine (the title of which was now shortened to simply *Flying Saucers*).[79] The column, written in the spring, suggests Barker thought interest in the hoax would dissipate, having been a momentary distraction during a lull in sightings. But it is an unpublished document that gives the clearest evidence that Barker hoped to bring the narrative surrounding the hoax to a conclusion. A final forged document kept in Barker's "Straith" file, dated May 25, 1958, and written on "United States Government Office Memorandum" letterhead, the typescript document presents itself as a letter from the office of Air Force Gen. G. K. Ganey to Straith. The text of the memo reads:

> With reference to your letter which Mr. George Adamski recently released to the world, I am hereby ordered to relieve you of your position on the Cultural Exchange Committee effective May 30, 1958, and to inform you that you have been transferred to a new post of duty in Beirut, Lebanon. Full travel orders are being forwarded now. You will be leaving almost immediately, so I suggest you prepare now.
>
> (signed)
>
> Major John Hallen, Adj.
> for Gen. G. K. Ganey, USAF[80]

There is no evidence that Barker arranged for the release or publication of this memo, and Moseley makes no reference to it in his memoir's detailed account of the hoax. There are two ways in which to read the document. On the one hand, it indicates the possibility of a desire to keep the mystery of Reynold E. Straith going and to provide further suggestions that there were those in the government who believed in the more outrageous claims of saucerdom's fringes—and those who wished to silence them. On the other hand, it hints at Barker's desire to banish the Straith character for good.

But Straith had now taken on a life of his own, driven by the amateur investigations of saucer enthusiasts.[81] By the fall of 1958, Barker had reason to worry about how close to him the investigations into the Straith letter, both amateur and official, were drawing. Sometime in September he was visited by an investigator from the State Department, though available details about the visit are unfortunately scant. Barker later published a brief and fairly vague account of the visit, indicating that the investigator's main concern was in getting "names of people publishing saucer magazines" and asking "questions about the saucer field in general."[82] The FBI apparently got involved as well: Adamski told Barker that they asked him about the matter in September.[83]

Toward the end of the year *Saucer News* contributor Lonzo Dove successfully cracked the case, sending Moseley "an accurate, detailed analysis of the [Straith] letter in which he demonstrated it had been typed on Gray's typewriter."[84] Moseley, hoping to protect both his friend and himself, attempted to stall: "Jim says he won't publish it, but will write Dove a glowing letter about it, saying that he likes it tremendously, but that the only issue he will put out before coming back from Peru is off the press. By time Jim comes back he will tell Dove he has met with Authorities, etc., who have asked him not to print anything more about the controversial matter, etc."[85] Nothing prevented Dove from sending the report elsewhere, however, and he shared it with both NICAP and the US State Department. A *NICAP Special Bulletin* released in November 1958 made it clear (without naming Barker directly) that Barker's involvement was known and that he was likely to find himself in trouble: "NICAP hopes the State or Justice Dept. will publicly expose the hoaxer and remove one of the trouble-makers in UFO investigation. If not, NICAP will do everything legally possible to reveal his identity."[86] Following this bulletin, Barker visited a lawyer for advice, and his communications regarding the Straith letter changed in tone from amusement to anxiety—and contained increasingly pointed claims of ignorance about the letter's origin.[87] He contacted NICAP, speaking with staffer Rose Campbell (formerly Rose Hackett):

> [She] confirms what I suspected[:] that they were trying to pin the Straith Affair on yours truly. She suggests that I challenge them and threaten them with dire law suits, etc., but as you know, they haven't named me publicly, but she says they are doing it privately. This of course I haven't been able to find

out definitely yet. She says they have letters from me which match up with the fake letter. . . . I have been able to confirm that the Justice Dept. HAS taken over the investigation from the State Dept. Although I am sure they would make no charges unless they were certain, it does worry me that some embarrassment may come out of this thing. I think we should do everything we can to unmask this hoaxter which is indeed giving saucer research—and myself, a bad name.[88]

According to Moseley, Barker also destroyed a key piece of evidence incriminating himself: "The investigation sent Gray into a panic, and he smashed the incriminating typewriter to bits and buried the mangled parts in wet cement at a Clarksburg construction site. He was so paranoid about the matter that he refused to tell even me where this was."[89]

According to letters Barker sent in early 1959, agents from the FBI visited him three times in the first few months of the year—but Barker's contemporary reports of these visits are the only available records to support this.[90] It is possible that Barker's account of the investigation was itself a hoax—or that it was not the FBI undertaking it, but the State Department or some other agency. In one letter Barker wrote that the FBI had questioned an associate of his who knew the source of the stationery.[91] On a third visit, later in the spring, agents collected "elaborate samples of my typewriters in the office, also collected samples of typing from other machines I traded off," according to Barker.[92] He also said that he helped them track down a typewriter of the same model as the one used for the Straith hoax, likely in the office of Lovett & Co.[93] And he reported that the investigators collected handwriting samples, asking Barker to sign the name "Kip"—the nickname used on the letter to CSI's officers.[94]

While this investigation was under way, Lonzo Dove's amateur investigation into Barker's hoaxes was heating up. But in addition to his accurate conclusion that Barker had authored the Straith letter, Dove came up with a more outlandish theory: that Barker had been the leader of the group of black-suited men who "silenced" Bender and others. Dove contacted several of Barker's correspondents, including Mitris and Daw, hoping to uncover evidence to support the theory.[95] In an effort to convince Mitris that Barker had been his strange, suntanned visitor, Dove sent him a photograph of Barker on which he had scribbled with a pencil to apply a false tan.[96] Moseley and Barker were both aware of Dove's investigation and hoped that its publication would show that Dove had a vendetta against Barker and thus cast doubt on his identification of the Straith hoaxer.[97]

When *Saucer News* published Dove's accusation in August, Moseley shared an advance copy of the issue with Barker, enabling him to print an official response in an issue of the *Saucerian Bulletin* released within a few days of the *Saucer News* piece.[98] Following this Barker sent *Saucer News* a letter, reproduced in the September 1959 issue, threatening legal action against Moseley and Dove, particularly if they published an article accusing him of writing the Straith letter.[99] Dove would ultimately self-publish his Straith article as a pamphlet, but without Barker or Moseley providing advertising or distribution, it reached few readers.[100]

Despite Barker's suggestion in early 1959 that the FBI was closing in on him, the bureau seems to have dropped the investigation not long after agents' apparent visits to him. Indeed, in the decade to come it would be Barker himself who would periodically attempt to revive interest in the Straith letter, as if in impish defiance of Dove and others who had come close to "remov[ing] one of the trouble-makers in UFO investigation."[101] He devoted a 1964 lecture in New York to the subject and wrote a long postmortem entitled "The Strange Case of R. E. Straith" for his 1965 book *Gray Barker's Book of Adamski*.[102] In this account of the Straith affair, Barker concludes that it was a hoax, but maintains ignorance about who may have been behind it. He directly addresses the rumor that Keyhoe had spread about his responsibility, but exaggeratedly proclaims: "MY GOD. I *HAVE* BEEN FRAMED."[103] But he adds a final hedge, claiming that Moseley uncovered evidence that the Straith letter was written on a typewriter other than Barker's, and that "a certain organization" was behind the hoax.[104] Barker concludes by stating: "If somebody or some agency was after ME, they have failed, for I have survived. I sincerely believe there have been other efforts to silence me. . . . In some ways I am GLAD these things happened, for I have been strengthened by the ordeals."[105]

"THIS BOOK IS GOING TO DO SOMETHING TO YOU": THE SAUCERIAN BOOK CLUB

By 1958 sales of *They Knew Too Much* had slowed. Evidence for this comes from an unusual source: the film *Bell, Book and Candle*, filmed from February to April 1958 and released in December.[106] The movie, adapted from a 1950 play by John van Druten, concerns a publisher of occult books (Jimmy Stewart) who becomes romantically involved with a practitioner of black magic (Kim Novak). Visible on the shelves of Stewart's office are several copies of *They Knew Too Much about Flying Saucers*, with their distinct blue-and-yellow color-burst design and black block lettering. Despite the similarities between the topics published by Stewart's character and Morrow, it's most likely that the shelves were stocked from remaindered titles acquired by the film's set dressers.[107] This would indicate that by the beginning of filming in 1958, Barker's book had run its course, at least as far as the mainstream book trade was concerned.

Nevertheless, in the summer of 1958, British publisher Werner Laurie issued the first British edition of *They Knew Too Much about Flying Saucers*.[108] This hardcover eschewed Morry Gropper's cover design, opting instead for a simple red jacket bearing a pencil drawing of a saucer by Peter Roberson. While reproducing the original text photographically, Werner Laurie avoided University Books' approach of designing the book to appear longer and more substantial, instead using lighter paper stock and cutting down the large margins for a smaller trim size. The resulting book comes across as both slighter and more generic than the original US edition. Sales figures for this edition are unknown, but in comparison to other editions of *They Knew Too Much* it is a scarce title, indicating that it may have sold poorly.[109]

The decline in sales of his book spurred Barker to continue his efforts for direct sales. In the spring of 1958, Barker expanded his book distribution business with a subscription-based Saucerian Book Club via which Barker would ship books to subscribers at a discount. After three purchases, each subscriber would also receive a "free dividend book" from a short list of available titles. Barker split his stock into two categories: "The SAUCER Section will be concerned with Flying Saucer books. The MYSTIC

Section will include the latest and most authoritative works about such subjects as THE OCCULT, SPIRITUALISM, YOGA, REINCARNA-TION, GHOSTS—or anything which is considered on the 'borderline' of 'recognized' science."[110] The initial saucer section selection was French author Aimé Michel's *Flying Saucers and the Straight-Line Mystery*, published through the efforts of Civilian Saucer Intelligence. For the mystic section, Barker offered Alexandra David-Neel's *Magic and Mystery in Tibet*. The earliest subscribers would also receive a free book, either Earl Nelson's *There Is Life on Mars!* or Harvey Day's *The Study and Practice of Yoga* (published by University Books). By mid-July, the book club had 125 subscribers—not an overwhelming number, but enough to keep it going and to guarantee book sales.[111]

Barker made Trevor James Constable's *They Live In the Sky* the club's second selection. The title was shipped to both saucer and mystic subscribers, indicating the increasing blurriness of the line between saucers and the occult. *They Live in the Sky*, published under the pseudonym Trevor James, posits three types of flying saucers: etherian craft, commanded by the likes of Ashtar, originate in space and are on the side of good; astral UFOs originate inside the earth and are hostile to humanity; and physical saucers originate on the moon and are allied with the evil astrals.

The *Saucerian Book Club News* presented Constable's book as the must-read saucer book of the year:

It will do one of four things to you:

(1) It will make you mad—at the author, at the publisher, but (we hope) not at Gray Barker.
(2) It will make you rave on and on about how wonderful it is, both to your friends and in letters to me.
(3) It will scare you so bad you will IMMEDIATELY DROP all your saucer and mystical readings and research.
(4) It will set you back a few dollars for infra-red film, while YOU try to catch some of the "things" the author was able to photograph.

"THEY LIVE IN THE SKY" is going to do SOMETHING to you. What we don't know. We only know that you SHOULD READ IT. . . . I, Gray Barker, go out on a limb and state that this is the most important book to come out since those of Adamski and Keyhoe. It is much better than my own.[112]

This hard-selling tactic—piquing the interest of potential readers by presenting them with a prescribed list of possible reactions, several of them negative—would recur in Barker's solicitation materials. Even those inclined to disbelieve in the book would be intrigued by the possibility of it angering or amusing them or would want to experience the thrill of frightening themselves by entertaining the dark possibilities at which the solicitation hints.

The book club's mystic section shows the growing importance of the occult and esotericism in Barker's portfolio. His column for *Flying Saucers* included a lengthy defense of Tuesday Lobsang Rampa in the summer of 1958.[113] In 1956 the British publishing house Secker & Warburg had released Rampa's *The Third Eye: The Autobiography of a Tibetan Lama*.[114] According to this memoir, Rampa was a native of Lhasa who entered a lamasery at the age of seven. Questions about the story's authenticity arose before it was published, but Rampa's book still became a bestseller. Recognizing the book's many falsehoods and inventions, scholars of the culture and history of Tibet were outraged.[115] A group of European scholars engaged a private investigator, who determined that T. Lobsang Rampa was an Englishman born in 1910 in Devonshire to Joseph and Eva Hoskin.[116] The exposure of these details did little to slow sales, however, and if anything the sensationalism helped the book. Warburg later estimated that it had sold over 250,000 copies and called it "one of the most profitable books we ever published."[117]

In his column for *Flying Saucers*, Barker indicates that when he read *The Third Eye* for the first time in the fall of 1957, he "could hardly put it down."[118] He comments on the fanciful spirit suffusing the would-be lama's account: "And, although [we] occasionally chuckled to [ourselves] and murmured, 'this guy surely has a lot of baloney,' it still remained one of our favorite books, along, perhaps, with 'THE COMPTE DE GABALIS,' 'FLYING SAUCERS HAVE LANDED,' and other volumes which broke through our hard crust of so-called reason and charmed us with a spell of might-be."[119] He concludes his write-up by repeating nearly word for word the conclusion of his review of Bethurum's *Aboard a Flying Saucer* for the

Saucerian, replacing the line "Some may call it Clarion" with "Rampa called it Lhasa."[120] By revisiting his wistfully romantic language about Bethurum's book, Barker attributes the same fairy-tale power to Rampa's discredited memoir and, by extension, to a larger category of pulp mysticism beyond the accounts of saucer seers.

On April 20, 1959, Morris Jessup, Barker's colleague in saucer authorship and publishing, died by suicide. Jessup was experiencing financial difficulties and turbulence in his private life at the time, and though his death was tragic, there was no mystery about it. Barker nevertheless sought to create one, devoting a full page of the September 1959 *Saucerian Bulletin* to a facsimile of his death certificate, purportedly "to eliminate the many wild rumors now circulating" about the saucer author's death.[121] There's little sign that any such rumors were actually circulating: the few saucerzines that mentioned Jessup's passing limited themselves to brief, speculation-free obituaries.[122]

Barker seems to have felt a more immediate impact from another 1959 death: the passing on May 11 of Franklin Thomas, proprietor of the New Age Publishing Co.[123] Barker corresponded with Trevor James Constable about Thomas's death, which seemed to inspire Barker to pick up where the Los Angeles occultist had left off. Barker was excited about the possibilities, if nervous about the investment required: "There seems to be a tremendous publishing field opening up to me—I only wish that I had the time, personnel and money in order to get into the thin[g] in the scope necessary."[124] But his focus had shifted: "As far as UFO's go, however, I think that this field, as an area of 'objective' investigation . . . is fast dying out. The Keyhoe's, the Jessups (rest his soul!), and the C.S.I.'s have had 10 years to cope with the mystery, but are no farther along on it than when they started—perhaps not as far along."[125] With the possibility of reaching any "objective" truth about unidentified flying objects fast receding, Barker saw publishing on new age topics as the best path forward.[126] James noted, "It has been my experience that all these new age things are moving so fast that you may well find yourself riding a very profitable wave."[127] The age of saucers was in decline—but a New Age was dawning.

7 "A VERY PROFITABLE WAVE": THE BEGINNING OF SAUCERIAN BOOKS

By 1958, a new contactee was rising to prominence: Howard Menger, a sign painter residing in High Bridge, New Jersey, who claimed that his contact with Venusians had begun in 1932, when he was ten years old. He offered proof of his account in the form of a number of photographs of glowing, Adamski-style saucers and blurry, humanoid space beings.[1] Long John Nebel had publicized Menger's story beginning in 1956, and two years later he was the most prominent contactee on the East Coast.[2] Believers in his story gathered regularly at his New Jersey farmhouse to witness alleged visits by luminescent landed saucers and their space-suited crews, while skeptics in the saucer scene attempted to catch Menger in lies and identify his accomplices.[3]

Both Barker and Menger attended the May 1958 Spacecraft Convention at Giant Rock, but it's unclear to what extent their paths crossed there. Two months later, however, Lucchesi and Roberts attended a large gathering at Menger's farm in New Jersey. About three hundred people attended the event, hosted by Menger, his first wife, Rose, and his new bride, Constance Menger (née Weber). Menger had divorced Rose following the death of their son from brain cancer in the summer of 1957 and quickly married Weber in May 1958.[4] Around the time of the wedding, Weber published an account of her mystic romance with Menger, entitled *My Saturnian Lover*, through the vanity house Vantage Press, under the pseudonym Marla Baxter. According to this account, Connie ("Marla") and Howard ("Alyn") were both reincarnated space beings and had been romantically involved in a prior life.

Of more immediate interest to Barker, however, was the business opportunity afforded by Menger's attempt to establish a California-style gathering on the East Coast. The July 1958 event was a trial run for a larger event Menger was planning for the fall, which he branded an "East Coast Giant Rock."[5] Lucchesi estimated that the July meeting had earned the Mengers at least $500, mainly through a suggested donation of $1.50 per attendee plus the sales of *My Saturnian Lover* and Howard's record album *Authentic Music from Another Planet* (an LP of piano music that he had heard during his space contacts, released by New Jersey label Slate Enterprises).[6] The Mengers were also accepting preorders for Howard Menger's book about his own experiences, which did not yet have a publisher.[7] Roberts suggested that Menger get in touch with Barker, who might be interested in releasing it.[8]

As the "serious" side of saucer investigation declined, Barker was increasingly inspired by the personalities circling the fringes of the field. For his column in the May 1959 issue of *Flying Saucers*, Barker abandoned his usual roundup of recent sightings, instead offering a narrative account of a trip he took to New York in January.[9] Barker describes, in lively prose, a stay at Moseley's apartment (maintaining the fiction that the two were feuding), visits with Leon Davidson and Yonah Fortner (who published under the name Y. N. ibn A'haron), a trip to see Bender in Connecticut, and an appearance on the Long John Nebel radio show.[10] The dialog-rich style of the column resembles that of *They Knew Too Much*, and at twenty-five pages the installment is over twice the length of the average Chasing the Flying Saucers column. This emphasis on people, rather than events, would become a prominent feature of Barker's writing going forward. And Howard Menger's colorful story of space contact made him a standout figure.

After hearing from Menger in the summer of 1958, Barker quickly confirmed his interest in the book and began advertising and accepting preorders for it by early December of 1958, likely as soon as he had received the manuscript. This represented a major turnaround from his initial reaction to hearing about Menger's authorial ambitions two years before, when he had told Lex Mebane, "I'm sure [Menger's book] would be commercial, but I suppose it's completely crackpot."[11]

Barker's solicitation letter for the book explains why Menger went with the unproven Saucerian Books rather than a larger publisher:

> But Howard Menger has been having the same difficulty getting his information before the public that many advocates of the New Age have experienced. One large firm wanted to publish this book, but they told Menger THEY WOULD HAVE TO SUBMIT THE MANUSCRIPT TO "CERTAIN SOURCES" FOR APPROVAL—just what the "sources" were we don't know, but we can guess!
>
> But Howard Menger turned thumbs down! "FROM OUTER SPACE TO YOU" must be published WITHOUT EVEN ONE PAGE DELETED! The same publisher also asked Menger to omit the actual photographs of space people and spacecraft, which Menger feels will PROVE his story is true.
>
> Hearing of this censorship, I told Menger I would publish the book JUST AS IT WAS—and that I would publish the photographs too, despite the threats. To make a long story short, Menger agreed, we shook hands, and the manuscript went to the printer.[12]

This supposed censorship certainly had more to do with economic concerns than conspiracy, particularly given the general decline in saucer-book publishing and sales that Barker had noted; the major publishers viewed saucers as a decade-old fad whose day had passed. Menger's reputation as a "new Adamski" didn't help, either, as it placed him in the role of an imitator of a celebrity whose own fame was quickly fading. But Barker's solicitation letter suggests that he alone was willing to stand up to the shadowy forces seeking to stop publication and encourages his audience to do the same by buying the book.[13] Barker would use the same tactic of presenting mainstream publishing's disinterest as a conspiracy of silence in promoting other works in years to come, including his own title *The Silver Bridge*.

Barker underestimated the amount of time and effort that he would need to spend on publishing *From Outer Space to You*. The editorial to the May *Bulletin* claimed that he had believed he "could get a manuscript to a printer and have a finished book in about 30 days"—an outrageous schedule, but the ostensible reason for Barker sending a solicitation letter so soon after receiving the manuscript.[14] He explained the delay as a result of Menger providing additional material after the book had gone to press, but an examination of the book's manuscript suggests a more likely explanation: the manuscript Menger submitted would make a book of only about 160 pages—not enough to justify the $3.50 price that Menger had been collecting for preorders since July.[15] Barker likely did not want to issue that slim a volume lest he risk appearing to be another vanity press. The decision to add more material to the book was probably Barker's alone, to provide a substantial enough volume to justify the asking price and launch Saucerian Books as a serious publishing concern.

Saucerian Books issued *From Outer Space to You* in July 1959.[16] The book narrates the complete story of Menger's ongoing contacts with space people, which began when he encountered a mysterious Venusian woman in the woods when he was ten years old. Menger's space contacts, according to the text, continued through his service in World War II and after; a long adventure-fiction-style section details his single-handed defeat of a group of Japanese soldiers at the Battle of Okinawa. He relates his side of the story of *My Saturnian Lover*, describing his first meeting with Marla Baxter (Constance Weber) at a 1956 lecture given by contactee George van Tassel. During telepathic journeys to other planets, Menger and Baxter realized that Menger was a Saturnian named Sol do Naro. This alien had transmigrated to Earth years earlier, taking over the life of the original Howard Menger, who died as an infant. Similar stories of spiritual replacement, later termed "walk-ins" by writer Ruth Montgomery, recurred in numerous contactee and new age narratives for decades to come: T. Lobsang Rampa, ViVenus, Omnec Onec, Prince Neosom, and many others recounted similar stories of their literal death and spiritual rebirth as a new being.[17] Not only was Menger secretly Saturnian: Baxter was the sister of the Venusian woman Menger met in his childhood, and the two had had a relationship spanning several lifetimes on other worlds—all of this much to the surprise of Menger's wife Rose, who divorced him on learning of the relationship.

Barker's solution to the insufficient length of the manuscript was to split *From Outer Space to You* into two sections, entitled "Takeoff" and "Landing." The first part contains the bulk of the manuscript: the narrative of his lifelong experiences with space people. The second section includes three chapters on the space people's pseudoscientific ideas about philosophy, nutrition, and free energy, which do little to advance the book's narrative. Menger's manuscript had lurched to an anticlimactic conclusion concerning his free energy experiments; Barker wisely closes the first half of the book with the natural conclusion of Menger's contact tale—his trip to the moon—and treats the pseudoscientific and philosophical material as a long appendix. To these three chapters from Menger Barker adds over a hundred pages of additional material, including three separate forewords, several poems, and a fifty-page article entitled "A New Concept of Nutrition" by G. H. Earp-Thomas, an eccentric nutritionist who had treated Menger's son. In one promotional piece for the book, Barker highlighted this expansion, calling *From Outer Space to You* "two books in one": "The hasty reader may wish to finish Book One and put the volume on the book shelf; but those who, after wetting their feet in the Milky Way, wish to gain a deeper insight into the teachings of the space people as expressed by the author, will find Book Two even more rewarding."[18]

Contrary to his claim that he was publishing Menger's book unaltered, Barker "went over [the manuscript] and jazzed it a bit."[19] The published text has many differences from the draft manuscript in Barker's files. The rhythm and pacing of the text is enormously different, largely a result of Barker breaking up Menger's long paragraphs (up to forty sentences long in the manuscript) into shorter ones rarely longer than three sentences. Virtually every descriptive passage has been expanded, with longer descriptions inserted, and conversations that are presented in summary in the typescript are expanded into dialogue in the published text. It's possible that Menger made these changes himself, but it is more likely that Barker rewrote the manuscript for publication using Menger's text as an outline, both to increase its length and to offer a more dramatic framing. Several of the inserted sections bear the hallmarks of Barker's style, like a nostalgic passage from the first chapter about wintertime activities on the Menger's farm, which may reflect Barker's reminiscences of his own rural upbringing.[20]

Elsewhere, the changes to Menger's original manuscript fundamentally alter aspects of the story. In Menger's typescript, his first encounter with the Venusian woman ends undramatically: she simply stands up to leave and shakes his hand before he walks out of the forest and goes home in an under-described state of semi-mystical reverie.[21] In the published text, Menger responds to her handshake with weeping, a longing inquiry about when he will meet other space people, and an emotional, unsettled conclusion: "I turned and ran, sobbing, first hardly audibly, then louder and louder, till my wails of a happy kind of sadness grew and filled the forest."[22] Menger's type-script is focused on providing an overview of his experiences; the rewritten version focuses more on emotions and setting, filling in significant details absent from the manuscript.

The jacket for *From Outer Space to You* features a painting provided by Calvin Girvin, author of *The Night Has a Thousand Saucers* (published by Daniel Fry's Understanding).[23] Girvin's artwork for *From Outer Space to You* depicts Menger's first encounter with the Venusian "Girl on the Rock" beneath an Adamski-style saucer. Barker noted to Sanders that the painting reflected a sanitized version of the event: "Researchers around New Jersey tell me that Menger's first version of the story had The Girl On The Rock IN THE NUDE, and they opined he had cleaned up the story after that."[24]

Barker printed six thousand copies of *From Outer Space to You* at a total cost of about six thousand dollars—"a buck a piece, which is pretty high," he confessed to Scully.[25] The production was undertaken by George McK-ibben & Son, the same Brooklyn-based bookbinder who handled University Books' publications.[26] Morrow seems to have been personally involved as an intermediary between Barker and the printer in resolving production issues.[27] By June Barker had already received preorders for three thousand copies.[28] These presales enabled Barker to fund the publication, which may not have happened at all without them, as he explained to Scully: "I had to bluff my way through this, for I had no money."[29] Nevertheless, he told James he still needed to sell a thousand more copies to break even on the publication.[30] In a letter to Scully, he expressed a more cautious approach to his future publishing plans than his enthusiastic statements from the spring, writing that Menger's book "may be the last contact book of any major sales value."[31]

In marketing *From Outer Space to You*, Barker faced an unexpected obstacle: Menger himself. As reported in the *Saucerian Bulletin*, as soon as the book was released Menger began "acting strangely," declining to appear on Nebel's radio program or engage in other publicity.[32] The following year, during an appearance on Nebel's short-lived television program on WOR-TV, Menger essentially recanted his entire story. Nebel later provided his own account of the television program:

> Howard said nothing, and un-said most of what he had originally claimed. . . . Where he had once sworn that he had seen flying saucers, he now felt that he had some vague impression that he might have on some half-remembered occasion possibly viewed some airborne object—maybe. Where he had once insisted that he had teleported himself he now speculated that strange things did happen to people and if it hadn't actually occurred to him, well, that's the way the story crumbles.[33]

This disappointing appearance potentially doomed Barker's prospects of recouping his losses on Menger's book. In the *Saucerian Bulletin* Barker hoped to wring a publicity angle out of Menger's intransigence, suggesting that he might be the victim of a "shush-up" and that *From Outer Space to You* might contain secrets that the likes of the "three men" didn't want getting out.[34]

"HUGE CASH SAVINGS FOR YOU": 1959–1960

Both the American and British publishers of *The Third Eye* had dropped T. Lobsang Rampa following the controversy over his identity. In London the book's two sequels, *Doctor from Lhasa* and *The Rampa Story*, were published by Ernest Hecht's Souvenir Press; in the United States, Dutton had declined the manuscript, opening an opportunity for Saucerian Books to make good on Barker's public promise the year before to publish it.[35] *Doctor from Lhasa*, which details Rampa's imagined experiences in China during the Communist Revolution, became Saucerian Books' second hardcover publication and appeared about six months after the British edition.

Rampa was a crossover figure between the worlds of nineteenth-century mysticism and flying saucers: in addition to his esoterically inflected memoir of Tibet, he had claimed saucer contacts of his own. In the April 1958 issue of the *Saucerian Bulletin*, Barker reprinted an article by Rampa from *Flying*

Saucer Review recounting his voyage to see and fly in a saucer that landed in a high-altitude Eden in the Changtang Highlands.[36] Rampa authored sequels that expanded the narrative to incorporate a trip to the planet Venus; Barker reprinted these texts separately and eventually compiled three of them under the title *My Visit to Venus*. In Rampa's 1976 book, *As It Was!*, he describes Barker—without naming him—as "a very peculiar sort of person, whenever he was tackled or threatened with a law case he conveniently went bankrupt and friends or relatives 'bought' his business, so there was not much redress, in fact there was none."[37] He minced no words in private correspondence, such as a 1980 letter: "This fellow, Barker really is a very evil fellow so far as I am concerned; for 26 years he has been plagiarizing my material, he has no agreement with me, and he never pays royalties."[38]

Barker was involved in detailed plans for several publications in addition to Rampa's book throughout the fall of 1959, but within a few months his plans for an expanded edition of Scully's *Behind the Flying Saucers* and a compilation of Jacqueline Sanders's contactee coverage had fizzled.[39] Sanders was facetiously blunt: she jokingly threatened to sue if he published any of her letters.[40] With the cancellation of these and other projects, Barker's publishing activities declined, and he issued nothing in the spring of 1960. He described his situation in a February letter to Constable: "I am at that stage of business which is like the darkest hour before the dawn. I have a number of personal debts facing me, which I am just finally clearing up. When I can throw my theatre money into publishing, as I will be able to do soon, I think you will see some rapid expansion in the Gray Barker camp."[41] The problem, however, was that in 1960 both the movie business and the saucer field were experiencing major declines, with sightings at a significant ebb throughout 1959.[42]

Nevertheless, 1960 saw the publication of a paperback edition of *They Knew Too Much about Flying Saucers* on the other side of the Atlantic. The book, with its title changed to the vague yet menacing *The Unidentified*, was issued by John Spencer & Co. under the Badger Books imprint, with a lurid painting by German illustrator Kurt Caesar of Adamski's saucers floating over a scene of urban destruction reminiscent of George Pal's *War of the Worlds*.

Barker shuttered the Saucerian Book Club sometime in 1960. While he had hoped the club structure would generate significant sales, in practice, the list of free dividend books had scarcely grown beyond the half-dozen mostly out-of-date and unpopular saucer and occult titles that Barker had offered at the club's inception. These titles didn't motivate sales, and Barker was reluctant to add new giveaway titles that he might otherwise be able to sell.

Barker's financial difficulties continued into 1961, when he released a sale catalog, described as an "Anniversary Tribute to Gray Barker on his Tenth Anniversary in UFO Research and Huge Cash Savings For You."[43] It was, in fact, several months before the *ninth* anniversary of Barker's saucer activities, but he clearly needed cash, and the catalog was soon followed by a one-page sale flyer extending the sale, which slashed prices on most of the books Barker distributed by 50 percent or more.[44]

Despite his financial difficulties, Barker attended the 1960 Giant Rock Space Craft Convention on May 28–29. He and Moseley flew together from Pittsburgh and set up a shared table selling books alongside subscriptions to the *Saucerian Bulletin* and *Saucer News*.[45] A photograph from the event shows Barker, wearing a rather ridiculous straw hat, standing behind a tiny card table on which copies of *They Knew Too Much*, *From Outer Space to You*, and other books are displayed.[46] Moseley and Barker attempted to spin one odd occurrence at the convention into a minor mystery, reporting after the event that mysterious drops of blood had appeared on several of the publications at their table.[47] Moseley and Barker had the "psychic blood" analyzed and revealed that substance was menstrual blood.[48] Nebel was less than amused by the story, later describing this event and Moseley's coverage of it as "the crudest and most offensive example" of bad taste in the realm of flying saucers.[49] The coverage given to the psychic blood story in *Saucer News* and elsewhere indicates the extent to which the beginning of the 1960s was a slow period for UFO news.

MULBERRY AVENUE AND THE ALPINE THEATRE

By early 1961 McCulty and Barker's living arrangements had changed, with McCulty moving into the adjoining apartment in their two-unit building.

In a document from 1962, Barker lists his address as "631 and/or 633 Mulberry," combining his and McCulty's apartments into a single domicile.[50] Barker jokingly described the reason for the change in a letter to Sanders, saying the move was necessary "because of the fact that the both of us accumulated too many copies of Mad magazines, Flying Saucer papers and movie trade papers."[51]

The move came at a period of change in the movie business brought on by a nationwide decline in theater attendance. Many drive-in theaters chased more adult audiences, and as the 1960s progressed they began showing sexploitation films and even hard-core pornography.[52] Barker seems to have begun to make such a switch in 1960, based on a letter to Sanders typed on an advertising leaflet for "the Nudist picture I'm distributing. Since saucering is bad just now I have to make a buck somehow."[53] Barker's problems in motion-picture booking and saucer book publishing were essentially the same: with limited access to the best-selling properties, he was resigned to making lower-quality product available during a period of general decline in the industry.

Many owners of traditional theaters were looking to get out of the business. Barker took advantage of this industry churn and in mid-1961 purchased the Alpine Theatre in Salem, thirteen miles west of Clarksburg.[54] In a letter to Moseley Barker gives a poetic portrait of the Alpine as a theater in decline:

> We often wonder just what did kill the movies, as they wonder what killed vaudeville. I don't know about vaudeville, but I think that our little Alpine Theatre would be the perfect laboratory whereby movie experts could witness and examine this demise—in fact it is a small stage where the Götterdamarung [sic] of the movies is nightly being staged. I feel that if Tennessee Williams were to write a play about a small theatre, he probably would select the Alpine as his subject—with its rotting upholstery and wall coverings, its invasion of roaches, its encouragement of various sexual deviations, and as Yul Brynner would say, "Et cetera, et cetera, et cetera."[55]

Barker undertook a renovation of the theater, purchasing new seats and other equipment from a nearby theater that had recently closed.[56] It was as manager of the Alpine that Barker began contributing brief movie reviews for *Boxoffice* in October, commenting on both the quality of films and the audiences they drew.[57] By late 1962 Barker had acquired a second theater, in Petersburg, West Virginia, about a hundred miles east of Clarksburg.[58] In managing these properties he probably relied on the assistance of McCulty, who was working as the manager of a theater in Clarksburg. McCulty, in turn, enlisted Barker's printing knowledge to publish a newsletter called *Moviews* for his theater.[59] McCulty had literary aspirations as well, and he and Barker briefly collaborated on a proposal for a book about great Hollywood actresses, to be entitled *The Durable Queens*.[60]

The combination of the slowness of flying saucer news and Barker's growing motion-picture responsibilities led to significantly reduced saucer output throughout 1960 and 1961. He put out only two books in 1960, both reissues of already available titles: Dino Kraspedon's contact account *My Contact with Flying Saucers* and Brinsley le Poer Trench's *The Sky People*. His only book in 1961 was *The Brotherhood of the Seven Rays* by Brother Philip, an apparent pseudonym for George Hunt Williamson.[61] There was a gap of more than a year between issues of the *Saucerian Bulletin*, prompting Moseley to print a rumor that the zine was no longer being published.[62]

Barker was martialing his energies for a major release, which would be Saucerian's first truly original publication since *From Outer Space to You*. Nearly a decade after closing the International Flying Saucer Bureau, Albert Bender was finally ready to tell the world the secret of his three mysterious visitors.

8 "A FAIRLY GOOD HACK WRITING STYLE": DECLINE AND RESURRECTION, 1962–1965

Albert Bender left the world of flying saucer research behind in 1953, but had indicated that the truth about the saucers was destined to come out soon enough. In 1962 he broke his silence, sending Gray Barker the manuscript that became *Flying Saucers and the Three Men*. Bender's book is essentially a sequel to Barker's *They Knew Too Much about Flying Saucers*, edited (possibly quite heavily) by Barker, who is credited as an "annotator."[1] Bender's book begins with a detailed account of his study of flying saucers and the founding and activities of the IFSB, with lengthy quotations from its publications and other documents. There are hints of the unusual in these early sections, notably a chilling sequence in which a ghostly figure with glowing eyes "like little flashlight bulbs lighted up on a dark face" manifests behind, and then beside, Bender in a movie theater.[2] (These glowing eyes inspired Gene Duplantier's design for the book's dust jacket, which features three pairs of eyes peering out from alternating bands of blue and white.) The ghostly figure's behavior is remarkably similar to a method of identifying an interested sexual partner in a movie theater, as described by gay writer Samuel R. Delany in *Times Square Red, Times Square Blue*.[3] Between this, the movie theater setting, Barker's tendency in *The Silver Bridge* and other books to reframe sexual encounters as extranormal experiences, and his private speculation about Bender's sexuality, it is likely that Barker invented or modified this sequence.[4]

The narrative turns further toward the fantastic beginning with the events of March 15, 1953, or C-Day—the day on which Bender urged the members of the IFSB and their associates worldwide to attempt to communicate a psychic message to the flying saucers.[5] Bender reveals that he received an immediate response to his psychic message in the form of a telepathic communication advising him to cease his investigations into the saucer mystery, and a warning: "We will make an appearance if you disobey."[6] Bender then recounts not one meeting with the men in black suits but a series of them, beginning on July 6, 1953, two months before the previously disclosed visit. Rather than threatening him, the three men informed him that he was "a very good contact for us on your planet of Earth" and gave him a small fragment of metal that he could use to summon them for further contacts by holding it in his hand and repeating the word *Kazik*—with a silent *z*.[7] This was apparently the name of the planet from which the glowing-eyed strangers originated; in their true form, they resembled the Flatwoods Monster.[8] The event at the end of August that precipitated the immediate closure of the IFSB was not a single, threatening visit but the culmination of these encounters, in which the extraterrestrials transported Bender to their base in the Antarctic. There, they engaged in a lengthy dialog in which the visitors gave detailed and complete answers regarding their origin and purposes on Earth. The dialog connects the dots between subjects covered in early issues of the *Saucerian*, including the Flatwoods Monster, the New Haven fireball, and a saucer occupant seen collecting water at Brush Creek, California. The beings swore Bender to secrecy, informing him that they could control him by means of the metal object. During a final visit at the end of 1954, a trio of beautiful extraterrestrial women in skintight white uniforms massaged a warm liquid onto "every part of [Bender's] body without exception" and subjected him to a ray that he was told would prevent disease, similar to Shaver's stim-rays.[9] Bender was warned again not to tell of his experiences until after the extraterrestrials have left our planet, an event that they would signal by causing the metal object to disappear.

Bender experienced headaches and other odd effects for several years, until one day in late 1960 he opened the box in which he had kept the metal disk and found it was gone.[10] This signaled that Bender was no longer under restriction by his strange visitors, enabling him to compose the manuscript of *Flying Saucers and the Three Men*. Bender's tale could at last be told.

Underneath the ghost story trappings, Bender's narrative was remarkably similar to those of George Adamski, Orfeo Angelucci, and Truman Bethurum.[11] The book represents a fundamental mutation of the metanarrative of the three men dressed in black. No longer government agents or representatives of earthly interests, they are now positioned as something far stranger: a secretive alien force.

Bender may have abandoned conspiracism, but Barker's marketing of the book embraced it. Barker received the manuscript in November or December 1961 and announced an unrealistic publication date of February 1962.[12] When the book was inevitably pushed back, Barker turned the delay into a marketing opportunity. The June issue of *Saucer News* carried an article under Barker's byline entitled "Why the Bender Book Has Been Delayed." It was unusual for Moseley to run an article under Barker's byline, given the ongoing feud the two were staging, and an editorial comment at the beginning of the issue attacks Barker for his "publicity-seeking antics."[13] Barker explains much of the delay as a result of customary problems with editing, designing, and printing the book. "I believe the reasons for this delay should not be construed as anything too far out of the ordinary," Barker claims, before launching into a numbered list of more unusual problems which, "to one given to more imagination than myself . . . would be credited to some organized interference of some sort."[14] These include the loss or delay of promotional mailings in transit, unusual telephone calls, weird visitors, a sustained illness, and being followed late at night by shadowy figures driving black sedans on multiple occasions. This insinuation is a hallmark of Barker's conspiratorial style: though the text states outright that Barker does not believe there is any connection between any of these events and the book manuscript, he hopes that readers "given to imagination" will draw a different conclusion and assume that Barker's publications contain a secret that the sinister forces—be they governmental or extraterrestrial—do not want known.

Barker sought to expedite the book's release by outsourcing its production to Exposition Press, a vanity publisher. This may have made the production go more smoothly, but Exposition would not extend credit, and the contract required Barker to pay the full $3,200 before he could receive a shipment of the finished book. In April 1962 he applied for a loan of $2,490. It is unclear what the lending institution was: no loan application form being available at the time, he filled out the application on a job application form from the National Cash Register Company. The stated purpose of the loan, however, was to cover production costs of "the Bender book."[15] The loan application shows that Barker was willing to go into debt to remain active in the saucer field and also reflects Barker's faith that Bender's book might finally pull Saucerian Books out of the red.

Barker's promotional material for the book made much of the importance of ensuring that as many readers as possible received it immediately upon publication.[16] A likely reason for this was that he feared his readers, who had waited nearly a decade to find out what Bender had been hiding, would conclude that "the Bender Mystery" was simply a shaggy dog story. Barker communicated a nuanced view of the supposed events in a letter to Constable: "I believe he believes the story. I do not think, however, that you or I, had we been present, would have seen the Three Men."[17] In the mid-1970s Barker commented that his initial impression was that Bender had written "either a piece of fair science fiction or . . . his recollections of a near commitment to the looney bin."[18] A typical reader view was expressed by H. P. Beasley and A. V. Sampsel, who concluded that the narrative Bender presented in his manuscript did not line up with the facts of the case as disclosed in 1953: "The book, taken at face value, doesn't make sense."[19] But the book sold fairly well; a few months after its release, Barker told one correspondent that "It has kept me going financially (We've sold about 4,000 copies) in a difficult time."[20]

"AGAINST THE PEACE AND DIGNITY OF THE STATE"

In March 1962 Barker (signing with the nickname Gig) began writing Jim Moseley (addressed by his nickname, Zo) a series of long letters describing aspects of his daily life. Under the collective title Mulberry Place—a variation on Mulberry Avenue, the street on which Barker and McCulty lived—the letters are presented as installments in a novel, with one letter carrying the disclaimer that "similarity to actual persons, places, or events, is purely coincidental."[21] The reason for this framing is that one of the primary topics of the letters is Barker's sexual life. He describes, in a frank and unflinching manner, his methods of identifying potential sexual partners, typically younger men—most, apparently, in their late teens or early twenties.

In the Mulberry Place letters, Barker euphemistically and humorously refers to sexual activity as "Communist Indoctrination," often extending the metaphor: men who may be willing to engage in sex have "a definite Marxist look," while those who appear less willing have a "John Birch aura about them"; sex itself is a "lecture" on the "decadent bourgeoisie," and so on.[22] Barker generally presents sex as something that men need to be persuaded or tricked into participating in, describing, for example, methods of getting prospective "indoctrinees" drunk. The relationships were typically ephemeral, and there appear to be few cases in which he had sex with the same partner more than once. Barker met his partners in "the low pool rooms and cafes on Pike St.," some of which were also semi-underground sports-betting establishments.[23] McCulty, nicknamed Dondon in the letters, is presented as an inhibiting force on Barker's sexual adventures, and McCulty taking a weekend trip becomes an opportunity for Barker to bring men home. But the letters establish that McCulty engaged in many of the same activities, in some cases even attempting to pick up the same men as Barker.[24] They also indicate that McCulty recognized few boundaries with Barker and would often enter his bedroom unannounced; Barker no doubt feared the embarrassment of an interruption from his roommate.

At the end of 1962, the life described in the Mulberry Place letters was thrown into disarray.[25] On November 15 McCulty was arrested, and two weeks later, on November 30, both he and Barker were indicted for several separate instances of homosexual activity in the preceding months. The charges against McCulty were for consensual sex acts with adults, which the indictment referred to as being "against the peace and dignity of the State."[26] Barker's indictment alleged that on two separate instances he had fondled boys aged fourteen and seventeen. Because of the nature of the laws criminalizing homosexuality, it was the extent of sexual activity itself that the state sought to punish. Thus McCulty faced a felony charge for sodomy, while Barker faced the relatively less serious (and more euphemistic) charge of contributing to the delinquency of a minor, a misdemeanor.[27]

Barker and McCulty were tried in quick succession on December 5 and 6.[28] Despite there being no connection between the specific occasions of sexual activity for which they were indicted, the prosecution presented a single witness list for the charges against both men. David Houchin describes this as "an attempt by the authorities to harass these particular homosexuals," noting that a statement to the court by McCulty specifically uses the word *harassment* to describe his treatment.[29] On November 24, a little over a week before the trial, McCulty traveled to Buffalo to marry his girlfriend, Alma Corder.[30] The timing of the wedding strongly suggests that this public display of heterosexuality was intended to influence the court's decision in his case. The court chose to prosecute Barker for only one of the two incidents specified in the indictment, to which he pled not guilty. McCulty, facing a significantly more serious penalty, pled guilty. The defense prepared by Barker's lawyer, Paul Poulicos, hinged on the euphemistic term *delinquent* and the question of whether the boy whom Barker had fondled "was *already a delinquent* when the offense occurred."[31]

Barker and McCulty were both found guilty on December 6. On January 5 the court committed McCulty to Weston State Hospital for a "presentence social and physical examination"; he remained there for two months and was sentenced to a five-year probation in June.[32] Barker was placed on probation on February 19, 1963, and was ordered by the court to undergo psychiatric treatment; he completed forty-eight sessions with Dr. Boylston Smith between his conviction and October 10, 1964.[33] Either as a logistical necessity following McCulty's marriage or because of a legal injunction, both Barker and McCulty moved out of their shared living arrangement on Mulberry Avenue. Barker relocated to 217 Austin Avenue, a narrow, residential street on a hillside southeast of downtown Clarksburg.[34]

At the close of 1963, the Harrison County Court challenged McCulty's employment at Saucerian Publications, presumably on the basis that his continued partnership with Barker represented, in the eyes of the court, an ongoing criminal association. On January 6, 1964, McCulty submitted a letter to the court listing reasons why he should be permitted to continue working for Barker's publishing firm. The letter indicates that McCulty had contributed one thousand dollars toward Saucerian Publications' expenses and that he was "a silent partner" in the firm who was essential to its continued operation. He described the nature of his work as "creative writing."[35] McCulty's anger at his and Barker's treatment by the court is palpable in the document: he describes his arrest and commitment to Weston State Hospital as "harassment by the Harrison County Court" that would prevent him from finding employment elsewhere, and notes that "not one friend or associate regards either Mr. Barker or myself as 'criminals' but victims of unfortunate circumstances."[36] It appears the letter was successful, as McCulty's name continued to appear in Saucerian publications for several more years.

It's important to understand the historical context of Barker's trial and the nature of the crimes for which he was prosecuted. If we view Barker's interest in legally underage, postpubescent boys as deviant today, it is not for the same reasons it was viewed as deviant in the context of West Virginia in the early 1960s.[37] Historian of sexuality Rachel Hope Cleves has written on the problem posed by the historical practice of pederasty for historians and biographers. Cleves makes the important point that the modern antipathy toward sex between adults and teenagers is a relatively modern invention, and in fact sexual relationships between adult men and teen-aged girls was absolutely normative throughout much of human history.[38] Indeed, in Barker's own time teenage girls were routinely sexualized: in the early 1960s nearly half of all brides in the United States were under twenty years old, and at the beginning of the 1950s about one marriage in twenty involved a bride younger than 16.[39] A letter Barker wrote to *Boxoffice* in 1965 reported on the success his theaters were having in showing the sexploitation film *Shotgun Wedding*, advertising materials for which promise it tells "the whole SHOCKING story of child brides in the Ozarks"—demonstrating that the culture that surrounded Barker was one that sexualized minors.[40] Definitions of childhood, adulthood, consent, and acceptable sexual practice are socially constructed and have always been in flux. For the court and for Barker's culture more broadly, it was not sexual relations between adults and teenagers that were stigmatized, but rather ones between individuals of the same sex.

This is made clear by the linked prosecution of Barker and McCulty and the discrepancy in the severity of the charges against them. McCulty's sexual partners were adults, but the sexual acts were penetrative, and thus felonies. Despite the ages of Barker's partners (or victims), the extent of his sexual activity with them—at least as attested in court—were less extensive, and thus he was charged with a lesser crime. It was the biological sex of Barker's and McCulty's partners alone that set their conduct "against the peace and dignity" of the State of West Virginia. This, for the court, was the beginning and end of their crime; the specific instances for which they were prosecuted were merely details—hence the prosecution of only one of the two counts against Barker. Regardless of our current understanding of the power dynamics at play in intergenerational sexual activity, in the context of their time, Barker and McCulty were both prosecuted, first, last, and foremost, for *being homosexual.*

In his introduction to the French translation of *They Knew Too Much about Flying Saucers*, Pierre Lagrange describes Barker as "doubly deviant": "Between his homosexuality—'sexually deviant' (especially in 1950's America)—and his practice of 'scientifically deviant' ufology, the only 'deviance' that he could display and take pleasure in was the latter."[41] David Houchin echoes this, suggesting that Barker's interest in UFOs may have been intended as a distraction from his less socially acceptable eccentricity. Small towns like Clarksburg tend to assign labels to marginal figures, and perhaps "it's better to have the 'UFO' tag than the 'dangerous sodomite' tag."[42] In later years Moseley wondered why Barker didn't just leave West Virginia for a city more welcoming of his sexuality.[43] Moseley may have been thinking of the contrasting experience of Ted Bloecher, cofounder of Civilian Saucer Intelligence, who was also a lifelong gay rights activist and a longtime member of the New York Gay Men's Chorus, thereby finding a depth of community that seemed to be unavailable to Barker.[44] But this attitude reflects what theorist Jack Halberstam has called "metronormativity," which "maps a story of migration onto the coming-out narrative . . . a spatial narrative within which the subject moves to a place of tolerance after enduring life in a place of suspicion, persecution, and secrecy."[45] But though Barker's work in publishing, motion pictures, and education gave him opportunities to relocate, he chose to remain in West Virginia—a choice

Figure 8.1

With *Bender Mystery Confirmed* in 1962, Barker abandoned hardcover publishing for fast, cheap reproduction on office copying equipment. Author's collection (public domain).

that New York–born Moseley could not understand. Instead of expressing bewilderment or derision at this choice, we should view it as Barker's conscious, resilient decision to define and hold a queer space in the place where he was born.[46]

Barker's arrest occurred just a few weeks after the release of the final issue of the *Saucerian Bulletin*. Amid the stress of his criminal trial, he issued what was, in some respects, one of the most important books of his career. *Bender Mystery Confirmed* marks a seismic shift in Saucerian's publishing. Prior Saucerian books had been relatively well-made hardcovers, produced with an eye toward bookstore sales—but Barker's self-distribution meant that none had a chance of bookstore success. *Bender Mystery Confirmed*, however, is a simply produced, staple-bound pamphlet printed on untrimmed letter-size paper, typeset, printed, and bound by Barker himself in an edition of five hundred copies.[47] Several years earlier Jessup had told Barker that he had wanted his *UFO Annual* to be produced in an inexpensive format like that of a telephone directory, and this seems to have informed Barker's decisions in preparing this volume.[48] Barker produced the book on office copying equipment—probably a Multilith 1250, a rotary offset duplicator introduced in 1954.[49] Barker's introduction includes a passage that could be considered a statement of purpose for Saucerian Books in general: "The book may not have the 'slick,' easy-reading characteristics of a commercially produced volume. Since this is a publication of limited circulation we believe readers prefer to receive it in this fashion. The public acceptance of the book in this form will determine how publication projects of similar nature may be carried out."[50] Barker also hyperbolically spins this approach as an assault against a conspiracy of silence: "IT DEFIES CENSORSHIP—IT SEEKS TO HIDE NOTHING! IT SEEKS TO DRAG INTO THE OPEN SUBJECTS OF OCCULT AND OTHER NATURE WHICH A FEW MAY HAVE TRIED TO KEEP SECRET!"[51] This kind of simply produced, crudely bound, samizdat-style volume immediately replaced the relatively luxurious hardcover books that Saucerian had thus far issued, and, with very few exceptions, the entire publishing output of Barker's press from this point on would be done in a similar style.

Bender Mystery Confirmed contains a wide range of responses to *Flying Saucers and the Three Men*, including some truly idiosyncratic comments. In the years to come, Barker would publish many bizarre and fringe theories, but no volume comes close to encompassing the sheer variety of eccentric beliefs represented here. The limited-circulation, cheaply produced book became a forum for ideas that were otherwise unlikely to be printed or distributed. Despite the title, none of the letters directly confirms Bender's experiences with the three men, though each contributor has their own opinion on what forces the mysterious three represent, from religious interpretations of the trio as a demonic force to antigovernment and anticommunist conspiracism to outright rejections of the whole story as a hoax. Some of the commentators were well-known in the flying saucer world, including Trevor James Constable and Jim Moseley, but most were simply readers of Saucerian's publications. With this assortment of views, the book becomes a public forum for occult knowledge and paranormal speculation.

Barker also sought a new model for selling *Bender Mystery Confirmed*, preselling the book along with two forthcoming titles at a steep discount to "Charter Subscribers."[52] This subscription model, which avoided the significant up-front payment required for hardcover publications like *Flying Saucers and the Three Men*, survived the imminent collapse of Barker's finances and would sustain the smaller scale of his publishing activities for the remainder of the decade. "Most of my business friends think I'm a fool and probably I am," he told Trevor James Constable, "but I'm in it till the last cup and saucer."[53]

"ATTACKS AND PERSECUTIONS": THE END OF *THE SAUCERIAN BULLETIN*

The winter of 1962–1963 was an exceptionally cold one in north central West Virginia. Following a series of severe cold snaps, freezing evening and overnight temperatures persisted into May.[54] The impact of this weather on drive-in theater business was devastating. In a mild season, drive-ins could open earlier in the year and stay open later, but in 1963 Barker's clients delayed their openings, and thus his booking income, for weeks.

On top of this, between borrowing money to produce *Flying Saucers and the Three Men*, purchasing a Multilith duplicator, and spending extravagantly on automobiles, Barker had overextended his finances. He had come up with a plan to use film booking money to pay off these loans, but the impact of the winter weather left his account empty, and he began missing payments.[55] In addition to reducing his publishing costs by shifting to in-house production, he took on a contract to print Duplantier's zine *Saucers, Space and Science* on his Multilith press.[56] But these efforts couldn't generate enough cash to pay off his loans.

In February 1963, hoping to raise some funds—or maybe to remove the possibility of his publication becoming the property of his creditors—Barker made arrangements to sell the *Saucerian Bulletin* to Moseley. The contract for the sale, dated February 23, includes the bulletin's subscriber list as well as the names *Saucerian Bulletin*, *The Saucerian*, and *Saucerian Review*, to James W. Moseley, in exchange for a single payment of five hundred dollars.[57] The contract calls for Barker to be named associate editor of *Saucer News* and specifies that he may publish books "of forty (40) pages or more," provided that they "shall not be numbered consecutively, nor shall they be purposely designed in such a fashion that the readers thereof would be likely to construe them as a continuation of the Magazine."[58] Moseley later stated that the merger nearly doubled the subscription rolls of *Saucer News*, bringing his zine to over four thousand bimonthly readers.[59]

The combination of *Saucer News* and the *Saucerian Bulletin* may have come as a surprise to Barker's and Moseley's readers, who had little reason to doubt that the feud between the two was serious. Moseley covered for both the fictional grudge and Barker's circumstances with an editorial announcing the merger in which he explained that, after a recent conversation in Clarksburg, "we became convinced of the reality of some of the persecutions which Mr. Barker has, for many months, been loudly proclaiming in his zine and elsewhere."[60] Moseley gave further information on Barker's "persecutions" in a *Non-Scheduled Newsletter* describing a visit to Barker on May 2, 1963:

> The Gray Barker who greeted us there was taciturn and frightened, much as Al Bender is said to have been after his "hush up" ten years ago. The Barker we had known before was arrogant, carefree, and apparently well off financially. He had had a comfortable office downtown and a pleasant apartment on Mulberry St., in a nearby residential area. Now the big office and apartment were gone, and Barker was living in a run-down old house on a high hill near

the edge of town. Barker asked us to be his guests rather than stay at a hotel. It was obvious that his new generosity was not altruism, but some sort of deep-rooted fear of being alone at night. . . .

When we saw Barker the next morning, he looked pale and nervous. He had obviously lost weight since our last visit. His forehead bore a small scar, which he said had been caused by a thug who assaulted him shortly before he moved out of his former apartment. His new quarters were in a terrible state of disorder, with books and papers scattered around haphazardly. We noticed that the printing press appeared to be damaged. Barker informed us that it had been sabotaged by the above-mentioned thug, whom he refused to describe in any further detail. . . .

Barker further stated that he had decided to dismiss his four employees "for their own protection," and was planning to go on alone with his book publishing business. . . . Although the term "Silence Group" was never used in our conversation, it was quite obvious that Barker felt there was some organized force behind the various attacks and persecutions which he has been suffering during the past several months.[61]

This announcement provides cover for Barker's legal and financial troubles. His sudden move from Mulberry Avenue, his firing of staff, and his sale of the magazine all become evidence of a potential "hush-up" and thus imply that Barker's publications might contain the secret to the UFO mystery.

"EVIL EXUDED FROM THE THING": *UFO WARNING*

In *They Knew Too Much about Flying Saucers*, Barker presented multiple cases of "silenced" saucer investigators, often using superficial similarities to fit disparate cases into the single metanarrative of "shush-ups." One case was that of John Stuart and Doreen Wilkinson, the sole members of the New Zealand organization Flying Saucer Investigators. Beginning with their first letter to Barker in 1954, the two recounted strange experiences, including hearing footsteps from an invisible source and receiving a phone call demanding that they stop investigating saucers.[62] Before long Wilkinson moved away, ostensibly out of fear for her safety, and the two discontinued their saucer research.

Stuart told his story to Barker several times over the ensuing years, culminating in a book manuscript, sent to Barker in August 1962, under the title *The Kiwi under UFO Attack*.[63] With each telling, Stuart added and removed details. In later versions of the story he described sighting a strange "green monster" in the lead-up to the FSI's closing, but a fistfight with a different, invisible monster disappeared from the narrative, as did a mysterious piece of metallic debris that Stuart claimed to have given to one strange visitor.[64] Stuart's main concern in spinning the tale seems to have been stemming rumors that he and Wilkinson were engaged in an affair— rumors that he admitted to Barker were accurate.[65] By 1958 he believed that all of his strange experiences, including the green monster, were the results of a hoax played on him by Wilkinson, who he said may have hypnotized him.[66] He later walked these claims back, concluding that Wilkinson had been just as frightened as he had been.[67] The instability of Stuart's narrative between 1954 and 1963 renders him an unreliable narrator of a story that was, by his own admission, difficult for many to accept.

Stuart's book, published by Barker as *UFO Warning*, details one version of the events that befell the Flying Saucer Investigators.[68] Undeterred by rumors about the true nature of their relationship, Stuart and Wilkinson— pseudonymized in the text as Barbara Turner—engage in a series of late-night conversations about flying saucers. They begin to theorize about an Antarctic origin of the saucers and discuss related mysteries, including archaeological enigmas and the strange experiences of "silenced" researchers Albert Bender and Edgar Jarrold. These bull sessions are interrupted by an increasingly bizarre series of events: threatening phone calls; strange odors; and mysterious footsteps, laughter, and other unexplained sensations with invisible sources. One evening a strange visitor with a "rather effeminate face" materializes in the room where they are speaking, claiming to be a spaceman and advising them to stop their investigations of flying saucers.[69] The two disregard the warning, but some time later they witness an eight-foot-tall green monster that advances on Barbara with carnal menace:

> The monster's head was large and bulbous. No neck. A huge and ungainly body supported on ridiculously short legs. It had webbed feet. The arms were

thin and not unlike stalks of bamboo. It had no hands, the long fingers jutting from the arms like stalks. Its eyes were about four inches across, red in color. There was no nose, just two holes, and the mouth was simply a straight slash across its appallingly lecherous face. The whole was a green lime in color, and it was possible to see red veins running through its ungainly form. The monster was definitely male.[70]

The monster approaches as if preparing to sexually assault Barbara, then disappears as suddenly as it had appeared. Several nights later, however, while alone in her home, Barbara is attacked and raped by an invisible intruder. Traumatized by the experience, Barbara leaves town. Shortly thereafter Stuart receives a final, strange visit:

> Its body resembled, vaguely, that of a human. From the waist up it was a man, and from the waist down that of a woman. Its flesh, stinkingly putrid, seemed to hang in folds. It was a greyish color. Evil exuded from the entire thing. The slack mouth was dribbling, and the horrible lips began to move. . . . The thing seemed to waver, and grow less distinct; then materialized again into solidity. I almost collapsed in horror and revulsion as the male and female areas of its body had suddenly changed places. "You have been warned! Take heed! Should you fail there will be others to suffer!"[71]

Terrified by the implications of this threatening visit, Stuart shuts down the FSI for good.

Sexual suggestiveness is central to *UFO Warning*, and the story is best remembered for its salaciousness. Jerome Clark described it as "steamy" and "creepy (on both levels of meaning)."[72] Barker later claimed it "had to be toned down when published due to explicit sexual references."[73] Barker made several additions to Stuart's text, adding descriptions of Barbara as "a sweet, kind, innocent girl" and representing Stuart and Wilkinson's relationship as a chaste friendship.[74] Barker's edit adds introductory phrases to passages in which Barbara is flirtatious or sexually suggestive, or removes her clothing, implying that these licentious moments are the result of extraterrestrial mind control.[75] Moreover, Barker deletes lines of dialog that reveal Stuart's participation in this flirtation and refer to their kissing. These adjustments necessitated a change in the illustrations supplied by Gene Duplantier, who

Figures 8.2–8.3
Gene Duplantier's original and Barker's censored illustration of "Barbara" from John Stuart's *UFO Warning*, 1963. Gray Barker UFO Collection, Clarksburg Harrison Public Library/Courtesy of the Gray Barker Estate.

had opted to illustrate a scene in which Barbara strips naked for a conversation with Stuart just prior to the effeminate visitor's arrival.[76] Duplantier's original illustration shows Barbara topless, albeit covered up with a sheaf of UFO-related papers; Barker censored this image on a Photostat used for the printed version, adding a longer skirt, a dark blouse, and, as if in wry Freudian commentary, a cigar on the ashtray beside her.[77]

Stuart's description of the green monster includes a reference to its genitalia more explicit than what appears in Barker's final copy. And in Stuart's version, Barbara strips her clothes off again as the creature approaches her, a series of events that Barker obscures with the text "I will spare the reader Barbara's actions."[78] Later, Stuart explicitly describes Barbara's rape by her invisible attacker, and the hermaphroditic alien that appears to Stuart at the end of the narrative makes similarly lascivious references to those events. Moreover, Stuart's manuscript gives a clearer explanation of why this being suddenly changes its bodily configuration, with its sexual transformation occurring in response to a question about the aliens' assault on Barbara.

The effects of Barker's changes to the narrative are to downplay the affair between Stuart and Barbara/Wilkinson and to make it appear that Barbara's sensual actions were the result of alien mind control rather than expressions of her own sexuality. Barker's manuscript is also significantly less explicit than Stuart's, even removing several instances of the word *rape* from the text. It's possible that Barker feared losing his more conservative readers, particularly since this was to be the first installment in his new charter subscription program. It's also possible that, following his arrest and conviction the year before, he feared the impact that publishing a sexually explicit book might have on his probation. Stuart was generally pleased with Barker's changes, particularly the more delicate treatment of Barbara's character.[79] After the book's publication, Barker told Stuart that he thought the unedited manuscript "would really make a hum-dinger of a pocket size book"—presumably from a publisher of sleaze paperbacks.[80]

BILL COLLECTORS AT THE DOOR: BANKRUPTCY

Barker had announced additional books to be released as early as March, but these were delayed significantly, almost certainly due to lack of funds to print them. In June Barker declared bankruptcy after selling some office equipment (probably including the Multilith) to his brother in hope of keeping it out of the hands of his trustee.[81] A hearing finalizing the process was held on

June 27, 1963, in the same courthouse where McCulty had been sentenced just two weeks before. Barker sent Moseley a detailed letter about both the hearing itself and events in Barker's life in the days around it.[82] These included his weekly visit to his psychiatrist; a recent fight between McCulty and his wife, Alma; and a particularly successful weekend at Lovett's Drive-In following a titillating advertising campaign for the film noir *Walk on the Wild Side*. Barker also discusses his continued pursuit of young men in and around Clarksburg, using "UFO research" as a euphemism in place of the "Communist indoctrination" of the Mulberry Place letters.[83] Though the letter is illuminating, there is some reason to doubt its veracity. Barker recounts an anecdote of an apparently recent cattle stampede on a drive-in lot—but the story is virtually identical to one he submitted to *Boxoffice* in 1949.[84] The recycling of this tale indicates that, even in reporting events of his own life to his closest friends, Barker was an unreliable narrator.

Arriving at the courthouse on June 27, Barker feared that the large number of people gathered in the courtroom were there to testify against him; he was both relieved and surprised to learn that they, too, were there to declare bankruptcy. Barker's case was among the last heard that day, likely due to the complexities of his intertwined businesses. Asked by the judge to explain the reason for his bankruptcy, Barker explained:

> I blamed this on "the decline of the theatre business," and the fact that the stuff I was selling and writing in book form had not been going as well as it once had (The judge did not ask me just what sort of material I wrote—if he had I was all set to call it "science fiction" instead of "flying saucers," feeling that would make a better impression—come to think of it, however, I was not there to make a Good Impression; instead I suppose the worse of an Impression I could have made would have been the better).[85]

At the conclusion of the hearing, the judge appointed Barker's trustee: the assistant district attorney who had prosecuted his criminal trial seven months earlier. Leaving the courthouse, Barker needed to decide what to do with his car, an ostentatious Continental Mark III convertible that the judge had ordered him not to drive until the trustee had determined its fate. He had parked the car outside the courthouse, however, and needed to move it. His lawyer's solution, which linked his previous legal troubles with his current financial situation, became the punchline to Barker's twenty-page account of his troubles:

> "What do I do," I asked him, "Go ahead and use the car anyhow[?]"
>
> The Bad Lawyer went into his usual deep contemplation, as he does when Important Matters are to be Decided, cleared his throat, and came out with a Classic Answer. I say "Classic," because it was the same answer he gave me when, after the trial, I asked him what I should do about Further Research [i.e., sexual activity].
>
> "ALL RIGHT," he said, "BUT USE DISCRETION."[86]

News of Barker's financial difficulties gradually spread through the saucer scene. Recalling Barker's fear, expressed in *They Knew Too Much*, that the three men would someday knock on his door, *Saucer News* reviewer Richard Wallace (a pseudonymous Eugene Steinberg) commented, "The only men Barker ever found at his door were the bill collectors."[87]

"THE MEN WERE COMPLETE FAILURES": THE PHILADELPHIA EXPERIMENT

The same week that he was in court for his bankruptcy hearing, Barker was also at work printing his book *The Strange Case of Dr. M. K. Jessup*. The book told a story that had begun nearly a decade earlier. Following the publication of *The Case for the UFO* in 1955, Morris Jessup received a series of strange letters, alternately signed Carlos M. Allende and Carl M. Allen.[88] Written in a fractured and disordered style, the letters describe a series of experiments in the Philadelphia Naval Yard in October 1943, during which a Destroyer-class ship was rendered invisible and teleported to the vicinity of Norfolk, Virginia, for a period of several minutes. Allen, then a crewman on the merchant marine vessel the SS *Furuseth*, claimed to have witnessed at least one of these experiments firsthand. The strange field that enabled invisibility and teleportation had devastating effects on the sailors caught within it, including "freezing" into a strange physical stasis, spontaneous combustion, and madness. Allen's second letter sums up the results of the event: "The expierement [*sic*] Was a Complete Success. The Men Were Complete Failures."[89]

Shortly before Jessup received these letters, the Office of Naval Research had received an anonymously mailed envelope containing a paperback copy of *The Case for the UFO*. The book contained extensive underlining and annotations in several different colors of ink, apparently in three different hands. The notes made oblique references to an ancient battle between two mysterious and apparently nonhuman species—and to the same experiment discussed in the letters from Allen/Allende. For reasons that remain murky, the ONR took an interest in the annotated book and called Jessup in to consult. He noted the similarity in handwriting and content between the annotations and the Allende letters, provided copies of these to the ONR, and commented on the matter to several colleagues.

The ONR hired the Varo Manufacturing Co., a small military contractor based in Garland, Texas, to transcribe the entirety of the book—Jessup's original text as well as all of the annotations, underlining, and other markings—and then produce a small mimeographed edition.[90] The Varo text identifies the three annotators as Mr. A, Mr. B, and Jemi, a nickname or salutation used periodically by the other two. Each annotation and mark is attributed to one of the three. Though few had seen Varo's printing of the book, some details about it were public; in fact, Barker had mentioned it in his Chasing the Flying Saucers column for the May 1959 issue of *Flying Saucers from Other Worlds*, which was probably on newsstands when Jessup died.[91]

Much of the evidence surrounding Allen/Allende suggested that his descriptions of the supposed experiment were either a hoax or the product of his mental illness.[92] But Barker saw in this bizarre and fragmentary narrative the beginnings of an insoluble—and thus endlessly extensible—mystery. *The Strange Case of Dr. M. K. Jessup* is Barker's first extended foray into this material, a compilation of bizarre theories concerning Jessup and what had become known as the Allende letters. Latching onto Allen's disordered and meandering prose style, Barker introduces the outlandish hypothesis that the Allende letters "MIGHT HAVE BEEN WRITTEN BY SOMEBODY FROM ANOTHER PLANET."[93] Barker concludes his commentary on the letters with a rhetorical question (and an emphatic line of eleven question marks), making clear the conclusion he wants his readers to reach about Jessup's death: "Did Jessup also 'know too much'???????????"[94]

As Barker was printing the book, it was coming up about ten pages short of its eighty-page target—the page count required for subscription books by the legal agreement between Moseley and Barker for the sale of the *Saucerian Bulletin*.[95] The final section of the book is an addendum containing a channeled message from a spirit implied, but pointedly not stated, to be Jessup's, received through an anonymous medium. In a letter to Moseley, Barker mentions the timely and fortuitous arrival of these unattributed materials in language that strongly suggests Barker had fabricated them, possibly with Lucchesi's help.[96] At the close of the addendum, Barker adds a comment summing up the book as a whole: "This book was in no way intended to represent a solution to the mystery surrounding the passing of Dr. Jessup. If it is therefore disappointing to those who expect complete answers, we are very sorry."[97] Indeed, the book was not intended to solve the mystery of Jessup's death—it was intended to invent one, and to turn Jessup into a blank canvas on which to project any number of unanswered questions.

John Keel later referred to the version of Jessup that Barker depicted as a narratological invention. Keel had played his own part in this invention, implying in a 1967 article for *Saga* that Jessup had been killed by "Gypsies . . . [who] know a great deal about flying saucers."[98] Barker's construction of the narrative was effective, and decades later the idea persisted that Jessup was keenly interested in the Allende material rather than bemused by it.[99] First by accident, and later deliberately, Barker succeeded in inserting the Allende material into the narrative of Jessup's death so deeply that even a debunking explanation cannot help but mention it.

"KER-FLUNK"

In mid-August 1963 Barker visited New York to deliver a lecture, the first in a series of monthly offerings hosted by *Saucer News* that lasted through much of the 1960s. The lecture was a success, in large part due to publicity from Nebel's radio show, and Barker referred to it as having had "a turnaway crowd."[100] Barker spent several days with the Moseleys on this trip, and Sandy Moseley contributed a brief profile describing his visit, entitled "What Gray Barker Is Really Like," to the December issue of *Saucer News*:

> Gray accepted our invitation and arrived with several suitcases and a box of books to sell. The first night we listened to a 'word jazz' [Ken Nordine] record album he had brought along. These records are very abstract, and although Jim enjoyed them, I found them depressing—like Gray's poetry. After a few beers, Gray's shyness started to disappear. He kicked off his white bucks and began exuding his charming personality. . . . We all have our secret ambitions, and Gray's is to re-make the silent picture classic, "Birth of a Nation." . . . He is an intellectual, a Christian, and an animal lover. While here he became attached to our cat Arnold, which he brought back to Clarksburg with him.[101]

This sketch of Barker is, in some respects, a puzzling one. His selection of D. W. Griffith's notorious *Birth of a Nation* as a film meriting a remake is provocative, particularly at the height of the civil rights movement. But there is little evidence in Barker's other activities to suggest a commitment to spreading white-supremacist attitudes. More likely, as a committed fan of the technical aspects of film production and presentation, he admired the film for its advances in cinematography. The passing reference to Barker's religious beliefs is similarly surprising. There are few signs of his religious beliefs in his contemporary writings, and in an interview after Barker's death, Moseley indicated that he had never heard Barker express any religious views before saying on his deathbed that he was "very religious"—a statement that surprised Moseley a great deal.[102] Barker published a wide range of spiritual material, and though he seemed almost envious of the worldview of the likes of Bethurum and Rampa, in his own life and writing it is difficult to see anything other than ironic detachment. If there were to be a god, he wanted it to be himself, pulling the world's strings.

But it's just as possible that at least some of the claims in Sandy Moseley's article were invented from whole cloth and tied to the article's true purpose: smoothing over the fake feud that Moseley and Barker had carried on and painting a picture of a growing, public friendship emerging in its place. Moseley continued this trend in an editorial in the June 1964 issue of *Saucer*

News, claiming that the two had quickly become friends after meeting in 1953, but had fallen out over a romantic dispute in 1954, when Moseley visited Clarksburg with his then-girlfriend: "As neither Barker nor Moseley wanted to publicly admit the real cause of their feud, they proceeded to attack each other in their respective magazines about other things not related to the incident that destroyed their friendship."[103] With this announcement—the details of which seem to be entirely fraudulent—Moseley and Barker officially, and publicly, buried the hatchet.

Since Barker had fired most of his staff in the lead-up to his bankruptcy proceedings, it appears that Saucerian Publications' sole employee in the winter of 1963–64 was McCulty, who was managing subscriptions, though a part-time assistant (dubbed by Barker "the Bad Secretary" in a letter to Moseley) also assisted in film booking and printing.[104] It's difficult to determine the extent of Barker's success in publishing, as his claims about book sales varied depending on whom he was speaking to and what he hoped to get from them. For prospective authors, sales were strong; for those requesting a royalty statement, they were stagnant. Prior to the release of a book by Virginia Brasington, Barker informed Brasington that he was regularly selling a thousand copies of every book he published, but immediately after the publication of *UFO Warning* he told Stuart that his book exemplified a general trend: "the Flying Saucer Book Market has gone 'ker-flunk.'"[105]

LAURA MUNDO, *THE FATHER'S PLAN*, AND THE BETTER BOOK LEAGUE

In the fall of 1963 Barker began soliciting a second charter subscription series, which was to begin with *Flying Saucers and the Father's Plan* by Laura Mundo. Few figures in the world of flying saucers were as colorful as Mundo. Initially active under her married name, Laura Marxer, she was a children's television presenter in the 1950s, appearing as the storyteller Midge on the Detroit-area preschool program *Playschool*.[106] She became interested in flying saucers shortly after reading Leslie and Adamski's *Flying Saucers Have Landed* and was active in the Detroit Flying Saucer Club in 1954, but left it soon after.[107] Around the same time, Marxer reverted to her maiden name,

Mundo; launched her own organization, variously called the Planetary Center and the Interplanetary Space Center; and became one of Adamski's chief promoters in the Detroit area. The Planetary Center issued mimeograph publications like the first edition of *Flying-Saucers and the Father's Plan* (title hyphenated in its original edition), containing the text of a lecture Mundo delivered in the summer of 1962. The introduction declares: "THIS MATERIAL may be re-copied and passed on to others, free."[108]

In the book Mundo recounts her association with saucers and contactees, including several sightings and encounters of her own, and seamlessly blends religious visions, psychism, and saucers: "A month after getting into saucer research (February 1954), while promoting Adamski's lecture, the Visitors came over my home, in their saucers, sending a beam of neutronic energy of the Father Frequency to my brain, re-activating brain cells that had been 'put to sleep' when I had also been demoted from more advanced planets."[109] The topics are far-ranging, and the text meanders from topic to topic, breaking apart its narrative aspects with lengthy discussions of Mundo's philosophical and religious ideas, presented, in the original edition, in densely compacted mimeographed text.

In his negotiations with Mundo, Barker made his customary offer of one thousand copies at a royalty rate of 10 percent for bookstore sales and 5 percent on discounted or direct-order sales (a subtle trick, since few Saucerian titles were sold in bookstores).[110] In response Mundo rejected any royalties for the publication and stated her belief that copyrighting the work would be "against universal law."[111] She forbade Barker from making edits of any kind to the introduction (written by Carmella Falzone, the codirector of the Planetary Center and an upholstery seamstress for General Motors), but advised him that he could make any changes he saw fit to her own text.[112] Barker took this literally and made extensive edits: in addition to spreading the text out into a more spacious layout and adding chapter and paragraph breaks, Barker's edition excises many of Mundo's philosophical passages and replaces them with material more directly related to flying saucers, "Visitors," and Adamski. The verso of the title page states, "No copyright is claimed, and the author encourages copying and further distribution of her Works, free of charge."[113]

When Mundo received her copies of the book in early November, she was furious at Barker's changes:

> The books arrived—and I am not pleased with what you have done to the script . . . you have stated some things, in re-writing, the opposite of what I know to be the truth. I had given you carte blanche, to rewrite, yes—with an eye to grammatical errors, punctuation, sentence structure, etc. Much you left out that is of vital importance, as well. . . . I am afraid I could not work with you in the future, in any way, unless you took my script exactly as it is written. . . . As it is, it is done up more amateurishly than I could have done, myself.[114]

Two weeks later Mundo wrote to Barker again, informing him of her intention to release her own revised edition of the book. Barker could continue to sell his edition, but her version would be distributed free of charge to anyone who requested it, "and will be competition for you."[115] Mundo followed through, issuing her "corrected version" of the book in January 1964, only two months after the release of the Saucerian edition.[116] Moreover, the Interplanetary Space Center actively discouraged potential customers from buying Barker's publication, with *Saucer News* running a letter from Falzone in their March 1964 issue announcing the new, free edition.[117]

Since Barker had agreed to publish the work without copyright, he had no real option to prevent the author pirating her own work. Mundo's edition, titled *The Father's Plan and Flying Saucers*, included a brief introduction concerning Barker, protesting perhaps too much that the issuing of this new edition was "in NO WAY an attempt to belittle Gray Barker, the editor."[118] Barker's response was a typically impish one: rather than challenge Mundo directly, he hoaxed her. In 1964 he called Mundo's Interplanetary Space Center, posing as a member of the "Better Book League" and offering to pay Mundo to take the book off the market.[119]

ANOTHER PRESENT FOR THE INNER CIRCLE: *UFO 96*

In December 1963 Barker privately printed a small-run publication as a Christmas card for the "inner circle," as he had done with *Youranus* six years earlier. *UFO 96* is a lively, jokey publication, primarily made up of correspondence sent to Barker and offering a decidedly satirical look at the world of saucers in general and contactees in particular. In the opening editorial, Barker describes *UFO 96* as "a rather fond look at the Early Days of Saucers, which, sometimes, have a way of stretching forward to yesterday."[120]

The compilation includes some previously released material, including one of Barker's past Christmas cards and Jacqueline Sanders's account of a channeling session at Giant Rock from the September 1954 *Saucerian*. Other material had never been published, including a condensed version of a letter he had sent to Sanders in 1956 detailing a trip to a contactee-themed convention in Detroit. Also included is a three-page *Mad*-style parody comic entitled "The Adventures of Jane Noseley," written by Barker and drawn by Duplantier.[121] The satire is less sharp than "They Knew Too Little about Flying Saucers" from *Youranus*, but Barker pokes fun at himself in the strip, where he appears as "Gay Parker," in an office with costumes of the Flatwoods Monster and a Silence Group member hanging on the wall. A similar joke appears in a fake advertising section, which lists for sale a particularly descriptive "Flatwoods Monster Suit": "Suit zips up back, packs in small carrying case so that you can get the suit off and packed away quickly and then get in on the fun of being the first to 'investigate' the site. Then make up stories on your own about the incident."[122] Barker's introduction notes with regret that he did not have room to include a "transcript of a Certain Trial" and "various 'Mulberry Place' writings," indicating that some of the details of his legal predicament and sex life may have been known to saucer-world friends besides just Moseley.[123]

"I HAVE ABANDONED UFO PUBLISHING"

UFO 96 may have been intended as a sort of farewell to the flying saucer world. In early February of 1964, Barker wrote to Roberts that he had taken a "real job," working "for a school projector equipment concern that I've been associated with for a number of years"—Lovett & Co.[124] Doc Lovett had suffered a stroke in February 1962, and Barker, feeling a sense of filial duty, wanted to help keep the business going.[125] His work now encompassed equipment sales as well as the production of short educational films, mainly about the history of West Virginia.[126] (Speaking of Barker's aspirations as a filmmaker, McCulty later recalled that "he always had a camera with him.")[127] Barker was also trying to sell the Alpine Theatre, suggesting that it, too, may have been operating at a loss following his bankruptcy. *They Knew Too Much* was out of print and no longer available from University Books. Book sales slowed as well, and by the spring he had shut down the operations of Book Tracers, his rare-book search service.[128] Saucerian Books published only a single title in 1964—*Without Figleaves* by contactee Dana Howard. The book is only tangentially related to saucers, focusing instead on Howard's ideas about the ability of "regenerative sex" to renew and revitalize human society. Shortly thereafter, Barker wrote to one correspondent, "I have abandoned UFO publishing as a full-time occupation."[129] Saucering was, once again, just a hobby.

Barker's legal jeopardy emerged again in early 1965.[130] On February 19, Barker's court-ordered therapy concluded, and he was placed on five years' probation. The terms of his parole allowed him to travel for business purposes, and March 1 found him in Elkins, West Virginia, sixty miles southeast of Clarksburg. According to court records, he picked up a fourteen-year-old boy at Wimpy's, a pool hall in Elkins, and brought him to a motel. Barker attempted sex with the boy, but—apparently overcome with guilt, or perhaps simply with fear over potential prosecution—he ceased his efforts after a few minutes and returned him to the pool hall. The boy's father went to the police, and the matter was referred to the prosecuting attorney for Randolph County, James Cain. Discovering Barker's prior conviction, Cain wrote to Robert Ziegler, the Harrison County prosecuting attorney, stating that he had intended to charge Barker and bring him to trial, but that it would be simpler to have his probation revoked rather than prosecute him anew in a different county. Ziegler concurred, and petitioned the court to have Barker imprisoned. The date of the initial hearing was set for May 6.

Barker again engaged the services of Paul Poulicos for his defense. Virginia Howell testified to Barker's character, and McCulty wrote a letter to the court urging against imprisonment: "We both know the pitfalls of confinement. Behind walls, Mr. Barker would soon fall prey to the very element he is trying so hard to fight."[131] But the key piece of testimony in Barker's defense came from his psychiatrist, Boylston Smith, who submitted a letter to the court on May 1. Smith argued that the events in Elkins were Barker's sole transgression since the conclusion of his trial and emphasized the abortive nature of the encounter: "If the patient is reporting accurately, then what occurred would represent a victory in regard to his ability to withstand temptation, which would mean that the patient is responding successfully to treatment."[132] The prosecutors of Randolph and Harrison Counties hoped that Barker's conduct in Elkins would become grounds for his immediate imprisonment, but under Smith's testimony it became instead evidence that his therapy had worked. Barker's probation was extended by two years (to conclude in 1970), but he remained free.

"OTHER, MORE SATISFYING REWARDS": *GRAY BARKER'S BOOK OF SAUCERS*

For most of 1965, Barker's saucer activities remained limited to selling increasingly out-of-date books through advertisements in the back of *Saucer News* and delivering a handful of lectures. But saucers were again emerging as a topic of interest in American culture. *Saucer News*'s declaration of a "giant 1964 saucer flap" was an exaggeration, but the number of sightings reported to the Air Force was gradually increasing, from 399 in 1963 to 562 the following year and nearly 900 in 1965.[133] Barker's lecture in New York on August 13, 1965, was a sold-out affair.[134] Perhaps as a distraction from his legal and financial troubles, perhaps detecting the reemergence of flying saucers as a business, Barker again turned his attention to publishing, asserting, "The editor will continue in other good-paying business, but only as a means of continuing with saucer publishing, which, if not financially rewarding, has its other, more satisfying, rewards."[135] However, he would reduce his direct involvement in printing: rather than producing his books in-house, for the next decade Barker outsourced his book production.[136]

As a lead-in to his revived publication program, Barker launched a new periodical, *Spacecraft News*. (Barker's agreement with Moseley prohibited him from using "Saucerian" in the title of a serial). Ostensibly intended as a way to quickly disseminate news about saucer sightings and landings, the newsletter's true, thinly veiled purpose was to plug upcoming publications. The free newsletter was announced as being available exclusively to members of Saucerian's charter subscription program, and "cannot be purchased nor subscribed for."[137] In the first issue Barker gave a rosy picture of Saucerian's future, declaring, "We have managed to pull through the financial vicissitudes of these [past] projects, and thanks to other business ventures of more conventional nature, now are in the best financial position we have been in for some years."[138] This editorial was accompanied by a smattering of sighting reports, sales listings, and a preview, written by McCulty, of Barker's latest book.

Gray Barker's Book of Saucers—primarily a roundup of news clippings of saucer sightings from 1962 to 1963—had a long, slow journey to market. Barker had first conceived of it as an annual roundup of sightings and pitched the idea to Ivan Sanderson in September 1963. "It will be a far cry from the Citadel ANNUAL by Jessup," he said, "in that some organization will be attempted and that a fairly good hack writing style will be employed."[139] The early chapters of *Book of Saucers* match this description, with brief introductions in Barker's breathless style to a litany of saucer sightings, landings, "spacenappings," and witness reports of strange creatures in much the same style as Barker's Chasing the Flying Saucers column. But this belated annual roundup occupies only about half of the book's page count. The remainder is newer material, including a long account of Barker's trip to New York in July and August 1965, entitled "The Dero and the Tero." Barker discusses his initial meeting with Erwin Vertleib and Norman Schreibstein, heads of the Rissler Observatory, who had reported being menaced by the three men in black and experiencing both psychic and corporeal contact from space beings, including the Flatwoods Monster itself. Though they had presented themselves, at least by implication, as scientists, Moseley states Vertleib and Schreibstein were teenagers, and their "observatory" was located in the basement of Schreibstein's parents' house. According to Moseley, Vertleib soon "found better things to do with his time (girls?), but Schreibstein became one of the (much) lesser players in Barker's sideshow, hanging around The Field into the early seventies."[140]

Gray Barker's Book of Saucers represents Barker's first engagement with a new metanarrative that began emerging in the 1960s and would eventually come to dominate the field. In 1962 a Brazilian ufological organization published an account of a farmer named Antônio Villas-Boas, who reported having been taken aboard a flying saucer and coerced into sexual relations with an alien woman five years earlier. Barker summarizes the story, apparently basing his text on both the original Brazilian publication and a summary by Gordon Creighton published in the January–February 1965 issue of *Flying Saucer Review*.[141] Barker goes into more detail than Creighton on the sexual aspects of the case, but still glosses over this portion of the account fairly quickly.[142] The main emphasis of his relatively long account is instead on the events surrounding the alien sexual encounter: the space-suited attackers who dragged Villas-Boas onto their ship; the "blood test" they administered; the strange, beaked appearance of their saucer; and speculations about the ship's origin, which give the chapter its title, "Visitors from the Bird Planet."

Barker correctly predicted that stories like this, in which strange, noncommunicative aliens kidnap human beings as test subjects, would prove more palatable than Adamski-style stories of friendly space brothers: "Saucerenthusiasts who gag at the usual 'contact' stories have little in common with them to find here. In this case nobody tells the witness what life is like on other planets. Nobody gives him sociological or religious instruction. Nobody tells him to stop smoking, drinking, or flesh-eating. In fact, the people are not very much interested in him, other than to use him to fulfill a biological mission."[143] The Villas-Boas case became a major UFO narrative, particularly after Coral and Jim Lorenzen included a detailed version of the story in their 1967 book *Flying Saucer Occupants*.[144] Similar stories of unwilling and sexualized alien contact would eventually come to the fore in UFO literature, in large part because of the lack of communication from the alien beings. These silent abductors would become a blank canvas on which all manner of anxieties and beliefs could be projected.

At some point Barker revisited the Villas-Boas case, focusing this time on aspects of the story he had glossed over in his 1965 summary. Barker's files contain a fragmentary document (missing at least its first page), undated but likely from the mid-1970s, that draws its inspiration from

Villas-Boas. The title, "Sexy Saucer People," is similar to *Those Sexy Saucer People*, a paperback issued in 1967 by the sleaze paperback house Greenleaf Classics, but the manuscript's content is completely different.[145] *Those Sexy Saucer People*, despite its packaging, had been a fairly straightforward and skeptical summary of a variety of contactee accounts, only a few of which had any sexual content.[146] The "Sexy Saucer People" manuscript, however, is a pornographic rewrite of the Villas-Boas contact case, with different names and significantly more details—particularly pertaining to what happened between the unwitting abductee and the alien woman aboard the saucer.[147] The manuscript may have been written for Timothy Green Beckley, who served as Barker's agent for magazine publications in the late 1970s and sold material both to newsstand magazines on UFOs and to pornographic publications. No evidence has emerged to indicate that this piece was published, but if it was, it likely appeared under a pseudonym.

9 THE SAUCER BOOM: THE PARANORMAL AS BUSINESS, 1966–1968

The middle of the 1960s may have been a slow period for Saucerian Publications, but it was an increasingly busy one for saucer sighters. A 1964 sighting in Socorro, New Mexico, by police officer Lonnie Zamora was well publicized, and a major new "flap" of sightings began in July 1965. Unlike in the past few years, mainstream media took notice. A series of sightings in Exeter, New Hampshire, in September 1965 and even more dramatic ones in Dexter and Hillsdale, Michigan, in March 1966 received levels of coverage not seen since the early 1950s. In 1966 the Air Force received more than a thousand reports of sightings for the first time since 1952.[1] The Michigan sightings in particular became a major source of public interest, amplified after J. Allen Hynek, investigating the flap for the Air Force's Project Blue Book, gave a press conference at which he explained some of the sightings as being the result of "swamp gas." Though Hynek intended this term to explain only a very narrow subset of the sightings, the media, many of the witnesses, and the public at large latched onto it as a catchall term for official dismissal of UFO sightings. Gerald Ford, then a congressional representative for Michigan's Fifth District, saw Hynek's explanation as symbolizing the Air Force's contemptuous attitude to UFO reports, declaring, "The American public deserves a better explanation than that thus far given by the Air Force."[2] In October 1966 the Air Force announced the formation of an independent committee to investigate UFO reports under the directorship of Edward Condon at the University of Colorado.

Along with this increased public interest in saucers came a new publishing trend of books about UFOs, as well as the first bestsellers on the topic

Inside the illustration:

DEDICATED

To all of Earth's People

.....Adoni Vasu

Figure 9.1
Gene Duplantier's frontispiece for *The Book of Space Ships and Their Relationship with Earth*, 1967. Author's collection/Courtesy of the Gray Barker Estate.

since the 1950s: Frank Edwards's general overview *Flying Saucers—Serious Business* and journalist John Fuller's *Incident at Exeter*, a detailed account of the 1965 New Hampshire sightings. Alongside these hardcover bestsellers, a new batch of pocket-size books on UFOs arrived to meet the reading public's desire for material on the topic, including Brad Steiger's *Strangers from the Skies*, Otto Binder's *What We Really Know about Flying Saucers*, and Coral and Jim Lorenzen's *Flying Saucer Occupants*. The increased public interest extended to the core of saucer investigators, increasingly called *ufologists*, and Moseley reported increasing fortunes as a result: "My circulation had been slowly increasing since Zamora's sighting. . . . Before long, it was in excess of eight thousand, and in the first six months of 1966, I grossed $10,000 in mail-order business. For the first time since 1953, saucering was profitable."[3]

Barker jumped into the fray with the first book dedicated specifically to the Michigan sightings: John Sherwood's *Flying Saucers Are Watching You*. Sherwood was a teenager who had started a UFO club, the Michigan Investigators of the Flying Saucer Phenomenon, in February 1966, and collected clippings on the sightings; he had compiled a book manuscript by that October, and Barker rushed it to press in the first few weeks of 1967.[4] Sherwood suggested the title *Behold! A UFO*, and Barker first solicited it under the title *Incident at Dexter* (in an obvious imitation of Fuller's recent bestseller).[5] But ultimately Barker assigned it the title *Flying Saucers Are Watching You*, explaining that this was "a title I've been trying to fit to a book for a long time, for most FS book buyers are paranoi[a]c and something watching them is most appealing."[6] Despite the manuscript's timeliness, Barker expected that an "objective type book" like Sherwood's "won't move like the nut books we sell," but was rather "a prestige item which will sell steadily over a very long period."[7]

Barker returned to the field with a keynote address at the third Congress of Scientific Ufologists, held in Cleveland from June 23 to 25, 1966. Among the congress's business was the adoption of a "Resolution for a Better NICAP"; in response to Barker's support for this resolution, Keyhoe's organization expelled him.[8] Chiefly organized by Cleveland researchers Rick Hilberg and Al Manak, the Congress of Scientific Ufologists became closely associated with Moseley and *Saucer News* and launched a movement called

Middle Ufology. The extremes between which this movement existed (thus the "middle") were, on one side, the overly stuffy NICAP, which had a single-minded focus on Congressional investigation of saucers, and on the other the contactees. Though the term Middle Ufology suggests a cool and rational approach, it in fact represented a wide array of opinions and hypotheses, distinguished from the two extremes not so much by a sense of compromise as a belief that both friendly space contacts and "nuts-and-bolts" investigations offered too simple an explanation for the increasing strangeness of saucer encounters. The middle, therefore, incorporated the fringe.

"THE MAN WITH THE BEARD": JOHN A. KEEL

A key figure in Middle Ufology was a new arrival in the UFO community: John Keel. Keel was a journalist who spent much of the early '50s traveling to Egypt, India, and Tibet, sending back tales of strange and dangerous adventures for publication in men's pulp magazines like *Cavalier, Escapade,*

Figure 9.2
John Keel, Gray Barker, and Jim Moseley at the 1967 Congress of Scientific Ufologists in New York. Photograph by George Earley, from *Saucer News* 14, no. 3. Author's collection/public domain.

and *Man's Conquest*. Keel avoided the well-worn tourist routes, seeking out danger and magic in hope of producing entertaining tales about "unusual people practicing lost and forbidden arts left over from another, darker age."[9] This writing culminated in his first book, *Jadoo*, which assembled his travel accounts into a single narrative. *Jadoo* and Keel's other writing of the 1950s fits squarely in a tradition of exoticizing, Orientalist travel literature that stretched back nearly three centuries and claimed to describe the vanishing vestiges of "a disappearing other."[10]

The 1966 wave of UFO sightings sparked Keel's interest, and he quickly pitched *Playboy* on what he believed would be the definitive magazine article on the topic.[11] *Playboy* ultimately rejected his draft, but by then he was several months into the research of UFOs, and rather than abandoning the project he resolved to turn it into a book.[12] Keel's investigation of UFOs and the paranormal in the late 1960s represents an ongoing descent into a rabbit hole of unreality that informed all of his later books on those topics. Works like *Operation Trojan Horse* and *The Mothman Prophecies* are travelogues, like *Jadoo*, but where Keel's earlier work presented clichés and fabulations about non-Western cultures, his later works turn the same exoticizing eye to the geographies of the mind.

One of Keel's emerging focuses was on cases of black-suited men silencing UFO witnesses, a metanarrative that he expanded from the core that Barker had established in the 1950s. Keel coined a new term to encompass this metanarrative: Men in Black, abbreviated MIB.[13] Barker had generally referred to these as "shush-up cases," but the term scarcely spread beyond his own writing; others in the contactee realm appropriated Keyhoe's term "Silence Group" to refer to the intimidators.[14] But Keel's appellation caught on, and it remains the standard term for a metanarrative that increased in strangeness under his authorial guidance. Keel presented the black-suited visitors that threatened UFO witnesses not as government agents but as the force behind the UFOs themselves:

The UFO pilots . . . [are] of medium height, with angular faces, pointed chins, high cheekbones, and long oriental-like eyes. Their complexion is usually described as "very dark, like a heavy suntan." Many witnesses compare them to Indians or Gypsies. Their manner of speech is said to be slow, halting, a curious monotone of clipped phrases, "as if they had taped thousands of conversations and memorized them."[15]

Keel's descriptions of the men in black suits are distinctly racialized and betray a tendency to present racial differences and neurodivergent behavior as signs of unearthly origin.[16] Under Keel's guidance, the Men in Black shifted from sinister silencers to far more ambiguous trickster figures.[17]

SAUCERS IN MOTION: THE LOST CREEK FILM

Barker had forged saucer photographs as early as 1961, when *Saucer News* ran an image created by Barker and a young associate, Joe Gonzales.[18] *Saucer News* carried a description of the ostensible circumstances for a sighting in Lost Creek, just south of Clarksburg, that was captured on film by an anonymous photographer and his employee John Sheets.[19] Sheets developed the film and, according to the published report, brought it to Barker. This conceals Barker's dual role in the narrative, as Sheets was his employee—making Barker the anonymous photographer in the published account.

A later account by Moseley makes it clear that while the location and date in this account may have been accurate, the rest of the narrative was pure invention. With an increasingly busy lecture schedule, Moseley was looking for an audiovisual component to include in his presentations and solicited Barker's assistance in creating a saucer film:

> Barker agreed that, if I footed the bill, we would do a brief saucer-sighting movie, complete with accompanying story. We made the film from my car. I drove, while Barker filmed out the window from the front passenger seat. [John] Sheets, a friend of Gray's, perched on the car roof, with a model saucer dangling off the end of a fishing pole. The complexity of the motion of the car and of the model, which bounced around like crazy, made it very difficult to tell how big the saucer was, or how far away. Befitting my bargain lecture fee, this was a very cheap production, just one roll of film, slightly edited by Barker, a silver-painted plastic saucer model, and a little gas.[20]

Barker later expanded the mystery surrounding the film, informing a correspondent that the Air Force had temporarily seized the film from the lab that was developing it.[21] In a 1968 letter to Barker, Moseley called it "the Last Crook saucer film."[22] By the close of the decade, Barker was offering the film clip for sale in multiple formats, along with additional, dubiously provenanced saucer footage.[23]

"WEST VIRGINIA HAS THE WEIRD MARKET CORNERED": INDRID COLD AND THE MOTHMAN

Though his career began with the Flatwoods Monster case, Barker rarely did on-the-ground investigation of unusual events. An important exception came at the end of March 1967, when he traveled west to the Ohio River Valley to look into unusual reports that had begun the previous fall. In Mineral Wells, a town just south of the city of Parkersburg, a salesman named Woodrow Derenberger had reported a meeting with a spaceman named Indrid Cold of the planet Lanulos on November 2, 1966. He had appeared on a local television program the following night to discuss the case and received a fair amount of press that winter as a result. Shortly thereafter, something even stranger occurred. On November 15 residents of the Point Pleasant area, about sixty miles southwest of Derenberger, had begun reporting sightings of a large, unusual bird that papers soon named Mothman, possibly in reference to the runaway popularity of ABC's television program *Batman*.[24] Barker wrote to Allen Greenfield about the strange events in the Ohio River Valley just a few days after the first Mothman report:

> Am busy following up some rumors here: Of course you've heard of the W. Va. "Moth-Man" that can fly 100 miles an hour and chased couples in cars; Derenberger is now rumored to be in a hospital suffering from radiation sickness; and in Ripley W. Va. a bank has in its vault a mysterious gold-plated sphere which resists all efforts to drill into it. West Virginia definitely now has the weird market cornered.[25]

But Barker's other business seems to have kept him occupied throughout the winter, and these investigations took place remotely, most likely over the phone.

It was over four months later, in March 1967, that Barker arrived in the Point Pleasant area to interview witnesses.[26] John Keel arrived at the same time, and the two interviewed Derenberger together on March 25. Keel later summarized the interview in a report circulated among his associates in ufology. He described Derenberger as a "charming, outgoing man" and his contacts with the denizens of the planet Lanulos as utterly unremarkable to anyone familiar with Adamski, Bethurum, or Menger: "Like most contactees of the old school, he seems to have an answer for every question. He is also able to reply to manufactured 'facts.' Yet he tells his story with incredible conviction and sincerity."[27] By the time of Woodrew Derenberger's contact with Indrid Cold from the planet Lanulos in 1966, the contactee metanarrative had largely run its course. Much of the apparent strangeness of Derenberger's story stems from its naïve charm, which disregards the general disrepute into which such stories had fallen in both mainstream culture and ufology.

The same weekend, Keel played a prank on Barker, "slip[ping] an obviously hoaxed up note under Gray's door in the Ohio motel, knowing full well that he would realize I had done it. So I was quite dismayed when I found he was later displaying this note as further proof of the sinister MIB."[28] Barker surely did know that Keel was behind the note, but Keel had misjudged what Barker's reaction would be. Barker and Moseley then targeted Keel with a campaign of pranks and hoaxes that ran for over a year—some of which found their way into Keel's *The Mothman Prophecies* and other works as authentic paranormal occurrences.[29] They subjected Keel to prank phone calls, consisting of strange beeps and otherworldly noises, and sent him odd letters, including one on the "International Bankers" letterhead Barker had created in 1957.[30] A passage in *The Mothman Prophecies* describing a strange phone call in which Barker sounds "like a man under duress . . . as though someone was holding a gun to his head" is one of the book's eeriest sections—but only if read without knowledge of Barker's pranksterism.[31] Keel knew that he was being targeted, even if he couldn't be sure of the source, and he ultimately identified the paranormal itself as his tormentor. Ufological historian David Clarke summarized his belief: "Once the investigator began to probe the mystery, the phenomenon would zero in on that person and play with their beliefs and prejudices."[32] The impact of the campaign is spelled out in a chapter title in *The Mothman Prophecies*: "Paranoiacs are made, not born."[33]

Keel remained in the Ohio River Valley for nearly three weeks, investigating reports of the Mothman and UFO sightings and other weird events in the area. But as with the Flatwoods case, Barker's work limited his presence to a single weekend. Keel's own investigation of the events in Point Pleasant was largely secondary to the work done by local journalist Mary Hyre, who covered strange occurrences for the *Athens Messenger* in Ohio. Hyre, approaching the end of a twenty-five-year newspaper career, accompanied Keel on many of his explorations in the Point Pleasant area and corresponded with him frequently in the following months, keeping him up-to-date on new UFO sightings and developments with some of the principal Mothman witnesses. Keel is most closely associated with the Mothman, primarily due to his book *The Mothman Prophecies*, published nearly a decade later, but it was Hyre who made his work possible.[34] Months after leaving the area, Keel was shaken by the collapse of the Silver Bridge, which connected Point Pleasant to Gallipolis, Ohio, in December 1967. Subsequently, he read the events of the previous year backward through the lens of this tragedy. But much of the mystique that surrounds the Ohio Valley bird creature, including its cultural identification as a harbinger of doom, can be traced to Keel's tendency to exaggerate and misrepresent the micronarratives he collected during the very strange first year of his acquaintance with Barker.[35]

THE 1967 CONGRESS AND *JIM MOSELEY'S BOOK OF SAUCER NEWS*

In June 1967 Moseley organized and hosted the fourth Congress of Scientific Ufologists in Manhattan. He published a special issue of *Saucer News* with a three-color cover as a sort of program book.[36] He also wanted a new book to sell at the event, but he failed to complete the long-promised manuscript of his book *UFO* in time.[37] Instead, shortly before the congress, Saucerian Books published *Jim Moseley's Book of Saucer News*, a compilation of Moseley's favorite material from his long-running saucerzine.

Barker traveled to New York for the gathering, appearing first on the event's list of featured guests. He assisted Moseley with promotion as well, including in a brief television appearance on the *Alan Burke Show*.[38] Roy Thinnes, the star of the saucer-themed television show *The Invaders* whom Moseley had hired to emcee the event, bowed out before the final day, and several of the promised speakers, including Ray Palmer, failed to appear. Despite its lack of organization, the convention was a success: Moseley broke even on his expenses and signed up more subscribers for *Saucer News*.[39] Barker also seems to have come out well, if the pace of Saucerian Books' publishing schedule in the months after the event is any indication. Among the books that followed was *The Shaver Mystery and the Inner Earth* by Timothy Green Beckley, a young associate of Moseley's who had been born in 1947, the year of Arnold's first sighting.

Barker sought to capitalize on the rising profile of UFOs in American culture, arranging for some of his past works to be reissued as pocket book paperbacks in 1967. In the spring Tower Books reissued *They Knew Too Much about Flying Saucers*; an announcement in *Spacecraft News* noted that "the publisher has assured Barker that the book will be published in its entirety, without any 'too hot to handle' parts out."[40] Pyramid Books followed later that year with a paperback reissue of Menger's *From Outer Space to You*, now under the simpler and more sober title *From Outer Space*. A third pocket book reprint followed in May 1968, when Paperback Library reissued Bender's *Flying Saucers and the Three Men*. But Donald Bensen, an editor for science fiction paperback house Pyramid, rejected Stuart's *UFO Warning*.[41] Barker issued his own reprint of Stuart's tale, along with *The Strange Case of Dr. M. K. Jessup*, in a format slightly more durable than that of the Multilith first printings.

SAUCER NEWS COMES TO CLARKSBURG

Moseley viewed the 1967 Congress of Scientific Ufologists as the peak of his career as a saucer figure, and after it he sought a way to bow out. On February 18, 1968, he sold *Saucer News*, along with the organization S.A.U.C.E.R.S. (the Saucers and Unexplained Celestial Events Research Society), to Barker.

Moseley retained a strictly honorary editorship, with Barker assuming the role of editor in chief. Barker changed the format of the publication, using professional typesetting rather than Moseley's offset-reproduced typescript format. To accomplish this work, he turned to Tomorrow River Printers, a Wisconsin press operated by a major ufological figure—Ray Palmer.[42] Palmer was responsible for the professionalization of Saucerian's publications during this period, visible in the sleek, minimally designed, and mysteriously titled *Document 96: A Rationale for Flying Saucers*. Palmer remained Barker's primary printer until his death in 1977. But the aesthetic changes in *Saucer News* came at a cost to the zine's readers, as the magazine's price immediately increased from fifty cents to one dollar per issue, and subscriptions from two dollars to four.

The content of Barker's first full issue of *Saucer News* is somewhat radical, albeit not significantly more so than material Moseley had been publishing prior to Barker's involvement. Included are a theoretical text on a possible mechanism for interdimensional transportation by Robert Morris, a report by Moseley (apparently ghostwritten) on an alleged spaceman who worked briefly for the *Los Angeles Times* in the 1950s, a channeled text by Diophantes of Sirius II on saucer technology, and a glossary of ufology terms compiled by Allen Greenfield.[43] The cover features a photograph of a ceramic lantern, sculpted in the shape of the Flatwoods Monster, produced by the Braxton County Chamber of Commerce as a fundraiser for the local Junior Chamber of Commerce.[44] The lantern also features prominently in a short, jokey photo feature showing Schreibstein's transformation when psychically taken over by the space being Zayron—likely a parody of psychic contactees rather than an authentic experience. Advertisements for works published or distributed by Saucerian Books abound, including an announcement of a "limited reprint" of Brasington's *Flying Saucers in the Bible*—potentially not a reprint at all but announced as a ploy to sell off old stock.

Barker kept *Saucer News* on schedule for his second issue, which he advertised with a solicitation letter summarizing Larry Klein's contribution, "The Fallen Angels."[45] The article argues that the saucers are piloted by Lucifer's cohort, who now "inhibit [*sic*] the bodies of murdered earth people, kept physically 'alive' by an advanced medical technology."[46] The article eventually makes some exceptionally specific claims, putting them in caps less any reader miss them: "ROBERT McNAMARA IS A CAPTAIN OF A FLYING SAUCER. HE IS A FALLEN ANGEL IN THE MURDERED BODY OF ROBERT McNAMARA. THIS MURDER TOOK PLACE IN 1959."[47] Klein gives no more details on this particular claim, but goes on to assert that Robert Six, president of Continental Airlines, is Satan himself. Barker later identified this as "by far the most unpopular [article] we have ever run."[48] A letter to the editor by Neil Gilchrist urges Barker not to "lower yourself to contactee claims and other yarns."[49] One can only assume Gilchrist was not happy with the new direction indicated by this article.

FRIENDS FROM LANULOS, LOVERS FROM SATURN

A little over a year after meeting Barker, Derenberger sent him the manuscript of *Visitors From Lanulos*, ghostwritten by Harold Hubbard. Barker responded with an offer to publish it, enclosing a one-hundred-dollar check as an advance and offering his standard 5 percent royalty (with the illusory promise of 10 percent on unlikely bookstore sales).[50] Barker began editing the manuscript, cleaning up Derenberger's phrasing, cutting passages, and inserting text.[51] But Derenberger declined Barker's offer, demanding a royalty of 50 percent or higher.[52] Derenberger's book—with the bulk of the text virtually unaltered from the original manuscript that he had sent to Barker, apart from several added chapters and a foreword by Keel—was ultimately published in 1971 by Vantage Press. The details of the publication arrangement are unknown, but there is little chance that Vantage, a vanity press, met his extraordinary demand of a 50 percent royalty rate.

Barker issued another contactee tale shortly after the arrangements for *Visitors From Lanulos* had fallen through—one that had first appeared as a Vantage Press title. Connie Menger's *Song of Saturn* repeats much of her pseudonymous earlier work *My Saturnian Lover*, omitting several key sections but appending a significant amount of new material. The book tells the story of Connie/Marla's youth, her first marriage and the death of her husband, her initiation into flying saucer and New Age groups, and her first encounters with Alyn—Howard Menger. The book describes the

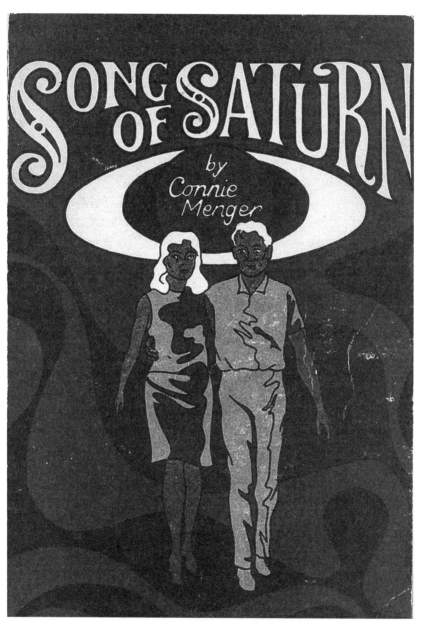

Figure 9.3
Duplantier's cover for Connie Menger's *Song of Saturn* (1968) blends contactee optimism with psychedelia. Author's collection/Courtesy of the Gray Barker Estate.

saucer group that Alyn organized, including its brief dalliance with Scientology before refocusing on saucers and the message of the space people who had contacted Alyn. The focus of *My Saturnian Lover* was on the romance between Marla and Alyn, but *Song of Saturn* downplays this aspect, as well as material related to Howard/Alyn's self-identification as a reincarnated Saturnian—a claim that he had recanted following the release of *From Outer Space to You*.

At the end of the summer of 1968, Barker organized "The First Annual Mothman 'Congress'" (quotation marks *sic*) at Point Pleasant. This small, hastily organized gathering attracted forty-six researchers to Point Pleasant, among them Moseley, Beckley, Greenfield, and Hyre. Barker had planned a similar event for the fifteenth anniversary of the Flatwoods Monster sighting in 1967, but the event hadn't come together.[53] He described the Mothman convention shortly afterward as "not only a social get-together for many top Ufologists, but . . . [an] opportunity for researchers to do on-the-spot investigation of the many UFO and 'monster' reports which have come from the area."[54] To commemorate the event, he issued a one-page publication, the *Mothman Times*. Keel did not look kindly on the Mothman gathering, writing to Barker six months later: "You, Moseley, Beckley, [Mark A.] Samwick, et al engaged in a typical buffery 'investigation.' You went down there and looked at the sky two years after the main incidents had occurred. This was tourism, not investigation, Gray."[55] Keel's aspersions aside, it is likely that Barker's intentions were more in line with "tourism" than "investigation"— not to identify some yet-undiscovered facts about the unusual bird or the events surrounding its appearance but to cement the place of the Mothman as a cultural touchstone. The influence of contactees like Derenberger and Menger was fading, but Barker was ready to explore new metanarratives.

10 "WHAT ELSE HAVE YOU GOT BESIDES FLYING SAUCERS?": SAUCERIAN BOOKS AFTER CONDON, 1969–1970

The Condon committee released its final report on unidentified flying objects to the public in January 1969. The published report runs to nearly 1,500 pages, but it is generally boiled down to a single sentence, which appears on the first page of text: "Careful consideration of the record as it is available to us leads us to conclude that further extensive study of UFOs probably cannot be justified in the expectation that science will be advanced thereby."[1] The government investigation into UFOs that NICAP and others in the UFO field had wanted for so long had come to an unexpected conclusion—that UFOs were a psychological phenomenon, not an interplanetary one. Barker offered his own response to the government's various UFO reports in an unpublished poem that has become one of his most quoted pieces of writing: "The A[ir] F[orce] investigated UFO / And issued a Report / Couched in polite language / which translated means / 'UFO is a bucket of shit.'"[2] The Air Force's response to the committee bears out Barker's characterization. On December 17, 1969, citing the committee's report, Air Force Secretary Robert C. Seamans announced that it was shutting down Project Blue Book.

Ironically, the Condon report ushered in Barker's busiest period as a flying saucer publisher: he issued nearly as many books in 1969 and 1970 as he had in the previous eight years combined.[3] He wasn't just publishing more titles; according to Gene Duplantier, Barker sold more books in 1969 than in any other year.[4] As the Condon report was being published, Barker issued a book that had little to do with establishing proof of physical UFOs: *Timothy Green Beckley's Book of Space Brothers*, a compilation of telepathic messages received from space beings by a variety of new age mediums and channels. The sourcebook illustrates the breadth of saucer-themed new age groups operating in the 1960s—groups that claimed firsthand experience of messages from space, on whose members the Condon report was unlikely to make much of an impression.

Books like *Timothy Green Beckley's Book of Space Brothers* and Ted Owens's *How to Contact Space People* can be considered indirect responses to the Condon report, but Barker's most direct reaction to the watershed of UFO skepticism came in *Saucer News* no. 74, released in the early summer of 1969.[5] In the opening editorial, entitled "A Lively Corpse," Barker discusses the report, writing that, despite its conclusions, "the saucers had not vanished . . . they were still flying, as thick as (or maybe even thicker) than usual!"[6] Barker's interest is not in the report's conclusions but in witnesses' continuing experiences and in the narratives he could spin from them. Barker turns the editorial into a campfire tale, coaxing his readers into spooky territory:

> Yes, the spacemen will still get you if you don't watch out; they will still take you for a ride if you can muster the nerve and the correct mental attitudes. And if you're alone in the house when you read this, in a second story room, if you listen . . . listen . . . LISTEN, you'll hear the stairway creak, and heavy breathing from outside the unlocked door. You'll be safe,—ONLY IF YOU DON'T KNOW TOO MUCH! If you DO know too much, maybe you can get by, simply by not telling! Otherwise the door will fly open, and there, phantasmagorically outlined in blue light will be THEM, three of them, staring THROUGH you with their piercing eyes, and—well, it is simply too frightening and terrible for us to tell you what happens next.[7]

Condon's report targets the rational mind, but Barker's editorial outflanks it by eliciting a visceral, emotional response.

The editorial addresses the Condon report directly, but the lengthy Recent News section takes a more poetic and contemplative approach to the topic. Barker presents the news section as a narrative with Condon as its central character wandering the streets of Boulder, Colorado, on Christmas Eve, 1968. Written in dreamlike prose, the text imagines Condon pondering the meaning of the customary string of one- to three-paragraph reports of UFO sightings, strange encounters, and Fortean mysteries. At the piece's conclusion, Condon encounters an unusual troupe:

> A group of bedraggled children shouted and screamed as they approached. They obviously were children from a poor neighborhood, for they wore cast-down adult clothing. One, with a grotesque necktie which reached almost to the street, clasped a toy camera which he aimed in all directions as he pretended to take pictures. Another held what appeared to be the remains of a discarded yellow notepad.
>
> "THE SPACEMEN! THE SPACEMEN HAVE LANDED!" they shouted.[8]

These children dressed in adult clothes, who reappear in a similar moment in Barker's *The Silver Bridge*, symbolize the world of ufology—as under-scored by this issue's publication of several letters and photographs of UFO researchers like the "Civilian Investigation Committee on Unidentified Flying Objects," the members of which appear to be between ten and fourteen years old.[9] Condon's report sought to redirect these children from fantasy to reality. But Barker's goal was to give them new stories with which to frighten themselves.

One such story, later revealed as a hoax, appears in the same issue under the byline of Dr. Richard H. Pratt. Barker rarely committed a hoax alone, often enlisting the help of an associate in constructing a false narrative. In 1969 John C. Sherwood became one such conspirator. According to Sherwood, he had sent Barker "a sci-fi piece I wrote about a scientific organization that discovers that UFOs are actually time machines, then encounters a more sinister enemy group of time-travelers who try to destroy them."[10] Sherwood's idea resulted in two stories that appeared under Pratt's byline: "Flying Saucers: Time Machines?" in *Saucer News* no. 74 and "The Strange B.I.C.R. Affair" in no. 75. After the first installment, Barker informed Sherwood that the magazine had received no reader responses about Pratt's article: "Evidently the fans swallowed this one with a gulp."[11]

Pratt's hoax about the B.I.C.R.—a deliberately meaningless acronym—seeks to convince readers that flying saucers were operated by time travelers who had become trapped in our era and sought the help of UFO researchers. To support the story, Sherwood submitted a notice to Palmer's *Flying Saucers* and enlisted the help of a friend in Worcester, Massachusetts, to make it appear that the group was active nationwide.[12] Sherwood's plan was to complete the story, then to "disclaim it, and then discuss its implications had I not denied the story; then add to it some essays of what I found in UFO research during my brief stay with it."[13] Ultimately, this is what he did—but it took nearly three decades for him to reveal the hoax, rather than the matter of weeks or months he had initially envisioned. In a 1998 essay for *Skeptical Inquirer*, Sherwood described his friendship with Barker and the background and development of the Pratt ruse. Sherwood suggests that Barker had manipulated him into something he later realized was unethical: "In my youthful naiveté and desire to be published, I didn't challenge the wrongness of this."[14] Sherwood did, in fact, submit a statement on the story's true nature to Barker, but left the decision about whether to include it up to the editor: "I typed up an attachment that you MAY or MAY NOT want to insert on page 4."[15] Naturally, Barker opted to present the articles as fact.

Following the final issue of *Saucer News*, Pratt's story faded into history, having made little impact outside the pages of the journal in which it appeared. It was Barker himself who revived it, including it in one of his final books, *M.I.B.: The Secret Terror among Us*, alongside other tales of mysterious vanishings and silencings.

THE PK MAN

In the second half of the 1960s, Ted Owens became a frequent correspondent to *Saucer News* and other periodicals, describing his mental contacts with the saucer intelligences, or SIs, and his ability to persuade these superpowerful beings to control events on our planet.[16] In *How To Contact Space People*, Owens describes in detail his interactions with these otherworldly beings—which, the book reveals, contrary to its title, originate in another dimension rather than in space.[17] Owens gives a chronological listing of the various predictions and miracles made by him through powers that the SIs granted him, along with quotations from news stories pertaining to events he predicted, notarized statements from hearers of his predictions, and excerpts from his letters to representatives of various agencies (most frequently George Clark of the CIA). Many of Owens's letters reprinted in the volume are signed with his supposed government code name, PK Man—short for Psychokinesis Man. The narrative that unfolds illustrates Owens's increasing frustration in his efforts to be taken seriously by those in positions of power.

Owens states that past efforts of the SIs to communicate more directly with individual human beings have resulted in madness or death; only Owens's near-superhuman mental abilities have enabled him to maintain a connection with them.[18] His powers were greater than those of any other human being since Moses. He could psychically ask the SIs to perform any number of extraordinary deeds: cause lightning strikes, initiate power blackouts, redirect the courses of hurricanes. Among the 181 miraculous events for which he claimed responsibility are the paths of Hurricanes Cleo, Betsy, and Inez; a "fireball" sighted across the Northeast in 1966; an attack on a young Michigan woman by a mysterious monster in 1965; and the Great Blackout of 1965 (plus a smaller one in Queens, New York, in 1967).

Owens distinguishes between the good SIs and more violent OIs (possibly meaning *other intelligences*), but the SIs themselves seem vindictive and mercurial: their primary means of communication with Earth is to cause natural disasters and attack government installations and innocent farmers alike with lightning. Owens's biographer, parapsychologist Jeffrey Mishlove, considered his use of his "PK" powers as an ethical conundrum: "From a moral perspective, how do we evaluate Owens' behavior? Should we hold him accountable for the damage to the Texas wheat crop or for the highway deaths during the freezing rainstorm? . . . If we are to take Owens' claims seriously, shouldn't we then also hold him accountable for his actions and responsible for reparations to his victims and to society?"[19] The individual expressions of Owens's PK abilities were unimportant: in claim after claim, his primary interest was simply to "prove that PK Man (Owens) is [the SIs'] representative, and that they can communicate with PK Man."[20] In place of the positive message of world transformation behind the narratives of contactees like Adamski and Bethurum is a shallower megalomania.

Owens had frequently changed cities and occupations throughout his adult life, but in 1969, shortly after the publication of *How to Contact Space People*, he gave up entirely on full-time employment "so that he could devote himself solely to his psychic work."[21] Following this, according to Mishlove, "Owens and his family lived almost like vagabonds. . . . Owens was not gainfully employed in any regular way. He was supported by a small coterie of true believers who accepted his claim that he was the messenger of other-dimensional Space Intelligences—which often guided him to relocate."[22] When Owens first contacted Barker in early 1968, he immediately pitched a series of three books in exchange for an unspecified but large advance, which he intended to use to launch a similarly unspecified project.[23] Barker's response has not survived, but Owens's next letter suggests that he offered a $500 advance on an edition of one thousand copies—an offer that Owens rejected, demanding at least $1,000 while predicting that, with the help of the SIs, Barker would sell no fewer than eight thousand copies.[24] Owens continued to make such grandiose claims throughout his correspondence with Barker, but downgraded his requests, ultimately foregoing a royalty structure and accepting a flat payment of $250 up front, along with as many copies of the book as he wished at half price.[25] He had negotiated himself into a significantly worse deal than Barker had offered to begin with. Barker's solicitation letter for the book revives a marketing idea Barker had initially used for Menger's *From Outer Space to You*, encouraging recipients to write in to have their names and addresses added to a "Space Scroll" that would be presented to the SIs.[26] The photograph of Owens on the back cover of *How to Contact Space People* shows him holding the scroll—a printout of mailing address labels rolled onto a wooden handle.

In addition to the Space Scroll, Barker offered another promotional item in connection with *How to Contact Space People*: a plastic "SI Disc." Owens had been offering similar objects to interested parties since 1967, announcing in *Saucer News* no. 70 that his "job for the SIs is to charge a 'disc' with power supplied from their dimension and send it to you. You will keep it from then on and it will change your life."[27] Barker's second solicitation for *How to Contact Space People* described (with a hedge that

Figure 10.1

The back cover of *Ted Owens, Flying Saucer Spokesman* (1970), advertising Owens's "SI Discs." Author's collection/public domain.

"we are still skeptical") the benefits that those who had already added their names to the scroll or received an SI disk had experienced—typically finding unexpected cash.[28]

Barker manufactured a new batch of these discs, but at a scale that prevented Owens from using his preferred method of "charging," which he claimed took twenty minutes of deep meditation for each individual disk.[29] Fortunately, Owens worked out a compromise with the SIs, enabling him to "charge" the discs en masse.[30] Owens may have been a mercurial figure, but he and his SIs always seemed willing to find expedient means for communicating his message more broadly.

Barker invited contributions to help Owens with his work, albeit with hedged language: "We do not solicit, but will accept donations and contributions to help Mr. Owens with his work."[31] He presumably assumed that such contributions would be welcome—not least of all because Owens had written to Barker to request a five-thousand-dollar "partnership" donation.[32] But when Barker sent a twenty-dollar check to transfer the donations he had received, Owens was furious. He informed Barker that he had not ever permitted and would never permit Barker to request donations on his behalf, adding that he had contacted a lawyer who believed Barker's action could constitute fraud.[33] In his response, Barker seeks to wash his hands of the matter, giving a superstitious rationale: "A few people have complained that they have had bad luck after receiving the Si Disc. . . . I feel that I may be playing with forces that I do not understand and that probably it would be best to drop the entire thing."[34] Those forces may have included the Food and Drug Administration: Barker later informed Owens that an attorney had advised him "that the only way I could offer the disc through the mail was simply as a 'good luck charm,' without any claims for other things it might do."[35]

FANTASTIC PEOPLE AND CRACKPOTS

In the second half of 1969, Barker began issuing a flurry of publications by deceased or inactive ufological and new age authors. The first of these was *The Hollow Earth* by Raymond Bernard, which hollow-earth historian David

Standish calls "the most 'definitive' (or at least exhaustive) recent elucidation of hollow-earth theory."[36] The pseudonymous author was Walter Siegmeister, who earned his doctorate in education from New York University in 1932 before establishing a series of health food miracle-cure businesses and utopian communities.[37] He eventually relocated to Brazil and adopted the Bernard pseudonym to avoid prosecution for mail fraud. Bernard and Barker had corresponded about reissues of his books in the 1960s, but Barker was unwilling to meet his demands for promotions and royalty payments.[38] But with Bernard's death in 1965, the door opened for Barker to republish the author's work on his own terms. Barker's solicitation seeks to turn Bernard's death into a mystery, asking: "Did Dr. Bernard vanish into the inner earth?"[39]

Barker stretched his finances to publish reissues of six books by the mysteriously named Californian author Michael X. This was the pseudonym of Michael Barton, who had become connected to the saucer and new age worlds through George Van Tassel's conventions. Beginning in 1957 and continuing throughout the 1960s, the Los Angeles–based Futura Press published a multitude of his new age pamphlets, collectively described as "Educational and Inspirational Course[s] of Study."[40] According to the solicitation letter for Saucerian's first batch of reissues of these works, Michael X retreated from public life in August 1969 to serve as a disciple to an otherworldly figure known as "The Voice of Two Worlds"—probably Edwin Dingle, founder of the Institute of Mentalphysics.[41] According to Barker's solicitation for the books, Michael X personally requested that Barker take over the publication of his works during his metaphysical absence.[42] Gorightly and Bishop give a different account of X's departure from the saucer scene—one more conspiratorial than mystical. According to their account, Barton traveled to the Mojave Desert on psychic instructions from his space contacts for a face-to-face meeting, but was overcome with "a sudden sense of dread" and left just as he realized that a glint of metal he saw in the distance was not a UFO but a reflection from an assassin's rifle.[43] Both of these accounts originate from unreliable sources—Barker for the former and Timothy Green Beckley for the latter—and their veracity is doubtful. The next step in Barton's life was a prosaic one: he became a delivery driver for UPS.[44]

To further encourage sales of Michael X's books, Barker offered a free pamphlet, *Gray Barker's Questions and Answers about Flying Saucers*, to anyone who preordered the complete series of six books.[45] The pamphlet contains a brief interview with Barker on saucer-related topics, and the text is likely reprinted from a magazine or newspaper, though its source is not identified. There is no guarantee that Barker's answers are entirely honest, but he comes across as generally skeptical on the nature and even existence of UFOs. The question of his opinions of contactees and other of the more outré subjects covered by Saucerian publications does not arise. He describes the contactees he has met as "fantastic people," though he also makes a distinction between contactees and mere saucer witnesses, "who are not crackpots."[46]

JOHN DEAN AND *FLYING SAUCERS CLOSEUP*

The most lavish publication issued by Saucerian Books is John Dean's *Flying Saucers Closeup*, a massive compilation and review of contactee material. Born in and raised in Nickerson, Kansas, Dean was in his late seventies when he compiled the work.[47] Following a sighting of an airborne object he later referred to as a "polarity tester" on June 28, 1957, Dean became interested in flying saucers, devising a lecture that eventually grew into his first saucer book, *Flying Saucers and the Scriptures*, issued by Vantage Press in 1964.[48] But Dean was dissatisfied by Vantage's poor marketing of the volume and sought a new publisher for his next work. Saucerian's advertising sheet hinted that the book was suppressed by mysterious forces, but in fact Vantage Press scarcely marketed any of its titles, leaving authors to publicize their own work.[49]

In both *Flying Saucers and the Scriptures* and *Flying Saucers Closeup*, Dean relates and attempts to correlate the accounts of a number of saucer contactees. He is particularly enamored of the rural, folksy contactees who congregated at Buck Nelson's annual spacecraft conventions in Mountain View, Missouri, from 1959 to 1966. At this nexus in the Ozarks, Dean met contactees like James Hill (who lived not far from Nelson's farm), Frank Buckshot Standing Horse, and a self-styled spaceman on Earth known only as Zagga of the Galactic Tribunal. The members of this loose coterie were more interested in the concrete facts of life on other worlds than the more

No. 4. Two planes chasing a space ship over Nickerson, Kansas, May 2, 1961. 2:30 P.M.

Figure 10.2
John W. Dean's retouched images of his saucer sightings seek to provide not photographic evidence, but a narrative experience. From *Flying Saucers Closeup*, 1970. Author's collection.

intangible interests of California-based new age contactees: rather than discussing etheric realms and vibrational densities, they preferred to swap tales about Venusian dogs, otherworldly farming methods, and restaurants on the moon.

Dean presents contactees' descriptions of life on other worlds with a naive innocence, seeming at turns bemused and frustrated that these claims are not accepted by the world at large. In *Flying Saucers and the Scriptures* he had taken a serious approach to the interplanetary travel claims of contactees like Buck Nelson and Bob Renaud, mapping charts of the distances between the worlds they claimed to have visited on the specific dates of their contacts and calculating the distances traveled.[50] He retains this scientific impulse in *Flying Saucers Closeup*, attempting a comprehensive catalog of information about spacemen, combining information from the accounts of dozens of contactees into topical chapters and charts: thirteen pages listing all of the inhabited worlds, their alliances, and their populations; fourteen pages detailing the comparative grammar of the Galinguan and Korendian languages; twenty pages of planet-by-planet details of the inhabited worlds of our solar system (including Clarion).

When it comes to narratives of space contact, Dean is trusting; after a radio appearance, he received "three letters from space folk in this area," accepting on no other basis than their own word that "there are ten space men living in Hutchinson and one or more in my old home town of Nickerson."[51] But he also makes the more traditional appeals to the "reliability" of certain witnesses: Renaud's description of his experiences on the moon are to be trusted because he "was a terran scientist among friendly lunar scientists, so I feel that we can accept his statements as very accurate."[52] Dean bemoans the difficulty of sifting through data in *Flying Saucers and the Scriptures*: "The sudden flood of space information makes it very difficult to eliminate fraud and half-truth from the hundred or more books in existence. We know some are factual, while others are by writers who tend to exaggerate their own philosophies, thinking no one will ever find them out."[53] By the time of *Flying Saucers Closeup*, his personal relationships with the contactees he writes about had bolstered his faith in their accounts: "I have weighed the evidence against my friends who would have no desire to deceive themselves or me and can only say that if all of them were deluded all of the time on every report, then I would also have to deny all of the alleged sightings that are claimed and reported and photographed, including my own. So they stand as given—the best we could do under the circumstances."[54] In Dean's flying saucer writing, we have moved far beyond the need for evidence that flying saucers are real. That they exist, in this text, is a basic assumption that needs no defense. The book communicates, instead, as full a picture as possible of a world in which spaceships and space contacts are self-evident—a psychogeography of an inhabited universe.

The same impulse guides Dean's approach to flying saucer photographs. Many of the illustrations in *Flying Saucers Closeup* are drawings of spacecraft, but several are photographs of the Kansas sky onto which Dean has clearly drawn saucers and other aircraft. Importantly, he does not consider these to be faked photographs. He describes the philosophy behind these illustrations in *Flying Saucers and the Scriptures*, explicitly describing such a touched-up image as "not faked": "That is the way they looked in the exact setting. A space ship does not wait for you to get your camera and filter. In all three cases, it would have been difficult to get a decent direct photo with my Kodak."[55] These illustrations are not intended to provide some visual proof of the objects that Dean saw. Rather, they represent attempts to capture and communicate the *experience* of those sightings. The photographic content is merely there to provide visual context, but the images—such as one of two jets chasing a saucer over the Nickerson, Kansas, water tower—encapsulate an entire micronarrative. In this sense, there is no real difference between Dean's photographs and his drawings; both embody an aesthetic response to flying saucer phenomena rather than any attempt at evidence.

Dean's voluminous and largely one-sided correspondence with Barker includes detailed background information on the publication of *Flying Saucers Closeup*. Dean submitted the manuscript to multiple publishers, Saucerian among them, and Barker urged him not to publish the work with a subsidy house like Vantage but accepted the work sight unseen based on Dean's past work and his outline.[56] Ironically, though, they ultimately settled on a subsidy agreement, albeit a more favorable one than typically offered by vanity houses. Dean paid three thousand dollars for the printing of two thousand copies of the book, of which an unspecified number were to be bound in hardcover; however, he was to receive royalties at the generous rate of 30 percent until he had recouped his subsidy payment.[57] Barker believed he could sell a thousand copies and was pleased with Dean's artistic contributions, telling him, "I have been wanting to do a book with a great deal of color in it."[58]

Within weeks of sending the final manuscript, Dean began sending changes and additional material, and even after publication Dean informed Barker that he was preparing a list of changes in the event of a second edition.[59] He also made arrangements with Barker for the publication of a manuscript not related to saucers, a memoir entitled *A Teacher Reminisces*. Though Dean intended to include material comparing the planet Korender's system of education with our own, Barker doubted he would be able to sell many copies of the work; he nevertheless made Dean an offer in October 1970: If Dean would forgo royalties and allow Barker to print a similarly royalty-free reissue of *Flying Saucers and the Scriptures*, he would publish *A Teacher Reminisces*, albeit printed and bound on demand and with little publicity. "I would propose to publish, keep in print, and market your book, as long as I am in business. . . . In other words, your book would get published, and we would make a continuing honest effort to sell it within the economies of mail order selling."[60]

Dean's health declined throughout 1970. He was harassed by a group of local toughs who claimed to be spacemen from the planet Zodiac; in the spring this group sabotaged his car, requiring him to spend the long, hot summer walking a mile or more to buy groceries.[61] This ordeal took its toll, and at the end of October he entered the VA hospital in Wichita on an emergency basis, where he died on November 10.[62] Following Dean's death, Barker received a letter from a lawyer who was settling his estate, inquiring about the status of the agreement regarding *A Teacher Reminisces*. Barker's response was as cold as it was final: "In regard to any unpublished works by this author, we would be interested in publishing them only on a subsidy basis since their commercial trade value is very limited."[63] His offer to Dean had appeared generous, but this generosity did not extend beyond the grave.

"A MONSTEROUS CHILD": *THE SILVER BRIDGE*

Though *They Knew Too Much about Flying Saucers*, which introduced the Men in Black to the world at large, is Barker's most influential book, *The Silver Bridge* is his most self-consciously literary work. In a certain sense it is the first book-length exploration of the Mothman sightings that took place in the Point Pleasant, West Virginia, in 1966 and 1967. But like its much better-known companion *The Mothman Prophecies*, it is also something much stranger and much more expansive. To say that either book is about the large bird that newspapers named the Mothman is a vast understatement. Barker's book is not a typical report on Fortean subjects but something more akin to a novel—it includes speculative chapters from the points of view of both a Man in Black and Indrid Cold, Derenberger's alien contact. But perhaps the most rewarding way to approach *The Silver Bridge* is as a psychic travelogue. Barker did not travel far geographically in researching the strange events in the Ohio River Valley in 1966 and 1967, but the book explores a vast terrain in the outlands of the human experience.

Barker began work on the book in 1968, telling Sherwood, "I'm now in the state of labor, in bringing forth a monsterous [*sic*] child, a book which I'm going to call 'MOTHMAN: THE GREAT BIRD THAT TERRIFIED POINT PLEASANT.'"[64] But it soon became apparent that the book was something else. Early in the writing process Barker told Sherwood that he was "throwing in a little fantasy," and that he expected the result to "transcend the usual crap such as GRAY BOOKERS BARK of this and that."[65] By the fall he no longer considered it to be about the phenomena so much as "the *people* who see monsters and saucers, etc."[66] He later told John Keel:

> I started writing this as a more or less straight account . . . but the other stuff got to creeping in. I figured that a straight saucer-monster book wouldn't get too much mileage in the trade anyhow, so I just went ahead and did it the way I really wanted to do it. To me, it captures the feelings and emotions I experienced while in Point Pleasant doing the investigations, which somehow, turned out to be a hauntingly beautiful thing.[67]

The Silver Bridge opens, straightforwardly enough, with an account of Barker's trip to interview Newell Partridge, a resident of New Martinsville, West Virginia, whose dog disappeared under mysterious circumstances in November 1966.[68] Ultimately, it is not the details of the interview on which Barker lingers, but on the impact of the events on Partridge's six-year-old son, who begins each day by going outside and calling for the missing dog. Barker also devotes his energies to a description of the West Virginia landscape and the perilous drive to Partridge's rural home. He gives an unflattering and ominous portrait of the rural western part of Harrison County as a primitive, decaying wasteland, suggesting, despite its similarity to the landscape of his childhood, that he is an urban interloper in this setting.

In the second chapter, however, Barker makes clear how different his intentions are from those of the usual paranormal book. The chapter describes a being identified only as "The Recorder" who arrives in the Ohio River Valley with sophisticated audiovisual equipment:

> So, laboriously, and panting, he climbed to the highest hill he could find, dragging the heavy gear with him, with many a stop for catching a breath and surveying the dizzying heights.
>
> Once at the top he set all of it up. The people down there, below, didn't have fine instruments like his, nor their capabilities; for, operating at this height, he had a power over them, and a cognizance of their activities of which they could never guess or dream.
>
> Now he could find out everything and properly Record it. Hooking up his sensitive instruments, powered by the movements of the Earth, the progression of the sun and the planets, and the Energy he sucked up from those Inferiors in the valley, he soon began to take down what had happened, what was happening, and what probably would happen.[69]

The Recorder harkens back to the isolated vigil of Barker's early poem "Mountain Poet," using his solitary vantage point to observe the human tapestry below. With his equipment in place, the Recorder collects information on the Mothman, the Men in Black, and flying saucers, before turning his attention to another activity on the hilltop:

> He turned his back to the valley and faced the vast unseen orchestra, pulled a limb from a tree which he employed as a baton. Grotesquely waving, this, he could hear the "Huff! Huff! Huff!" of the great Steam Horns well up, the Academic Horns chime in, the Seagulls adding their peculiar squawking. The German Horns added their subtle, deliquescent airs to the otherwise somewhat cacaphonous though awe-inspiring performance. Suddenly he dropped the baton and quietness descended. Taking his pen from his pocket, he knew he *had it* at last! With one neat incision he deleted the Far-Away Horns for a full measure.
>
> Then, for the first time, he performed the first highly satisfactory rendition of *The Symphony of the Horns*.
>
> As he led the great orchestra he knew that, as in the past, this music had provided the inspiration, almost the stage itself, for setting the drama that was transpiring in the valley below.[70]

As the initial moments of the chapter borrowed from "Mountain Poet," this bizarre scene draws from Barker's unpublished poetical work *Seven Sagas* and its "Symphony of the Horns"—a Dadaist collection of sound effects that attempts to translate a bizarre, imagined musical piece into language. Once the symphony is playing, the Recorder performs a final series of tasks:

> He turned on all of his equipment. From his Television Kit he withdrew great Idiot Cards, and hung them on over-size easels. Throwing away all pens and selecting a huge black marker from his chest, he filled the Cards with large characters, telling the story that was occurring below.
>
> Now he could see all things in the valley. He could penetrate the walls, see through the curtains, and behind the masks. Suddenly he *knew* what was happening. He knew the secrets of everything and everybody.
>
> And he knew all the things the people of the valley were thinking, and they were good. At last he knew that they loved him, and that he loved them, and that he loved all mankind.
>
> And so it was that the greatest power of his experience came upon the Recorder, and he became capable of Recording all things.
>
> And he became capable of the gift of Reorientation, so he took liberties with time and space, and he reassigned names, and he lifted people from one place and put them down into another, and the people below loved him more, and they applauded, and they gathered in a great moving human throng, advancing upon the Recorder.
>
> They carried him off the mountain, into the valley, across the great bridge into Ohio, shouting.[71]

The Recorder chapter provides context for the remainder of the book: It is not science, but art, in which a godlike, sometimes invisible witness has altered the events described to create a more beautiful symphony. And rather than seeing this as a betrayal of his scientific Recording, the people of the world love him all the more for it.

The Recorder is at once an authorial stand-in and a commentary on the entire field of ufology. Barker said as much in a letter to Robert Sheaffer in 1980: "I tried to clue my own role as that of The Recorder, who also, I thought, could be a composite of UFO 'researchers' in general."[72]

Figure 10.3
The "hornblower" image, reflecting the mischievous Recorder, was first used on the cover of *The Silver Bridge* (1970) and appeared in advertising materials for Barker's publications and businesses for the next fifteen years. *Saucerian Books 1971 Catalog*. Author's collection/public domain.

Convinced of his unique importance and insight, the Recorder believes he is the only one capable of accurately describing the events he witnesses. But he willfully distorts the events to fit the metanarrative he is crafting. In one sense this is a confession, since *The Silver Bridge* contains fictional material, but it is also a comment on UFO authors in general, who are more than willing to leave out details that would tend to overcomplicate a story or contradict a chosen metanarrative. Barker had done this in *They Knew Too Much*, shoehorning the stories of "Gordon Smallwood" (Laimon Mitris) and John Stuart into the "three men in black" metanarrative he was crafting out of Bender's experiences.

Though Barker periodically appears as a first-person narrator in *The Silver Bridge*, most of the book is written in third-person omniscient narration, and this chapter suggests that the Recorder—whose vision can "penetrate the walls"—is the omniscient narrator. Gene Duplantier's jacket illustration depicts a jagged, twisted suspension bridge in the foreground, but in the background, in the upper right corner of the jacket, is a small, robed figure on a hilltop, playing a horn. This is the Recorder, conducting his strange symphony over Point Pleasant. Following the book's publication, this image of the horn-playing Recorder appeared on numerous Saucerian catalogs and publications as a sort of logo or emblem, suggesting that Barker saw his role as publisher as an extension of the Recorder's artistic distortion as depicted in *The Silver Bridge*.

Barker's exploration of other events from the Ohio Valley similarly foregrounds his artistic interpretations of events. A chapter concerning Men in Black sightings culminates in an invented narrative from the point of view of Agar, one of the inscrutable MIB, as he attempts without success to intimidate a young boy who has taken a picture of a UFO.[73] Barker depicts Agar as a weird, emergent being, somehow created by humankind:

> Agar had never analyzed himself, except that he believed he was forever condemned to walk in sidewise motion, and that it had been these people who had so condemned him. He felt that he was a part of them, though an evil part of them, a *fear* part of them; and that since he was a part of so many people he would live forever—though he wondered if he really liked living as these people liked living.[74]

But despite Agar's inhumanity and his threatening nature, the boy befriends him, ultimately telling him, "I know that you are dying, and I don't want you to go!"[75] The boy, perhaps a young UFO enthusiast or a stand-in for Keel, clings to that which tries to frighten him, just as the realm of ufology—a field that Barker frequently equates with childhood—had embraced Barker's, Bender's, and Keel's stories of enigmatic MIBs.

A similar chapter presents Indrid Cold of the planet Lanulos as a viewpoint character. Cold and his copilot, Carl Ardo, travel in a strangely dilapidated spacecraft, constructed with walls salvaged from abandoned houses and threadbare, secondhand furniture. Just as Agar's identity seems subordinate to the human beings he was compelled to terrify, Cold seems unaware of his origins or mission. The only self-knowledge he possesses has been communicated him through the intermediary of "the Interpreter." This distant being has "imposed certain limits" on what Cold and Ardo can do and provides them with knowledge about their own origins: "Indrid had once listened raptly, as the Interpreter, in a talkative mood, had told him of the people who moved among the stars, who explored the universe. . . . The Interpreter had shown some of these places on the screen, and Indrid was very thankful to him for doing this."[76] The scene concludes with a bizarre image of silver cords penetrating Cold's ship: "Indrid would like to be free, to fly to these outer climes, but of course there were the silver cables, tied to his hands and feet, also similarly to Carl's body, and to the spaceship itself. Through the walls of the spaceship, they stretched downward, sometimes hanging loosely in great arcs, sometimes taut."[77] These puppet strings further emphasize the extraterrestrial's lack of agency and subordination to the will of the Interpreter. Barker privately identified the Interpreter as Derenberger himself:

> [Cold and Ardo] are real in some ways, but also disquietly unreal when we get the impression that their "reality" depends a great deal on the authority of the "Interpreter" who of course is Derenberger. . . . While I may not be able to admit that Derenberger's account is untrue, I can cloak my doubts in a kind of middle-ufological kind of thinking, and ask, do these spacemen exist as independent entities, or has Derenberger wholly or partially created them into a powerful and compelling myth? Can the "myth" become "real" if enough people believe?[78]

In this way of thinking Barker is similar to Keel, whose book *Operation Trojan Horse*, released just a few weeks before *The Silver Bridge*, explored his conception of "ultraterrestrials, or superior humanlike nonhumans" behind UFO sightings and contact accounts.[79] These enigmatic, cosmic pranksters, capable of manipulating human perception, represent a mutation of Charles Fort's statement in his 1919 work *The Book of the Damned*: "I think we're property."[80] For Keel, we are not simply subjugated to a this unknowable external force; we are the targets of "cosmic jokers."[81] But where Keel would tie Cold's puppet strings to an unseen, unknowable ultraterrestrial source, Barker suggests that they originate instead on Earth, in the hands of Derenberger himself.

Barker returned to this image in one of his final books, describing a "remarkable Vision" that summed up his view of the universe, God, the flying saucer mystery, and the meaning of his own life: "In this vision an incomprehensible Being of enormous size and power—perhaps larger than our Globe itself—dangled huge cables from the sky. Like some gargantuan giant wielding enormous fishpoles, this Force cast bait consisting of disc-shaped objects not unlike modern UFOs."[82] In *The Silver Bridge* Barker left some mystery as to what was on the other ends of the cables controlling Cold and his ship. Here he shows us who is pulling the strings. This is God as a hoaxer, or the hoaxer as God, dangling bait with which to capture earthbound explorers of the unknown—and a fitting description of Barker himself.

Religious language does appear in *The Silver Bridge*, but it is explicitly and intentionally opaque. In one chapter Mary Hyre visits the "T.N.T. area," an abandoned munitions testing site that was the primary locus of the initial Mothman sightings. She sees, among the gathered crowd, a manic preacher standing atop a car, quoting from Ezekiel's vision of wheels in the heavens:

> Punctuating the reading with an admonition that the bird creature was a sign sent by God, he continued by describing how the strange beings in Ezekiel's vision *"went upon their four sides: and they turned not as they went."*
>
> At this point, as Mary was walking away, the speaker suddenly repeated the phrase, *"and they turned not as they went"*. Then he repeated it over and

over, his manner becoming frenzied. The small group of followers responded at each repetition with "Amen!" To [Mary] the statement was meaningless.[83]

This preacher appears several more times in Barker's later writings, sometimes ranting, sometimes merely muttering, but always repeating in isolation the phrase "they turned not as they went."[84] If the character is a prophet, he is an incomprehensible one—or at least one whose message is only interpretable by those who already believe, as if it is communicated in code.

The narratives of Agar, Cold, and the Recorder all orbit around the purportedly central subject of *The Silver Bridge*: the Mothman itself. Barker spends two chapters recounting the stories of witnesses Linda and Roger Scarberry and Steve and Mary Mallette, but much of the Mothman content in the book is entirely fictional. Barker was particularly proud of chapter 7, "The Winter Wind," which tells the invented story of Jimmy Jamison, a borderline juvenile delinquent living with foster parents whose sighting of the bird creature is related to his compulsion to "wander the back streets."[85] The narrative strongly hints that, on one of his nocturnal jaunts, Jamison had had sex with an alcoholic drifter—possibly a stand-in for Barker—in exchange for a single dollar bill, which then becomes a sort of totem for him: "the only evidence that, for him, had separated this real experience from fantasy."[86] When Jamison sees the Mothman through his bedroom window, he associates the bird creature with his absent father, known to him only from a photograph, prompting him to call out: "Mothman! Please come back, Mothman! . . . I love you, Mothman!"[87] Sending this chapter to Sherwood in advance of publication, Barker noted its fictional status, adding, "The tale is, of course, not about mothman, but the sympathetic treatment of a disturbed child."[88] Another Mothman witness is repurposed from Barker's memories: the dog Old Ponto, Barker's own childhood pet, in the chapter "The Dog Who Saw Mothman."[89]

Barker's theory of a connection between the paranormal and the human sexual drive emerges in chapter 14 of *The Silver Bridge*, "The Voice in the Night," which describes a young man named Jennings "Red" Buckley and his relationship with a man who seems to be a cross between Barker and Derenberger: he lives alone, is interested in technological gadgets, has a large collection of saucer books on his shelves, and claims to have gone for a ride in a flying saucer.[90] Buckley wants this unnamed man to teach him the secret of contacting the space people. In light of the Mulberry Place letters' euphemistic descriptions of sexual activity, Buckley's subsequent "occult studies" and "experiments" are suggestive. The secret of space contact is also presented in sensual terms: "When you want to contact them . . . you can do this by thinking of orange leather. You have to imagine it very strongly. You have to almost see it. Then you create the mental attitude of actually feeling it, experiencing the smell of it; finally you imagine you are snapping it in your hands. You must do all this, however, in strict privacy, perhaps in your room at night before retiring."[91] Later, at a party at the T.N.T. area, Buckley initiates a sexual encounter with a girl his own age, but they are interrupted when she sees the glowing eyes of the Mothman. Later that night Buckley is awakened by the voice of a space being: "Then, booming through the entire upstairs floor, the voice, still with the odd accent, said: '*Have you called us? What do you want?* . . . I replied: 'WHAT ELSE HAVE YOU GOT BESIDES FLYING SAUCERS?'"[92] Having achieved his sought-after connection, Buckley is dissatisfied and seeks something else—some other form of escape. The stories of Jimmy Jamison and Red Buckley both hint at a connection between sexuality, social disaffection, and paranormal experience.

A chapter late in the book depicts the collapse of the eponymous Silver Bridge, framed with a Mothman story that Barker privately admitted was "constructed out of whole cloth."[93] This chapter presents the story of a fictional man named Frank Wentworth, whose wife, Ida, has left him, and is staying with her sister across the Ohio River. Distraught, Frank visits a bar on December 16, 1967, and while there imagines Ida transforming into a bird: "He had often looked at her and mentally transfigured her into an old hen, pecking at him in great frenzy."[94] From this reverie he begins to imagine that Ida is traveling back to him, and at this moment the bridge collapses with a horrendous roar. Frank rushes home to find his house in disarray and a strange shape occupying his bed:

> Red flashing eyes burned into his. Then with seeming confusion, and a flapping and gurgling sound, the thing tumbled sidewise to the floor, flapped

again, upset a lamp, and then righted itself unsteadily. He retreated to the living room, tripped on the edge of the rug, and fell. As he was getting up, hoping to run and escape from the incomprehensible horror in the bedroom, it waddled through the door. He noted another facial feature besides the eyes: It had a long sharp beak which slanted downward, almost corresponding to a nose. . . . The great bird—that was as close as he could describe it to himself—again righted itself, leaped toward the large picture window, and with a crashing and splintering of glass, disappeared.[95]

The creature Barker describes in this chapter is clearly a mud-drenched sand-hill crane, made strange mainly by its dirtiness and its unexpected appearance inside Frank's bedroom. But in the context of Frank's perception and this narrative of it, it is surely something else as well—either Ida transformed or a harbinger of her death in the bridge disaster. Ultimately, however, it doesn't matter; the description of Frank's confused experience is all we have access to and all that the book hopes to communicate. Whether bird, angel, demon, or something stranger, the Mothman grows from witnesses' ideas about it—and from readers'.

Barker shared portions of the manuscript with Keel as he was writing them. Keel was critical of the work, and particularly a chapter describing the meeting between the two and their joint interview with Derenberger. In a letter dated October 18, 1968, he writes, "It isn't very accurate, Gray, and since I have articles coming out which mention this (as well as my intro. to Woody's book) I think we ought to get the facts straight."[96] The following day Keel sent Barker edited material to replace some of Barker's original draft. "I don't object to being 'glamorized,'" he writes, "but I do object to being turned into some kind of 'mysterious' character."[97] Barker does not seem to have retained a copy of the original chapter, but the revised material in Keel's letter of October 19 indicates changes to only a few sections: the first meeting between the two investigators, an incident involving Keel's attempt to cross a cow pasture in the face of a potentially violent bull, and Keel's concluding theoretical remarks about saucers and Men in Black. In all, it appears that Keel reworked about a quarter of the chapter from Barker's original.[98]

Keel was not the only one disappointed with the liberties taken in Barker's book. Allen Greenfield, who had written an introduction for the volume, was frustrated with edits that Barker made to his essay. On March 4, as the book was going to press, he sent a pointed note requesting "that my text be left basically unaltered, or not used at all."[99] Barker's response is not retained in his files—but the published introduction is significantly shorter than Greenfield's original. Barker in fact made significant cuts to Greenfield's text, removing references to several of the narratives in the book.[100] The cut sections, amounting to a full page of Greenfield's manuscript, summarize and comment on several of the book's enigmatic passages, and Barker's reason for cutting them was likely that they risked giving the game away, spelling out too clearly what he wanted his readers to experience for themselves: "Is the author engaging in a long figure of speech to explain to us that he may have changed some names, that he may have changed a few events in time and space, and have spoken in allegory at times? I think so."[101]

Barker's advertising circular for *The Silver Bridge* was a form letter that, while signed by Moseley, reads more like Barker's prose. It was sent as a direct mailing to Barker's customers and was included in Duplantier's *Outermost*, alongside a condensed chapter from *The Silver Bridge*.[102] The letter states that Barker had sent the book "to a national paperback firm which was immediately interested in publishing the book"—but only with substantial edits, which Barker felt would "talk down to" his readers.[103] The letter goes on to claim that Barker made an unusual arrangement with this paperback house: "Barker accepted the agreement for the publishing of the 'watered down' paperback, to come out in 1971, WITH THE CONDITION THAT HE FIRST BE ALLOWED TO PRIVATELY PUBLISH A COMPLETE AND UN-CUT EDITION OF '*THE SILVER BRIDGE*' FOR HIS FAITHFUL READERS, HIS BOOK AND MAGAZINE CUSTOMERS OVER THE YEARS."[104]

A letter to Keel in 1970 makes it clear that the entire narrative of the book's publication described in the solicitation letter was fiction. "I tried sending the book to a couple of publishers, but got rejection slips. I had no agent, so things sorta ended there. The publishers (one LJ's [Long John Nebel's] and the other a West Coast concern whose names I forget) did point out the weirdness of construction."[105] He also sent the manuscript to an agent in New York and paid a one-hundred-dollar fee to try to have it placed: "Instead, I got a masterpiece of a letter, about three pages, pointing out the good points of the book, but with suggestions that I change the plot to have Mrs. Ralph Thomas convert Woody Derenberger to her faith as a high point in the book. Evidently they were completely confused and felt I was trying to write a novel. I guess I dropped a hundred bucks to no good purpose there."[106] (This, perhaps, was the origin of the "watered-down" version of the book to which the letter refers). Neville Spearman expressed interest, but was put off by the admission that some of the material in the text was less than factual. His outside options exhausted, Barker resolved to put out the book himself, for a much more limited audience than he had hoped to reach.

THE END OF GIANT ROCK

Barker wound down his activity as the publisher of *Saucer News* in late 1970 and sold the publication to Palmer early the next year to be combined with his *Flying Saucers*.[107] Another mainstay of the early days of saucers was also drawing to a close: on October 10–11, 1970, Barker and Moseley—accompanied by Barbara Hudson—attended the seventeenth Annual Space Convention, which would prove to be George Van Tassel's final UFO meeting at the Giant Rock Airport. Moseley called the 1970 convention "a mere ghost of the past."[108] A Lt. Philip Cestling (possibly a pseudonym), writing in the premiere issue of Gene and Geneva Steinberg's ufological fanzine *Caveat Emptor*, painted a grim portrait of "bands of hippies and motorcycle toughs who smoked marajuana [sic] openly in the hills overlooking the Rock, and yelled obscenities down at the 'hard core.' Drunkenness, drugs and violence were the order of the day."[109] Barker sold few books, telling John Dean that his entire revenue from the weekend totaled twenty-eight dollars.[110]

Barker published an unreliable account of the weekend six years later in *Gray Barker at Giant Rock*. He combines elements of past visits to Giant Rock with the 1970 event and even reworks Jacqueline Sanders's account of attending one of Van Tassel's early channeling sessions, previously published in *The Saucerian* no. 4 and *UFO 96* under Sanders's name, but here presented as an experience of his own. But he also describes the changing culture of the Giant Rock convention, increasingly attended by young members of the counterculture with little connection to the flying saucer scene of the previous two decades. The two worlds did not blend smoothly. Barker describes coming across "a group of young people, some bearded, all with long hair and shabbily dressed. . . . When they spotted us, there was some commotion as many of them quickly stamped out cigarettes. 'We're sorry to butt in,' Jim apologized. 'We're not cops,' he added."[111] Elsewhere at the convention, a car was set on fire: "There was a report of some kids seeing a saucer which set the car on fire, but it's my opinion that a bunch of hippies got stoned on pot or speed and were careless with their 'joints.'"[112]

Barker's account of the weekend incorporates surreal moments reminiscent of the magical realism of *The Silver Bridge*. In one anecdote he recounts seeing an elderly man standing outside the wire fence surrounding the unfinished Integratron, a domed wooden structure Van Tassel had constructed based on plans received in channeled messages. Van Tassel claimed the structure, once completed, would be able to rejuvenate anyone who entered it, and, according to Barker, the elderly man has "vowed to stay here until I am allowed to enter the Integratron and regain my youth so that I can preach the Bible to all the world!"[113] A group of long-haired youths surrounds the man, perplexed that he sees the shoddy fence as a barrier: after a brief conversation, they simply cut a hole in the wire to allow him access, leading to a moment of transcendent strangeness in the text:

> The elderly gentleman with the bleached white face stood there for a moment, incredulously viewing the cutting of the wire. He looked upon the limp, severed strand with a kind of ecstasy. Then he cautiously put his hand on the remaining strand. With a sudden shout he leaped over it, clearing it by about six feet, surprising all of us with his agility. . . . The man tore off his shirt. . . . His face became muscular, severe and full. His hair was no longer grey. His naked shoulders were suddenly powerful. Then he jerked off his trousers, and then his underpants. In the confusion, I could swear that his body had taken on a *golden tone*, like a gold statue. With a loud shout he made enormous leaps into the darkness of the desert.[114]

Though there is no clear sign that Barker intends the character as a stand-in for any individual, the elderly gentleman, in his fascination with scripture, his obsession with "rejuvenation," and even his youthful tormenters, resembles John Dean. This bizarre and fanciful anecdote suggests both a disconnect between the older contactee subculture and youth counterculture and the potential of some manner of mystical transformation emerging from a combination of the two. At several points in Barker's text, he mentions the music of Creedence Clearwater Revival, including their UFO-based "It Came Out of the Sky" and the apocalyptic "Effigy." Barker's inability to understand the lyrics to their songs becomes a running joke throughout the book: the kids are saying something about UFOs, transcendence, and the future, but he can't understand the words.

1971: HUSH-UP!

In early 1971 Saucerian Books issued James Moseley's long-delayed monograph, once titled simply *UFO*, now rechristened *The Wright Field Story*. In his memoir, *Shockingly Close to the Truth!*, Moseley claims that the book that was ultimately published was entirely ghostwritten by Barker, Moseley having essentially retired from the saucer field. He describes the book as "an absurdly fictionalized version of my great saucer odyssey of 1953–54. . . . I was never proud of this book, and it's so shockingly *far* from the truth that I literally have never even *read* all of it and probably never will."[115] Despite this claim, it's clear that at least some of the text did indeed originate in Moseley's typewriter. But the recurring framing sequence—describing the August 23, 1959, episode of Long John Nebel's radio show, which was mysteriously cut off the air during a discussion between Barker and Moseley about the Men in Black—is undoubtedly Barker's. (Rather than being numbered, the chapters progress through the hours of the lengthy overnight radio program, from 11:45 p.m. through the final chapter, detailing the sudden and unexpected conclusion of the radio program: "4:30: Hush-up!") Within this frame Barker inserts a variety of material going all the way back to Moseley's initial saucerological investigations for Ken Krippene. *The Wright Field Story* was a slow seller, and in 1981 Barker reported that it had taken over ten years to sell through its first and only printing of a thousand copies.[116] These figures suggest that the sales boom that Barker had experienced in the aftermath of the Condon report had finally subsided.

On May 24, 1971, Virginia Howell, the longtime manager of Lovett & Co., died unexpectedly, leaving the business in disarray.[117] Writing several months later to Rose Hiett, Barker explained his position: "I was next in line—so I had to take over. When this happened, I knew that something had to give so I made the decision that I would phase down considerably my writing and publishing about UFOs."[118] Following a prodigiously productive two years, Saucerian Publications was suddenly "hushed up"—not by mysterious or sinister forces, but by sheer lack of time.

11 "THOROUGHLY DEDICATED TO PROMOTING UFO CRACKPOTTERY": BARKER IN THE 1970s

The hardcover publication of *The Silver Bridge* was an expensive undertaking; Barker explained to Laura Mundo that he had "what amounts to half of my life's savings tied up in this project."[1] Moreover, Doc Lovett's health was continuing to decline, and his wife, his primary caretaker, had recently been involved in a car accident.[2] Government funding for Lovett & Co.'s education work was also drying up.[3] As in 1963, when Barker declared bankruptcy following the poor sales of Saucerian's expensive hardcovers, the combination of book production debt and the tightening of his regular work led to a significant contraction in the press's publishing over the next few years.

Barker's work for Lovett & Co. occupied virtually every moment of his time through the summer of 1971. He explained to a correspondent that September: "Have sort of let the UFO and book part of the scene go, and have partially closed my mail order business, just taking care of the residual business that's trickling in. That doesn't mean I'm out of it. I'm still going to do a limited amount of saucering and publishing."[4] Barker maintained a certain level of activity, attending the 1971 Congress of Scientific Ufologists (where he was named Ufologist of the Year). But his publishing lull continued for more than a year, exacerbated by cataract surgery in February 1972; though his recovery progressed smoothly, it required him to avoid straining his eyes with extensive reading or writing.[5]

Doc Lovett died on March 20, 1973.[6] As the manager of Lovett's firm, Barker kept the business operating through the loss of its founder. Barker's managerial role gave him significant leeway in the operation of the business, and he worked out an arrangement whereby Saucerian Publications would share its office and staff (including McCulty) with Lovett & Co.[7] He moved both businesses into a single office, located at Lovett's Weston Drive-In on a rural stretch of road about halfway between Weston and the smaller town of Jane Lew.[8] Barker had little time to devote to publishing activities, and closed the Clarksburg office from which Saucerian had been operating.[9]

Chief among his terrestrial responsibilities was a new movie theater. By the fall of 1973, nearly a decade after selling the Alpine Theatre, Barker had leased the Colonial Theatre in Buckhannon from Ota West, widow of the theater's former exhibitor.[10] Barker soon rechristened the theater the Cinema V, and his press announcement promised it would be a family venue: "We're betting a lot of money that you don't want to see X-rated movies but do want to see pictures with famous stars, good acting, exciting plots, colorful locales, etc."[11] Barker stuck to this policy for the opening months of his operation, and the theater became a success. He had initially planned to operate it only on weekends, but within a month of its opening the theater operated full-time, and he renewed his initial, short-term lease for five years in mid-1974.[12] Once again, motion-picture promotion was a primary part of Barker's day-to-day work.

A letter to British publisher Neville Armstrong in September 1973 gives a picture of the state of Barker's businesses six months after his mentor's death:

> I am still in the publishing/bookselling business, though I have been able to cut it down to a size where it is profitable. . . . We do a steady business all of the time of around $50.00 a day from bookstores, plus the business that comes in from our retail customers when we mail to our 6,000 list.
>
> I am also operating a motion picture theatre on the side, so you can see that I must budget my time. We have our mailing list, and most of our shipping "out of the house" so that our book operation is fairly simple and getting to be profitable.
>
> Although we have an excellent back list of items that move steadily, we need a mail promotion about four times a year. I do not have proper time to write and/or develop that much new material, although we are now doing mainly reprints. . . . (We do not do well with Keyhoe or Hyneck [sic], but authors such as Trench, Dr. Bernard and the like are quite profitable for us).[13]

This picture of a routinized, if slow-moving, book trade characterizes Barker's publishing activities throughout the 1970s, a period in which he published very little new material. With Tomorrow River handling the bulk of Sau-cerian's printing, and storage and order fulfillment handled by an offsite warehouse in New Jersey, Barker was able to reprint his most profitable titles with very little prearrangement, maintaining a steady line of income.[14] He periodically expanded his sales list with new reprints of titles by the likes of Michael X and Raymond Bernard. But compared to the printing exper-iments of the late 1950s and early 1960s, this was not a period in which Saucerian Books tried new things—with one notable exception when, after a decade-long search, Barker finally uncovered a text he'd once doubted even existed.

"YOU ARE NOT AFRAID OF THE IMPLICATIONS": THE VARO EDITION

After *The Strange Case of Dr. M. K. Jessup*, other researchers kept interest in the Allende letters and the annotated edition of Jessup's book alive. Most notable of these was Brad Steiger, a magazine and paperback writer who obtained a microfilm copy of the Varo edition from a Michigan ufologist named Stephen Yankee. Steiger's 1967 article for *Saga*, "Fantastic Key to the UFO Mystery," brought the Allende material before a national audience.[15] The following year Steiger adapted his *Saga* article into a chapter in a book coauthored with *Saucer Scoop* editor Joan Whritenour for Award Books. Though entitled *New UFO Breakthrough*, the cover text of the paperback gives more prominence to the Allende letters than to the book's title itself. The same year Steiger and Whritenour also produced *The Allende Letters*, a booklet in magazine format packaged for newsstand sales.[16] Steiger and Whritenour's writings on the subject incorporate the Men in Black, sup-posed archaeological mysteries, and accounts of UFO hostility into a specu-lative proposition that extraterrestrials, including the annotators of Jessup's book, walk among us. Steiger and Whritenour had built the Philadelphia Experiment into a major subcategory of paranormal research.

Barker, however, was growing skeptical about the matter. After reading Steiger's article, he commented to Keel, "In fact I have almost come to the conclusion that there never was a Varo Edition and that its alleged existence was a hoax, probably perpetrated by Jessup."[17] But Keel quickly countered

Barker's doubts: Not only was the Varo edition real, he told him, but he had seen Jessup's personal copy and read through it twice. This copy contained additional handwritten annotations by Jessup himself, who "appeared to regard the whole thing as some kind of hoax."[18] Now convinced that the book did indeed exist, Barker contacted the Varo Company in 1968. Their response confirmed the book's existence but informed him that it was no longer in stock.[19]

In 1971 Texas UFO researcher and illustrator Hal Crawford wrote to Barker to announce that he had obtained a complete photocopy of the Varo edition.[20] Crawford wouldn't tell Barker the name of his source for the photocopy, but indicated that he was an aerospace industry worker who contacted him through an intermediary. Barker and Crawford soon began discussing plans to reprint the Varo text from Crawford's photocopy, and Crawford even wrote a brief "Introduction to the Saucerian Edition," including a questionnaire for readers to use to identify any strange phenomena they encountered after purchasing the book.[21]

Anticipating the imminent release of the annotated book, Barker got to work, contacting Citadel Press in April 1971 to obtain reprint rights for Jessup's original text "in a paperback edition"; the agreement makes no reference to the annotations.[22] He then drummed up interest with an article for the September 1971 issue of *Flying Saucers* entitled "The Enigma of M. K. Jessup." The article summarized the story of Jessup and Allende, with heavy emphasis on the Varo edition. A sidebar issues a call to the magazine's audience: "If any FLYING SAUCERS readers have actually seen a copy of this book, and can verify its existence, please write to Gray Barker, Box 2228, Clarksburg, W. Va. 26301."[23] The call is odd, since Barker had known about Crawford's photocopy for several months, but it serves to amplify the enigma surrounding the mysterious book.

Barker's request bore fruit within weeks of the article's publication. On September 11 Barker received a letter from Rose Hiett (formerly Rose Campbell), who had worked as an administrator for NICAP in its earliest days, before being expelled for her support of contactees.[24] Hiett wrote to him to inform him that she owned a copy of the book—in fact, she owned the copy from which the BSRA's Riley Crabb had reprinted selections, which Barker had reproduced in his own publications.[25] Moreover, she was interested in disposing of not only this scarce book, but her entire collection of flying saucer publications, clippings, and notes.[26] The two soon made arrangements for Barker to purchase her entire collection for a lot price of one hundred dollars, and she mailed him the Varo book on November 17, 1971, with the remainder of the collection following in late January 1972.[27]

Barker delayed countersigning the Citadel reprint agreement until December 20, 1972, over a year after he obtained the original Varo edition.[28] He contacted Ray Palmer in February 1973 requesting a price quote for printing a two-color facsimile of the book, with Jessup's text in black and the annotations in red. Palmer informed him that an exact facsimile would not be possible: the original had indicated the annotator's underlining with red underlining beneath black text, and it was impossible to separate these in duplicating the mimeographed text. Barker's facsimile would need to print these underlines in black.[29] In their book *The Philadelphia Experiment*, Charles Berlitz and William Moore claim that five hundred copies of this edition were printed; if accurate, this suggests both that Barker's funds may have been tight and that he doubted he'd be able to sell as many copies of the book as his more straightforward ufological publications.[30]

As Crawford had suggested he do, Barker waited until the book was printed and waiting in his warehouse before soliciting sales. In October 1973 Barker sent an advertising circular that stressed the conspiracism surrounding the book. The sales flyer came in a sealed envelope containing a warning: "NOTICE—THIS ENVELOPE CONTAINS AN AD ON CONTROVERSIAL UFO INFORMATION. . . . If you feel you do not wish to know this information or have this information in your possession, destroy this envelope immediately or return to sender."[31] Those who ignored the warning and opened the envelope anyway found a message marking them as one of the fearless UFO elite: "The fact that you opened this envelope tells me something about your personal character. . . . YOU ARE SERIOUSLY INTERESTED IN THE UFO MYSTERY, and you are NOT paranoid or crazy! . . . AND YOU ARE NOT AFRAID OF THE IMPLICATIONS THAT THE 'FLYING SAUCER' MYSTERY might bring."[32] These "select few" were offered the book at the discounted price of $12.50 per copy, discounted from the retail price of $25.[33] The elusive document was at last available. But the mailing was hardly sent only to the elite—Barker sent out eight thousand copies.³⁴ This book had the highest retail price of any of Barker's publications to date, and by encouraging any of the recipients who actually opened the tantalizing envelope to view themselves as a self-selecting few, he sought to justify the significant markup on the publication. Keel described the advertising promotion as "a masterpiece. Too bad you never got into a legitimate line of work. You could have made a fortune."³⁵

One recipient of the solicitation letter was particularly surprised by it: Hal Crawford, who had spent more than a year expecting that Barker would be reproducing a black-and-white reissue of the Varo edition from his photocopy. On October 22 he wrote to Barker to express his confusion at seeing the advertisement, since he had never sent the photocopy to Barker for reproduction.³⁶ Apparently Barker had not bothered to tell one of his most interested correspondents about this new development in the Allende saga.

Jessup's original text was about far more than UFOs. His interests extended into Forteana more broadly, and his book includes long passages on mysterious objects falling from the skies, archeological oddities, inexplicable teleportations, and maritime mysteries like the case of the *Marie Celeste*. In all cases, he is interested more in mysteries than their solutions, and his book is essentially a catalog of oddities rather than the sustained argument the title suggests. The annotations purport to provide solutions, but in fact they create mysteries of their own. They concern warring saucer occupants, identified only as the sinister, extraterrestrial "S-Ms" and the relatively peaceful, undersea-dwelling "L-Ms" (a term explained in one annotation as "Lemurian-Muanians" or "Little Men").³⁷ Frequent reference is made to the Navy's 1943 experiments in the Philadelphia Navy Yard and to related subjects mentioned in the Allende letters. Ufologists latched onto the Philadelphia Experiment as the main mystery explored by the annotations, but the annotator seems far more concerned with an ancient war between spacemen and Lemurians.

Moreover, the annotator is concerned about Jessup's knowledge of mysteries he seems to believe only he holds the keys to: as "Mr. B" states, "He *Knows* Something but *How* Does He know."³⁸ Allende's annotations provide an explanation for virtually every mystery that Jessup raises. Fallen organic matter is "SPOILED FOOD, DROPPED."³⁹ The ship *Ourang Medan* (a ship supposedly lost in the South Pacific the 1940s) exploded due to "More Work of 'The Little Men' of Mu & their force-ships."[40] A sheet of ice forming in the sky is "a Gigantic Lens for close observation of Humankind or Merely for amusement."[41] For every unsolved mystery Jessup raises, the annotator has a solution: the S-Ms and L-Ms are a complete system for explaining the unexplained. Considered in context, they bear more than a passing resemblance to Shaver's dero, at whose feet Shaver laid the blame for every ill.

In fact, there was only one annotator in the Varo edition: Allende himself claimed responsibility for all of the added text. Allende did not merely admit to, but insisted on his authorship of this material when he traveled to Clarksburg to be interviewed by Barker and Moseley in 1979.[42] In an article on Allende in the October 1980 issue of *Fate*, Robert Goerman quotes the letter that Allende sent to his parents along with a copy of the Varo edition: "Enclosed is a book I *co-authored* with professor Morris K. Jessup of the University of Michigan *nigh* 24 years ago . . . *and so this book I helped to write (alone by myself with no* 'Mr. A. or Mr. B.') . . ."[43] In a letter to Goerman in 1983, John Keel wrote, "Varo was behind the 'hoax,' not Allende or anyone else. Jessup . . . myself and everyone else knew that Allende had written the annotations."[44]

The production of the Varo edition sparked a lengthy, voluminous, and one-sided correspondence between Allende and Barker. Allende continued to add to his annotations, as illustrated by a later printing of Barker's reissue to which Allende has added additional handwritten annotations in brown and red ink. Allende has altered the author credit on the cover of this copy, adding "+ Carlos Allende" beneath Jessup's name. He adds a long, handwritten preface in which he states that the purpose of the annotations is "to spur science onwards and upwards in removing the level of ignorance then so transparently & generally prevalent."[45] Allende alludes to the material on S-Ms, L-Ms, and gypsies as a clever fiction: "annotations based on . . . anthropology Navajoe [*sic*] Indian pantheon of both 'Enemy gods' & 'Beneficial gods' and the heavily dramatized 'MYSTERIOUS GYPSIES' of anthropological puzzlement."[46] To the final page, he adds a note thanking "humble men like Carlos Allende for they dared give us a larger view of the universe."[47]

The low-maintenance book distribution system that Barker had established came undone at the end of 1974 when the New Jersey warehouse that had been storing and drop-shipping Saucerian publications declared bankruptcy after several months of declining service. In early 1975 Barker reclaimed his stock and once again began handling order fulfillment from his own office, hiring a new staffer, Donna Darlene Helmeck, to help sort out the warehouse's errors and missed shipments.[48] He found, among the returned material, copies of several titles he had thought were entirely out of stock. To announce the surprise availability of these titles, Barker drew up a two-page letter in early 1975 to enclose in book shipments that winter, entitling it *Gray Barker's Newsletter*. This and the subsequent issue, which followed in July, were single-page newsletters, comparable in size and content to the *Saucer News Non-Scheduled Newsletter*, and the second issue explicitly identifies it as a continuation of that miniature publication.

With its third full issue, in January 1976, *Gray Barker's Newsletter* expanded from a single leaf to a corner-stapled zine, essentially a smaller-scale version of *Saucer News* itself. (Barker retained ownership of the S.A.U.C.E.R.S. organization, and the indicia of this and future issues refer to this as an official publication of the group.) The back cover, containing the address panel for mailing the publication, bears the hornblower image of the Recorder from the cover of *The Silver Bridge* beside the return address. It would remain there on most future issues of the newsletter, becoming the de facto logo of Barker's publishing operation.

PROMOTIONS AT THE CINEMA V

Throughout 1974 and 1975, Barker's energies were primarily directed toward the Cinema V. McCulty's career moved in parallel to Barker's, and by late 1975 he was also a theater owner, operating the Kanawha Theatre in Buckhannon, just a few blocks away from the Cinema V.[49] Rather than competing, Barker and McCulty cross-promoted, showing trailers and displaying advertising material for films showing at the other theater.[50] The two likely collaborated on film booking to ensure no direct competition between the two movie houses.

Barker undertook some renovations and equipment purchases for the Cinema V. He put a disused stereo sound system to use by playing music "fitting the mood of the feature picture . . . before the show and during intermissions."[51] He upgraded the projection equipment with an EPRAD SWORD (Show without Rewind) film transport system (which let film be shown without a projectionist changing reels). Though it would have little effect on theatergoers' experience, the system nonetheless became a marketing tool; Barker branded it the "Mighty Sword Projector."[52] In addition to these technical upgrades, Barker apparently revised the "family-friendly" policy under which he had opened the Cinema V: in late 1975 he told Sherwood, "We've had some of the townspeople complaining about the filthy movies and dirty 'Prevues.'"[53] Possibly in reaction to this, when he added a second screen to the theater in 1976, he emphasized the family-friendly nature of the entertainment on offer: "Barker adopted the promotional name 'Sky Porch' for the piggyback twin and in his advertisements has dedicated it 'to the young persons of Buckhannon.' The second screen will be used for G and PG pictures whenever possible."[54] The "Sky Porch" moniker was an attempt to put a good spin on a change that would make the theater less pleasant for attendees: turning the balcony of the auditorium into a second theater would reduce the screen size, and acoustically isolating the two auditoriums was all but impossible. Richard Haines minces few words in declaring that, in comparison to the large auditoriums they replaced, "many twinned theaters were horrible."[55] Overall, however, business at Barker's theater seemed to be doing well, and it was there he chose to invest most of his time and money in the mid-1970s.

NOSTALGIA AND DISILLUSIONMENT

In 1975 and 1976 a growing sense of nostalgia developed around ufologists of Barker's generation, reflected in Moseley's 1976 revival of his publication, which changed its name every month before settling on *Saucer Smear* in 1981. Barker's wistfulness for the joys of his past saucer activity is reflected

Figures 11.1 and 11.2

Duplantier's jokey cover to *Gray Barker at Giant Rock* (1976). Author's collection/courtesy of the Gray Barker Estate.

GRAY BARKER AT GIANT ROCK

By GRAY BARKER

SAUCERIAN PUBLICATIONS, CLARKSBURG, W.VA.

"Thoroughly Dedicated to Promoting UFO Crackpottery"

in the reissue, in February 1976, of his own first book, *They Knew Too Much about Flying Saucers*, and the nostalgic *Gray Barker at Giant Rock*, which followed shortly thereafter.[56] As with *The Silver Bridge* several years before, the latter title was solicited with a letter bearing James Moseley's name, though it was not necessarily written by him.[57] The sales pitch for the book hyperbolically compares it to the *Decameron*, but ultimately sums it up as an "attempt to preserve the atmosphere of this and past conventions he has attended [at Giant Rock], so that the saucer 'fan' of the future, and those of you who have never attended one, can vicariously experience these fabulous meetings."[58] Gene Duplantier provided the book's humorous cover: the front shows a grinning photographic portrait of Barker (bespectacled, with a receding hairline, shoulder-length hair, and a vividly patterned jacket), with Giant Rock drawn into the background; the back shows a photograph of Barker from the rear, facing the Integratron. In addition to depicting the landscape of Giant Rock and its surroundings, Duplantier has drawn in the imaginary photographers taking each of the back- and front-facing portraits. The cover hints at the book's lighthearted nature—an ode to an era of saucering that was already fading quickly into the past when the work was finally published in 1976.

Alongside this cheerful nostalgia, though, was regret. In responding to a reader's letter in *Gray Barker's Newsletter* no. 3, Barker gives a picture of his own developing attitude toward the UFO subject. He seems jaded and increasingly skeptical. He even undercuts the quality of his own current writing: "With a very few exceptions I find the new books on UFOs, particularly the proliferating paperbacks, quite boring, for it all seems to be a rehash of what I have read so many times. . . . I'm certain that my new MIB book will not be greatly satisfying to me, and my soon due off the press *Gray Barker at Giant Rock*, will be largely a rehash of contactee stories."[59] Reflecting on Bender's narrative specifically, he also shows greater skepticism than ever before:

> For about three years after *They Knew Too Much* was published the Bender mystery became quite a fixation in my mind. What Bender had "found out" was the topic of discussion with all my friends in saucer research. I collected reams of notes, and summaries of different conclusions. . . . In the years that

followed I have become somewhat more skeptical and hopefully more objective about Bender, but although . . . my instincts tell me it was all a leg-pull, I cannot help believing there was truly *something there* that still hasn't been solved.[60]

Barker leaves open the possibility of a lingering mystery, admitting that "Bender still has me by the saucerian balls."[61] Whether this indicates a truth that he still felt was out there or a metanarrative monster of his own creation from which he could not escape is left to the reader.

NEW NARRATIVE ROUTES: AUDIOTAPES AND NEWSSTAND MAGAZINES

Barker had been gathering audio recordings for years, chiefly in reel-to-reel format, and by 1979 had acquired the collections of several ufologists, including saucer audiophile Adolph Dittmar and the late Jack Robinson.[62] The increasing popularity and affordability of the compact cassette format opened up a new line of production. Barker announced his first cassette, entitled *Gray Barker on the Air*, in *Gray Barker's Newsletter* no. 7, in early 1977, and within a few months the tape list had grown to ten titles. These included interviews Barker conducted with monster witness Jennings Frederick and with Carlos Allende, but most of them were culled from Barker's collection of sound recordings going back nearly three decades. Among them were audio recordings sent to Barker for personal use or limited distribution, including John Stuart's narration of his frightening experiences and Albert Bender's report of his experiences with the black-clad men from Kazik, produced for the closed sessions of the 1970 Congress of Scientific Ufologists.[63] Others were recorded from radio or television, such as tapes of contactees Reinhold Schmidt and Woodrow Derenberger. And one is a simple bootleg: a reissue of Howard Menger's space music LP, *Authentic Music from Another Planet*. Easy to produce and cheap to ship, these cassettes were likely produced on demand or in small batches rather than in bulk.

In addition to producing these audiocassettes, Barker began a prolific period of writing in the second half of the 1970s. In 1976 he had written to Timothy Green Beckley, complaining that his audiovisual business was declining but he hoped to revitalize his customer base and earn more income from UFO writing and publishing.[64] Barker wrote at a fortuitous moment: Beckley had recently launched a firm, Global Communications, that operated as an agent to writers and photographers, especially those seeking to publish in men's magazines, tabloids, and pornographic publications.[65] Among Beckley's clients was the men's magazine *Saga*, which had just launched a UFO-focused newsstand publication called *UFO Report*, part of a trend of nationally distributed UFO magazines. Beckley served as Barker's agent for about a dozen contributions to these magazines.[66] Beckley's advice makes the aims of these publications clear: he told Barker that editor Marty Singer wanted the magazine to contain recent sighting reports—and encouraged him to invent stories if it helped him meet that demand.[67]

Barker also began producing a regular column for Beckley's new saucer tabloid *UFO Review*, which launched in 1978. Barker's column was a revival of his Chasing the Flying Saucers column from Palmer's *Flying Saucers*; it even reused the old heading designed by Gene Duplantier (and Barker's old headshot, now over two decades old). The revived column follows the same format as the original: a collection of brief sighting and creature reports, often strung together with a loose narrative framework. Barker's first column recounts a saucer crash or landing in Wetzel County, West Virginia, and a phone call with Anna Genzlinger, an investigator who suspected a conspiracy surrounding the death of M. K. Jessup, both placed in the framework of a January 1978 blizzard that left his office snowbound. Barker blends his folksy narrative style with brief accounts of the strange and sinister.[68]

UFO Review also inspired Barker to investigate cheaper printing methods, and beginning with its eighth issue *Gray Barker's Newsletter* appeared in a similar tabloid format on newsprint, probably using the same printer as Beckley. This was the most cost-effective printing method available to Barker, and he saw no reason that this format—which could fit up to 2,500 words on a page—could not be used for book-length works as well as periodicals. Barker launched the short-lived Giant Tab series, which could fit the entire text of a book on about twenty tabloid-sized pages, describing it in a letter to Crawford as "an experimental type of book."[69] The prices of the Giant Tab publications were indeed low, but it appears that the difficulty of reading a book on tabloid pages put off his readers. Barker published only a handful of titles in the format, and when he returned to tabloid printing for *Worlds beyond the Poles*, a compilation of Ray Palmer's hollow-earth writings, he cut the pages down, roughly and by hand, and bound them in stiff paper boards to produce something more like the books his customers expected.

CLOSE ENCOUNTERS WITH E.T.

On November 16, 1977, thousands of people gathered to see an enormous extraterrestrial "mothership" slowly descend to Earth. But this mass sighting took place not in a single location but on movie screens across the country, during the climax of Steven Spielberg's film *Close Encounters of the Third Kind*. Though not a "real" saucer sighting, the visual effects in the film (supervised by Douglass Trumbull) created a template for extraterrestrial encounters in its audience. Moreover, Spielberg's film drew directly and explicitly on ideas from the realm of ufology, marking the first time since the 1956 film *Earth vs. the Flying Saucers* (ostensibly based on Keyhoe's *Flying Saucers from Outer Space*) that a major Hollywood production had drawn so directly on UFO literature. *Close Encounters of the Third Kind* brought ideas previously known only to dedicated readers of flying saucer books to a mass audience, most notably the ideas of J. Allen Hynek, whose typology of UFO sightings in his 1972 book *The UFO Experience* provides the film's title.[70] Hynek himself has a six-second cameo in the film's final reel, standing among the throng of scientists gazing in wonder at the descending extraterrestrial mothership.[71] *Close Encounters* was a hit and proved to movie studios that the runaway success of *Star Wars* six months earlier had been not a fluke, but a sign that audiences hungered for science fiction spectacle. David Clarke and Andy Roberts describe the film's release as "the 'high water mark' of popular belief in UFOs as extraterrestrial spacecraft," and it led to the publication of dozens of paperback books on UFOs and extraterrestrial life, many of which adopted the film logo's font in an attempt to cash in on its success.[72]

Gray Barker was less impressed. Hynek's serious and scientific approach had always clashed with Barker's freewheeling mischievousness, and Barker seems to have resented the astronomer's growing success. According to

Moseley, Barker altered the prints of *Close Encounters* that passed through his booking business, targeting Hynek's brief on-screen cameo: "Gray carefully and professionally edited that tiny section of the film out of all the prints he handled before distributing them to his customers. Thus, at least in West Virginia, Hynek wound up on the cutting room floor."[73] Barker minced few words about *Close Encounters*, calling it "pretty ridiculous" in a 1977 solicitation letter.[74] Barker's mailings had typically appealed to his mailing list as a discerning elite. With a UFO movie enjoying broad cultural success, Barker sought to preserve his audience's sense of being special. Nevertheless, Barker recognized that the film's success represented a shift in public interest. Unfortunately, though, it came at a time when his publishing activity was at an ebb—he published very little from 1977 through 1979, with most of his available capital going to the Cinema V.[75]

Where possible, Barker sought to exploit the synergy between Hollywood movies and UFO metanarratives. In 1974 he screened Erich von Däniken's ancient aliens documentary *Chariots of the Gods* at the Cinema V, showing it in a double bill with a pilot Frank Edwards shot for a television show called *Flying Saucers Here and Now*, but found the response at the box office disappointing.[76] Barker also appeared on a WDTV television program in November, promoting the low-budget flying saucer thriller *UFO: Target Earth*.[77] Another, more subtle sign of the blend between Barker's two main areas of activity appears on a surviving handbill from the Cinema V. The hornblower figure—the Recorder from Gene Duplantier's cover design for *The Silver Bridge*—appears prominently as a logo for the theater, suggesting conceptual overlap between Barker's film promotions and his UFO publishing.[78] Barker also apparently produced short films on ufological subjects, likely using Lovett & Co.'s equipment. A 1975 newsletter listed the titles of two of these films: *MIB—The Secret Terror among Us* and *Giant Rock Saucer Convention*.[79] In 1980 he arranged to screen a rough cut of the low-budget film *Hangar 18* in advance of its release for the National UFO Conference, hosted by Moseley in Manhattan.[80]

In mid-1979 Barker received word that his first book might soon become a movie. Moseley announced in his newsletter: "As amazing as it may seem, a minor-league movie company is seriously considering making a film based on Barker's classic UFO book, 'They Knew Too Much About Flying Saucers.' Production is scheduled to start in the Fall."[81] But beyond printing a script excerpt and some Duplantier illustrations (presented as storyboard images) in *UFO Review*, there's little indication that the project ever got close to production. By the time Barker's most influential literary creation finally reached cinemas, in the form of the 1997 movie *Men in Black*, the metanarrative of terror had been transformed into comedy.

"GO FORTH AND BE CRAZY": *THE PHILADELPHIA EXPERIMENT* AND *THE JESSUP DIMENSION*

Six years after Barker made the Varo edition available, the metanarrative of the Philadelphia Experiment began reaching a larger audience than ever. In the spring of 1979, Grosset & Dunlap published *The Philadelphia Experiment: Project Invisibility* by Charles Berlitz and William L. Moore.[82] Berlitz lent his name to the project largely to increase its appeal following the success of his earlier work *The Bermuda Triangle*; by all accounts, the bulk of the book was written by Moore alone.[83] The book expands on the brief and spotty narrative of the Allende letters, investigating the various people, places, and ships that Carl Allen had claimed were involved in experiments in invisibility and teleportation in 1943 and exploring the supposed mystery of Jessup's death. The book was a hit: according to Moore, it sold sixty thousand copies and went through five printings in the first few months of its release.[84]

To trade on Moore and Berlitz's success, Barker made the Philadelphia Experiment the central topic of the ninth issue of *Gray Barker's Newsletter* in late 1979. The lead story is a lengthy summary of the Philadelphia Experiment narrative, printed alongside an interview Barker conducted with Moore in August. Barker illustrates his lead text with a morgue photograph of Jessup's body. The authenticity and provenance of the photograph are unclear, but the decision to print it is decidedly ghoulish and exploitative. The rest of the issue expands on the metanarrative, with the decidedly overstated front-page headline "Navy Admits Reality of the Philadelphia Experiment."

One of Moore and Berlitz's readers was inspired to launch her own investigation of the subject, and of Jessup's death in particular: Anna Lykins

Figure 11.3
Barker with his TRS-80 computer at the Barker family home in Exchange, ca. 1980–1984. Gray Barker UFO Collection, Clarksburg-Harrison Public Library/courtesy of the Gray Barker Estate.

Genzlinger, whom Moseley describes as "psychically oriented, wealthy, and well-intentioned" in her investigation of the cold case.[85] *The Jessup Dimension*, apparently written at Barker's urging, details her investigation and its conclusions. Genzlinger believed that Jessup's death in 1959 was not a typical suicide, and that he may have been under mind control when it occurred. Genzlinger writes, "Gray Barker asked me to write this book in the form of a detective story."[86] Barker made significant changes to Genzlinger's typescript, most notably building on a brief passage in which Genzlinger briefly discusses her feeling of connection with Jessup's spirit, turning it into a device running through the book wherein Genzlinger's investigation is guided by Jessup's ghost.[87] At least some of the work of editing and laying out Genzlinger's book was done on a new piece of equipment: a TRS-80 computer, which Barker purchased in November 1978—a little over a year after the early personal computer model became available.[88]

Barker further promoted the book by suggesting in a Chasing the Flying Saucers column that its author had been targeted by the Men in Black.[89] But an "open letter to the M.I.B." by Genzlinger, published in *Gray Barker's Newsletter*, casts doubt on these persecutions, as she demands to know: "So why haven't you come after me? I'm waiting! . . . If you don't come forward, then I intend to find you. You cannot be allowed to go on as you have been doing."[90] Genzlinger clearly expected that her research would expose her to the Men in Black, and her lack of persecution produced an anxious sense that her research didn't matter enough to merit silencing.

ABDUCTIONS AND SAUCER CRASHES

The release of the Condon report in 1969 resulted in the collapse of the reigning metanarratives about UFOs, and in the 1970s the ufological community scrambled for new metanarratives to explain new and old sightings. The contactee metanarrative, in particular, was no longer viable: decades after Adamski's encounter with Orthon, the space brothers had not arrived en masse. Hopeful stories of friendly, human-appearing space beings were being replaced with more sinister stories of abduction by UFO occupants.[91] This emerging metanarrative was inaugurated by John Fuller's 1966 bestseller, *The Interrupted Journey*, detailing the experiences of New Hampshire couple Betty and Barney Hill.[92] The abduction metanarrative remained mostly dormant for several years before erupting into predominance in the 1970s. It initially appeared as a subset of contactee narratives, and the magazine *Look* serialized Fuller's book with the title "Aboard a Flying Saucer"— the same as Truman Bethurum's 1954 book describing his meetings with Aura Rhanes.[93] Though the Hills' case was disseminated widely, it was not until the 1970s that further high-profile abduction cases emerged. The metanarrative expanded with the 1981 publication of *Missing Time* by Budd Hopkins. Hopkins's book is built on the idea that most abductees suppress their memories of their experiences, thus essentially severing the abduction metanarrative from UFOs proper. After Hopkins, the sighting of an aerial object was no longer necessary for investigators to suspect an abduction. Any sense of unaccounted time, even a vague unease, could become a rationale for the use of hypnosis and the emergence of a new abduction narrative.[94] Barker put it more bluntly in a 1981 catalog: "You may have been abducted and not even know it!"[95]

From Barker's perspective, there was not much new about these abduction cases; in *Gray Barker's UFO Annual 1981* he declared that they were "quite similar to the contact cases of the Adamski era but in different guise."[96] Scott Scribner, in elucidating the differences between contactees and abductees, declares that the former "relate how they meet space people, ride in spaceships, receive higher knowledge, and take physical or out-of-body trips to other planets."[97] But these features are present in many abduction narratives, and some of the major figures in the metanarrative, including Betty Andreasson and Whitley Strieber, report *all* of them. Barker saw this overlap, and in the final years of his publishing career he struggled to preserve a place for contactees in the world of ufology: after all, it was a metanarrative that had been a primary focus of his work for more than two decades. Proponents of the abduction metanarrative wanted to downplay the relationship between their cases and those of contactees, but Barker saw them as part of the same story.

Another dominant metanarrative to emerge in the 1970s was that of saucer crashes. Throughout the 1950s and '60s, mainstream ufology had generally viewed saucer crash stories as hoaxes. Charles Ziegler notes that the revelation of the hoax at the core of Scully's *Behind the Flying Saucers* "created within the UFO community a strong and long-lasting bias against crashed saucer stories."[98] Barker was one of the few to air saucer crash and retrieval narratives. In addition to Moseley's "Wright Field Story," Barker also publicized the claims of Californian George Tyler, who spun a complex tale alleging that expatriate Estonian Baron Nicholas von Poppen had taken hundreds of photographs of saucer wreckage at a military base in the early 1950s. Jacqueline Sanders had investigated Tyler's story in the 1950s and, after meeting von Poppen and hearing his exasperated denials, concluded that it was a bizarre hoax. But Barker revived the story several times, eventually claiming Sanders's investigative work as his own but leaving out her conclusions about Tyler's reliability.[99]

The revival of the crashed-saucer metanarrative in the 1970s is chiefly due to the work of ufologist Leonard Stringfield, whose presentation at the 1978 MUFON Symposium presented the case that the US government was in possession of at least one crashed spacecraft and an extraterrestrial corpse. Stringfield's talk sent shock waves through the world of ufology. Its title, "Retrievals of the Third Kind," proved him as much a showman as a scientist, trading on Spielberg's success just as Beckley and Barker had. An updated version of Stringfield's talk was serialized in two 1978 issues of the *MUFON UFO Journal*, presenting brief accounts of eighteen alleged cases of crashed saucers retrieved by the US military.[100] Case number XVIII in Stringfield's catalog of crashes, added to the paper after the MUFON conference, describes a purported crash at a locale that had been scarcely mentioned in ufological publications for over thirty years: Roswell, New Mexico.[101] Stringfield does not emphasize the Roswell narrative in particular, but the 1980 publication of *The Roswell Incident* by Moore and Berlitz turned that event into a metanarrative magnet, attracting details from a number of distinct stories of alien craft and in turn becoming a core component of further metanarrative mutations.[102]

Barker gave front-page placement to an interview with Stringfield in *Gray Barker's Newsletter* no. 8, opening with a long summary of the metanarrative going back to Scully's book:

> From a "political" standpoint, [Stringfield's] position was extremely unwise. The UFO establishment was rapidly changing in view from the "nuts-and-bolts" interplanetary school to a gradual acceptance of the alternate theories proposed by Keel and others of the "new wave." Although the alleged retrievals of crashed saucers and their occupants indicated physical and likely interplanetary origins and thus did not jibe with the "new wave," even worse, the idea was still tarred by the Scully brush.[103]

Surprisingly, Barker's article makes no reference to his own promotion of the Tyler and von Poppen story. But he ties virtually every item in this issue of the newsletter to the Stringfield interview: the headline of the catalog section stridently asks, "IS THE GOVERNMENT HOLDING CRASHED UFOS?," and the zine review section appears beneath a header reading

"Doctor examines alien." Alongside the metanarrative of alien abductions, Stringfield's theories concerning crashed saucers were soon to grow into a dominant metanarrative of their own, and Barker's choice to overprint and broadly distribute this particular issue of the newsletter may have had an impact on the increasing acceptance of the formerly taboo topic. If his stated print run is accurate, Stringfield's story was now put before ten thousand readers in addition to the significantly smaller number who subscribed to the *MUFON UFO Journal*.

As the dominant metanarratives surrounding UFOs changed, Barker's public persona shifted to one of a broader skepticism surrounding the chief theory that these new ideas sought to bolster: the extraterrestrial hypothesis. In a "position statement" written for Ronald Story's 1980 *Encyclopedia of UFOs* (to which he also contributed the entry on Mothman and his own biography), Barker writes: "The phenomena has not responded to scientific investigation. . . . Closely allied to scientific investigation has been the Extra-terrestrial Hypothesis, which has been similarly unsuccessful."[104] He instead suggests that alternative theories like Keel's are more likely to prove productive, and that "the UFO mystery . . . should be more closely studied by the sociologist, the psychologist, and the established clergy along with radical metaphysicians."[105] This statement was written for a broad public audience, and in such venues Barker always maintained a pseudo-skeptical support for all manner of paranormal narratives. But he underscored this particular point in a letter to UFO skeptic Robert Sheaffer the same year in which he commented on fairy and ghost stories, noting, "I'm rather convinced that whatever the UFOs are, they are a part of the same above phenomena."[106] This was essentially the argument that Jacques Vallee had made in *Passport to Magonia* (a foundational text of Middle Ufology) and continued to elaborate on in his books into the 1990s. In another letter, though, Barker jokingly—though perhaps accurately—described his public persona: "I AM thoroughly dedicated to promoting UFO crackpottery."[107] And the lead article to the tenth newsletter, written for the narrower audience of Barker's own readers, closes with a paean to the crackpot—and the liar:

> Sometimes we wonder why we persist in trying to separate legend from fact, old wives' tales from truths, Philadelphia Experiments from souped-up gener-

ators. We can argue that the proving of a crashed saucer tale could reveal what might be the most important event in history, our contact with an extraterrestrial race. But what if we are "wrong" and these things are only the products of our over-wrought imaginations and our proneness for paranoia?

Of course, there may be a beneficial spinoff to anything, even crackpottery: Don Juan's jousting with windmills has implanted an energy-saving symbol in the minds of millions; Baron Manchausen's [sic] perfidious prevarications have inspired countless bureaucrats.

The saucer nut's badgering of the Government over things such as UFOs and the Philadelphia Experiment may represent a technomorphization of far more serious anxieties, and help push the terrible Orwellian deadline of 1984 back a few notches on the calendar.

Subscribers:—GO FORTH AND BE CRAZY![108]

Though Barker privately joked with Sheaffer about his promotion of "crackpottery," his public statements published in the newsletter often presented such defenses of his authors, subjects, and readers from ostracism.[109]

Similarly, Barker attacked those who sought to augment their own respectability by putting down those beyond their particular pale. The twelfth issue of the newsletter contained an editorial assault on Hynek and Vallee, who had blocked an extraterrestrial conspiracist named Colman von Keviczky from a United Nations meeting related to UFOs.[110] Though he does not name them directly, Barker makes it clear from the context of the editorial that its closing salvo is directed at Hynek and Vallee:

We have long wanted the opportunity to speak about those persons, whose reputations in Ufology hang precariously upon media attention and the prestige of their doctoral degrees rather than "dirt farmer" accomplishments in a field somewhat removed from their valid academic specialties; those whose poverty of practicality lead them . . . into esoteric wastelands where they may wander and pontificate without accountability; those who depend upon their publicity in the National ENQUIRER rather than engage in genuine National INQUIRY. In their exclusion of VonKeviczky from the UN discussion they have shown, perhaps, their fears and doubts of their own self-images.[111]

Hynek and Vallee also placed a premium on a certain kind of seriousness, one that sought to broaden ufology's impact by narrowing its scope to something more scientific and academic. Barker, on the other hand, wanted to broaden ufology's scope, to make room for voices not heard elsewhere, even if that diminished the general public's ability to take the topic seriously.

Barker was an invited speaker at the nineteenth National UFO Conference in Cleveland, held on May 29, 1982. Organizer Rick Hilberg promoted Barker's talk as his "first presentation to a major UFO convention in over ten years"—but Moseley reported a rumor that it would be his final public appearance.[112] The concluding words of the lecture betray a curious finality, as Barker exhorted the audience to seek mystery:

> I hope that, if you all haven't seen a flying saucer, that eventually you will see one. If you haven't seen one, my advice would be not to look for them in outer space, or even in another dimension, into the oceans, or not even in the Hollow Earth. But the next time you go outside on a starry night and you do not see a UFO, I guarantee you this. If you look deep inside yourself, there you will see them.[113]

12 "DEEP PEACE AND DROWSINESS": NEW AGE BOOKS AND BARKER'S FINAL YEARS, 1982–1984

At the close of 1981 Barker began a phase of semiretirement.[1] From the end of 1981 until the end of his life, Barker lived with his sister Blanche and her family in Exchange, West Virginia, just a few miles from where he was born.[2] He expanded the available living space on the property by purchasing a trailer home to install alongside the main house, which had been built by his brother Walter.[3] He spent much of his time with family; Gene Duplantier recalled: "Gray was very fond of his little grandnephew Christopher, who was five years old in 1982. At that time, it seems that Christopher came up with the words 'MIB' before he could print even his own name."[4] His increase in publishing activity in the following years may have resulted from this opportunity to spend more time with his family: his nephew Joe worked with him as a press operator.

Barker had difficulties finding a new printer after Palmer's death in 1977, complaining that new printing technologies provided excellent prices for mass-producing books, "but IMPOSSIBLY high per-copy prices for mini-publishers (such as we) who may not be able to sell more than 500 copies of a book."[5] With his customer base shrinking, Barker no longer needed to print in anything like the quantities he had in earlier years. In 1983 Barker returned to in-house production, leasing a new photocopier "that offers greater economy than the previous Xerox."[6] Barker's first production on this machine was a black-and-white reissue of the Varo edition—a book he knew he could sell at a high price.[7] Barker returned to hands-on book production with enthusiasm, reflected in the detail with which he described the

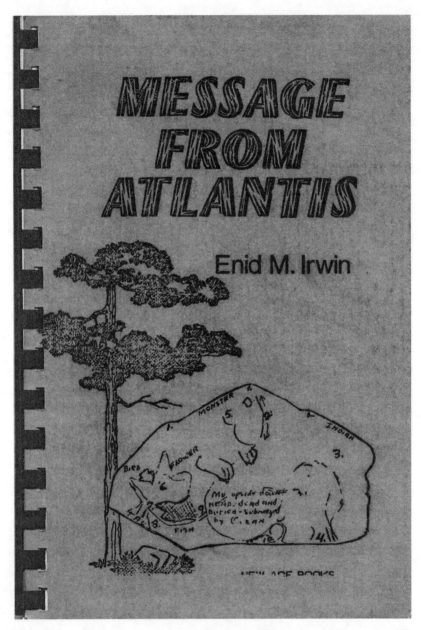

Figure 12.1

The change from Saucerian Books to New Age Books reflected a change in production methods, with all printing and binding once again done in-house. Enid M. Irwin's *Message from Atlantis*, 1983. Author's collection.

design, layout, and printing of several of his later publications.[8] With these changes came a new name: Barker abandoned the "Saucerian" brand he had established three decades before and rechristened the press New Age Books.

The books issued under the New Age imprint are crude affairs, with smudged printing, roughly trimmed page edges, and plastic comb bindings. But this roughness bespeaks their handmade nature: if Barker's offset books under the Saucerian imprint were made for a mass audience, albeit one that didn't care much about the aesthetics of their reading material, New Age publications are bespoke, if rustic—and, in many respects, made just for Barker and his family. Moseley was blunt in his assessment of their "primitive home printing," but Barker presented this roughness as an aesthetic selling point, the result of an artisanal process of handcrafting.[9] In the advertising copy for Bruce Walton's hollow-earth bibliography *A Guide to the Inner Earth*, Barker reports that he "'splurged' and purchased expensive, off-white paper, with a texture suggesting parchment and creating a 'feel' of antiquity!"[10] As with most of Barker's statements about paper quality in the New Age Books period, this is an exaggeration; the highly acidic, textured paper is more akin to construction paper than parchment, and it may in fact have been cheaper than standard letter paper. Nevertheless, the experience of reading a book on such rough stock is a fundamentally different aesthetic and tactile experience than reading a slick magazine or a cheap paperback. It may not communicate a "feel of antiquity" but rather convey the sense of encountering something intended for a select few. Barker's emphasis on the production process glosses over the reduction in print runs: whereas he had previously averaged a thousand copies on each print run of his books, he was now printing drastically fewer copies of each title. Exact edition sizes are unknown for most of the publications Barker issued in 1983 and 1984, but it is likely that he prepared very few copies of each book—dozens rather than hundreds.

STORIES IN STONE

Barker's final publications of 1983 seem rooted in nostalgia for the past and for the subterranean enigmas of the Shaver Mystery in particular. Walton's *A Guide to the Inner Earth*, an extensive annotated bibliography of hollow-earth

Figure 12.2
Dominick Lucchesi provided detailed illustrations for his cryptic *Flying Saucers from Khabarah Khoom* (1983). Author's collection.

theory and the Shaver Mystery, has its roots in Ray Palmer's publications.[11] Enid Irwin's *Message from Atlantis* does not reference Shaver directly, but its author's discernment of antediluvian images in rocks she found on her wilderness hikes resembles Shaver's own interest in Atlantean "rock books."[12] In

1984 Barker published a book by Palmer himself—*Worlds beyond the Poles*, a compilation of Palmer's hollow-earth editorials for *Flying Saucers*.

Subterranean caverns also provided the basis for one of the largest New Age Books publications, Lucchesi's *Flying Saucers from Khabarah Khoom*. Lucchesi's only book describes the experiences of saucer witness "Mr. H." and Lucchesi's own encounters with a resident of a terrestrial saucer base called Rin-2, located in a cavern somewhere in South America. The base is underneath a mountain that is also the site of the ancient city of Khoom, a "pre-ancient" site that was a major city of a lost civilization. Rin-2 struggles against "the Group," an evil organization that inhabits an enormous "Sky Island" and pilots saucers of its own, many of which are crewed by "acromegalic cephelocephalic anomalies (small men with large heads)."[13] Lucchesi's text, which totals scarcely more than thirty pages, is fragmented and nonlinear. However, the writing is not the real focus of the work, which is dominated by Lucchesi's illustrations. These include highly detailed drawings of the lost city of Khoom and its environs, as well as detailed saucer schematics, a map, transcribed alien mathematical notation, and samples from a deck of Khoom tarot cards that Lucchesi planned to publish.

Lucchesi's introduction states that he began work on the book no earlier than 1978, but Barker's past publications show that it may have originated in some sense two decades earlier. Barker quotes Lucchesi using the phrase "Khabarah Khoom" in a Chasing the Flying Saucers column from 1959:

"Kabarah Khoom," he intoned deeply.

"Kabarah what?" asked Mike.

"Kabarah KHOOM. Say it, very slowly, and with feeling. Kabarah KHO-O-O-O-M-M-M!"

"What does it mean?"

"That doesn't matter. Doesn't it give you a feeling of deep peace—and drowsiness?"[14]

The basic outline of Mr. H's story—encountering a landed saucer in a rural area, then meeting and speaking with its crew—is essentially the same as the one that Lucchesi gave Barker for his column in 1961 and 1962, which, like his later book, concluded with a lengthy question-and-answer dialog.[15]

Another seed was planted in *Flying Saucers and the Three Men*, suggesting that Lucchesi knew the secret of the saucers and had diverted the investigation into Bender's experiences when it came too close to the truth.[16] Barker and Lucchesi could have presented *Khabarah Khoom* as the culmination of a three-decades-long mystery, but instead treated it as an entirely new narrative, making no reference to Lucchesi's previous contact tales or use of the phrase "Kabarah Khoom." To anyone who may have remembered, the introduction renders Lucchesi an unreliable narrator from the beginning.

At least one reader did remember Lucchesi's pre-1978 references to "Khoom": Jim Moseley. In a review of the book for *Saucer Smear*, he wrote: "Hopefully these [tarot cards] are not connected with the text, as we remember seeing a couple of them in Lucchesi's apartment many years ago. . . . Your humble editor has known Dominick Lucchesi since 1953, and even then—or thereabouts—he was talking about writing a book some day called 'Flying Saucers from Khabarah Khoom.' (He now says he liked the title, and the story came along later to fit it!)"[17]

THE END

Barker was hard at work in 1984, despite his declining health. He planned a new issue of the newsletter, and acquired the *New Atlantean Journal* from the estate of its late editor, Joan (Whritenour) O'Connell.[18] Gene Duplantier visited Barker in September 1984, and later described him as extraordinarily busy but clearly unwell: "The printing press was going full steam ahead belting out a new book on Blavatsky. . . . My wife and I noticed Gray was coughing more than normally, and had only recently gone back to cigarette smoking after the doctor told him to quit. Two ashtrays overspilled with butts on the old wooden floor attested to his reliance on the devil's coffin nails."[19]

Barker was still reacting quickly to new developments in ufological culture. On August 3, 1984, Roger Corman's New World Pictures released the science fiction thriller *The Philadelphia Experiment*.[20] Following a dramatic reenactment of Allende's supposed invisibility experiment, the film's plot follows a pair of sailors whom the experiment transports four decades into the future. The film performed moderately well, particularly considering its relatively limited distribution, but made little impact compared to the year's top-grossing paranormal film, *Ghostbusters*.[21] In his final Chasing the Flying Saucers column, Barker criticized the film and commented on its declining box office receipts. The main fault, in his opinion, was that "the movie was NOT based on the best-selling Moore/Berlitz book. . . . It is too bad that the film couldn't have been more of a documentary and more actual research done."[22]

Despite his negative appraisal of the film, Barker couldn't pass up the free publicity that even a modestly performing Hollywood film could provide. In September 1984 he produced what was to become his final book, *After the Philadelphia Experiment*. The book is primarily a compilation of the extensive material on the Philadelphia Experiment that originally appeared in *Gray Barker's Newsletter* nos. 9 through 16, including virtually all of the reader letters that the newsletter had carried on the topic. The book is a rehash, but the long text from issue 9 was detailed and entertaining, and it is likely that Barker had written it with an eventual book publication in mind. *After the Philadelphia Experiment* serves as the culmination not just of a metanarrative he had spent two decades guiding, but of his career as a whole.

In October his health took a turn for the worse. Moseley reported: "Publisher Gray Barker . . . almost became the late Gray Barker following a severe heart & lung problem of some sort. Gray spent some time in the hospital, but as of this writing he is on the road to recovery."[23] Beckley ran a notice in *UFO Review* as well, calling for readers to get in touch to wish him well.[24] Barker returned home, but his recovery proved short-lived, and within just a few days he returned to the hospital, where his condition continued to decline.[25] He spoke on the phone with Moseley—whom he surprised by confessing his rarely voiced religious convictions—and McCulty, who had not seen him in about two years.[26] At the beginning of December he entered intensive care with kidney failure and other mounting problems.[27] He died on December 6, 1984, at the age of fifty-nine.

The exact nature of his fatal illness is unclear. His sister Blanche said the cause of death was "cigarette smoking and alcohol, combined."[28] Jerome Clark claimed that the assumption in ufological circles was that his addictions had culminated in a "suicide by alcohol."[29] Moseley raised a different, speculative possibility: "I think Gray Barker died of AIDS. I think in those days it was not diagnosed as easily as it is today. The name AIDS was known and was in the papers and was talked about, but in an area such as West Virginia I would not be surprised if the doctors were not able to recognize it or didn't expect to see the symptoms."[30] Barker's niece Sharon Stump, who settled his estate, rejects Moseley's hypothesis, noting a family history of heart disease and his doctor's explanation that "his heart muscle just gave out."[31] And Barker's death certificate identifies his cause of death as pneumonia—the culmination of thirty years of chronic lung disease in a lifelong smoker.[32] The competition between these claims is fitting: they render Barker's death a mystery.

Saucer Smear announced Barker's passing in mid-December. "Gray Barker should have lived forever," Moseley wrote, "but he didn't."[33]

CONCLUSION

In a 1996 issue of *UFO Magazine*, columnist Richard Hall called Barker "a pure opportunist who engaged in hoaxes, fake feuds with James Moseley and other game playing, while he milked every dollar he could out of 'flying saucers.'"[1] But such a conclusion must disregard the fact that it seems to have been a rare occurrence for Barker to turn a profit on his writing and publishing. Detailed business records are not preserved in Barker's archive, but those that remain suggest that, though Saucerian Books was a business, it was by and large a losing one. From the 1960s onward, Barker's own relevance in the ufological community declined, and following the Condon report, so did his customer base. His bankruptcy in 1963 was driven in large part by debts he had undertaken in his hardcover publications, but there's little sign that his profit margins were any better on the smaller-run publications he issued thereafter; they simply required less initial funding to get off the ground. In the early 1970s he nearly ceased his ufological publishing entirely, shifting his attention to the businesses that were actually enabling him to pay his bills—Lovett & Co. and Cinema V.[2] His national magazine contributions in the latter 1970s represent an effort to broaden his audience, but these writings produced scarcely a ripple in the wider world of ufology. Saucers were an expensive hobby, and his business was intended primarily to help him recoup what he could of his losses.

James Lewis offers a more accurate characterization, that Barker "considered himself an entertainer and folklorist rather than a factual reporter."[3] This assessment comes across as a dismissal, implying that Barker was *merely* a spinner of tales, and that those tales are of little import if he did not consider them to be occulted truths. And yet his influence is enormous, albeit scarcely traceable, affecting the rhetoric of UFO literature more than its substance. (One sign of this hidden influence: the issue of *UFO Magazine* containing Hall's condemnation of Barker as a "pure opportunist" has a cover story promising to reveal the strange but true story of the Men in Black.)[4]

As a storyteller Barker utilizes a rhetorical style calculated to draw in an audience. One key aspect of Barker's authorial style is the use of abrupt, unresolved endings, like those of ghost stories or campfire legends. His conclusions frequently leave the reader in a place of tension, compounded through the use of second-person narration to directly involve the audience in the narrative. The concluding sentences of *They Knew Too Much*, for example, leave the reader waiting for a sinister apparition:

> I have a feeling that some day there will come a slow knocking at my own door.
>
> They will be at your door, too, unless we all get wise and find out who the three men really are.[5]

The closing of *M.I.B.* recapitulates this conclusion, at greater length and with far less subtlety:

> Maybe you have read something in this book, added this to knowledge you already had, and then got creative and started to put some pieces together! You suddenly may have developed a theory of your own which might really expose the Men In Black and reveal what they are really up to!
>
> This may be why you hear the little creaks in the hallway just outside your room. Oh yes, you say, it's just the old house settling. But could it be—yes it could be, secret footsteps creeping toward your door, ready to burst it open with a phantasm of horror that could turn your hair white overnight!
>
> And what about the light you've noticed down in the alley? Isn't it too bright to be automobile headlights?
>
> What about the sing-song voice, muted intermittently by the wind that threatens to tear your house apart!
>
> Oh yes, you say, "It's my old man's voice. He's coming home late as usual tonight, and he's had a few too many. It's his car lights, not a UFO!"

There you go, spoiling things for me! But even if you protest, I know you dare not look outside. And did you notice the peculiar chill in your room—often associated with psychic phenomena, and sometimes with UFO and MIB!

Pull the covers up more tightly around your neck, dear reader. Put this book on the bedside stand.

Remember, if you don't know too much, there is nothing to worry about.

OTHERWISE THE MIB WILL GET YOU IF YOU DON'T WATCH OUT![6]

Barker's apparent intention with this conclusion is not to spur the audience to better research but to frighten them. In an interview Barker's nephews Jimmy and Joe commented that their uncle "liked scary things" and that he would often dress up like a monster or stage fake murder scenes "to scare us kids."[7] The same impulse guided Barker's writing: to provide entertainment through fright.

MIB FROM "SECRET TERROR" TO "GALAXY DEFENDERS"

The Men in Black remain Barker's most notable and lasting legacy in both ufology and popular culture. The 1980 film *Hangar 18*, which identifies its nameless government agents tasked with silencing UFO witnesses as "MIB," may be the first big-screen appearance of Barker's saucer silencers.[8] A pair of far more alien Men in Black feature in the 1984 film *The Brother from Another Planet*, an allegorical satire directed by John Sayles. The two MIB, played by David Strathairn and Sayles himself, are bizarre detectives tasked with tracking down the eponymous, fugitive alien. They communicate with one another in batlike, electronic screeches, and they move strangely, a result of Sayles filming several of their scenes backwards.[9] A farcical take on the MIB appears in the 1996 *X-Files* episode "Jose Chung's 'From Outer Space,'" in which a comical pair of black-suited silencers are portrayed by professional wrestler Jesse Ventura and *Jeopardy* host Alex Trebek.[10] In this metafictional episode, FBI agents Fox Mulder and Dana Scully—themselves described at several points in the series as Men in Black—attempt an investigation of an alien abduction in which no narrator is reliable and every event is depicted from multiple conflicting and absurd points of view. Barker would have loved it.

The culmination of the Men in Black as a pop cultural phenomenon came in 1997 with the release of the film *Men in Black*. The film is based, rather loosely, on a comic book miniseries by Lowell Cunningham and Sandy Carruthers that was first published in 1990 by indie comics publisher Aircel. The comic book presents a pair of violent secret agents tasked, in their first storyline, with fighting against demons, drug-smuggling satanists, and insectoid alien monsters. In an interview in the first issue, Cunningham explains that he had sought to separate the MIB from the context of UFOs entirely: "Anything that could upset the normal flow of society should attract their attention . . . [and] I thought UFOs every issue might get boring after a while."[11] The film, directed by Barry Sonnenfeld, disregards this shift in focus, placing the MIB squarely back in alien territory. But their nature is vastly different from that depicted in Barker's accounts and their direct heirs. Rather than being sinister and intimidating figures, the eponymous figures in *Men in Black* are "galaxy defenders" tasked with guarding the privacy of a plethora of extraterrestrial beings living in secrecy on Earth—and, when needed, with protecting Earth from alien threats. Instead of intimidating witnesses into silence, they use a high-tech device to erase inconvenient memories and ensure that no one knows too much—a procedure that is generally played for laughs. The film's success led to three sequels and a Saturday morning cartoon.

The MIB metanarrative became multivalent following Keel's revival of interest in it. Folklorist Peter Rojcewicz contextualized MIB narratives with pre-UFO legends of black-clad strangers, particularly those related to the devil; David Halperin similarly identifies analogues to the Bender Mystery in early modern narratives.[12] Keel's interpretation emphasized strange and otherworldly behavior, and many MIB narratives have picked up this thread, attributing unearthly abilities like telepathy and telekinesis to the sometimes-trio.[13] The conspiracist facet of the metanarrative remains, however: in a 2005 interview, actor and enthusiast of the paranormal Dan Aykroyd suggested that his television show *Out There* was canceled due to interference from MIB.[14]

Recent compilations of MIB narratives acknowledge Barker's role in inventing the core metanarrative that is their subject. Nick Redfern notes that our ideas about the Men in Black "as derived from the works of Barker and Keel should be viewed through careful filters."[15] But divorcing the metanarrative from these key sources is impossible.

Barker's conception of the Men in Black produced monstrous figures that became lasting cultural phantoms. William Clements argues that the existence of all such monsters "menaces the culture's system of distinctions, the categories of the universe which the culture has created."[16] But such challenges to cultural boundaries can be as much a function of humor as of horror: both the jester and the ogre upend our ordering of the world. Thus, the connotation change of the Men in Black may not be so absurd. Commenting on the film *Men in Black* in 1998, Barker's correspondent and Saucerian author John Sherwood commented on the shift of MIB from objects of terror and suspicion to humor: "That's appropriate, because so much of it really is a huge joke. And that weird laughter you hear is coming from Gray Barker's grave."[17]

The Philadelphia Experiment has a legacy as well, and has undergone further mutations. The changes are largely the work of author Al Bielek, who claimed in 1990 to have witnessed the original experiment—though his memories of the event were suppressed, unlocked only by a viewing of Roger Corman's 1984 film.[18] But far from being a novice to the topic in 1984, Bielek had long been interested in Jessup and Allende. A 1962 letter from Riley Crabb names Bielek as a Philadelphia Experiment enthusiast, proving that he was deeply invested in the metanarrative more than twenty years before his alleged epiphany.[19] In the early 1990s, author Preston Nichols elaborated even further on Bielek's version of the metanarrative, proposing that the experiment was linked to a series of even more bizarre experiments at a government laboratory at Montauk, at the easternmost tip of Long Island.[20] With each new iteration, the story that had emerged from Allende's pen became ever stranger.

The monsters whose narratives Barker helped popularize are now tamed: both the Mothman and the Flatwoods Monster, redubbed "Braxxie," are now the subject of museums–*cum*–visitors' centers that drive tourism—patron monsters of a tourist economy.[21] For West Virginia poet Robert Wood Lynn, the Mothman has become a symbol for the uniqueness, the forgottenness, the tragedy of the Mountain State. His book *Mothman Apologia* intersperses poems with titles like "(The Mothman Leaves the Used Car Lot Empty-Handed)" and "(The Mothman Picks Up a Misdemeanor)" with a series of "Elegies for Fire and Oxycodone," which explores the impact of the opioid epidemic on the residents of West Virginia.[22] The cultural legacy of the Mothman is filtered chiefly through the lens of Keel's *Mothman Prophecies* rather than Barker's more limited explorations. But Barker's influence is present, if camouflaged, in the 2002 film adaptation of Keel's book, directed by Mark Pellington.[23] A central scene in the film concerns the protagonist, reporter John Klein, receiving a strange phone call from "Indrid Cold"—no longer Derenberger's kindly space contact, now an undefinable paranormal presence. Though the details of the scene differ greatly, its apparent inspiration is the strange call Keel reported receiving from a robotic voice identifying itself as Gray Barker. With similar subtlety, the individual first contacted by Indrid Cold in the film is a psychologically fragile man named Gordon Smallwood—the pseudonym Barker had used for Laimon Mitris in *They Knew Too Much*. The laughter from the grave continues.

TRUTH AND FICTION IN SAUCER LITERATURE

The intended fright in Barker's unresolved endings as well as his pranks on his nephews hinges on a tension between reality and fiction: Was that ketchup splashed on Barker as he lay motionless in bed, or blood? Would the Men in Black really show up at the reader's door if their research succeeded in uncovering the secret, or is that just a story? It couldn't be true . . . or could it?

This lack of resolution is a definitive part of certain kinds of folk literature. Jan Harold Brunvand notes that this kind of ending is a key part of legends and folktales about shocking and unusual events: "The abrupt, unresolved ending leaves open the possibilities of what 'really happened.'"[24] Ashley Lister, discussing first-person narratives of ghost encounters, notes that "the narrator, typically, wants to leave the audience with a lingering feeling of unease. The absence of a coda . . . means the audience are left in a supernatural story that could be perceived as continuing."[25] The lack of resolution leaves the audience in suspense, but also blurs the line between reality and fiction by leaving people unsure where they stand in relation to the narrative: "The audience is not being given explicit instructions for how to escape the supernatural world of the narrative."[26] Lister views this narrative indeterminism as a source of fear, but Susan Lepselter sees further dialectical possibilities: "The uncanny story denaturalizes dominant histories, imagining ghostly pasts and potential futures in elaborated discourses of nostalgia and apocalypse. But the story's endings are not predetermined. Out of such longings emerge restriction and possibility, containment and freedom, and license to imagine."[27] Barker's early poem "Behold the Behemouth" gestures at this sense of freedom, positing that describing oddities has a self-transformative purpose:

Because things like this
Sound like they do strange things
to people when they say them.[28]

This tension is at the core of both oral folk legends and paranormal literature. Bill Ellis notes the ambiguity at play between truth and fiction in certain kinds of belief-legend and folktale. Speaking of a summer camp horror story, Ellis identifies a paradoxical tension in both the telling and reception of the story:

Yes, ostensibly the narrator and his audience regard the story as true, and, yes, their actions show they do not take it seriously. Such narratives are neither "real" legends nor tales but narratives deliberately designed to fit the gray area between. . . . Legends actually believed and told as literally true may be stylistically similar to legends meant as fiction and told to an audience that demands the illusion of strict realism. In such cases the actual nature of the narrative is determined, not by its style, nor by its content, nor even by the teller's degree of belief, but *by the audience's perception of the narrative in context.*[29]

Tanner Boyle places literature of the paranormal into a similarly ambiguous category he terms *maybe-fiction,* defined by its tension with observable reality.[30] A narrative that is maybe-*fact* can be simply wrong, but one that is maybe-*fiction* is placed in an ambiguously negative relationship with reality, leaving the audience questioning not whether the story is false but whether it could be true. The distinction is subtle, but powerful. The tension is negotiated in intertextual interactions and also in communication between narrator and audience. Barker's paeans to Bethurum and Rampa suggest an infatuation with this mode of literature, which invites the reader into an alternative reality by presenting the impossible not merely as possible, but as *already present*.

In a letter to *Saucer Smear* following Barker's death, John Keel expressed exasperation at Barker's fictionalization of Mothman narratives in *The Silver Bridge*: "I asked him then what sense of mischief was driving him and why he presented a novel as non-fiction. He answered me with jokes."[31] For Keel these were true stories, and Barker's fast-and-loose attitude toward presenting them was baffling. But far from placing Barker beyond the pale of paranormal investigation, the authorial processes of elision, conflation, and fabrication were and remain commonplace in Fortean writing (Boyle's "maybe-fiction"), arguably even forming one of the genre's defining characteristics: it is deeply resistant to letting the facts get in the way of a good story.[32]

On the other side, the "scientific" approach to ufology, which frequently seeks to reduce witness narratives to narratologically neutral "data," requires casting aside details from witnesses' actual descriptions of what they saw. Keel's insistence that his 1970 book *Operation Trojan Horse* emerged from treating UFO reports as scientific data reflects this impulse. His yearlong task of "sorting this great mass of material, categorizing it, and boiling it down into valid statistical form" in fact means taking that so-called data—much of which was already filtered through the agendas of either newspaper reporters or UFO investigators—out of its narrative context and constructing a new, metanarrative context by excising details.[33] The same impulse to transform narratives into data became the guiding principle behind the Center for UFO Studies (CUFOS), founded in 1973 by former Project Blue Book investigator J. Allen Hynek. Throughout the 1970s CUFOS published a series of summary reports that reduced hundreds of micronarratives into rows on a spreadsheet, shorn of context.[34]

Though he briefly toyed with using computer programs to analyze UFO sightings in the 1970s, Barker quickly abandoned the approach in favor of a more narrative method.[35] Barker's particular blend of fact, fiction, and audience interaction can be read as a form of *kayfabe*—a term originating in carnival speak now most often used in the world of professional wrestling.[36] *Kayfabe* refers to the taboo against a carnival performer breaking character or acknowledging the fakery behind the performance. But the term reflects a mutual relationship between the performer, who implies a particular reality, and the audience, which infers an interpretation of what has been presented. The same compatible collaboration occurs in the interplay between Barker (as author and publisher) and the ufological reader. Rarely does Barker declare that a narrative is simply true. Far more often he uses hedging language, distancing himself from assertions about the truth of any specific claims.[37] The headlines on his advertising materials are frequently questions rather than statements of fact: "Did Dr. Bernard vanish into the Inner Earth?," "'Longevity seeds' from outer space?," "Have space people communicated with Earth?"[38] Barker's hoaxing ancestor P. T. Barnum similarly avoided truth claims, instead promoting his attractions as controversial; he chose to invite, rather than discourage, his audience's doubts.[39] As Kevin Young summarizes, Barnum told his audiences: "You're smart, or better yet, you think you're so smart: *come see and decide for yourself.* He made everyone an expert."[40] Like Barnum, Barker never explicitly states his own belief: he frames himself as an unbiased facilitator who merely presents the evidence, a predecessor of the post-truth internet's "just asking questions."

Barker's place in ufological history is primarily that of a storyteller, and Lewis's appraisal of him as a "folklorist" suggests that this must mean a bounded reach, a perpetual grain of salt. But Barker understood, perhaps better than any other figure in "The Field," that stories are what really matter. His style—vivid, breathless, anxious, ambiguous—influenced the writing of those that followed him far more than the dry prose of more "scientific" UFO authors. Barker told stories, and there is surely cause to doubt the factual basis of many—even all—of them. But UFOs are, after all, stories: stories that researchers tell to readers, that witnesses tell to investigators, and that human minds tell to themselves. They're all stories: And stories like these do strange things to people when they tell them.

Acknowledgments

When I began the project that became this book over a decade ago, I had no idea that my idle hobby of assembling a spreadsheet listing the weird books put out by a publisher in West Virginia would eventually grow into the present work. This transformation would not have been possible without the assistance of many people who have supported and guided the research behind it.

Above all, I am indebted to David Houchin of the Clarksburg-Harrison Public Library, who has been a stalwart caretaker of the Gray Barker UFO Collection for over two decades. David shared the many wonders of this archive with me, including his original, enormously in-depth research, with generosity, kindness, and patience. Of comparable excellence is the staff of the Archives for the Unexplained, including Anders Liljegren and Leif Åstrand, who were extraordinarily generous with scans and digital photographs (thus saving me the expense of traveling to to Sweden—though their library certainly seems worth the trip). Thanks are also due to Stewart Plein and Lemley Mullett of the West Virginia and Regional History Center at the University of West Virginia at Morgantown, and to the New York Public Library's Manuscripts and Archives Division, which houses the archive of ufologist Ted Bloecher. I am also grateful to those who knew Barker and shared their memories of him: John Sherwood, Richard Wilt, Sharon Stump, Allen H. Greenfield, and one other who wishes to remain anonymous.

This work was supported in many ways by the New York University Division of Libraries, not only through access to secondary research materials but also through a generous Goddard Junior Faculty Fellowship that supported travel, research materials, and much-needed time.

My thanks are also due to Jack Womack, whose collection of flying saucer books first introduced me to Gray Barker's strange world, and Michael P. Daley, whose persistent encouragement was essential in seeing the work through to completion (and whose monumental biographical experiment, *Bobby BlueJacket: The Tribe, the Joint, the Tulsa Underworld*, served as an inspiration). I am especially grateful to Erik Davis, who kindly put me in touch with Matthew Browne at the MIT Press, who saw potential in my project. My wonderful MIT Press team—Anthony Zannino, Deborah Cantor-Adams, Janice Audet, Lorelei Horrell, and Nicholas DiSabatino—have been invaluable in guiding it into its final form. Kristen Holt Browning and Lily Burana both provided excellent editorial assistance that reduced the pain of the revision process significantly.

I am also thankful to all those who assisted me in locating and accessing materials, responded to my email inquiries, or just talked with me about the project, including David Halperin, Doug Teifel (@dark_siege_), Doug Skinner (johnkeel.com), Isaac Koi (isaackoiup.blogspot.com), Erik A. W. Östling, Joseph Laycock, Natasha Mikles, Joe Vergolina, Rachel Herschman, Aaron Gulyas (saucerlife.com), Jeffrey J. Kripal, Theo Paijmans, William J. Dewan, Michael David Strayer (a.k.a. Mothboy Mike), Robert Goerman, Bryan Cipolla, Julie Carlsen, David Ratzan, Kate Thomson, and Shannon Monroe.

My utmost thanks are reserved for my best editor and eternal partner, Gwynne Watkins, who tolerated the stacks of books I have left in various places around our house for the past few years, and was kind enough to tell me when my first draft wasn't a book yet.

Notes

INTRODUCTION

1. *UFO* (Showtime, August 22, 2021), 5:20, https://www.sho.com/ufo/season/1/episode/3/103.

2. The list of UFO reports and publications including this phrase, or variations on it, is too extensive to cite; the phrase provided the title of a 2009 History Channel documentary on the subject (*I Know What I Saw*).

3. Michael P. Daley, "Concerning the Discovery, Taxonomic Implications, & Initial Impressions of a Whispering Mold," in *Echoes of a Natural World: Tales of the Strange & Estranged*, ed. Michael P. Daley (Chicago, IL: First To Knock, 2020), 46.

4. According to Joseph Blake, "The UFO experience . . . is essentially an altered state of consciousness, akin to dreams, trances, hypnagogic and hypnonomic phenomena." Joseph A. Blake, "Ufology: The Intellectual Development and Social Context of the Study of Unidentified Flying Objects," in *On the Margins of Science: The Social Construction of Rejected Knowledge*, ed. Roy Wallis (Keele: University of Keele, 1979), 323. On the question of nonfalsifiability, see Colin Dickey, *The Unidentified: Mythical Monsters, Alien Encounters, and Our Obsession with the Unexplained* (New York: Viking, 2020), 273–274.

5. On the "unconscious and general conception of what the extranormal, extraterrestrial 'should' be like," see Virginia A. P. Lowe, "A Brief Look at Some UFO Legends," *Indiana Folklore* 12, no. 1 (1979): 71.

6. Jack Womack, *Flying Saucers Are Real!: The UFO Library of Jack Womack*, ed. Michael P. Daley, Johan Kugelberg, and Gabriel Mckee (New York: Anthology Editions, 2016), 157.

7. For similar summaries of the narrative aspects of UFOs, see Keith Thompson, *Angels and Aliens: UFOs and the Mythic Imagination* (Reading, MA: Addison-Wesley / William Patrick, 1991), 36–37; Benson Saler, Charles A. Ziegler, and Charles B. Moore, *UFO Crash at Roswell: The Genesis of a Modern Myth* (Washington, DC: Smithsonian Institution, 1997), 30.

8. On this process, see Thomas E. Bullard, *The Myth and Mystery of UFOs* (Lawrence: University Press of Kansas, 2010), 10–11, https://muse.jhu.edu/book/48323; Diana G. Tumminia, "From Rumor to Postmodern Myth: A Sociological Study of the Transformation of Flying Saucer Rumor," in *Encyclopedic Sourcebook of UFO Religions*, ed. James R. Lewis (Amherst, NY: Prometheus Books, 2003), 103–119. For a similar narrative process describing alien abduction narratives specifically, see Scott R. Scribner, "Alien Abduction Narratives: A Proposed Model and Brief Case Study," in *The Supernatural in Society, Culture, and History*, ed. Dennis D. Waskul and Marc A. Eaton (Philadelphia: Temple University Press, 2018), 219–222.

9. In using such metaphors, I deliberately avoid referring to the terminology of "memetics" proposed in Richard Dawkins, *The Selfish Gene*, 40th anniversary ed., Oxford Landmark Science (Oxford: Oxford University Press, 2016), 245–251. Elliott Oring has provided a detailed explanation of the limited applicability of memetics to folklore; see Elliott Oring, "Memetics and Folkloristics: The Theory," *Western Folklore* 73, no. 4 (2014): 432–454, https://www.jstor.org/stable/24551136; Elliott Oring, "Memetics and Folkloristics: The Applications," *Western Folklore* 73, no. 4 (2014): 455–492, https://www.jstor.org/stable/24551137; see also Adam Kuper, "If Memes Are the Answer, What Is the Question?," in *Darwinizing Culture: The Status of Memetics as a Science*, ed. Robert Aunger (Oxford: Oxford University Press, 2000), 174–188, https://doi.org/10.1093/acprof:oso/9780192632449.003.0009. For a use of biological terminology in folkloristics independent of Dawkins, see Barre Toelken, *The Dynamics of Folklore*, rev. and expanded ed. (Logan: Utah State University Press, 1996), 47–49.

10. On the dissemination of folklore in general and paranormal narratives in particular, see Lauri Honko, "Memorates and the Study of Folk Beliefs," *Journal of the Folklore Institute* 1, no. 1 (1964): 5–19; Linda Dégh, "UFO's and How Folklorists Should Look at Them," *Fabula* 18 (1977): 242–48, https://doi.org/10.1515/fabl.1977.18.1.242; David J. Hufford, *The Terror That Comes in the Night: An Experience-Centered Study of Supernatural Assault Traditions* (Philadelphia: University of Pennsylvania Press, 1982); Linda Dégh and Andrew Vázsonyi, "Does the Word 'Dog' Bite? Ostensive Action: A Means of Legend Telling," *Journal of Folklore Research* 20, no. 1 (January 1983): 5–34; Linda Dégh, *American Folklore and the Mass Media* (Bloomington: Indiana University Press, 1994), 20; Linda Dégh, *Legend and Belief: Dialectics of a Folklore Genre* (Bloomington: Indiana University Press, 2001); Bill Ellis, *Aliens, Ghosts, and Cults: Legends We Live* (Jackson: University Press of Mississippi, 2003); William J. Dewan, "Occam's Beard: Belief, Disbelief, and Contested Meanings in American Ufology," PhD diss., University of New Mexico, 2010, https://digitalrepository.unm.edu/amst_etds/10; Shira Chess and Eric Newsom, *Folklore, Horror Stories, and the Slender Man: The Development of an Internet Mythology* (New York: Palgrave Macmillan, 2014), https://doi.org/10.1057/9781137491138.

11. Mark Featherstone, *Knowledge and the Production of Nonknowledge: An Exploration of Alien Mythology in Postwar America* (Cresskill, NJ: Hampton, 2002), 4.

12. Carl Wilhelm von Sydow, "The Categories of Prose Tradition," in *Selected Papers on Folklore: Published on the Occasion of His 70th Birthday*, by Carl Wilhelm von Sydow, ed. Laurits Bødker (Copenhagen: Rosenkilde and Bagger, 1948), 87. Dégh cautions that von Sydow's definition of these and related terms were somewhat unstable (Dégh, *Legend and Belief*, 35).

13. On the definition of *legend*, see Herbert Halpert, "Definition and Variation in Folk Legend," in *American Folk Legend: A Symposium*, ed. Wayland D. Hand (Berkeley: University of California Press, 1971), 47–54; Robert A. Georges, "The General Concept of Legend: Some Assumptions to Be Reexamined and Reassessed," in *American Folk Legend: A Symposium*, ed. Wayland D. Hand (Berkeley: University of California Press, 1971), 1–20; Gillian Bennett, "Legend: Performance and Truth," in *Monsters with Iron Teeth*, ed. Gillian Bennett and Paul

Smith (Sheffield: Sheffield Academic Press, 1988), 13–36; on the field investigator, see Bullard, *Myth and Mystery*, xv.

14. Susan Lepselter, *The Resonance of Unseen Things: Poetics, Power, Captivity, and UFOs in the American Uncanny* (Ann Arbor: University of Michigan Press, 2016), 4, https://doi.org/10 .3998/mpub.7172850; Thompson, *Angels and Aliens*, 15.

15. For similar approaches to UFO literature using different terminology, see Lepselter, *Resonance of Unseen Things*; Thompson, *Angels and Aliens*; Curtis Peebles, *Watch the Skies! A Chronicle of the Flying Saucer Myth* (Washington, DC: Smithsonian Institution, 1994).

16. Saler, Ziegler, and Moore, *UFO Crash at Roswell*, esp. 1–73.

17. Works focusing on the oral exchange of UFO narratives include Lepselter, *Resonance of Unseen Things*; Dewan, "Occam's Beard."

18. On such mediation, see Diana Walsh Pasulka, *American Cosmic: UFOs, Religions, Technology* (Oxford: Oxford University Press, 2019), 100; Dewan, "Occam's Beard," 245.

19. In her review of alien abduction narratives, Bridget Brown notes that the initiatory event for many experiencers occurs through "an act of reading." Bridget Brown, *They Know Us Better than We Know Ourselves: The History and Politics of Alien Abduction* (New York: NYU Press, 2007), 178, https://doi.org/10.18574/nyu/9780814739174.001.0001.

20. Saler, Ziegler, and Moore, *UFO Crash at Roswell*, 35.

21. William J. Dewan, "'A Saucerful of Secrets': An Interdisciplinary Analysis of UFO Experiences," *Journal of American Folklore* 119, no. 472 (2006): 186, http://www.jstor.org/stable /4137923.

22. On the definitions of these fields of study, see G. Thomas Tanselle, *Literature and Artifacts* (Charlottesville: Bibliographical Society of the University of Virginia, 1998), esp. 50; Robert Darnton, "What Is the History of Books?," in *The Book History Reader*, ed. David Finkelstein and Alistair McCleery (1982; repr., London: Routledge, 2002), 9–26.

23. See, for example, Elizabeth L. Eisenstein, *The Printing Press as an Agent of Change: Communications and Cultural Transformations in Early-Modern Europe*, combined paperback ed. (Cambridge: Cambridge University Press, 1980); Marshall McLuhan, *The Gutenberg Galaxy: The Making of Typographic Man* (1962; repr., Toronto: University of Toronto Press, 2011).

24. Ian Batterham has provided an indispensable guide to copying techniques, but focuses mainly on the processes themselves and says little about their broader cultural impact. Ian Batterham, *The Office Copying Revolution: History, Identification and Preservation* (Canberra: National Archives of Australia, 2008).

25. Tom Lind, *The Catalogue of UFO Periodicals*, Said of Saucers Research Publications (Hobe Sound, FL: privately printed by the author, 1982), i.

26. Gérard Genette, *Paratexts: Thresholds of Interpretation*, trans. Jane E. Lewin (Cambridge: Cambridge University Press, 1997), 1.

27. Jonathan Gray cautions against making too clean a distinction between text and paratext, but still argues for the usefulness of the term. Jonathan Gray, "Afterword: Studying Media with and without Paratexts," in *Popular Media Cultures: Fans, Audiences and Paratexts*, ed. Lincoln Geraghty (Houndmills: Palgrave Macmillan, 2015), 233, https://doi.org/10.1057/9781137350374_12.

28. Jerome J. McGann, *The Textual Condition* (Princeton, NJ: Princeton University Press, 1991), 56, https://doi.org/10.1515/9780691217758.

29. David J. Halperin, *Intimate Alien: The Hidden Story of the UFO* (Stanford, CA: Stanford University Press, 2020), 150, https://doi.org/10.1515/9781503612129. The documentaries are *Shades of Gray: A True Story* (Seminal Films, 2010); and *Whispers from Space* ([West Virginia?]: The Last Prom, 1995).

30. Barkun defines "stigmatized knowledge" as "claims to truth that the claimants regard as verified despite the marginalization of those claims by the institutions that conventionally distinguish between knowledge and error." Michael Barkun, *A Culture of Conspiracy: Apocalyptic Visions in Contemporary America*, Comparative Studies in Religion and Society (Berkeley: University of California Press, 2003), 26.

31. Barkun, *Culture of Conspiracy*, 28; see also Brenda Denzler, *The Lure of the Edge: Scientific Passions, Religious Beliefs, and the Pursuit of UFOs* (Berkeley: University of California Press, 2001), 90, https://doi.org/10.1525/9780520930278. For a detailed early-modern case study, see Lorenzo Montemagno Ciseri, "Can Failing to Check Sources Give Rise to Monsters? The Iconographical History of a Paradigmatic Case," *Preternature: Critical and Historical Studies on the Preternatural* 2, no. 2 (2013): 139, https://doi.org/10.5325/preternature.2.2.0139; for a distinctly ufological one, see Paul C. W. Davies, "The Piri-Reis Map: Fact and Fiction," *Flying Saucer Review* 18, no. 2 (April 1972): 21–23.

CHAPTER 1

1. On the history of West Virginia generally, see Stephen W. Brown and Otis K. Rice, *West Virginia: A History*, 2nd ed. (Lexington: University Press of Kentucky, 1993), chaps. 1–5, https://muse.jhu.edu/book/671; Roxanne Dunbar-Ortiz, *An Indigenous Peoples' History of the United States* (Boston: Beacon, 2014), chap. 4; Alexander Scott Withers, *Chronicles of Border Warfare, or, A History of the Settlement by the Whites, of North-Western Virginia; and of the Indian Wars and Massacres, in That Section of the State; with Reflections, Anecdotes, &c.* (Clarksburg, WV: Joseph Israel, 1831), https://n2t.net/ark:/13960/t2q59506z; John Davison Sutton, *History of Braxton County and Central West Virginia* (Sutton, WV: privately printed by the author, 1919), https://n2t.net/ark:/13960/t44q8z189; Henry Haymond, *History of Harrison County, West Virginia: From the Early Days of Northwestern Virginia to the Present* (Morgantown, WV: Acme, 1910), https://n2t.net/ark:/13960/t8gf12020.

2. "George E. Barker (10 November 1871–1 April 1950)," Family Search, 2022.

3. Sutton, *History of Braxton County*, 216.

4. "George E. Barker (10 November 1871–1 April 1950)."

5. "Marie Barker," September 12, 1922, West Virginia Deaths, 1804–1999.

6. "Henry Graceland Barker," November 8, 1922, West Virginia Deaths, 1804–1999.

7. E.g., Antoinette Long, "Rosa Lee Barker (Frame)," Geni, May 24, 2018, https://www.geni.com/people/Rosa-Barker/6000000076892853875.

8. Gray Barker to Jacqueline Sanders, November 24, 1956, Folder "Sanders, Jacqueline—1956," GBC.

9. Barker to Sanders, November 24, 1956, 4. Exchange's small town center was abandoned after the railroad ceased operating in the 1960s. Adam Burns, "Elk River Railroad," American-Rails.com, January 12, 2024, https://www.american-rails.com/elk.html; Bob Weaver, "'Exchange' Faded from Glory: Braxton Ghost Town," Hur Herald, February 23, 2024, https://www.hurherald.com/obits.php?id=74926.

10. Barker to Sanders, November 24, 1956, 4–5.

11. Gray Barker, "Reflection: About the Author," *The Saucerian* 2, no. 1 (whole no. 3) (February 1954): 28.

12. Gray Barker to Jacqueline Sanders, March 30, 1959, 1, Folder "Sanders, Jacqueline—1959," GBC.

13. "Pupil's Monthly and Term Report Card: Gray Barker," March 23, 1933, Barker chronology folder, GBC.

14. Barker to Sanders, November 24, 1956, 4.

15. Barker to Sanders, November 24, 1956, 4.

16. Barker to Sanders, November 24, 1956, 4.

17. Rose [i.e., Gray] Barker, "The Lady in White," *Fate* 9, no. 7 (whole no. 76) (July 1956): 103. Barker informed Sanders that he wrote and published this brief account of the narrative under his mother's name. The dates in "The Lady in White" do not entirely line up with public records; Florence's death is recorded in 1900, but it was Lela who was born in that year, not Walter. Gray Barker to Jacqueline Sanders, [June 9–10, 1956?], 1, Folder "Sanders, Jacqueline—Special letters," GBC.

18. "History of GSC," Glenville State College, 2022, https://www.glenville.edu/about-us/history-gsc.

19. "Barker, Gray," *Who's Who among Students in American Universities and Colleges* 12 (1945–1946): 30, https://graybarker.wordpress.com/2017/03/30/gray-barker-in-whos-who-among-students.

20. "Semester Enrollment down; Night, Extension Students Will Boost Semester Total," *Glenville Mercury*, September 29, 1942, 1.

21. "Freshmen Get into 'Swing of Things' and Start Careers in Higher Education," *Glenville Mercury*, September 26, 1944, 1.

22. H. Bailey, "On the Campus," *Glenville Mercury*, January 22, 1946, 4.

23. "Gray Roscoe Barker," May 2, 1943, U.S., World War II Draft Cards Young Men, 1940–1947; Gray Barker, "Qualification Record [Loan Application]," April 12, 1962, 2, Barker chronology folder, GBC. On homosexuality and the draft, see John D'Emilio, *Sexual Politics, Sexual Communities: The Making of a Homosexual Minority in the United States, 1940–1970*, 2nd ed (Chicago: University of Chicago Press, 1998), 24–25.

24. "Braxton Students Organize Club Here," *Glenville Mercury*, October 27, 1942, 4; "Canterbury Club Has Four New Members," *Glenville Mercury*, February 23, 1943, 4; "Ohnimgohows Initiate 12 Pledges Wednesday," *Glenville Mercury*, January 19, 1943, 4.

25. Gray Barker, "Blindness Isn't Keeping This College Soph from Working toward Goal," *Glenville Mercury*, November 17, 1942, 1, 3.

26. "Campus Capers," *Glenville Mercury*, February 16, 1943, 2.

27. "Evelyn Finster . . . ," *Glenville Mercury*, May 30, 1944, 4; "Heckert Heads 'YM' Chapter on Campus," *Glenville Mercury*, October 17, 1944, 1.

28. Eunice Wilfong, "Freshman Ohnimgohow Pledge Scores with Parody on 'Man with the Hoe,'" *Glenville Mercury*, January 19, 1943, 4; "Ohnimgohows Initiate."

29. "'Glenville Smirkury' Makes Debut at April Fools' Day Party Held Saturday," *Glenville Mercury*, April 4, 1944, 1.

30. "Minstrel, Fashion Show, Play, Songs, B'shop Quartet, Etc., in Big Variety Show to Be Presented Tomorrow at 8 PM," *Glenville Mercury*, April 30, 1946, 4; "White Masters Ceremonies for Show Featuring Vocals, Minstrel, Style," *Glenville Mercury*, May 7, 1946, 1.

31. "Nominated: King and Furr Typical G.S.C. 'Bouncers,'" *Glenville Mercury*, October 23, 1945, 3.

32. Gray Barker, "Some Ills of Film Instruction," *West Virginia School Journal* 74, no. 10 (May 1946): 5–6.

33. Gray Barker, "Believes in Flying Saucers," *Nicholas County News Leader*, September 15, 1954, 6.

34. Gray Barker, "Guest Editorial," *Flying Saucers*, no. 73 (June 1971): 3.

35. "Halloween Party in Science Hall Is a Major Highlight of Social Season," *Glenville Mercury*, November 7, 1944, 4.

36. "Nominated."

37. On the nature and history of spook shows generally, see Jim Knipfel, "Midnight Spook Shows: A Brief History," Den of Geek, October 29, 2014, https://www.denofgeek.com/movies/midnight-spook-shows-a-brief-history.

38. Gray Barker, "Mercury Musings," *Glenville Mercury*, February 6, 1945, 1.

39. Gray Barker, "The Campus at Night: A Description," *Glenville Mercury*, February 15, 1944, 3.

40. Barker donated a copy to Glenville's Robert F. Kidd Library, now in the collection of the West Virginia and Regional History Center at West Virginia University's Morgantown campus. Gray Barker, "Who Knows" (Typescript, 1946), P8921, West Virginia and Regional History Center, University of West Virginia at Morgantown, Printed Ephemera Collection.

41. Barker, "Who Knows," [11].

42. Barker, "Who Knows," [16].

43. Barker, "Who Knows," [6].

44. Barker, "Loan Application (4/12/1962)," 2. In an account of his past employment completed in 1962, Barker gives the dates of his employment for Howard County as April–December 1945, but this does not line up with his activities as reported at the time in the *Mercury* and appears to be a typographical error.

45. Gray Barker, "The Early Poems of Gray Barker, Edited by Alexander Queen" (Typescript, [1960?]), [40], Box "Moseley/Private Writings," GBC (emphasis original).

46. Barker, "Loan Application (4/12/1962)," 2. David Houchin speculates that Barker may have been fired due to his sexuality. David Houchin, personal communication with author, October 11, 2021.

47. *Whispers from Space*, 46:45.

48. "Exhibitor Turned Outdoors Sets Up 16mm Drive-In," *Boxoffice* 51, no. 8 (June 28, 1947): 88; Gray Barker to August C. Roberts, August 5, 1953, Folder "Roberts, August/Correspondence with Gray Barker," GBC.

49. Nina Craigo, "Screen Sketches," *Glenville Mercury*, May 13, 1947, 2; Barker to Roberts, August 5, 1953, 2. On the movie being shown, see "Pictureland Theater [Advertisement]," *Glenville Mercury*, May 6, 1947, 3.

50. Craigo, "Screen Sketches."

51. Barker to Roberts, August 5, 1953, 2.

52. Virginia Howell to Gray Barker, August 27, 1947, Folder "Lovett & Co.," GBC.

53. Kerry Segrave, *Drive-in Theaters: A History from Their Inception in 1933* (Jefferson, NC: McFarland, 2006), 235.

54. Segrave, *Drive-in Theaters*, 235.

55. Gray Barker to James W. Moseley, "The Hearing: Consisting of a Letter from Gig to Zo," [June 30–July 4, 1963?], 3, Box "Moseley/Private Writings," GBC.

56. Gray Barker, "Atomic Projection Made Easy in Ten Simple Lessons (Lesson I)," *Boxoffice/The Modern Theatre* 52, no. 13 (January 31, 1948): A44, A47.

57. Gray Barker, "On Cue: Easy Ways for Projectionists to End It All," *Boxoffice/The Modern Theatre* 53, no. 23 (October 9, 1948): A34.

58. For a brief summary of film distribution in the 1960s (and relevant to this period), see Richard W. Haines, *The Moviegoing Experience, 1968–2001* (Jefferson, NC: McFarland, 2003), 12–13.

59. Gray Barker to Ernest Garrett, December 21, 1953, Folder "G-1"; item G1-4-1, GBC. Garrett had just purchased the Pictureland Theater, where Barker had gotten his start as a projectionist, and Barker notes his personal interest in the venue.

60. Barker, "Loan Application (4/12/1962)," 2; Houchin, personal communication.

61. Charlotte Johnson, "George Elliott Barker," Find a Grave, March 26, 2017, https://www.findagrave.com/memorial/177786130/george-elliott-barker; Houchin, personal communication.

62. Gray Barker, "Chasing the Flying Saucers [No. 14]," *Flying Saucers*, no. 28 (FS-14) (February 1960): 16.

63. Unfortunately no copy of this publication survives in the Barker Collection, though it is mentioned in Gray Barker, *The Trip to the Moon: A Story* ([Clarksburg, WV]: [privately printed by the author], 1951), [2].

64. Barker, *Trip to the Moon*, [5].

65. Gray Barker to Cinema Research Corp., June 9, 1952, Folder "C-5," item C5-1-1, GBC; "Delbert Lovett Succumbs; Projection-Airer Veteran," *Boxoffice* 102, no. 25 (April 2, 1973): E-7.

66. Gray Barker to Dominick Lucchesi, August 24, 1953, Folder "Lucchesi, Dominick," GBC.

67. Barker to Roberts, August 5, 1953, 4.

68. "Drive-in Film Stampedes Cattle in Nearby Field," *Boxoffice* 55, no. 4 (May 28, 1949): 69.

69. "Drive-in Patrons View Extra Horror Picture," *Boxoffice* 58, no. 1 (November 4, 1950): 32; "Two British Showmen Win Bonus Awards for October," *Boxoffice* 58, no. 2 (November 11, 1950): 35.

70. Michelle Pautz, "The Decline in Average Weekly Cinema Attendance: 1930–2000," *Issues in Political Economy* 11 (2002): 14.

CHAPTER 2

1. There are numerous histories of the phenomena known as "unidentified flying objects," from which this brief account is summarized. The best are David Michael Jacobs, *The UFO Controversy in America* (Bloomington: Indiana University Press, 1975); and Peebles, *Watch the Skies*. For sheer depth, the unsurpassed record of unidentified flying objects from the beginning through the early 1960s is Loren E. Gross's *UFOs: A History*, a day-by-day annotated chronology of sightings from 1972 to 2008 and now available as a collection of over

one hundred PDFs from the Sign Oral History Project: Loren E. Gross, "UFOs: A History/ The Fifth Horseman of the Apocalypse," Sign Oral History Project, 2022, https://sohp.us /collections/ufos-a-history/. For the earliest period of saucer sightings, see Gordon B. Arnold, *Flying Saucers over America: The UFO Craze of 1947* (Jefferson, NC: McFarland, 2022); Ted Bloecher, *Report on the UFO Wave of 1947*, updated version (N.p.: NICAP, 2005), http:// kirkmcd.princeton.edu/JEMcDonald/bloecher_67.pdf.

2. Quoted in Peebles, *Watch the Skies*, 9.

3. Kenneth Arnold and Ray Palmer, *The Coming of the Saucers: A Documentary Report on Sky Objects that Have Mystified the World* (Boise, ID, and Amherst, WI: privately printed by the authors, 1952).

4. For detailed overviews of Shaver's and Palmer's careers, see Richard Toronto, *War over Lemuria: Richard Shaver, Ray Palmer and the Strangest Chapter of 1940s Science Fiction* (Jefferson, NC: McFarland, 2013); Fred Nadis, *The Man from Mars: Ray Palmer's Amazing Pulp Journey* (New York: Jeremy P. Tarcher / Penguin, 2013); see also Gabriel Mckee, "'Reality—Is It a Horror?': Richard Shaver's Subterranean World and the Displaced Self," *Journal of Gods and Monsters* 1 (Summer 2020): 1–17, https://doi.org/10.58997/jgm.v1i1.1.

5. Fred Crisman [as "ex-Capt. A.C."], "Encounter in the Caves," *Amazing Stories* 20, no. 3 (June 1946): 178, https://n2t.net/ark:/13960/t0sr1jk1m; Fred L. Crisman, "Report from Alaska," *Amazing Stories* 21, no. 5 (May 1947): 168, https://n2t.net/ark:/13960/t0jt51b57.

6. Andrew May, *Pseudoscience and Science Fiction* (Cham: Springer International, 2017), 46, https://doi.org/10.1007/978-3-319-42605-1.

7. Edward J. Ruppelt, *The Report on Unidentified Flying Objects*, 1st ed. (Garden City, NY: Doubleday, 1956), 37–39.

8. Charles Fort, *The Book of the Damned* (New York: Boni and Liveright, 1919), 7, https://n2t .net/ark:/13960/t3125rm6k; on Fort in general, see Jim Steinmeyer, *Charles Fort: The Man Who Invented the Supernatural* (New York: J. P. Tarcher / Penguin, 2008).

9. Kenneth Arnold, "I *Did* See the Flying Disks!," *Fate* 1, no. 1 (Spring 1948): 4–10, https:// s3.us-west-1.wasabisys.com/luminist/OC/FATE_1948_1.pdf.

10. See, e.g., Peebles, *Watch the Skies*, 1–3.

11. Jacobs, *UFO Controversy*, 50.

12. Sidney Shalett, "What You Can Believe about Flying Saucers, Part One," *Saturday Evening Post*, April 30, 1949, 20–21, 136–39; Sidney Shalett, "What You Can Believe about Flying Saucers, Conclusion," *Saturday Evening Post*, May 7, 1949, 36, 184–86, https://n2t.net/ark :/13960/t3wv17j74; see also Arnold, *Flying Saucers over America*, 147.

13. Donald Keyhoe, "Flying Saucers Are Real," *True Magazine*, January 1950, 11–13, 83–87, https:// www.saturdaynightuforia.com/library/fsartm/truemagazinetheflyingsaucersarcreal1950 .html; Donald Keyhoe, *The Flying Saucers Are Real* (New York: Fawcett Publications, 1950).

14. On the role of science fiction magazines in the spread of the ETH, see May, *Pseudoscience and Science Fiction*, 64–70.

15. Frank Scully, *Behind the Flying Saucers* (New York: Henry Holt, 1950).

16. Jerome Clark, *The UFO Encyclopedia: The Phenomenon from the Beginning*, 3rd ed. (Detroit, MI: Omnigraphics, 2018), 2:1044–1047 ("Scully Hoax").

17. H. B. Darrach Jr. and Robert Ginna, "Have We Visitors from Space?," *Life*, April 7, 1952, 80–96.

18. Peebles, *Watch the Skies*, 65.

19. Clark, *UFO Encyclopedia*, 1:496–497 ("Florida Scoutmaster Case").

20. Jacobs gives the date of this group's founding as 1952, but Clark places it in December 1951. See Jacobs, *UFO Controversy*, 84; Clark, *UFO Encyclopedia*, 1:241 ("Civilian Saucer Investigation").

21. Clark, *UFO Encyclopedia*, 1:49 ("Aerial Phenomena Research Organization").

22. Clark, *UFO Encyclopedia*, 1:623 ("International Flying Saucer Bureau").

23. The BSRA provided a fantastic explanation for an aerial sighting in 1946, making them an important precursor to the post-Arnold macronarrative. Meade Layne, "Welcome? Kareeta!," *Round Robin* 2, no. 10 (October 1946): 6, https://borderlandsciences.org/journal/vol/02/n10/Welcome_Kareeta.html).

24. "Flying Saucers Placed in Autos for 'Collide,'" *Boxoffice* 61, no. 20 (September 13, 1952): 213. Notably, the *Boxoffice* report on the promotion was published the same week as the Flatwoods sighting.

25. Quoted in Gray Barker, "W.V.A. 'Monster': A Full Report," *The Saucerian* 1, no. 1 (September 1953): 9, from which the account of Barker's investigation here is summarized.

26. Frank C. Feschino Jr., *The Braxton County Monster: The Cover-up of the Flatwoods Monster Revealed* (Charleston, WV: Quarrier, 2004), 7; Ivan T. Sanderson, *Uninvited Visitors: A Biologist Looks at UFO's* (New York: Cowles, 1967), 39.

27. Barker, "W.V.A. Monster," 17.

28. Gray Barker, "The Monster and the Saucer," *Fate* 6, no. 1 (January 1953): 12–17; Gray Barker to the British Interplanetary Society, December 5, 1952, Folder "B—Misc.," item B-15, GBC.

29. The letter is not present in Barker's archive, but is mentioned in Gray Barker, *They Knew Too Much about Flying Saucers* (New York: University Books, 1956), 65–66; and Albert K. Bender, *Flying Saucers and the Three Men*, ed. Gray Barker (Clarksburg, WV: Saucerian Books, 1962), 57; the notice to which Barker responded is Albert K. Bender, "The International Flying Saucer Bureau," *Other Worlds*, no. 24 (December 1952): 156, https://n2t.net/ark:/13960/s2xwgpsqvtn.

30. Johan Kugelberg, Jack Womack, and Michael P. Daley, eds., *The Tattooed Dragon Meets the Wolfman: Lenny Kaye's Science Fiction Fanzines 1941–1970* (New York: Boo-Hooray, 2014), [18].

31. Gary Hubbard, "Lettercolumn," *Trap Door*, no. 4 (May 1985): 25, https://fanac.org/fanzines /Trap_Door/Trap_Door04.pdf.

32. William Sims Bainbridge, *The Sociology of Religious Movements* (New York: Routledge, 1997), 378 (quotation marks removed); for thorough explorations of this phenomenon, see May, *Pseudoscience and Science Fiction*; Tanner F. Boyle, *The Fortean Influence on Science Fiction: Charles Fort and the Evolution of the Genre* (Jefferson, NC: McFarland, 2021).

33. On the earliest SF fanzines, see Sam Moskowitz, *The Immortal Storm: A History of Science Fiction Fandom* (1954; repr., Westport, CT: Hyperion, 1974), especially 8–17; see also Stephen Duncombe, *Notes from Underground: Zines and the Politics of Alternative Culture* (London: Verso, 1997), 6–7; Kugelberg, Womack, and Daley, *Tattooed Dragon*.

34. Gray Barker to Dean Grennell, January 26, 1955, 1, Folder "G-1"; item G1-62-1, GBC.

35. On Tucker's career in fandom, see Harry Warner, *All Our Yesterdays: An Informal History of Science Fiction Fandom in the 1940s*, ed. Joe D. Siclari (Framingham, MA: NESFA, 2004), 166–172; Harry Warner, *A Wealth of Fable: An Informal History of Science Fiction Fandom in the 1950s*, [2nd ed.] (Van Nuys, CA: Scifi, 1992), 74–76.

36. International Flying Saucer Bureau, "Directory of Representatives," *Space Review* 2, no. 1 (January 1953): 8, https://n2t.net/ark:/13960/t47q6zg7t.

CHAPTER 3

1. On the spirit duplicating process, see Batterham, *The Office Copying Revolution*, 51–56; for further details on Barker's printing methods, see Gabriel Mckee, "Office Copying Technology in the Flying Saucer Subculture: Gray Barker's Saucerian Books," *Book History* 27, no. 2 (Fall 2024): 375–404.

2. Gray Barker, *Hoaxoffice* ([Clarksburg, WV]: [privately printed by the author], 1952), [4].

3. Barker, *Hoaxoffice*, [9].

4. W. C. DeVry to Gray Barker, November 24, 1952, Folder "Hoaxoffice," GBC; Morris Schlozman to Gray Barker, November 20, 1952, Folder "Hoaxoffice," GBC; Chester Friedman to Gray Barker, November 14, 1952, Folder "Hoaxoffice," GBC.

5. Friedman to Barker, November 14, 1952.

6. Gray Barker to Ben Shylen, November 28, 1952, Folder "Hoaxoffice," GBC; Gray Barker to Chester Friedman, December 1, 1952, Folder "Hoaxoffice," GBC. The letter to Friedman mentions Barker's *Fate* contribution, but the letter to Shylen does not, suggesting that Barker may have received a copy of the magazine during the three days between the letters.

7. Gray Barker, "Mountain Poet," *Echoes of West Virginia* 4, no. 3 (Winter 1953): 13.

8. The earliest reference to the title I have located is a letter Barker sent to *Time* on February 1, 1953. See New-York Historical Society, "A Flying Saucer Sighting in the Time Inc. Records," *From the Stacks* (blog), September 4, 2019, https://blog.nyhistory.org/a-flying -saucer-sighting-in-the-time-inc-records.

9. S. L. Daw to Gray Barker, February 7, 1953, 1, Folder "Daw, S. L.," GBC.

10. Albert K. Bender to August C. Roberts, February 14, 1953, Folder "Bender, Albert K.— Roberts correspondence," GBC.

11. Albert K. Bender, "'Masonick Saucer Report' and 'Greenway Saucer Report'" (June 8, 1953), Folder "IFSB," GBC. The spelling of Lucchesi's first name is variable, and he used both Dominic and Dominick. For the sake of consistency I have opted for the latter throughout.

12. Lonzo Dove to Gray Barker, June 24, 1953, 1, Folder "Dove, Lonzo," GBC.

13. Gray Barker to S. L. Daw, February 13, 1953, Folder "Daw, S. L.," GBC.

14. Barker to August C. Roberts, August 5, 1953, 1. In a later publication, Barker gave the edition size as two hundred rather than three hundred. Gray Barker, ed., *The Saucerian Review* (Clarksburg, WV: Gray Barker, 1956), 7. I believe the contemporary, private report to Roberts to be the more reliable figure.

15. Barker to Roberts, August 5, 1953, 1.

16. Bender, *Flying Saucers*, 25.

17. Gray Barker, "Editorial," *The Saucerian* 1, no. 1 (September 1953): 1.

18. Barker, "Editorial," *The Saucerian, 1*.

19. Barker, "Editorial," *The Saucerian, 2*, paragraph break removed.

20. Barker, "W.V.A. Monster," 8.

21. Barker, "W.V.A. Monster," 13.

22. Barker, "W.V.A. Monster," 8.

23. Albert K. Bender to August C. Roberts, July 15, 1953, 2, Folder "Bender, Albert K.—Roberts correspondence," GBC.

24. Barker registered to attend about a week after finishing the first issue of *The Saucerian*. The signatures are recorded in Barker's copy of the program. Gray Barker to World Science Fiction Convention Committee, August 11, 1953, Folder "Philcon 1953," GBC; David A. Kyle, ed., "11th World Science-Fiction Convention [Program Booklet]," 1953, Folder "Philcon 1953," GBC. For accounts of Philcon II, see Warner, *Wealth of Fable*, 366–371; Earl Kemp, "Bye Bye Bellevue," *Nite Cry*, no. 1 (December 1953): 3–10, https://www.fanac.org/fanzines /Nite_Cry/Nite_Cry01.pdf.

25. Barker, *They Knew Too Much*, 90–91. Barker elides Barbieri, Lorenzen, and Moseley from the account, suggesting that it was Roberts alone who collected the samples.

26. James W. Moseley and Karl T. Pflock, *Shockingly Close to the Truth! Confessions of a Grave-Robbing Ufologist* (Amherst, NY: Prometheus Books, 2002), 40.

27. Moseley and Pflock, *Shockingly Close*, 42.

28. Barker's account of these events is in Barker, *They Knew Too Much*, 94–98.

29. Albert K. Bender to August C. Roberts, September 9, 1953, Folder "Bender, Albert K.—Roberts correspondence," GBC.

30. For Barker's account, see Barker, *They Knew Too Much*, 99–106.

31. Gray Barker to Harold Fulton (with "Chronology"), December 18, 1954, 7, Folder "Fulton, Harold," GBC.

32. Barker, *They Knew Too Much*, 95–96; Gray Barker to Richard Toronto, July 21, 1980, Folder "Shavertron," GBC.

33. Gray Barker, "Telephone Conversation between Gray Barker and S. L. Daw, April 5, 1954" (Carbon copy of typescript, April 5, 1954), 2–3, Folder "Daw, S. L.," GBC (hereafter "Barker-Daw Telephone Transcript"). UFO and conspiracy researcher Nick Redfern found no record of the interview in the few FBI documents related to Barker in response to a Freedom of Information Act request. Redfern offers two possible explanations: the interview was off the record, or the FBI is hiding the interview. He does not mention a third option: that there is no record of an FBI interview with Barker because none took place. Nick Redfern, *The FBI Files: The FBI's UFO Top Secrets Exposed* (New York: Pocket Books, 1998), 331.

34. Timothy Green Beckley, "Gray Barker: The Man Who Knew Too Much about Flying Saucers," Exploring the Bizarre, January 31, 2016, YouTube video, 1:05:00–1:08:00, https://youtu.be/0m8weYukun4.

35. Barker, "Barker-Daw Telephone Transcript," 1.

36. Barker, "Barker-Daw Telephone Transcript," 2.

37. Barker, "Barker-Daw Telephone Transcript," 5.

38. Barker to Fulton, December 18, 1954, 7; Gray Barker to Jacqueline Sanders, September 29, 1956, 1, Folder "Sanders, Jacqueline—Special letters," GBC; see also Gray Barker, ed., *UFO 96* (Clarksburg, WV: The International Bankers, 1963), [54], https://www.davidhalperin.net/ufo-96-the-ufo-world-of-50-years-ago.

39. Albert K. Bender to Dominick Lucchesi, September 9, 1953, Folder "Bender, Albert K.—Lucchesi correspondence," GBC.

40. Bender to Roberts, September 9, 1953. Unfortunately, Barker's letter to Bender does not seem to have survived, and we cannot know if Bender conflated their stories or if Barker explicitly told him that he had spoken with an FBI agent.

41. Bender to Roberts, September 9, 1953.

42. Albert K. Bender to S. L. Daw, Carbon copy of manuscript (copy in Daw's hand), September 9, 1953, Folder "Daw, S. L.," GBC.

43. Halperin, *Intimate Alien*, 202.

44. Barker, *They Knew Too Much*, 92–93 (emphasis original).

45. Albert K. Bender to August C. Roberts, September 14, 1953, Folder "Bender, Albert K.—Roberts correspondence," GBC. The letter also suggests that Bender believed it was the FBI, rather than the local police, who had contacted Roberts about Lucchesi's lost-and-found report.

46. Barker, *They Knew Too Much*, 127–135. The exact date of the visit is from Bender, *Flying Saucers*, 135.

47. Albert K. Bender to August C. Roberts, November 12, 1953, Folder "Bender, Albert K.—Roberts correspondence," GBC; quoted in Aaron John Gulyas, *Extraterrestrials and the American Zeitgeist: Alien Contact Tales since the 1950s* (Jefferson, NC: McFarland, 2013), 180.

48. International Flying Saucer Bureau, "Late Bulletin," *Space Review* 2, no. 4 (October 1953): 1. Paragraph breaks removed.

49. International Flying Saucer Bureau, "Statement of Importance," *Space Review* 2, no. 4 (October 1953): 1.

50. International Flying Saucer Bureau, "A Special Announcement," *Space Review* 2, no. 4 (October 1953): 7.

51. Gray Barker to Arthur Godfrey, October 13, 1953, Folder "G-1"; item G-5, GBC.

52. Gray Barker to Laimon Mitris, October 19, 1953, Folder "Mitris, Laimon," GBC.

53. Date inferred from Gray Barker to Jacqueline Sanders, October 14, 1953, Folder "Sanders, Jacqueline—1953," GBC.

54. Lem M'Collum, "Mystery Visitors Halt Research, Saucerers Here Ordered to Quit," *Sunday Herald*, November 22, 1953; reprinted in Gray Barker, *The Saucerian: December, 1953 Bulletin* (Clarksburg, WV: Gray Barker, 1953); see also Loren E. Gross, *The Fifth Horseman of the Apocalypse: UFOs: A History, 1953 August–December, Supplemental Notes* (Fremont, CA: [The author], 2002), 38, https://sohp.us/collections/ufos-a-history/doc/1953-Aug-Dec-SN.php.

55. Gray Barker to Dominick Lucchesi, November 30, 1953, 1, Folder "Lucchesi, Dominick," GBC.

56. Gray Barker, "Editorial: The I.F.S.B. Closing," *The Saucerian* 2, no. 1 (whole no. 3) (February 1954): 3.

57. Barker, "Editorial: The I.F.S.B. Closing," 5–6; Coral E. Lorenzen, "The Editorial," *APRO Bulletin* 2, no. 3 (November 1953): 2; Coral E. Lorenzen, "The Bender-IFSB Affair," *APRO Bulletin* 2, no. 4 (January 1954): 4–5. Lorenzen later privately theorized that Bender was being blackmailed, though she was vague about what secret he wanted kept (Coral Lorenzen to Ted Bloecher and Lex Mebane, [May 24, 1956?], 1, Folder 2.3, TBP).

58. Gray Barker, "Editorial: The I.F.S.B. Closing," 5.

59. Gray Barker to Richard S. Shaver, [November–December 1953?], Folder "Shaver, Richard S.," GBC; Richard Kelsey, "Notes on Shaver" (December 25, 1953), Folder "Shaver, Richard S.," GBC; Gray Barker to Dominick Lucchesi, November 11, 1953, Folder "Lucchesi, Dominick," GBC (mentioning Layne); Harold Fulton to Gray Barker, January 5, 1954, Folder "Fulton, Harold," GBC.

60. Gray Barker to Laimon Mitris, December 17, 1953, Folder "Mitris, Laimon," GBC; Gray Barker to Dominick Lucchesi, December 17, 1953, Folder "Lucchesi, Dominick," GBC.

61. Barker refers to receiving a copy of the issue in Barker to Dominick Lucchesi, November 30, 1953, 2.

62. Gray Barker, "Nexus," *The Saucerian* 2, no. 1 (whole no. 3) (February 1954): 40.

63. Barker, "Editorial: The I.F.S.B. Closing," 6.

64. Barker, "Editorial: The I.F.S.B. Closing," 9.

65. Halperin, *Intimate Alien*, 153–155.

66. "UFOs," FBI Records: The Vault, 2013, https://vault.fbi.gov/UFO. It is worth noting that Coral Lorenzen had been visited by Air Force representatives who wanted her to "reduce the excitement around UFO cases" in June 1953, just a few months before Bender's experience. Michael D. Swords and Robert Powell, *UFOs and Government: A Historical Inquiry* (San Antonio: Anomalist Books, 2012), 197.

67. H. P. Beasley and A. V. Sampsel, "The Bender Mystery: Still a Mystery?," *Flying Saucers*, no. FS-30 (May 1963): 20–27; George Hunt Williamson, "The Silence Group," *Saucerian Bulletin* 1, no. 5 (whole no. 11) (November 1956): 6. The article was later adapted as part of one of Williamson's books: George Hunt Williamson and John McCoy, *UFOs Confidential!* ([Corpus Christi, TX]: Essene, 1958), 40–53; see also George Hunt Williamson to Gray Barker, April 30, 1956, 3–4, Folder "Williamson, George Hunt," GBC.

68. Brian Burden, "MIBs and the Intelligence Community," *Awareness* 9, no. 1 (Spring 1980): 6–13.

69. Lonzo Dove, "Gray Barker's 'Three Men in Black,'" *Saucer News* 6, no. 3 (whole no. 36) (June 1959): 6–13; Lonzo Dove to James W. Moseley, January 5, 1959, Folder "Straith," GBC; Lonzo Dove to James W. Moseley, March 2, 1959, Folder "Dove, Lonzo," GBC; Loren E. Gross, *UFOs: A History, 1953 August-December* (Fremont, CA: privately printed by the author, 1990), 41, https://sohp.us/collections/ufos-a-history/doc/1953-Aug-Dec.php.

70. Gray Barker to Jacqueline Sanders, November 14, 1953, 1, Folder "Sanders, Jacqueline—1953," GBC.

CHAPTER 4

1. *Fate* published a portfolio of Adamski's saucer photos in 1951. George Adamski, "I Photographed Space Ships," *Fate* 4, no. 5 (July 1951): 64–74, http://www.adamskifoundation.com/gafhtml/News8Fate.htm.

2. On the connections between the Royal Order of Tibet and Adamski's later "cosmic philosophy," see Lou Zinsstag and Timothy Good, *George Adamski: The Untold Story; the Latest and Most Complete Evidence on the First Man to Claim That Extraterrestrials Live among Us* (Beckenham: Ceti, 1983), 188–191; Gulyas, *Extraterrestrials*, 75, 80. A much-repeated theory holds that Adamski founded the organization as a front for bootlegging operations, but it rests on a single source: an interview with Ray Stanford, a ufologist and disgruntled former associate of Adamski. See Douglas Curran, *In Advance of the Landing: Folk Concepts of Outer Space* (New York: Abbeville, 1985), 72.

3. For Adamski's own account of this contact, see Desmond Leslie and George Adamski, *Flying Saucers Have Landed* (London: Werner Laurie, 1953), 185–222; see also Gulyas, *Extraterrestrials*, 60–72; Clark, *UFO Encyclopedia*, 1:39–40 ("Adamski, George"); Peebles, *Watch the Skies*, 93–99; Jacobs, *UFO Controversy*, 110–111. Detailed, if less than objective, accounts of the November 20 contact story can be found in Michel Zirger and Maurizio Martinelli, *The Incredible Life of George Hunt Williamson: Mystical Journey, Itinerary of a Privileged UFO Witness*, ed. Warren P. Aston (Baiso: Verdechiaro Edizioni, 2016), 41–66; Colin Bennett, *Looking for Orthon: The Story of George Adamski, the First Flying Saucer Contactee, and How He Changed the World* (New York: Cosimo Books, 2008), 33–46.

4. Gulyas, *Extraterrestrials*, 88.

5. On contactees in general, see Gulyas, *Extraterrestrials*; Nick Redfern, *Contactees: A History of Alien-Human Interaction* (Franklin Lakes, NJ: New Page Books, 2010); Mikael Rothstein, "The Rise and Decline of the First-Generation UFO Contactees: A Cognitive Approach," in *Encyclopedic Sourcebook of UFO Religions*, ed. James R. Lewis (Amherst, NY: Prometheus Books, 2003), 63–76; John A. Saliba, "UFO Contactee Phenomena from a Psychosociological Perspective: A Review," in *The Gods Have Landed: New Religions from Other Worlds*, ed. James R. Lewis (Albany: State University of New York Press, 1995), 207–250; Christopher Bader, "The UFO Contact Movement from the 1950's to the Present," *Studies in Popular Culture* 17, no. 2 (1995): 73–90, https://digitalcommons.chapman.edu/sociology_articles/3/; J. Gordon Melton, "The Contactees: A Survey," in *The Spectrum of UFO Research: Proceedings of the Second CUFOs Conference*, ed. Mimi Hynek (Chicago: J. Hynek Center for UFO Studies, 1988), 99–108, http://www.cufos.org/books/The_Spectrum_of_UFO_Research .pdf; David Stupple, "Mahatmas and Space Brothers: The Ideologies of Alleged Contact with Extraterrestrials," *Journal of American Culture* 7, no. 1/2 (Spring/Summer 1984): 131–139, https://doi.org/10.1111/j.1542-734X.1984.0701_131.x; J. Gordon Melton, "UFO Contactees: A Report on Work in Progress," in *Proceedings of the First International UFO Congress*, ed. Curtis G. Fuller (New York: Warner Books, 1980), 378–395; David Stupple et al., "Visiting with Space People: A Symposium on the Contactee Phenomenon," in *Proceedings of the First International UFO Congress*, ed. Curtis G. Fuller (New York: Warner Books, 1980), 305–321. David Jacobs's treatment of the subject in *UFO Controversy* has been influential, but his conclusions on the subject reveal biases regarding the relative roles of contactees and "serious" ufologists; see Pierre Lagrange, "Close Encounters of the French Kind: The Saucerian Construction of 'Contacts' and the Controversy over Its Reality in France," in *Alien*

Worlds: Social and Religious Dimensions of Extraterrestrial Contact, ed. Diana G. Tumminia (Syracuse, NY: Syracuse University Press, 2007), 156–160.

6. Orfeo Angelucci and Paul M. Vest, "I Traveled in a Flying Saucer," *Mystic*, no. 1 (November 1953): 52–68; Gray Barker, "A Ride in a Flying Saucer," *The Saucerian* 1, no. 2 (November 1953): 30–31.

7. David Stupple cautions against making too clean a distinction between "psychic" and "non-psychic" contactees, noting that "the two constitute ideal types, theoretical constructs that are more or less approximated by empirical cases," but "there is some overlap." Stupple, "Mahatmas and Space Brothers," 135.

8. Sanders discussed Van Tassel in one of her first letters to Barker. Jacqueline Sanders to Gray Barker, October 26, 1953, Folder "Sanders, Jacqueline—1953," GBC. See also, e.g., Jacqueline Sanders, "The Van Tassel Saucer Meeting," *The Saucerian* 2, no. 2 (whole no. 4) (September 1954): 15–17.

9. Gulyas, *Extraterrestrials*, 103–104. Roth notes that Adamski, too, owed a debt to Theosophy. Christopher F. Roth, "Ufology as Anthropology: Race, Extraterrestrials, and the Occult," in *E.T. Culture: Anthropology in Outerspaces*, ed. Debbora Battaglia (Durham, NC: Duke University Press, 2005), 52, https://doi.org/10.1515/9780822387015-003.

10. Zirger and Martinelli, *Incredible Life*, 178–180.

11. Barker attended the fifth of these gatherings in May 1958 (meeting Sanders in person there), and returned in 1960 and 1970. Ruth Netherton to James Villard, June 5, 1958, Folder "Giant Rock Convention," GBC; Moseley and Pflock, *Shockingly Close*, 163–166, 218; James W. Moseley, "Report on the Giant Rock Convention," *Saucer News* 7, no. 3 (whole no. 41) [September 1960]: 3–9; Gray Barker to John W. Dean, October 16, 1970, Folder "Dean, John W.," GBC; Gray Barker, *Gray Barker at Giant Rock* (Clarksburg, WV: Saucerian Publications, 1976).

12. George Adamski to Gray Barker, November 18, 1953, in Gray Barker, ed., *The Adamski Documents, Part One* (Clarksburg, WV: Saucerian Press, Inc., 1980), [29].

13. Gray Barker, "New Saucer Books," *The Saucerian* 2, no. 1 (whole no. 3) (February 1954): 56.

14. Gray Barker to Laimon Mitris, November 12, 1953, 2, Folder "Mitris, Laimon," GBC.

15. Barker to Mitris, November 12, 1953, 2.

16. Gray Barker, "The New Saucer Books," *The Saucerian* 2, no. 2 (whole no. 4) (September 1954): 38–39.

17. Moseley and Pflock, *Shockingly Close*, 98.

18. Moseley and Pflock, *Shockingly Close*, 26–32. Moseley and Pflock consistently spell Krippene's name as Krippine; I use here the spelling that appears in the author's own published works.

19. Gray Barker to Dominick Lucchesi, November 30, 1953, 1, Folder "Lucchesi, Dominick," GBC.

20. Gray Barker to Dominick Lucchesi, [January 20, 1954?], Folder "Lucchesi, Dominick," GBC.

21. Moseley and Pflock, *Shockingly Close*, 98–99.

22. Specifically, January 22nd or 23rd (inferred from Gray Barker to Bob Farnham, January 20, 1954, Folder "C-5," item C5-74-1, GBC). Farnham was editor of the fanzine *Chigger Path of Fandom.*

23. Barker, "Editorial: The I.F.S.B. Closing," 10.

24. The illustration had first appeared in the Sam Johnson's fanzine *Sfanzine*. R. Monger [pseud.], "The Wild Rumor Column," *The Saucerian* 2, no. 2 (whole no. 4) (September 1954): 25.

25. Gray Barker to Dominick Lucchesi, February 1, 1954, 1, Folder "Lucchesi, Dominick," GBC.

26. The inner circle is mentioned in, e.g., Gray Barker to Jacqueline Sanders, July 12, 1958, Folder "Sanders, Jacqueline—1958," GBC.

27. A different drawing of the space woman also appeared on the cover of the sixth issue of *Nexus*.

28. E.g., Dominick Lucchesi to Gray Barker, June 2, 1954, Folder "Lucchesi, Dominick," GBC.

29. Gray Barker to Dominick Lucchesi, September 14, 1954, 1, Folder "Lucchesi, Dominick," GBC.

30. Dominick Lucchesi to Gray Barker, [February 1, 1954?], 1, Folder "Lucchesi, Dominick," GBC; James W. Moseley to Ted Bloecher, September 22, 1954, Folder 1.7, TBP; James W. Moseley to Ted Bloecher, October 16, 1954, Folder 1.7, TBP.

31. Gray Barker to Dominick Lucchesi, [January 25, 1954?], 1–2, Folder "Lucchesi, Dominick," GBC.

32. Moseley and Pflock, *Shockingly Close*, 106.

33. James W. Moseley to Ted Bloecher, July 10, 1954, Folder 1.7, TBP.

34. James W. Moseley, "Gossip Column," *Nexus* 1, no. 2 (August 1954): 4.

35. James W. Moseley to Ted Bloecher, August 5, 1954, Folder 1.7, TBP.

36. Gray Barker to Jacqueline Sanders, November 21, 1954, 1, Folder "Sanders, Jacqueline—1954," GBC.

37. Barker's first letter to Jessup is Gray Barker to Morris K. Jessup, November 11, 1954, Folder "Jessup, Morris K.," GBC; parts of the New York trip are detailed in James W. Moseley to Ted Bloecher, December 6, 1954, Folder 1.8, TBP; and Ted Bloecher to James W. Moseley, December 6, 1954, Folder 1.8, TBP.

38. Gray Barker to James W. Moseley, November 22, 1954, 1, Folder "Moseley, James W.," GBC.

39. James W. Moseley, "Who's Lying? The Wright Field Story," *The Saucerian* 3, no. 1 (whole no. 5) (January 1955): 32–36; for an entertaining overview of the afterlife of the story sketched by Moseley, see Aaron John Gulyas, "Storm Hangar 18!," *The Saucer Life*, September 18, 2019, podcast, 41:58, https://saucerlife.com/2019/09/18/storm-hangar-18.

40. Gray Barker to Harold Fulton, November 20, 1954, 1–2, Folder "Fulton, Harold," GBC.

41. Laimon Mitris to Gray Barker, November 19, 1954, Folder "Mitris, Laimon," GBC; see also Gray Barker, "The Mitris Mystery: Code Name: Delores" (Spirit-duplicated document, November 23, 1954), Folder "Mitris, Laimon," GBC.

42. Doreen A. Wilkinson and John E. Stuart to Gray Barker, December 5, 1954, Folder "Stuart, John—Correspondence," GBC.

43. E.g., Gray Barker, "Saucernews: What's Doin' with the Saucers," *The Saucerian* 2, no. 2 (whole no. 4) (September 1954), 7.

44. Gray Barker to Jacqueline Sanders, December 23, 1954, Folder "Sanders, Jacqueline—1954," GBC; "Rosa Lee Frame," Family Search, January 26, 2022.

45. Barker to Sanders, November 21, 1954, 10–11.

46. Gray Barker, "From 'Seven Sagas'" (Typescript, [1955–1961?]), B, Box "Moseley/Private Writings," GBC.

47. On the car, see Jacqueline Sanders to Gray Barker, January 18, 1955, 1, Folder "Sanders, Jacqueline—1955," GBC; Gray Barker to James Villard, [October 1956?], Folder "Villard, James," GBC; on the secretary and typewriter, see Gray Barker to Jacqueline Sanders, February 12, 1955, Folder "Sanders, Jacqueline—1955," GBC.

48. Barker to Grennell, January 26, 1955, 1.

49. Leon Festinger, Henry W. Riecken, and Stanley Schachter, *When Prophecy Fails* (Minneapolis: University of Minnesota Press, 1956), https://catalog.hathitrust.org/Record/000818353. For an essential critique of Festinger et al., see Diana G. Tumminia, *When Prophecy Never Fails: Myth and Reality in a Flying-Saucer Group* (New York: Oxford University Press, 2005), 33–37, 155–158, https://doi.org/10.1093/0195176758.001.0001; on the continuation of Martin's career following Festinger's observations, see Jerome Clark, "The Odyssey of Sister Thedra," in *Alien Worlds: Social and Religious Dimensions of Extraterrestrial Contact*, ed. Diana G. Tumminia (Syracuse, NY: Syracuse University Press, 2007), 25–41.

50. Gray Barker to Dominick Lucchesi, [May 22, 1954?], Folder "Lucchesi, Dominick," GBC. The letter's stated date of February 22 must be incorrect; I have dated it May 22 based on evidence from other letters in Barker's files from that date.

51. Gray Barker to Jacqueline Sanders, May 22, 1954, 2, Folder "Sanders, Jacqueline—1954," GBC.

52. For a more detailed summary of Barker and Martin's communications, see Clark, "The Odyssey of Sister Thedra," 31–32.

53. Gray Barker, "Editorial: The End of the World," *The Saucerian* 3, no. 2 (whole no. 6) (Spring 1955): 57–58.

54. Barker, "Editorial: The End of the World," 59.

55. Barker, "Editorial: The End of the World," 59–60.

56. James W. Moseley, "Some New Facts about 'Flying Saucers Have Landed,'" *Nexus* 2, no. 1 (whole no. 7) (January 1955): 7–17; Desmond Leslie, "Leslie Strikes Back (Part One)," *Nexus* 2, no. 5 (whole no. 11) (May 1955): 7–8; Harold T. Wilkins, "Is Mr. Scully a Cynic?," *Saucer News* 2, no. 6 (whole no. 12) (July 1955): 14–17; Lonzo Dove, review of *Inside the Space Ships*, by George Adamski, *Saucer News* 2, no. 8 (whole no. 14) (November 1955), 14–17; Justin Case [pseud.], review of *Space, Gravity and the Flying Saucer*, by Leonard G. Cramp, *Saucer News* 2, no. 7 (whole no. 13) (September 1955), 6–8.

57. Gray Barker to Laimon Mitris, February 4, 1955, 2, Folder "Mitris, Laimon," GBC.

CHAPTER 5

1. Gray Barker to Jacqueline Sanders, October 31, 1955, 1, Folder "Sanders, Jacqueline—1955," GBC.

2. Segrave, *Drive-in Theaters*, 74.

3. Segrave, *Drive-in Theaters*, 76.

4. Lillian Lazarus, "Cincinnati Realart Celebrates 40 Years," *Boxoffice* 67, no. 4 (May 21, 1955): 74.

5. Barker to Sanders, October 31, 1955, 4.

6. Barker to Sanders, October 31, 1955, 4.

7. On the introduction of Thorazine (chlorpromazine) in American psychiatry, see Judith P. Swazey, *Chlorpromazine in Psychiatry: A Study of Therapeutic Innovation* (Cambridge, MA: MIT Press, 1974), 191–224.

8. Gray Barker to the *Exhibitor*, September 10, 1955, 1, Folder "E—Misc.," item E-30, GBC.

9. Jacobs, *UFO Controversy*, 140.

10. Leon Davidson, *Flying Saucers: An Analysis of the Air Force Project Blue Book Special Report No. 14*, 4th ed. (Clarksburg, WV: Saucerian Publications, 1971), 102; see also Jacobs, *UFO Controversy*, 138–143; Peebles, *Watch the Skies*, 109–111.

11. Davidson, *Flying Saucers*, 117.

12. Peebles, *Watch the Skies*, 110.

13. Gray Barker, "Memo from the Saucerian" (Clarksburg, WV: The Saucerian, October 29, 1955), [2], Folder "Saucerian News Releases," GBC.

14. Gray Barker to George Adamski, November 15, 1955, in Barker, *The Adamski Documents, Part One*, 56; Jacobs, *UFO Controversy*, 139.

15. The date is confirmed in James W. Moseley, "News Briefs," *Saucer News* 2, no. 8 (whole no. 14) (November 1955): 11.

16. Donald Keyhoe, *Flying Saucers from Outer Space* (New York: Henry Holt, 1953); Donald Keyhoe, *The Flying Saucer Conspiracy* (New York: Henry Holt, 1955).

17. Peebles, *Watch the Skies*, 112.

18. Gray Barker to Jacqueline Sanders, December 13, 1955, 3, Folder "Sanders, Jacqueline—1955," GBC.

19. Barker to Sanders, December 13, 1955.

20. Barker to Sanders, December 13, 1955, 1.

21. Gray Barker to Harold Fulton, October 25, 1955, 2, Folder "Fulton, Harold," GBC.

22. Gray Barker to Lonzo Dove, November 5, 1955, Folder "Dove, Lonzo," GBC; Barker to Sanders, December 13, 1955, 1.

23. For an overview of Morrow's departure from communist politics and his publishing career, see Alan M. Wald, *The New York Intellectuals: The Rise and Decline of the Anti-Stalinist Left from the 1930s to the 1980s*, 30th anniv. ed. (Chapel Hill: University of North Carolina Press, 2017), 287–289.

24. Wald, *The New York Intellectuals*, 288.

25. Gary Lachman, *Turn Off Your Mind: The Mystic Sixties and the Dark Side of the Age of Aquarius* (London: Sidgwick & Jackson, 2001), 280.

26. Barker to Sanders, December 13, 1955, 1.

27. Morrow may have taken his inspiration from the film *The Man Who Knew Too Much*, released on May 16, 1956, the day before Barker's book. The earliest reference to the title seen is in Gray Barker to Harold Fulton, January 25, 1956, Folder "Fulton, Harold," GBC.

28. Gray Barker, "About This Publication," *Saucerian Bulletin* 1, no. 1 (whole no. 7) (March 1956): 1.

29. Barker highlighted the incongruity of this title in a letter to Sanders. Barker to Sanders, November 21, 1954, 9.

30. Gray Barker to Morris K. Jessup, March 23, 1956, 2, Folder "Jessup, Morris K.," GBC.

31. Jacqueline Sanders to Gray Barker, March 13, 1956, 1–2, Folder "Sanders, Jacqueline—1956," GBC.

32. Barker, *Saucerian Review*, 6.

33. Barker, *Saucerian Review*, 30.

34. Gray Barker to Jacqueline Sanders, June 7, 1956, 2, Folder "Sanders, Jacqueline—1956," GBC.

35. Barker, *Saucerian Review*, 41.

36. Gray Barker to Jacqueline Sanders, February 11, 1956, 2, Folder "Sanders, Jacqueline—1956," GBC.

37. Barker to Sanders, February 11, 1956, 2.

38. Gray Barker to Dominick Lucchesi, March 3, 1956, 1, Folder "Lucchesi, Dominick," GBC.

39. Barker to Lucchesi, March 3, 1956.

40. "Books Published Today," *New York Times*, May 17, 1956; Gray Barker to Morris K. Jessup, March 3, 1956, Folder "Jessup, Morris K.," GBC; Gray Barker to Morris K. Jessup, March 29, 1956, Folder "Jessup, Morris K.," GBC. Barker received his first advance copy of the book on April 20; see Gray Barker to Ted Bloecher, April 20, 1956, Folder 2.2, TBP.

41. Barker, *They Knew Too Much*, 11–12.

42. John Hitchcock, "More Reviews," *Umbra*, no. 14 (June 1956[?]): 13, https://www.fanac.org/fanzines/Umbra/Umbra14.pdf.

43. Barker, *They Knew Too Much*, 234. Moseley made similar claims in private correspondence and told Bloecher that he had been pressured into silence by a "visitor." James W. Moseley to Ted Bloecher, September 28, 1954, Folder 1.7, TBP; Ted Bloecher to Isabel Davis, October 8, 1954, Folder 1.7, TBP.

44. Lex Mebane to Gray Barker, May 2, 1956, 1, Folder "Civilian Saucer Intelligence," GBC.

45. Mebane to Barker, May 2, 1956.

46. Barkun, *A Culture of Conspiracy*, 3–4 (emphasis original).

47. Barker, *They Knew Too Much*, 246.

48. Gray Barker to Jacqueline Sanders, [April–May 1956?], 4, Folder "Sanders, Jacqueline—Special letters," GBC.

49. Barker to Sanders, April–May 1956[?], 5.

50. Laimon Mitris to Gray Barker, March 28, 1956, 1, Folder "Mitris, Laimon," GBC. Australian researcher Fred Stone was similarly upset that Barker had used his correspondence without permission. John E. Stuart to Gray Barker, December 4, 1956, 3, Folder "Stuart, John—Correspondence," GBC; Lex Mebane to Gray Barker, December 4, 1956, Folder "Civilian Saucer Intelligence," GBC.

51. Gray Barker to Laimon Mitris, April 3, 1956, Folder "Mitris, Laimon," GBC.

52. Laimon Mitris to Gray Barker, June 5, 1956, 2, Folder "Mitris, Laimon," GBC.

53. Gray Barker to Jacqueline Sanders, [June 18, 1956?], 3, Folder "Sanders, Jacqueline—Special letters," GBC. I assume that Barker's original phrasing ("my word not to keep his story secret") is a typographical error.

54. Barker to Jacqueline Sanders, [June 9–10, 1956?], 2.

55. Barker to Sanders, [June 9–10, 1956?], 5. Moseley published a photograph from the broadcast: James W. Moseley and August C. Roberts, "This Unusual Picture," *Saucer News* 3, no. 5 (whole no. 19) (September 1956): 6.

56. Barker to Sanders, [April–May 1956?], 2.

57. Barker to Sanders, [June 18, 1956?], 6.

58. Barker to Sanders, [June 9–10, 1956?], 9.

59. Lex Mebane to Felix Morrow, June 12, 1956, Folder 2.4, TBP; Ted Bloecher to Felix Morrow, July 1, 1956, Folder 2.4, TBP.

60. Mebane to Morrow, June 12, 1956; see also "A report on receipts during the third winter season," Barker, "Early Poems of Gray Barker," [36].

61. Barker to Sanders, [June 9–10, 1956?], 10.

62. Barker to Sanders, [June 9–10, 1956?], 11. Details of the Q&A are given in Civilian Saucer Intelligence of New York, "Reported Intimidation of UFO Researchers," *CSI-NY*, no. 15 (May 1956): 4.

63. Barker did not know the man's name at the time, but got to know him several years later. Gray Barker, *Gray Barker's Book of Saucers* (Clarksburg, WV: Saucerian Books, 1965), 73.

64. Barker to Sanders, [June 9–10, 1956?], 11–12.

65. Gray Barker to Jacqueline Sanders, June 24, 1956, Folder "Sanders, Jacqueline—Special letters," GBC.

66. "Booker's Flying Saucer Hobby Makes Him Author and Film Aide," *Boxoffice* 69, no. 17 (August 18, 1956): 27; Roger Pierce, "Barker Speaks in Cleveland," *Cosmic News* ([1956?]): 7–8, https://files.afu.se/Downloads/Magazines/United%20States/Cosmic%20News%20 (Pierce%20and%20Neuberger)/Cosmic%20News%20-%201956a.pdf.

67. Jacqueline Sanders to Gray Barker, April 17–May 1, 1956, 3, Folder "Sanders, Jacqueline—1956," GBC.

68. See Jodi Dean, *Aliens in America: Conspiracy Cultures from Outerspace to Cyberspace* (Ithaca, NY: Cornell University Press, 1998), 40–41; for a contemporary example, see Isabel L. Davis, "Meet the Extraterrestrial," *Fantastic Universe* 8, no. 5 (November 1957): 31–59.

69. Ted Bloecher to Gray Barker, February 23, 1956, Folder 2.1, TBP; Ted Bloecher to Gray Barker, March 3, 1956, Folder "Civilian Saucer Intelligence," GBC (also folder 2.1, TBP).

70. Gray Barker to Ted Bloecher, February 25, 1956, Folder 2.1, TBP.

71. Gray Barker, "The Inside of the 'London Story,'" *Saucerian Bulletin* 1, no. 4 (whole no. 10) (October 1956): 2; Gray Barker and Jacqueline Sanders, "'Mon-Ka' Doesn't Come Through," *Saucerian Bulletin* 1, no. 5 (whole no. 11) (November 1956): 1–3; Gray Barker to Jacqueline Sanders, November 7, 1956, Folder "Sanders, Jacqueline—1956," GBC; see also Adam

Gorightly, "Dick Miller's Favorite Martian," *Chasing UFOs* (blog), January 15, 2020, https://chasingufosblog.com/2020/01/15/dick-millers-favorite-martian.

72. Gray Barker, "And the Inevitable Would Come—Accounts of Having Met the Space People Themselves," *Saucerian Bulletin* 2, no. 4 (whole no. 15) (November 1957): 3.

73. Gray Barker to Jacqueline Sanders, September 5, 1956, 1, Folder "Sanders, Jacqueline—1956," GBC; *Polk's Clarksburg (Harrison County, W. Va.) City Directory, Vol. 30, 1957–58* (Pittsburgh: R. L. Polk, 1958), 120.

74. Barker to Sanders, November 24, 1956, 1.

75. Gray Barker to *One Magazine*, [July 1954?], Folder "Barker, Gray—Biography and chronology," GBC. On the history of *ONE*, see C. Todd White, "Drama, Power and Politics: ONE Magazine, Mattachine Review and The Ladder in the Era of Homophile Activism," in *Gay Press, Gay Power: The Growth of LGBT Community Newspapers in America*, ed. Tracy Baim (Chicago: Prairie Avenue Productions / Windy City Media Group, 2012), 141–152.

76. McCulty briefly recounts the meeting in *Whispers from Space* (26:00), but does not specify a date.

77. Moses Edward Naedele, "Don Leigh McCulty: A Remembrance," October 2018, 1, Folder "Barker, Gray—Biography and chronology," GBC.

78. *Whispers from Space*, 26:00; Naedele, "Don Leigh McCulty: A Remembrance," 3.

79. Gray Barker, "Dear _____," in *Youranus* ([Clarksburg, WV]: [Gray Barker], 1957), [45] (emphasis original).

80. On Alma's position at the newspaper, see Barker, "Dear _____."

81. Barker to Sanders, September 5, 1956, 3.

82. Gray Barker to James W. Moseley, "The Books of Charles Fart," October 14, 1957, [11], Box "Moseley/Private Writings," GBC.

83. Gene Duplantier, "I Remember Gray Barker," circa 1985, 1, Box "Moseley/Private Writings," GBC.

84. Adam Gorightly and Greg Bishop, *"A" Is for Adamski: The Golden Age of the UFO Contactees*, color ed. (n.p.: Gorightly, 2018), 36.

85. On the sales: Gray Barker to Morris K. Jessup, October 1, 1956, Folder "Jessup, Morris K.," GBC; on the print run: Morris K. Jessup to Gray Barker, October 4, 1956, 1, Folder "Jessup, Morris K.," GBC.

86. Barker to Sanders, November 24, 1956, 1.

87. Gray Barker to [recipient redacted], [November 27, 1957?], [folder name redacted by request of the correspondent], GBC.

88. Barker to Sanders, November 24, 1956, 2.

89. Jessup to Barker, October 4, 1956, 1.

90. Jessup to Barker, October 4, 1956, 3; see also Morris K. Jessup to Ted Bloecher, November 1, 1956, Folder 2.6, TBP.

91. Gray Barker, "The Inside on Why 'Cosmic News,'" *Saucerian Bulletin* 1, no. 5 (whole no. 11) (November 1956): 4. The terrible pun that emerged when Von Mobile's first name was revealed to be Otto suggests a prank rather than anything more mysterious. Gray Barker, "The International Bankers," in *Youranus* ([Clarksburg, WV]: [Gray Barker], 1957), 31–32.

92. Barker and Sanders, "'Mon-Ka' Doesn't Come Through."

93. Barker to Sanders, September 29, 1956, 7.

CHAPTER 6

1. Gray Barker to Lex Mebane, July 17, 1957, Folder "Civilian Saucer Intelligence," GBC.

2. Lex Mebane to Gray Barker, July 10, 1957, Folder "Civilian Saucer Intelligence," GBC; Lex Mebane to Gray Barker, March 8, 1958, Folder "Civilian Saucer Intelligence," GBC.

3. Barker to Mebane, July 17, 1957.

4. Ted Bloecher to Richard Hall, August 10, 1957, 4, Folder 3.1, TBP.

5. Barker first appeared on the program in January 1957 (Gray Barker to Lex Mebane, December 18, 1956, 2, Folder "Civilian Saucer Intelligence," GBC). The year before he had recorded a conversation for an unspecified New York radio program that may have been Nebel's, but the January program would have been his first live appearance (Barker to Jacqueline Sanders, [June 9–10, 1956?], 13). Palmer named Barker as his "official representative" on the radio program, particularly in matters relating to the Shaver Mystery (Ray Palmer to John Nebel, February 4, 1957, 4, Folder "Shavertron," GBC). On Nebel generally, see Donald Bain, *Long John Nebel: Radio Talk King, Master Salesman, and Magnificent Charlatan* (New York: Macmillan, 1974); Michael C. Keith, *Sounds in the Dark: All-Night Radio in American Life* (Ames: Iowa State University Press, 2001). For a recording of one of Barker's early appearances on the program, see Long John Nebel, *Long John Nebel—WOR—11.16.1958*, AM FM Archives, 1958, https://www.bitchute.com/video/WiHVlB8R4EMZ.

6. For a detailed, if somewhat conspiracist, overview of NICAP's early days, see Jack Brewer, *Wayward Sons: NICAP and the IC* (N.p.: published by the author, 2021), esp. 14–43.

7. Morris K. Jessup, "A Report on Washington D.C.'s NICAP (National Investigations Committee on Aerial Phenomena)," *Saucer News* 4, no. 2 (whole no. 22) (March 1957): 5, 16. Jacobs cites this same figure, but gives it as the entire operating budget for the organization, not just its payroll; see Jacobs, *UFO Controversy*, 146.

8. On Keyhoe's interim appointment, see Jessup, "A Report on Washington D.C.'s NICAP (National Investigations Committee on Aerial Phenomena)," 5; on his tenure as the group's leader, see Jacobs, *UFO Controversy*, 145ff.; Peebles, *Watch the Skies*, 115ff.

9. Jacobs, *UFO Controversy*, 148.

10. Donald Keyhoe to Gray Barker, March 7, 1957, Folder "Straith," GBC.

11. Gray Barker, "James Moseley," *Saucerian Bulletin* 2, no. 2 (whole no. 13) (May 1957): 2–3.

12. Barker, "James Moseley," 3.

13. Quoted in Gray Barker, "Chasing the Flying Saucers [No. 2]," *Flying Saucers from Other Worlds*, no. 25 (August 1957): 33.

14. Laura Mundo, *The Mundo UFO Report* (New York: Vantage, 1982), 53. Mundo also gives the date as March 1956, a year before the call recounted here, and it is possible she is conflating Barker's contemporarily reported prank call with another.

15. Coral E. Lorenzen, "Quotes and Comments," *APRO Bulletin*, March 1957, 3.

16. Barker, "Chasing the Flying Saucers [No. 2]," 33–34.

17. Moseley and Pflock, *Shockingly Close*, 156.

18. On this hoax, see Moseley and Pflock, *Shockingly Close*, 201.

19. Dégh, *Legend and Belief*, 97; on another folkloristic aspect of hoaxes, see Dégh and Vázsonyi, "Does the Word 'Dog' Bite?," 19.

20. Christopher L. Miller, *Impostors: Literary Hoaxes and Cultural Authenticity* (Chicago: University of Chicago Press, 2018), 37–38.

21. Barker, *UFO 96*, [5].

22. Gray Barker to John C. Sherwood, December 11, 1966, Folder "Sherwood, John," GBC.

23. According to psychologist Peter Hancock, "The very best of deceptions play directly into . . . desperate aspirations. Deception provides a material foundation for some dearly held hope or belief." Peter A. Hancock, *Hoax Springs Eternal: The Psychology of Cognitive Deception* (New York: Cambridge University Press, 2014), 68).

24. On Reich's life and theories, see Myron R. Sharaf, *Fury on Earth: A Biography of Wilhelm Reich* (New York: Da Capo, 1994); Robert S. Corrington, *Wilhelm Reich: Psychoanalyst and Radical Naturalist* (New York: Farrar, Straus and Giroux, 2003); for his trial and imprisonment, see Wilhelm Reich, *Where's the Truth?: Letters and Journals, 1948–1957*, ed. Mary Boyd Higgins (New York: Farrar, Straus and Giroux, 2012), 202–244, 252–255 passim.; for his interest in saucers, see James Reich, *Wilhelm Reich versus the Flying Saucers: An American Tragedy* (Santa Barbara, CA: Punctum Books, 2024).

25. Wilhelm Reich, *Contact with Space: Oranur Second Report, 1951–1956* (1957; repr., Haverhill, MA: Haverhill House Publishing, 2018), 7; Reich, *Wilhelm Reich*, 28.

26. Sharaf, *Fury on Earth*, 413–14.

27. Corrington, *Wilhelm Reich*, 239.

28. Corrington, *Wilhelm Reich*, 235.

29. Barker, "Dear _____," [46].

30. Barker, "Dear _____," [46].

31. Barker, "Dear _____"; the "battle" to which Reich referred is detailed in Reich, *Contact with Space*, 138–211.

32. Barker, "Dear _____," [47].

33. Barker, "Dear _____," [46].

34. See, e.g., Brad Steiger and Joan Whritenour, *New UFO Breakthrough* (New York: Award Books, 1968), 29–37.

35. Gray Barker, "In and out of Zines," *Gray Barker's Newsletter*, no. 5 (March 1976): 2.

36. SF historian Mike Ashley presents editor Hans Stefan Santesson's willingness to provide coverage to flying saucers as a sign that he was out of touch with the world of SF fandom. Mike Ashley, *Transformations: The Story of the Science-Fiction Magazines from 1950 to 1970* (Liverpool: Liverpool University Press, 2005), 182. CSI's column began with Civilian Saucer Intelligence, "Shapes in the Sky [No. 1]," *Fantastic Universe* 7, no. 3 (March 1957): 82–87.

37. Bill Meyers, "Spreading the Fertilizer," *Cry of the Nameless*, no. 108 (October 1957): 21, https://fanac.org/fanzines/Cry_of_the_Nameless/Cry108.pdf.

38. Gray Barker to Ruth E. Landis, April 15, 1957, Folder "London SF Convention," GBC.

39. Gray Barker to Jacqueline Sanders, June 21, 1957, 1, Folder "Sanders, Jacqueline—1957," GBC.

40. For a photograph of Barker's costume, see Gene Duplantier, "Gray Days at Clarksburg," *Ufolk*, no. 1 (1978): 12.

41. Gray Barker to Jacqueline Sanders, September 15, 1957, 4–5, Folder "Sanders, Jacqueline—Special letters," GBC. The decampment of Barker and others from the unsuitable hotel led to significant problems for the convention organizers, who were responsible for the full amount of their hotel bills. The ensuing fracas in SF fandom culminated in several lawsuits, but Barker stayed largely out of it. See Warner, *Wealth of Fable*, 388–389; "Plane Trip," Fancyclopedia 3, July 24, 2020, https://fancyclopedia.org/Plane_Trip.

42. Gray Barker to the *Exhibitor*, September 26, 1957, Folder "Exhibitor, The," GBC; ". . . And Now Back to Earth?," *Psychic News*, no. 1328 (November 16, 1957): 4, http://hdl.handle.net/10719/2953345.

43. Fanzine contributor Walt Willis identified Barker this way in an account of Loncon. Walt Willis, "The Harp That Once or Twice," *Oopsla*, no. 23 (November 1957): 12, https://fanac.org/fanzines/Oopsla/Oopsla23.pdf.

44. "Serious Constructive," Fancyclopedia 3, accessed January 10, 2023, https://fancyclopedia.org/Serious_Constructive.

45. Jacobs, *UFO Controversy*, 155.

46. Quoted in Jacobs, *UFO Controversy*, 155.

47. Jacobs, *UFO Controversy*, 155.

48. Gray Barker to [recipient redacted], December 13, 1957, [folder name redacted by request of the correspondent], GBC (emphasis original).

49. Gray Barker, "The Great Green God," in *Youranus* ([Clarksburg, WV]: [Gray Barker], 1957), [6].

50. Gray Barker to Jacqueline Sanders, January 4, 1958, Folder "Sanders, Jacqueline—1958," GBC; Frank Scully to Gray Barker, January 4, 1958, Folder "Scully, Frank," GBC.

51. Barker used the *Books of Charles Fart* cover sheet on a bound letter he sent to Moseley around the time that he was preparing this publication. The *Other Tongues, Other Cash* page appears as the back cover to both copies of *Youranus* in the Gray Barker collection. See Barker to Moseley, "The Books of Charles Fart,"; James W. Moseley, "Letters to U-No-Hu," *Saucer Clues* [*Saucer Smear*] 24, no. 3 (March 5, 1977): 3.

52. Barker, "Great Green God," [4]. All foliation from *Youranus* is counted from Moseley's copy, beginning with the first interior page and including blank leaves; the pages are printed on the recto only. The collation of other copies may vary.

53. Barker, "Great Green God," [4].

54. Barker, "Great Green God," [4].

55. Barker, "Great Green God," [4].

56. Batterham, *Office Copying Revolution*, 102–103.

57. Duplantier had begun corresponding with Barker after buying a copy of the *Saucerian Review* in 1956, and not long afterward Barker asked him to create saucer-themed artwork, following his *Youranus* contribution with a cartoon in the April/May 1958 issue of *Saucer News*, which Barker had sent to Moseley on the artist's behalf. See Duplantier, "I Remember Gray Barker," 1; Davis and Gene Duplantier, "Cartoon," *Saucer News* 5, no. 3 (whole no. 30) (April–May 1958): 17; Barker to Moseley, "The Books of Charles Fart," 13.

58. Gray Barker and Gene Duplantier, "They Knew Too Little about Flying Saucers," in *Youranus* ([Clarksburg, WV]: [Gray Barker], 1957), [53–54]; on Barker's appreciation of *Mad* see Gray Barker to James Villard, February 4, 1957, Folder "Villard, James," GBC.

59. Barker, "International Bankers," [28].

60. Gray Barker, "International Bankers," *Saucerian Bulletin* 7, no. 1 (whole no. 25) (October 1962): 16–18.

61. Barker and Sanders, "'Mon-Ka' Doesn't Come Through." Barker credited at least one "Von Mobile" hoax letter to *Psychic News* editor John Pitt, but implies his own participation as well. Barker to Sanders, November 24, 1956, 2.

62. Barker, "International Bankers," [31–32].

63. Barker, "International Bankers," [34].

64. "International Bankers" to Gray Barker, September 22, 1957, [Folder name redacted by request of the correspondent], GBC.

65. The correspondent was a minor at the time of the events discussed here, and Moseley declined to name them publicly, even after other ufological publications had done so. To protect their privacy I have redacted their name and am not citing the article that named them in its publication of the letters referred to here, and at their request I do not quote from their letters to Barker.

66. Barker to [recipient redacted], [November 27, 1957?]. Keel reproduced a hoax missive typed on the letterhead in John A. Keel, "Three Letters of Undetermined Origin," *Anomaly*, no. 3 (December 1967): 45–49.

67. Gray Barker to [recipient redacted], November 22, 1957, [Folder name redacted by request of the correspondent], GBC.

68. Moseley and Pflock, *Shockingly Close*, 124.

69. Five of these forgeries survive in Barker's files: "R. L. Andrews" to Laura Mundo, carbon copy and photocopy of typescript, December 16, 1957, Folder "Straith," GBC; "A. G. Matthews" to Manon Darlaine, carbon copy and photocopy of typescript, December 1957, Folder "Straith," GBC; "Kip" to Lex Mebane [and Ted Bloecher], Verifax copy and carbon copy of typescript, [December 1957?], Folder "Straith," GBC; "E. R. Stryker" to George Van Horn Moseley, carbon copy of typescript, December 1957, Folder "Straith," GBC; "R. E. Straith" to George Adamski, Verifax and photostat of typescript, December 16, 1957, Folder "Straith," GBC. For details on some of the letters, see Moseley and Pflock, *Shockingly Close*, 124–125; Laura Mundo, "[Letter to R. L. Andrews]," *The Open Letter*, April 1959, 14–17; Laura Mundo, *Flying-Saucers and the Father's Plan* (Dearborn, MI: Planetary Center, 1962), 9; Civilian Saucer Intelligence, "The Straith Letter," *CSI News Letter* 11, no. (CSI Publication No. 25) (July 15, 1959): 2.

70. Moseley and Pflock, *Shockingly Close*, 124.

71. "R. E. Straith" to Adamski, December 16, 1957.

72. "Reynold E. Straith," "Memorandum of Conversation" (Typescript, January 14, 1958), Folder "Straith," GBC.

73. Ted Bloecher to Coral Lorenzen, January 1, 1958, Folder 3.5, TBP; Ted Bloecher to Donald Keyhoe, January 6, 1958, Folder 3.5, TBP; Donald Keyhoe to Ted Bloecher, January 10, 1958, Folder 3.5, TBP. Bloecher soon began to doubt his initial, correct conclusion and began to suspect that Moseley had acted alone. Ted Bloecher to Coral Lorenzen, January 13, 1958, Folder 3.5, TBP.

74. Brinsley le Poer Trench, "U.S. Govt. Has Evidence of Extra-Terrestrials," *Flying Saucer Review* 4, no. 2 (April 1958): 2–3.

75. Gray Barker, "You Have Just Read a Letter from George Adamski," *Saucerian Bulletin* 3, no. 2 (whole no. 17) (May 1958): 6.

76. Barker, "You Have Just Read a Letter from George Adamski."

77. Gray Barker, "More on the Controversial State Department Letter," *Saucerian Bulletin* 3, no. 3 (whole no. 18) (June 1958): 12–13.

78. Barker, "More on the Controversial State Department Letter," 13.

79. Gray Barker, "Chasing the Flying Saucers [No. 8]," *Flying Saucers*, no. 32 [= 8] (December 1958): 43–44.

80. "G. K. Ganey" to "R. E. Straith," May 25, 1958, Folder "Straith," GBC. Hallen's signature bears a strong resemblance to Barker's own handwriting.

81. Max B. Miller, in particular, conducted a detailed investigation. Max B. Miller, "That State Department Letter," *Saucers* 6, no. 2 [Summer 1958]: 8–12; see also James D. Villard, "The 'R. E. Straith' Case," *Saucers* 6, no. 4 (Winter 1958–Winter 1959): 2–6.

82. Gray Barker, ed., *Gray Barker's Book of Adamski* (Clarksburg, WV: Saucerian Books, 1966), 68.

83. George Adamski to Gray Barker, September 19, 1958, in Barker, *The Adamski Documents, Part One*, [76].

84. Moseley and Pflock, *Shockingly Close*, 126–127.

85. Gray Barker to [recipient redacted], September 24, 1958, [Folder name redacted by request of the correspondent], GBC. Typographical errors corrected.

86. "Justice Dept. Hunting 'Straith' Hoaxer," *NICAP Special Bulletin*, November 1958, 4, https://retroufo58.tumblr.com/post/633938260867072000/nicap-special-bulletin-november-1958.

87. Barker, *Barker's Book of Adamski*, 69.

88. Gray Barker to [recipient redacted], November 19, 1958, [Folder name redacted by request of the correspondent], GBC. Paragraph break removed and typographical errors corrected.

89. Moseley and Pflock, *Shockingly Close*, 126. Decades later Moseley published a dubious, anonymous comment concerning the typewriter: "You are probably not aware of the fact that in 1980 the expansion of a shopping center parking lot in Clarksburg, W. Va. uncovered a strange parcel that was so odd it was turned over to the police, who sent it to the FBI laboratory believing that it must have figured in some crime. It was half a Remington typewriter, disassembled, flattened with a sledge hammer, burned with gasoline, doused with battery acid and then caustic lye. It had been put into a 5-gallon paint bucket and filled with roofing tar and then buried deeply in what had been a flower planter at the edge of the shopping center, and then a cubic foot of portland cement was poured on top of the hole. In spite of all that, the FBI lab identified the keys as belonging to the long-sought typer." However, Moseley prefaces the comment by stating that it comes from "a usually *un*reliable source." Its presence in the April 1 issue should also be taken into consideration. James W. Moseley, "Miscellaneous Ravings," *Saucer Smear* 32, no. 3 (April 1, 1985): 3.

90. A Freedom of Information Act request to the FBI turned up no documents related to this investigation.

91. Gray Barker to [recipient redacted], March 3, 1959, [folder name redacted by request of the correspondent], GBC.

92. Gray Barker to George C. Wilson, July 18, 1959, 1, Folder "Straith," GBC.

93. Barker to Wilson, July 18, 1959, 1.

94. Gray Barker to [recipient redacted], June 23, 1959, [Folder name redacted by request of the correspondent], GBC. Like Hallen's signature on the undistributed hoax Ganey memo, the "Kip" signature bears a strong resemblance to Barker's own.

95. Dove to Moseley, January 5, 1959; Dove to Moseley, March 2, 1959.

96. Lonzo Dove to Laimon Mitris, March 10, 1959, Folder "Dove, Lonzo," GBC; Laimon Mitris to Gray Barker, March 14, 1959, Folder "Mitris, Laimon," GBC. Mitris's visitor was almost certainly Australian eccentric Gordon Deller; see Clark, *UFO Encyclopedia*, 1:633 ("Jarrold Affair").

97. Gray Barker to Laimon Mitris, March 18, 1959, Folder "Dove, Lonzo," GBC.

98. Dove took this timing, as well as a joint appearance on the August 23 episode of "Long John's Party Line" in which Moseley and Yonah Fortner confronted Barker over the accusations, as evidence that Moseley and Barker were secretly working together. Richard Ogden, "Special Note" [September 5, 1959?], Folder "Dove, Lonzo," GBC; Gray Barker to [recipient redacted], September 11, 1959, 1, [folder name redacted by request of the correspondent], GBC.

99. Gray Barker, "[Letter to the Editor]," *Saucer News* 6, no. 4 (whole no. 37) (September 1959): 3.

100. Lonzo Dove, *The "Straith" State Department Fraud* (Broadway, VA: privately printed by the author, 1959). I have not seen a copy of this publication. No copies are recorded in OCLC and it is not held in either the Barker Collection or the Archives for the Unexplained; it appears in the bibliography of Clark, *UFO Encyclopedia*, 2:1320.

101. "Justice Dept. Hunting 'Straith' Hoaxer."

102. James W. Moseley, "Latest News about New York Lecture Series," *Saucer News* 11, no. 3 (whole no. 57) (September 1964): 4–5; Gray Barker, "The Strange Case of R. E. Straith," in *Gray Barker's Book of Adamski*, ed. Gray Barker (Clarksburg, WV: Saucerian Books, 1966), 61–78.

103. Barker, *Barker's Book of Adamski*, 68 (emphasis original).

104. Barker, *Barker's Book of Adamski*, 73.

105. Barker, *Barker's Book of Adamski*, 77–78.

106. American Film Institute, "Bell Book and Candle (1959)," AFI Catalog of Feature Films, 2019, https://catalog.afi.com/Catalog/moviedetails/52477.

107. The other titles visible on screen—which include William James's *The Will to Believe*, a biography of Rachmaninoff, and *How To Massage*—have nothing to do with saucers or the occult.

108. The date is inferred from Harold Fulton's report of when he had received his copies of the book in New Zealand. Harold Fulton to Gray Barker, September 4, 1958, Folder "Fulton, Harold," GBC.

109. OCLC records only thirteen copies, compared to over sixty for the book's first edition.

110. Gray Barker, *A Note from the Desk of Gray Barker* (Clarksburg, WV: Saucerian Book Club, [1958?]), [6].

111. Barker to Sanders, July 12, 1958.

112. Gray Barker, "Dear Saucerian Book Club Member," *Saucerian Book Club News* 1, no. 1 ([September–October 1958?]): 1.

113. For a robust, if not wholly unbiased, gathering of both positive and negative materials on Rampa's life and career, see Karen Mutton, *Lobsang Rampa, New Age Trailblazer*; a memoir by Rampa's longtime secretary, Sheelagh Rouse, is also a rich source of material, and a detailed account of the publication of *The Third Eye* appears in Warburg's memoir. Karen Mutton, *Lobsang Rampa, New Age Trailblazer* (Frankston, TX: Hidden Mysteries / TGS, 2006); Sheelagh Rouse, *Twenty-Five Years with T. Lobsang Rampa* (N.p.: published by the author, 2006); Fredric Warburg, *All Authors Are Equal: The Publishing Life of Frederic Warburg, 1936–1971* (New York: St. Martin's, 1974), 220–247.

114. T. Lobsang Rampa, *The Third Eye: The Autobiography of a Tibetan Lama* (London: Secker & Warburg, 1956).

115. David Snellgrove, review of *The Third Eye: Autobiography of a Tibetan Lama*, by T. Lobsang Rampa, *Oriental Art* 3, no. 2 (Summer 1957), 75; see also Donald S. Lopez Jr., *Prisoners of Shangri-La: Tibetan Buddhism and the West*, 20th anniv. ed. (Chicago: University of Chicago Press, 2018), 97; Agehananda Bharati, "The Origin and Persistence of Rampaism," The Life and Career of Prem Rawat aka Maharaji, accessed June 7, 2022, http://prem-rawat-bio.org /nrms/info/rampaism.htm.

116. I do not propose to solve here the controversy over the idea of transracialism, of which Rampa could be considered an example. It is clear, however, that Rampa centered his entire life around his self-identification as Tibetan for nearly three decades, and he legally changed his name to T. Lobsang Rampa. He never mentioned his birth name in his publications, even when discussing his former existence, and it was primarily used and publicized by those who wished to discredit him. From both a bibliographical and a legal standpoint, by the end of his life his name was indeed T. Lobsang Rampa, which is the name that I will use here rather than his birth name. On the controversial subject of transracialism, see Rebecca Tuvel, "In Defense of Transracialism," *Hypatia* 32, no. 2 (Spring 2017): 263–278, https://doi.org/10.1111/hypa .12327; and Jana Cattien, "Against 'Transracialism': Revisiting the Debate," *Hypatia* 34, no. 4 (Fall 2019): 713–735, https://doi.org/10.1111/hypa.12499.

117. Warburg, *All Authors Are Equal*, 244.

118. Gray Barker, "Chasing the Flying Saucers [No. 6]," *Flying Saucers*, no. 30 [= 6] (August 1958): 26.

119. Barker, "Chasing the Flying Saucers [No. 6]," 26.

120. Barker, "Chasing the Flying Saucers [No. 6]," 26.

121. Gray Barker, "To Eliminate the Many Wild Rumors . . . ," *Saucerian Bulletin* 4, no. 2 (whole no. 21) (September 1959): 24.

122. See, e.g., "Morris Jessup," *The U.F.O. Investigator* 1, no. 8 (June 1959): 8; "Obituary: M. K. Jessup," *The Spacecrafter*, December 1959, 27.

123. "Franklin Thomas (California, County Birth and Death Records, 1800–1994)," accessed June 5, 2022.

124. Gray Barker to Trevor James, June 10, 1959, 2, Folder "James, Trevor," GBC.

125. Gray Barker to Trevor James, June 14, 1959, Folder "James, Trevor," GBC.

126. "New Age" is a contentious term; for a definition, including summaries of the major counterarguments, see George D. Chryssides, "Defining the New Age," in *Handbook of New Age*, ed. Daren Kemp and James R. Lewis (Leiden: Brill, 2007), 5–24. Outside of quotations from Barker and other primary sources, I use it not to suggest a single, discrete movement, but rather a general milieu.

127. Trevor James to Gray Barker, June 12, 1959, Folder "James, Trevor," GBC.

CHAPTER 7

1. The photographs were first published by George van Tassel in "The Howard Menger Contact," *Proceedings of the College of Universal Wisdom* 5, no. 2 (November 1956): 1, 3–10, https://integratron.com/wp-content/uploads/2018/12/NOV-1956.pdf. For an early critique of the images, see Lonzo Dove, "Menger's Adamski-Type Saucers," *Saucer News* 4, no. 2 (whole no. 22) (March 1957): 6–7.

2. Mebane indicated that Menger had first appeared on the radio in late 1956, and Barker first noted Menger's narrative around the same time. Mebane to Barker, December 4, 1956; Gray Barker, "Newest 'Contact' Story," *Saucerian Bulletin* 1, no. 5 (whole no. 11) (November 1956): 5; Gray Barker, "Serious Doubt Has Been Cast on the 'Contact' Story," *Saucerian Bulletin* 2, no. 1 (whole no. 12) (January 1957): 2.

3. Civilian Saucer Intelligence, "'Very Sincere Fellow' Howard Menger Returns to Long John Nebel Program," *CSI News Letter* 9, no. (CSI Publication No. 21) (November 1957): 14–16; Richard Harpster to Ted Bloecher, June 10, 1957, Folder 3.2, TBP; Ted Bloecher to Richard Hall, October 14, 1957, Folder 3.2, TBP.

4. For further details on Menger's life during his son's illness, see Berthold Eric Schwarz, *UFO-Dynamics: Psychiatric and Psychic Aspects of the UFO Syndrome*, 3rd ed. (Moore Haven, FL: Rainbow Books, 1988), 110–112.

5. Barker to [recipient redacted], September 24, 1958. The official name for the event was either the East Coast Interplanetary Spacecraft Convention (according to some contemporary press coverage) or the Howard Menger Space Convention (according to the official event program). See Jules St. Germain, "Out of This World," *Argosy* 348, no. 1 (January 1959): 34–35, 100–101; "An Inner Space Convention in Outer Jersey," *New York Post*, September 15, 1958; Howard Menger, "Program for Howard Menger Space Convention, Sept. 13, 14th" (Swiftstream Farm, Lebanon, NJ, September 13, 1958), Folder "Menger, Howard—Articles," GBC.

6. Dominick Lucchesi to Gray Barker, July 15, 1958, 1, Folder "Lucchesi, Dominick," GBC; August C. Roberts to Gray Barker, July 24, 1958, 2, Folder "Menger, Howard—Correspondence," GBC.

7. Roberts to Barker, July 24, 1958, 2.

8. Howard Menger to August C. Roberts, July 18, 1958, Folder "Menger, Howard—Correspondence," GBC.

9. Gray Barker, "Chasing the Flying Saucers [No. 10]," *Flying Saucers*, no. 34 = FS-10 (May 1959): 19–43.

10. On Fortner, see Erik A. W. Östling, "Yonah Fortner and the 'Historical Doctrine' of 'Extraterrestrialism'" (American Academy of Religion Annual Meeting, Denver, 2018).

11. Gray Barker to Lex Mebane, December 7, 1956, Folder "Civilian Saucer Intelligence," GBC.

12. Gray Barker, "[Solicitation Letter for 'From Outer Space To You']" (Saucerian Press, Inc., December 1958), Folder "Menger, Howard—Correspondence," GBC.

13. Barnum employed a similar tactic in advertising the "Feejee mermaid" by allowing newspapers to freely reproduce a woodcut of the creature while claiming that the specimen's owner had prohibited it from being exhibited publicly. Neil Harris, *Humbug: The Art of P. T. Barnum* (Boston: Little, Brown, 1973), 63–64.

14. Gray Barker, "Editorial," *Saucerian Bulletin* 4, no. 1 (whole no. [20]) (May 1959): 2.

15. Howard Menger, "From Outer Space to You" (Carbon copy of typescript, [1958?]), Folder "Menger, Howard—FOSTY ms.," GBC.

16. The book was printed and shipped by July 2. Copies were shipped to preorder customers by July 20, based on a letter from reader Bernie Babcock. Gray Barker to James W. Moseley, "Ogden Out-Mongered: A Full (and Expensive) Report," Typescript, July 2, 1959, Box "Moseley/Private Writings," GBC; Bernie Babcock to Howard Menger, July 24, 1959, Folder "B—Misc.," item B-13-A, GBC.

17. Ruth Montgomery, *Strangers among Us: Enlightened Beings from a World to Come* (New York: Coward, McCann & Geoghegan, 1979), 13 & passim.

18. Gray Barker, "Dear Book Club Member," *Saucerian Book Club News* 2, no. 1 ([July–September 1959?]): 3.

19. Barker to Sanders, March 30, 1959, 2.

20. Howard Menger, *From Outer Space to You* (Clarksburg, WV: Saucerian Books, 1959), 24; Menger, "From Outer Space," 2.

21. Menger, "From Outer Space," 6.

22. Menger, *From Outer Space*, 28.

23. According to Barker's account, Girvin declined payment for the jacket painting, but Barker insisted on paying him "whatever we can afford based on sales." Barker, "Editorial," *Saucerian Bulletin* 4, no. 1: 3.

24. Barker to Sanders, March 30, 1959, 2.

25. Gray Barker to Frank Scully, September 14, 1959, Folder "Scully, Frank," GBC.

26. Gray Barker to Trevor James Constable, December 10, 1962, Folder "James, Trevor," GBC. Producing the jackets cost eight hundred dollars, and it is unclear if this figure is included in the unit price mentioned to Constable. Gray Barker to Joseph J. Badamo, September 16, 1959, Folder "Scully, Frank," GBC.

27. Barker to James, June 10, 1959; Barker to Moseley, "Ogden Out-Mongered," 2.

28. Gray Barker to Trevor James, June 4, 1959, Folder "James, Trevor," GBC; Barker to James, June 10, 1959, 2; Gray Barker to James Villard, July 30, 1959, Folder "Villard, James— correspondence 1959," GBC.

29. Barker to Scully, September 14, 1959.

30. Gray Barker to Trevor James, August 6, 1959, Folder "James, Trevor," GBC.

31. Barker to Scully, September 14, 1959.

32. Gray Barker, "Now Let's Beat the Deadline," *Saucerian Bulletin* 4, no. 2 (whole no. 21) (September 1959): 22.

33. Long John Nebel, *The Way-out World* (Englewood Cliffs, NJ: Prentice-Hall, 1961), 66; see also James W. Moseley, "Recent News Stories," *Saucer News* 7, no. 2 (whole no. 40) (June 1960): 18.

34. Barker, "Now Let's Beat the Deadline"," 22.

35. Gray Barker, "The Lama's Story," *Saucerian Bulletin* 3, no. 4 (whole no. 19) (October 1958): 14.

36. The text first appeared as T. Lobsang Rampa, "Saucers over Tibet," *Flying Saucer Review* 3, no. 2 (April 1957): 10–12.

37. T. Lobsang Rampa, *As It Was!* (London: Corgi / Transworld, 1976), 182.

38. Quoted in Mutton, *Lobsang Rampa*, 169.

39. Gray Barker to Joseph J. Badamo, October 14, 1959, Folder "Scully, Frank," GBC; Gray Barker to Jacqueline Sanders, September 24, 1959, Folder "Sanders, Jacqueline—1959," GBC.

40. Jacqueline Sanders to Gray Barker, April 12, 1960, Folder "Sanders, Jacqueline—1960," GBC.

41. Gray Barker to Trevor James, February 29, 1960, Folder "James, Trevor," GBC.

42. Edward Uhler Condon, *Final Report of the Scientific Study of Unidentified Flying Objects Conducted by the University of Colorado*, ed. Daniel S. Gillmor, Internet edition (Washington, DC: National Capital Area Skeptics, 1999), 861; Edward Uhler Condon, *Final Report of the Scientific Study of Unidentified Flying Objects Conducted by the University of Colorado*, ed. Daniel S. Gillmor (New York: Bantam Books, 1969), 514.

43. Saucerian Publications, "Anniversary Tribute to Gray Barker," [April–June 1961?], Folder "Promo—Sales," GBC.

44. "Sale! U.F.O. and New Age Book Bargains!," [June 1961?], Folder "Promo—Sales," GBC.

45. For Moseley's account of the convention, see Moseley and Pflock, *Shockingly Close*, 163–166; Moseley, "Report on the Giant Rock Convention."

46. Moseley, "Report on the Giant Rock Convention," 5.

47. Moseley, "Report on the Giant Rock Convention," 6; Gray Barker, "Chasing the Flying Saucers [No. 24]," *Flying Saucers*, no. FS-26 (July 1962): 30–33.

48. James W. Moseley, "Saucer News Non-Scheduled Newsletter #11," September 10, 1960.

49. Nebel, *Way-out World*, 70.

50. Barker, "Loan Application (4/12/1962)," 1.

51. Gray Barker to Jacqueline Sanders, February 17, 1961, Folder "Sanders, Jacqueline—1961," GBC.

52. Segrave, *Drive-in Theaters*, 153–168 passim.

53. Gray Barker to Jacqueline Sanders, [April 13, 1960?], Folder "Sanders, Jacqueline—1960," GBC.

54. Gray Barker to Jacqueline Sanders, August 8, 1961, 1, Folder "Sanders, Jacqueline—1961," GBC.

55. Gray Barker, "An Evening with [Name Redacted]," [March 6, 1962?], 6, Box "Moseley/Private Writings," GBC.

56. Barker to Moseley, "The Hearing," 5.

57. See, e.g., Gray Barker, "The Exhibitor Has His Say about Pictures: Snow White and the Three Stooges," *Boxoffice* 80, no. 2 (October 30, 1961): 182.

58. "Pittsburgh," *Boxoffice* 82, no. 4 (November 12, 1962): E-6.

59. "Eight-Page Moviews Being Published at Clarksburg," *Boxoffice* 78, no. 10 (December 26, 1960): 206; see also "Theatres Need Voice Like TV Guide, so West Virginia Editor Offers Moviews," *Boxoffice* 80, no. 81 (March 12, 1962): 42.

60. Gray Barker to Ivan Sanderson, February 20, 1962, Folder "Sanderson, Ivan," GBC; Ivan T. Sanderson to Gray Barker, May 12, 1962, Folder "Sanderson, Ivan," GBC; Gray Barker to Ivan Sanderson, May 23, 1962, Folder "Sanderson, Ivan," GBC.

61. John J. Robinson presented conclusive evidence that identified Williamson as the book's author; however, Zirger, referring to Williamson's private writings, asserts that Williamson distinguished between himself and "Brother Philip," who was "an entity regarded as distinct from himself," and further notes that some of the material was channeled by Dorothy Martin, Betty Jane Williamson, and Charles Laughead. Further complicating matters, Ray Stanford later claimed that he had channeled the material, and Williamson published it without his consent. John J. Robinson, "The Three-Faced Idol, or, The Identity of Brother Philip Hidden in the Secret of the Andes," *Saucer News* 9, no. 2 (whole no. 48) (June 1962): 10–13; Zirger and Martinelli, *Incredible Life*, 310–313; Zarkon 2, "Ray Stanford Uncensored," *The Truth Uncensored* (blog), November 21, 2009, http://the-truth-uncensored.blogspot.com/2009/11 /ray-stanford-is-researcher-of-things.html.

62. James W. Moseley, "Recent News Stories," *Saucer News* 8, no. 1 (whole no. 43) (March 1961): 11.

CHAPTER 8

1. Barker insisted on several occasions that his editing of Bender's text was minimal, but Barker himself may have been behind rumors that sinister forces had successfully pressured him to make drastic changes. In the absence of Bender's original manuscript, the question of what, if anything, Barker may have added to Bender's narrative remains open. Gray Barker, "Publisher's Introduction," in *Flying Saucers and the Three Men*, by Albert K. Bender, ed. Gray Barker (Clarksburg, WV: Saucerian Books, 1962), 9–12; Gray Barker, "Letters," *Gray Barker's Newsletter*, no. 3 (January 1976): 11; James W. Moseley, "Recent News Stories," *Saucer News* 9, no. 3 (whole no. 49) (September 1962): 20–21.

2. Bender, *Flying Saucers*, 45–46.

3. Samuel R. Delany, *Times Square Red, Times Square Blue* (New York: New York University Press, 1999), 15; see also Marcus McCann, *Park Cruising: What Happens When We Wander off the Path* (Toronto: Anansi, 2023), 179–80.

4. In letters to both Lucchesi and Sanders, Barker described a theory that Bender was gay. Gray Barker to Dominick Lucchesi, [July–October 1954?], 1, Folder "Lucchesi, Dominick," GBC; Barker to Jacqueline Sanders, November 21, 1954, 5.

5. C-Day was not announced in *Space Review*, and the printed announcement that Bender describes seems to have been scarce, if it ever existed; no copy is present in Barker's archive. The sole extant source of the announcement appears to be Bender, *Flying Saucers*, 83–84. The text of Bender's C-Day psychic broadcast was later adapted into the Klaatu song "Calling Occupants of Interplanetary Craft," which became a minor hit for the Carpenters in 1977.

6. Bender, *Flying Saucers*, 84–85.

7. Bender, *Flying Saucers*, 89–92. Bender only mentions it being a July evening, but the circumstances immediately preceding the apparition match the events of July 6 as given by Barker to Harold Fulton (with "Chronology"), December 18, 1954, 6.

8. Bender does not explain the word "Kazik" in *Flying Saucers and the Three Men*, but later made its meaning clear. Bender, *Flying Saucers*, 99; Albert K. Bender, *The World of Kazik*, audio recording, 1970, https://archive.org/details/HighStrangenessGuide/02.mp3.

9. Bender, *Flying Saucers*, 154–156.

10. Bender, *Flying Saucers*, 175.

11. Gulyas observes that the book "reads like a pastiche of . . . contactee literature." Gulyas, *Extraterrestrials*, 187.

12. The date of Barker's receipt of the manuscript is inferred from a reference to it in Gray Barker to Laimon Mitris, December 9, 1961, Folder "Mitris, Laimon," GBC; on the February release date, see Gray Barker, "Chasing the Flying Saucers [No. 23]," *Flying Saucers*, no. FS-25 (May 1962): 53; Gray Barker, "Why the Bender Book Has Been Delayed," *Saucer News* 9, no. 2 (whole no. 48) (June 1962): 6–7.

13. James W. Moseley, "Publicity-Seeking Antics by Gray Barker," *Saucer News* 9, no. 2 (whole no. 48) (June 1962): 2.

14. Barker, "Bender Book Has Been Delayed," 6.

15. The loan application may have been submitted to Lovett. Barker, "Loan Application (4/12/1962)," 3.

16. Gray Barker, "Personal News Release Re: Albert K. Bender" (Saucerian Publications, [January 12, 1962?]), 2, Folder "Promo—FS & Three Men," GBC.

17. Gray Barker to Trevor James Constable, [October 3, 1962?], 1, Folder "James, Trevor," GBC.

18. Barker, "Letters," *Gray Barker's Newsletter*, no. 3 (January 1976): 11.

19. Beasley and Sampsel, "The Bender Mystery," 21–22.

20. Barker to Constable, [October 3, 1962?], 1.

21. Gray Barker to James W. Moseley, "Mulberry Place," [March 3, 1962?], i, Box "Moseley/Private Writings," GBC.

22. Barker to Moseley, [March 3, 1962?], 3–4, 6.

23. Barker to Moseley, [March 3, 1962?], 3.

24. Gray Barker to James W. Moseley, "More Mulberry Place," [April 6, 1962?], 7, Box "Moseley/Private Writings," GBC.

25. The documents related to Barker and McCulty's trial are not sealed but are largely inaccessible in the archive of the Harrison County courthouse. For the discussion here, I am indebted to David Houchin, who has reviewed and summarized the surviving documents. David

Houchin, "Review of the Barker and McCulty Court Documents," July 2010, Folder "Barker, Gray—Biography and chronology," GBC.

26. Houchin, "Review of Court Documents," 3.

27. On the application of this charge during this time period, see Neil Miller, *Sex-Crime Panic: A Journey to the Paranoid Heart of the 1950s* (Los Angeles: Alyson Books, 2002), 130.

28. "Jury to Resume Studies; Barker Trial in Progress," *Clarksburg Exponent*, December 6, 1962.

29. Houchin, "Review of Court Documents," [1]. For examples of larger-scale harassment of gay communities in other towns around the same time, see Miller, *Sex-Crime Panic*; John Gerassi, *The Boys of Boise: Furor, Vice, and Folly in an American City* (New York: Macmillan, 1966).

30. "Alma M. Corder," November 24, 1962, New York State, Marriage Index, 1881–1967.

31. Houchin, "Review of Court Documents," 1.

32. Houchin, "Review of Court Documents," 3.

33. Houchin, "Review of Court Documents," 2.

34. David Houchin, "Gray Barker: Notes from City Directories," [2001?], 1, Folder "Barker, Gray—Biography and chronology," GBC.

35. Quoted by Houchin, personal communication with author.

36. Quoted by Houchin, personal communication with author.

37. For further context on the sexual dynamics in play in Barker's world, see George Chauncey, *Gay New York: Gender, Urban Culture, and the Makings of the Gay Male World, 1890–1940* (New York: Basic Books, 1994), esp. 86–91; Colin R. Johnson, *Just Queer Folks: Gender and Sexuality in Rural America* (Philadelphia: Temple University Press, 2013), esp. 55–60, 88–97.

38. Rachel Hope Cleves, "The Problem of Modern Pederasty in Queer History: A Case Study of Norman Douglas," *Historical Reflections* 46, no. 1 (Spring 2020): 49, https://doi.org/10.3167/hrrh.2020.460104.

39. U.S. Department of Health, Education, and Welfare, Anthony J. Celebrezze, and Luther L. Terry, *Vital Statistics of the United States, 1960*, vol. 3, *Marriage and Divorce* (Washington, DC, 1964), 1–9, https://www.cdc.gov/nchs/data/vsus/mgdv60_3.pdf; Gordon B. Dahl, "Early Teen Marriage and Future Poverty," *Demography* 47, no. 3 (August 2010): 693, https://doi.org/10.1353/dem.0.0120.

40. "Pittsburgh," *Boxoffice* 87, no. 14 (July 26, 1965): E-8; "Shotgun Wedding: Taglines," IMDB .com, 2022, http://www.imdb.com/title/tt0057496/taglines.

41. Pierre Lagrange, ed., "Avant-propos: Gray Barker et l'invention des Men in Black," in *Ils en savaient trop sur les soucoupes volantes*, by Gray Barker, trans. Vincent Carénini, Bibliothèque des prodiges (Paris: Presses du Châtelet, 2002), 44 (my translation).

42. *Shades of Gray*, 1:03:00.

43. *Shades of Gray*, 1:02:00.

44. Liavon Yurevich, "Ted Bloecher Papers, 1950–2000," New York Public Library Archives & Manuscripts, 2013, https://archives.nypl.org/mss/5984.

45. Jack Halberstam, *In a Queer Time and Place: Transgender Bodies, Subcultural Lives* (New York: New York University Press, 2005), 36–37, https://doi.org/10.18574/nyu/9780814790892 .001.0001. On the related concept of the "Great Gay Migration" narrative and rural spaces as a national "closet," see Kath Weston, *Long Slow Burn: Sexuality and Social Science* (New York: Routledge, 1998), 29–56; John Howard, *Men like That: A Southern Queer History* (1999; repr., Chicago: University of Chicago Press, 2001), 63; Christopher J. Stapel, "Dismantling Metrocentric and Metronormative Curricula: Toward a Critical Queer Pedagogy of Southern Rural Space and Place," in *Queer South Rising: Voices of a Contested Place*, ed. Reta Ugena Whitlock (Charlotte, North Carolina: Information Age Publishing, 2013), 59–72.

46. For comparison, see West Virginia native Jeff Mann's detailed description of the unity of his rural and queer identities. Jeff Mann, *Loving Mountains, Loving Men* (Athens: Ohio University Press, 2005).

47. Gray Barker, "Should You Burn the Bender Book? [Solicitation Letter for Bender Mystery Confirmed]" (Saucerian Publications, 1962), 3, Folder "Promo—Bender Mystery Confirmed 1962," GBC. For details on Barker's production methods, see Mckee, "Office Copying Technology."

48. Morris K. Jessup to Gray Barker, December 22, 1956, Folder "Jessup, Morris K.," GBC.

49. Barker mentions his plans to purchase an offset press from the Addressograph company in a letter to James W. Moseley, "More Mulberry Place," [April 6, 1962?], 2. A photo published in Gene Duplantier's zine *UFOlk* shows the Saucerian staff (Mae Britton, John Sheets, and Thelma Atha) unloading the machine upon its arrival at Barker's office. Duplantier, "Gray Days at Clarksburg," 12. On the Multilith, see Batterham, *Office Copying Revolution*, 110–111; Laurens Leurs, "The History of Prepress & Publishing: 1950–1959," *Prepressure* (blog), [2010?], https://www.prepressure.com/prepress/history/events-1950-1959.

50. Gray Barker, ed., *Bender Mystery Confirmed: Consisting of Comments by Readers of "Flying Saucers and the Three Men"* (Clarksburg, WV: Saucerian Books, 1962), 7–8.

51. Barker, "Should You Burn the Bender Book?," [2].

52. Barker, "Should You Burn the Bender Book?," [3–4].

53. Barker to Constable, [October 3, 1962?], 2 (paragraph breaks removed).

54. "Elkins 1963 Past Weather (West Virginia, United States)," Weatherspark, [2010–2022?], https://weatherspark.com/h/y/19634/1963/Historical-Weather-during-1963-in-Elkins -West-Virginia-United-States.

55. Barker to Moseley, "More Mulberry Place," 2; Gray Barker to the Bank of Gassaway, March 3, 1963, Folder "G-1"; item G1-86-1, GBC.

56. Before this, Duplantier's zine had been produced on a spirit duplicator. The first issue printed by Barker was the December 1962 issue, in an edition of 130 copies. Gene Duplantier to Gray Barker, August 29, 1962, 1, Folder "Stuart, John—Correspondence," GBC.

57. Gray Barker and James W. Moseley, "Contract of Sale" (February 23, 1963), Folder "Barker, Gray—Biography and chronology," GBC.

58. Barker and Moseley, "Contract of Sale," 1.

59. Moseley and Pflock, *Shockingly Close*, 182–183.

60. James W. Moseley, "Editorial: Saucer News Combines with 'The Saucerian Bulletin,'" *Saucer News* 10, no. 2 (whole no. 52) (June 1963): 2.

61. James W. Moseley, "Saucer News Non-Scheduled Newsletter #16," May 15, 1963.

62. Wilkinson and Stuart to Barker, December 5, 1954.

63. John E. Stuart, "Concerning the 'Strange Experiences' during 1953/54" (Typescript, October 4, 1956, Folder "Stuart, John—UFO Warning," GBC; John E. Stuart to Gray Barker, April 9, 1955, Folder "Stuart, John—Correspondence," GBC; John E. Stuart to Gray Barker, March 1, 1959, Folder "Stuart, John—Correspondence," GBC; John E. Stuart, *Warning from the UFO*, 1962, Box "Audiocassettes," GBC; John E. Stuart, "The Kiwi under UFO Attack" (Typescript, 1962), 21, Folder "Stuart, John—UFO Warning," GBC.

64. The metal fragment and fistfight each receive only one mention, in, respectively, Stuart to Barker, April 9, 1955; and Stuart, "Concerning the Strange Experiences".

65. John E. Stuart to Gray Barker, October 2, 1956, 1, Folder "Stuart, John—Correspondence," GBC.

66. John E. Stuart to Gray Barker, April 8, 1958, Folder "Stuart, John—Correspondence," GBC.

67. John E. Stuart to Gray Barker, April 8, 1962, Folder "Stuart, John—Correspondence," GBC.

68. A prepublication announcement of the book lists its title as *John Stuart Speaks–Researcher Hushed Up*. Saucerian Publications, "U.F.O. and New Age Books from Saucerian Publications" (Saucerian Publications, [1962?], Folder "Promos—Michael X," GBC.

69. John E. Stuart, *UFO Warning* (Clarksburg, WV: Saucerian Books, 1963), 54.

70. Stuart, *UFO Warning*, 67.

71. Stuart, *UFO Warning*, 80.

72. Jerome Clark, *Unexplained!: Strange Sightings, Incredible Occurrences, and Puzzling Physical Phenomena*, 3rd ed. (Detroit: Visible Ink, 2013), 349.

73. Gray Barker, "Kollector's Korner," *Gray Barker's Newsletter*, no. 7 (March 1977): 17.

74. Stuart, *UFO Warning*, 35.

75. See, e.g., Stuart, *UFO Warning*, 43; compare Stuart, "Kiwi under UFO Attack," 21.

76. Gray Barker to Gene Duplantier, [September 1962?], 1, Folder "Stuart, John—Correspondence," GBC; Gene Duplantier to Gray Barker, October 12, 1962, Folder "Stuart, John—Correspondence," GBC.

77. Gene Duplantier, *Barbara (Illustration for UFO Warning)*, 1962, ink on paper & photostat, 1962, Folder "Stuart, John—UFO Warning," GBC.

78. Stuart, *UFO Warning*, 67; compare Stuart, "Kiwi under UFO Attack," 38–39.

79. John E. Stuart to Gray Barker, June 20, 1963, 1–2, Folder "Stuart, John—Correspondence," GBC.

80. Gray Barker to John Stuart, June 29, 1963, Folder "Stuart, John—Correspondence," GBC.

81. Barker to Moseley, "The Hearing," 13.

82. Barker to Moseley, "The Hearing," 3; Houchin, "Review of Court Documents," 3.

83. For example, he refers to someone he sees at the courthouse as "a Young Man, dressed in Semi-JD fashion, who appeared rather interesting from a UFO Research standpoint." Barker to Moseley, "The Hearing," 6.

84. "Drive-in Film Stampedes Cattle."

85. Barker to Moseley, "The Hearing," 20.

86. Barker to Moseley, "The Hearing," 20.

87. Richard E. Wallace, review of *Gray Barker's Book of Saucers*, by Gray Barker, *Saucer News* 13, no. 1 (whole no. 63), (March 1966), 15.

88. The story of the Allende letters and the Varo edition has been reproduced in multiple places; the summarization here draws on William L. Moore and Charles Berlitz, *The Philadelphia Experiment: Project Invisibility* (New York: Grosset & Dunlap, 1979); Jacques Vallee, "Anatomy of a Hoax: The Philadelphia Experiment Fifty Years Later," *Journal of Scientific Exploration* 8, no. 1 (1994): 54; Steiger and Whritenour, *New UFO Breakthrough*, 56–77; Gray Barker, ed., *The Strange Case of Dr. M. K. Jessup* (Clarksburg, WV: Saucerian Books, 1963); Riley Crabb, ed., *M. K. Jessup and the Allende Letters* (Vista, CA: Borderland Sciences Research Associates Foundation, 1962); and Barker's own preface to Morris K. Jessup and Carl M. Allen, *The Case for the UFO: Unidentified Flying Objects*, annotated ed. (Clarksburg, WV: Saucerian Press, 1973), (unpaginated front matter).

89. Crabb, *M. K. Jessup and the Allende Letters*, 27.

90. Robert A. Goerman, "Michael Ann Dunn: In Memoriam," Alias Carlos Allende, 2007, https://windmill-slayer.tripod.com/aliascarlosallende/id12.html; see also Gray Barker, "The Enigma of M. K. Jessup," *Flying Saucers*, no. 74 (September 1971): 12, https://www.debunker.com/historical/GrayBarkerPapers.pdf. Estimates of the print run range from 25 to 127 copies. Brad Steiger, "Fantastic Key to the Flying Saucer Mystery," *Saga* 35, no. 2 (November 1967): 60; Steiger and Whritenour, *New UFO Breakthrough*, 62; Rose Hiett to Gray Barker, November 17, 1971, Folder "Hiett, Rose," GBC; Moore and Berlitz, *Philadelphia Experiment*, 38; Vallee, "Anatomy of a Hoax," 54; P. J. Dowers, *Hoax: The Philadelphia Experiment Unraveled* (N.p.: Pandora's Press, 2012), 86.

91. Barker, "Chasing the Flying Saucers [No. 10]," 36.

92. The supposed mystery was largely explained in a 1980 article in *Fate*; see Robert A. Goerman, "Alias Carlos Allende," *Fate* 33, no. 10 (October 1980), http://windmill-slayer.tripod.com/aliascarlosallende/.

93. Barker, *Strange Case of M. K. Jessup*, 61.

94. Barker, *Strange Case of M. K. Jessup*, 62.

95. Barker and Moseley, "Saucerian Bulletin Contract of Sale," 1.

96. Barker to Moseley, "The Hearing," 21–22. One participant in the séance is identified as "L."

97. Barker, *Strange Case of M. K. Jessup*, 79.

98. John A. Keel, "UFO Kidnappers!," *Saga*, February 1967, 60–61.

99. In the early 1990s, Jacques Vallee attested in a summary of Jessup's death that "the Allende revelations became an obsession for Jessup" and suggested that they were a key contributor to the "emotional turmoil" that led to his suicide. Vallee, "Anatomy of a Hoax," 54.

100. Gray Barker to Aden R. Major, August 21, 1963, Folder "Jessup, Morris K.—Suicide," GBC.

101. Sandy Moseley, "What Gray Barker Is Really Like," *Saucer News* 10, no. 4 (whole no. 54) (December 1963): 14 (paragraph break removed).

102. *Whispers from Space*, 1:15.

103. James W. Moseley, "The Inside Story Regarding Our Feud with Gray Barker," *Saucer News* 11, no. 2 (whole no. 56) (June 1964): 2 (spelling error corrected).

104. Gray Barker to Virginia Brasington, January 4, 1964, Folder "Brasington, Virginia," GBC; Gray Barker to James W. Moseley, October 30, 1963, Folder "Xmas," GBC.

105. Gray Barker to John Stuart, June 24, 1963, Folder "Stuart, John—Correspondence," GBC.

106. Elizabeth X, "Laura Charlotte (Mundo) Marxer (1913–1989)," Wikitree, May 30, 2022, https://www.wikitree.com/wiki/Mundo-10; Mundo, *Mundo UFO Report*, 4.

107. The DFSC was under investigation by the FBI at the time of her involvement, and the drama surrounding her departure appears in the publicly available records of the period. See Aaron John Gulyas, "And Then the Feds Showed Up . . . ," *The Saucer Life*, November 26, 2017, podcast, 28:06, https://saucerlife.com/2017/11/26/encounter-206-and-then-the-feds-showed-up/; and the original documents in "FBI Vault," file 13, 26–31.

108. Mundo, *Flying-Saucers and the Father's Plan*, inside front cover.

109. Mundo, *Flying-Saucers and the Father's Plan*, 15.

110. Gray Barker to Laura Mundo, December 12, 1962, Folder "Mundo, Laura #1," GBC.

111. Laura Mundo to Gray Barker, April 26, 1963, Folder "Mundo, Laura #1," GBC.

112. Laura Mundo to Gray Barker, August 8, 1963, Folder "Mundo, Laura #1," GBC.

113. This is below an abortive statement reading only "No copyright is claimed, and the author gives." Laura Mundo, *Flying Saucers and the Father's Plan* (Clarksburg, WV: Saucerian Books, 1963), [4].

114. Laura Mundo to Gray Barker, November 15, 1963, Folder "Mundo, Laura #1," GBC (paragraph break removed; the punctuation given as dashes replace the original's two-period ellipses).

115. Laura Mundo to Gray Barker, November 30, 1963, Folder "Mundo, Laura #1," GBC.

116. Laura Mundo to Gray Barker, January 1964, Folder "Mundo, Laura #1," GBC.

117. Carmella Falzone, "Letter to the Editor," *Saucer News* 11, no. 1 (whole no. 55) (March 1964): 4.

118. Laura Mundo, *The Father's Plan (and Flying Saucers)* (Dearborn, MI: Planetary Space Center, 1964), i.

119. Moseley recounts the hoax but is unaware of the rationale behind it. Moseley and Pflock, *Shockingly Close*, 171; see also Gabriel Mckee, "A Contactee Canon: Gray Barker's Saucerian Books," in *The Paranormal and Popular Culture: A Postmodern Religious Landscape*, ed. Darryl V. Caterine and John W. Morehead (New York: Routledge, 2019), 284–285.

120. Barker, *UFO 96*, [5].

121. Barker, *UFO 96*, [31–33].

122. Barker, *UFO 96*, [65].

123. Barker, *UFO 96*, [5].

124. Gray Barker to August C. Roberts, February 3, 1964, Folder "Roberts, August/Correspondence with Gray Barker," GBC.

125. "Pittsburgh," *Boxoffice* 81, no. 8 (June 12, 1962): E-6; "Pittsburgh," *Boxoffice* 83, no. 11 (July 8, 1963): E-6; Gray Barker, "A Weekend with James W. Moseley, with Complete Details of the Mongers Thereof" (Bound typescript, April 25, 1962), Box "Moseley/Private Writings," GBC.

126. Fannie Hoffman, ed., *Gray Barker's Questions and Answers about UFO's* ([Clarksburg, WV]: [Saucerian Books], 1969), [6].

127. *Whispers from Space*, 45:00.

128. Gray Barker to Lon Dunaway, May 23, 1964, Folder "D—Misc.," item D-26, GBC.

129. Gray Barker to Joseph H. Davis, April 11, 1964, 2, Folder "Jessup, Morris K.—Suicide," GBC.

130. I am again indebted to David Houchin's summary of documents from the Harrison County Courthouse for this information.

131. Quoted in Houchin, "Review of Court Documents," 4.

132. Quoted in Houchin, "Review of Court Documents," 4.

133. James W. Moseley, "Recent News," *Saucer News* 11, no. 3 (whole no. 57) (September 1964): 8–23; Condon, *Final Report*, 1999, 861; Condon, *Final Report*, 1969, 514.

134. James W. Moseley, "Recent News," *Saucer News* 12, no. 4 (whole no. 62) (December 1965): 21.

135. Barker, *Barker's Book of Saucers*, 11.

136. Barker had tested outsourcing with Virginia Brasington's *Flying Saucers in the Bible*, issued at the end of 1963 on a subsidy basis. Gray Barker to Virginia Brasington, February 21, 1963, Folder "Brasington, Virginia," GBC; Virginia Brasington to Gray Barker, April 27, 1963, Folder "Brasington, Virginia," GBC; Virginia Brasington to Gray Barker, June 9, 1963, Folder "Brasington, Virginia," GBC.

137. Saucerian Publications, "Spacecraft News, Issue No. 1," November 1965, [5].

138. Saucerian Publications, "Spacecraft News," [4].

139. Gray Barker to Ivan Sanderson, September 6, 1963, Folder "Sanderson, Ivan," GBC.

140. Moseley and Pflock, *Shockingly Close*, 172.

141. W. Buhler, "The A.V.B. Contact Case," *SBEDV Boletim*, no. 26–27 (April–July 1962): 1, 7–9, 14, https://files.afu.se/Downloads/Magazines/Brazil/SBEDV/SBEDV%20-%20No%20026-27%20-%201962.pdf; Gordon Creighton, "The Most Amazing Case of All: Part 1—A Brazilian Farmer's Story," *Flying Saucer Review* 11, no. 1 (January–February 1965): 13–17. Barker's text seems to follow Creighton's version, but Duplantier's accompanying illustrations more closely match the crude witness drawings from the SBDEV account than those published by Creighton.

142. "Some of the details must need be missing, for we could not with propriety interview him too closely on this matter; for he seemed very reticent and ashamed, and blushed much when this was discussed. Suffice it to say that he acquiesced to the rather persuasive demands of the female"; in contrast, Creighton's gloss mentions only the alien woman's open arms, with a suggestive ellipsis. Barker, *Barker's Book of Saucers*, 55.

143. Barker, *Barker's Book of Saucers*, 55.

144. Coral Lorenzen and Jim Lorenzen, *Flying Saucer Occupants* (New York: Signet, 1967), 42–72.

145. A rumor emerged in the 2010s that Barbara Hudson had been the book's author, but Adam Gorightly has demonstrated that this was not the case. The book's author was Jan Hudson, apparently a pseudonym of George H. Smith. See Adam Gorightly, "Barbara Hudson & Those Sexy Saucer People," *Chasing UFOs* (blog), February 3, 2019, https://chasingufosblog.com/2019/02/03/barbara-hudson-those-sexy-saucer-people.

146. Jan Hudson, *Those Sexy Saucer People* (San Diego: Greenleaf Classics, 1967; repr., n.p., 2019).

147. Gray Barker, "Sexy Saucer People" (Typescript, [1977?]), Folder "Barker, Gray—Sexy Saucer People," GBC.

CHAPTER 9

1. Condon, *Final Report*, 1999, 861; Condon, *Final Report*, 1969, 514.

2. Quoted in Jacobs, *UFO Controversy*, 204.

3. Moseley and Pflock, *Shockingly Close*, 193.

4. Gray Barker to John C. Sherwood, February 3, 1967, Folder "Sherwood, John," GBC; Gray Barker to John C. Sherwood, February 25, 1967, Folder "Sherwood, John," GBC; John C. Sherwood, interview by Gabriel Mckee, June 22, 2022.

5. Sherwood, interview; Gray Barker, "The Big Flap of '66," *Spacecraft News*, [new series] no. 2 (Fall 1966): 4.

6. Barker to Sherwood, December 11, 1966.

7. Barker to Sherwood, February 25, 1967.

8. Gray Barker, "Your Editor Expelled from N.I.C.A.P.," *Spacecraft News*, [new series] no. 2 (Fall 1966): 14. The letter informing Barker of his expulsion is reproduced in Michael Strayer, ed., *UFO Is a Bucket of Shit: A Gray Barker Zine* (N.p.: Mothboys Podcast / Strange Days Zine, 2023), [1].

9. John A. Keel, *Jadoo* (New York: Julian Messner, 1957), 28.

10. Ali Behdad, "Orientalism and Middle East Travel Writing," in *Orientalism and Literature*, ed. Geoffrey P. Nash (Cambridge: Cambridge University Press, 2019), 197, https://doi.org/10.1017/9781108614672.011; on Keel's writing style in general, see Deborah Dixon, "A Benevolent and Sceptical Inquiry: Exploring 'Fortean Geographies' with the Mothman," *Cultural Geographies* 14, no. 2 (2007): 189–210, https://www.jstor.org/stable/44251140.

11. Doug Skinner, "That 'Playboy' Article," *John Keel: Not an Authority on Anything* (blog), February 11, 2015, http://www.johnkeel.com/?p=2482.

12. The magazine opted instead to run an article by J. Allen Hynek. J. Allen Hynek, "The UFO Gap," *Playboy* 14, no. 12 (December 1967): 143–146, 267–271, https://n2t.net/ark:/13960/t1f5hr6g.

13. Keel's first published use of term "Men in Black" was in John A. Keel, "UFO 'Agents of Terror,'" *Saga* 35, no. 1 (October 1967): 28–31, https://files.afu.se/Downloads/Magazines/0%20-%20Articles/United%20States/SAGA/1967%2010%2000_SAGA%20-%20John%20Keel%20-%20UFO%20Agents%20of%20Terror.pdf; the abbreviation MIB first appeared in John A. Keel, "UFO Report: The Sinister Men in Black," *Fate* 21, no. 4 (April 1968): 32–39.

14. For an early example of this that precedes the release of Keyhoe's *Flying Saucer Conspiracy*, see John Otto, "Come In, Outer Space," *The Saucerian* 3, no. 2 (whole no. 6) (Spring 1955): 37–40.

15. Keel, "UFO 'Agents of Terror,'" 78.

16. Dixon, "Benevolent and Sceptical Inquiry," 200–201.

17. See Thompson, *Angels and Aliens*, 95. Eventually the metanarrative of the Men in Black would come to encompass a "typical" series of events based largely on Keel's conceptualization; researcher Hilary Evans offers a succinct summary. However, even in Evans's account, the MIB phenomenon is a chimera, with no single case containing all of the "standard" elements, and most differing significantly from the template. Hilary Evans, *Visions, Apparitions, Alien Visitors* (Wellingborough: Aquarian, 1984), 138–139.

18. James W. Moseley, "Recent News Stories," *Saucer News* 8, no. 4 (whole no. 46) (December 1961): 14. Moseley later published a photograph of the making of this hoax image. Moseley is uncertain of the identity of the individual in the behind-the-hoax photo, but the model appears to be the one used in the Gonzales photograph. In later years, however, Moseley misidentified the photograph as representing the Lost Creek hoax. James W. Moseley, "In Which We Attempt to Take Another Look at the Famous 'Lost Creek' Saucer Case," *Saucer Smear* 33, no. 2 (March 1, 1986): 2; James W. Moseley, "Editorial," *Saucer Smear* 58, no. 5 (May 2011): 1.

19. James W. Moseley, "Recent UFO Sightings," *Saucer News* 13, no. 4 (whole no. 66) (Winter 1966–Winter 1967): 33.

20. Moseley and Pflock, *Shockingly Close*, 201. The prop used to make this film is part of Barker's archive at the Clarksburg-Harrison Public Library, and Moseley demonstrated the fishing pole rig for Ralph Coon's film *Whispers From Space*. Gray Barker, *Lost Creek Saucer Prop*, 1966, 1966, Artifacts Box, GBC; *Whispers from Space*, 38:00.

21. Gray Barker to Ronald C. Calais, May 8, 1967, Folder "C-6," item C6-44-1, GBC.

22. James W. Moseley to Gray Barker, January 4, 1968, Folder "Keel, John—#2," GBC.

23. Part of the cost for the film's reproduction was covered by television producer Ronald C. Calais. Gray Barker, "Invoice for Ronald Calais" (June 14, 1967), Folder "C-6," item C6-7-1, GBC; see also Gray Barker, "Recent News," *Saucer News* 15, no. 1 (whole no. 71) (Spring 1968): 14. The origin of the "Airport Saucer" film is less clear than that of the Lost Creek film. Moseley admitted to being present at its creation, but shortly thereafter retracted the claim, saying instead that he was involved in creating only the Lost Creek hoax. James W. Moseley, "Ye Olde Misc. Ravings," *Saucer Wit* [*Saucer Smear*] 26, no. 3 (March 1979): 1; James W. Moseley, "Ye Olde Mail Bag," *Son of Saucer Wit* [*Saucer Smear*] 26, no. 5 (April 30, 1979): 3.

24. Some sources point specifically to the villain Killer Moth as a possible origin of this name, but while this character had appeared in comic books by 1966, he had not appeared on television. See Richard Moreno, *Myths and Mysteries of Illinois: True Stories of the Unsolved and Unexplained* (Guilford, CT: Globe Pequot, 2013), 142; "Killer Moth," 1966 Batman Pages, May 20, 2020, https://www.66batmania.com/bios/villains/killer-moth/.

25. Gray Barker to Allen Greenfield, November 19, 1966, Folder "Greenfield, Allen," GBC.

26. An article in the *Parkersburg News* for December 5, 1966, suggests that he may have been in the area briefly in November; see Raymond A. Keller, "Lessons Learned from a Contactee:

Woodrow W. Derenberger (1916–1990), Part II," *Phantoms & Monsters* (blog), July 21, 2020, https://www.phantomsandmonsters.com/2020/07/lessons-learned-from-contactee -woodrow_21.html.

27. John A. Keel, "Special Report on Incidents in Ohio and West Virginia (2)" ([1967?]), 6–7, DS, http://www.johnkeel.com/?p=2808; see also Gray Barker, "Names of Space People" (March 25, 1966), Folder "Derenberger, Woody—Correspondence," GBC. In their initial notes, both Keel and Barker spell the planet's name as Lanolus.

28. John A. Keel to James W. Moseley, July 30, 1970, Folder "Keel, John—#2," GBC. An undated note in Barker's files on Keel may be the note Keel wrote. Written in red ink and signed with a stylized *M*, it reads: "They warneb [*sic*] you now we are / Stop your research or we will!." M, "They Warneb [*sic*] You" (Manuscript, ca. 1967), Folder "Keel, John—#2," GBC.

29. Barker's pranks primarily consisted of phone calls and fake letters, but he and Moseley also enlisted a Long Island saucer enthusiast named Joseph Henslik to pretend to Keel that he had been silenced by the Men in Black; see John A. Keel, "Another 'Man in Black' Case," *Saucer News* 14, no. 3 (whole no. 69) (Fall 1967): 14–15; John A. Keel, "The B-M Swindle: Continued" ([November 1967?], DS, http://www.johnkeel.com/?p=489). Barker and Moseley may also have been involved in an elaborate story communicated to Keel by Long Island radio host Jaye Paro (and involving unusual characters named Apol and Princess Moon Owl) in 1967. Many of Keel's primary notes from this period have been made available online by Doug Skinner; see, e.g., John A. Keel, "The Answer: A Series of Brief Articles Based upon the Special Cases Files" ([October 1967?], DS, http://www.johnkeel.com/?p=4752). Paro's initial contacts with Keel occurred around the time of Moseley's UFO Congress, and may have been intended to help publicize it. Keel summarizes some of the pranks that are attributable to Barker in a dossier assembled in early 1968: John A. Keel, "Organized Harassment of Individuals" (Typescript, January 1968), DS, https://www.johnkeel.com/?p=2133). In his published works and in notes that he distributed to other researchers, Keel has a tendency to duplicate characters with pseudonyms and multiply singular events in a manner that exponentially increases their apparent strangeness. See, e.g., John A. Keel, *The Mothman Prophecies* (1975; repr., New York: Signet, 1976), 170–176 (§16); Robert A. Goerman, "The True Story of Mothman," [2021?], https://robertgoerman.wixsite.com/mothman.

30. Gorightly and Bishop, *"A" Is for Adamski*, 125–126; Doug Skinner, "John Keel and 'The International Bankers,'" *John Keel: Not an Authority on Anything* (blog), December 12, 2012, https://www.johnkeel.com/?p=1667; Keel, "Three Letters."

31. Keel, *Mothman Prophecies*, 204–205, ellipsis original. Asked about the call in 2001, Moseley commented: "Knowing Gray, he was probably drunk." John C. Sherwood, "Gray Barker's Book of Bunk: Mothman, Saucers, and MIB," *Skeptical Inquirer* 26, no. 3 (June 2002): 42, https://skepticalinquirer.org/2002/05/gray-barkers-book-of-bunk/; see also Jesse Walker, *The United States of Paranoia: A Conspiracy Theory* (New York: Harper Perennial, 2014), 225–226.

32. David Clarke, *How UFOs Conquered the World: The History of a Modern Myth* (London: Aurum, 2015), 239. Compare George P. Hansen's description of a similar long-form hoax on alien abduction researcher Budd Hopkins, in which "the victims interpreted the handiwork as due to beings with virtually unlimited magical powers." George P. Hansen, *The Trickster and the Paranormal* (Philadelphia: Xlibris, 2001), 266.

33. Keel, *Mothman Prophecies*, chap. 16; see also Keel, "Organized Harassment of Individuals," sec. 2, pt. 4; on the "beep" calls in particular, see Gorightly and Bishop, *"A" Is for Adamski*, 125–126. In this discussion I have avoided the term *paranoid*, which originated in a clinical setting and has an imprecise meaning in the broader culture. See Jovan Byford, *Conspiracy Theories: A Critical Introduction* (New York: St. Martin's / Palgrave Macmillan, 2011), 120–126, https://doi.org/10.1057/9780230349216; and Debbora Battaglia, "Insiders' Voices in Outerspaces," in *E. T. Culture: Anthropology in Outerspaces*, ed. Debbora Battaglia (Durham, NC: Duke University Press, 2006), 14, https://doi.org/10.1515/9780822387015-002.

34. Hyre's reporting on the Mothman is compiled in Donnie Sergent and Jeff Wamsley, *Mothman: The Facts behind the Legend* (Point Pleasant, WV: Mothman Lives, 2002), 68–125.

35. For example, Eleanor Hasken notes Keel's claim that there were "hundreds" of Mothman sightings, despite his own data including scarcely more than two dozen. Eleanor Ann Hasken, "The Migration of a Local Legend: The Case of Mothman" (PhD diss., Indiana University, 2022), 60–61; see also John A. Keel, "Table of 'Mothman' Sightings–1966–67" ([1968?]), DS, https://www.johnkeel.com/?p=5395.

36. James W. Moseley, ed., *Saucer News: Special Convention Issue* (Fort Lee, NJ: S.A.U.C.E.R.S., 1967).

37. Barker announced that *UFO* would be published in the fall of 1967, but it never appeared. "Letters to the Editor," *Spacecraft News*, [new series] no. 3 (June 1967): 27.

38. Moseley and Pflock, *Shockingly Close*, 210.

39. For a detailed account of the 1967 Congress of Scientific Ufologists, see Moseley and Pflock, *Shockingly Close*, 204–213.

40. Randy Parks, "Gray Barker Is Happy to Announce . . . ," *Spacecraft News*, [new series] no. 3 (June 1967): 10.

41. Donald R. Bensen to Gray Barker, March 1, 1967, Folder "Stuart, John—UFO Warning," GBC.

42. Though there is no direct evidence of Tomorrow River printing Barker's first issue of the magazine, several elements of the design match both later Saucerian publications for which evidence does exist and Palmer's own publications of the same period. For details on Palmer's business in Amherst, including a photograph of his high-speed offset press, see Toronto, *War over Lemuria*, 200.

43. Moseley contends that most of the material that appeared under his name during Barker's tenure was written by Barker himself. Moseley and Pflock, *Shockingly Close*, 214.

44. Barker identifies the sculptor of the piece as Andrea Flammonde. A recent documentary produced for the Flatwoods Monster Museum in Sutton discusses the manufacturing of the lanterns in detail, but does not mention Flammonde or provide further details about her, and it is possible her existence is a fiction. Barker reported Flammonde's death in 1969. *The Lantern*, dir. Andrew Smith, YouTube video, 22:19, 2020, https://www.youtube.com /watch?v=C2PeOMIwk8Y; Gray Barker, "Necrology," *Saucer News* 16, no. 4 (whole no. 74) (Spring–Summer 1969): 55.

45. Gray Barker, "[Subscription Letter for 'Saucer News' ('The Fallen Angels')]" (Saucerian Publications, [December 1963?]), Folder "Promo—Saucer News," GBC.

46. Larry Klein, "The Fallen Angels," *Saucer News* 15, no. 2 (whole no. 72) (Summer 1968): 6.

47. Klein, "Fallen Angels," 7.

48. Gray Barker, ed., "Letters to the Editor," *Saucer News* 16, no. 4 (whole no. 74) (Spring–Summer 1969): 48.

49. Neil Gilchrist, "[Letter to the Editor]," *Saucer News* 15, no. 2 (whole no. 72) (Summer 1968): 26.

50. Woodrow W. Derenberger to Gray Barker, June 3, 1968, Folder "Derenberger, Woody—Correspondence," GBC; Gray Barker to Woodrow Derenberger, July 27, 1968, Folder "Derenberger, Woody—Correspondence," GBC. Duplantier issued a premature announcement of the book in "A Look at Books," *Saucers, Space and Science*, no. 52 (Summer 1968): 17, https://n2t.net/ark:/13960/t6q035q4h.

51. Barker's editorial suggestions appear in only the first half of the text. Woodrow W. Derenberger, "Visitors from Lanulos" (Annotated photocopy of typescript, [1968?]), Folder "Derenberger, Woody—Book ms.," GBC.

52. Woodrow W. Derenberger to Gray Barker, August 15, 1968, Folder "Derenberger, Woody—Correspondence," GBC.

53. Gray Barker to John A. Keel, November 11, 1967, 1, Folder "Keel, John—#2," GBC.

54. Gray Barker, "Editorial Notes," *Saucer News* 15, no. 3 (whole no. 73) (Autumn–Winter 1969): 1.

55. John A. Keel to Gray Barker, March 15, 1969, 2, Folder "Mothman 1970," GBC; quoted in part in Sherwood, "Barker's Book of Bunk"; and reproduced with erroneous emendations (including a misidentification of Mark Samwick as Charles Samwick) in John A. Keel, *Searching for the String: Selected Writings of John A. Keel*, ed. Andrew Colvin (Seattle, WA & Point Pleasant, WV: Metadisc Productions / New Saucerian Books, 2014), chap. 19.

CHAPTER 10

1. Condon, *Final Report*, 1999, 1; Condon, *Final Report*, 1969, 1. Within a month of the report's publication, David Saunders, who had been fired from the committee, issued an

unofficial minority report. David R. Saunders and R. Roger Harkins, *UFOs? Yes!: Where the Condon Committee Went Wrong*, Signet Books (New York: Signet, 1968).

2. Gray Barker, "UFO Is a Bucket of Shit" ([1969?]), Box "Moseley/Private Writings," GBC. The date of this poem is unclear, and it could have been written virtually any time after 1959; I believe a date after the release of *Flying Saucers and the Three Men* in 1962 is likely. The poem has been published online; see, e.g., Greg Bishop, "Interview with J. Moseley," The Excluded Middle, 1994, https://web.archive.org/web/20110610232500/http://www.excludedmiddle .com/J.%20Moseley.html.

3. Melton notes that, though the Condon report "killed and weakened so many UFO groups," it had little impact on the occult and contactee-focused side of the field, and sees the persistence of these groups as an "indication of [the] essentially religious nature" of the UFO macronarrative. Melton, "The Contactees: A Survey," 10.

4. James W. Moseley, "Missives from the Masses," *Saucer Wit* [*Saucer Smear*] 26, no. 3 (March 5, 1979): 4.

5. Barker told Sherwood he had received the shipment of issues from Tomorrow River on July 2, but had sent Greenfield an advance copy before June 30. Gray Barker to John C. Sherwood, July 3, 1969, Folder "Sherwood, John," GBC; Allen H. Greenfield to Gray Barker, June 30, 1969, Folder "Greenfield, Allen," GBC.

6. Gray Barker, "Editorial Notes: A Lively Corpse," *Saucer News* 16, no. 4 (whole no. 74) (Spring–Summer 1969): inside front cover.

7. Barker, "Editorial Notes: A Lively Corpse," 1.

8. Gray Barker, "Recent News," *Saucer News* 16, no. 4 (whole no. 74) (Spring–Summer 1969): 23.

9. "New Utica, N.Y. Group," *Saucer News* 16, no. 4 (whole no. 74) (Spring–Summer 1969): 37.

10. John C. Sherwood, "Gray Barker: My Friend, the Myth-Maker," *Skeptical Inquirer* 22, no. 3 (May–June 1998): 38–39, http://www.csicop.org/si/show/gray_barker_my_friend_the _myth-maker.

11. Gray Barker to John C. Sherwood, August 7, 1969, JCS; see also Sherwood, "My Friend, the Myth-Maker," 39.

12. Richard H. Pratt [John C. Sherwood], "The Strange B.I.C.R. Affair," *Saucer News* 17, no. 1 (whole no. 75) (Spring 1970): 12. For the original notice of the BICR, see Ray Palmer, "Saucer Club News," *Flying Saucers*, no. 63 (April 1969): 35–37, 46; John C. Sherwood to Gray Barker, [1969?], Folder "Sherwood, John," GBC; Sherwood, interview.

13. John C. Sherwood to Gray Barker, July 20, 1968, Folder "Sherwood, John," GBC.

14. Sherwood, "My Friend, the Myth-Maker," 39.

15. John C. Sherwood to Gray Barker, December 11, 1968, Folder "Sherwood, John," GBC.

16. On Owens generally, see Jeffrey Mishlove, *The PK Man: A True Story of Mind over Matter* (Charlottesville, VA: Hampton Roads, 2000); Jeffrey J. Kripal, *Mutants & Mystics: Science Fiction, Superhero Comics, and the Paranormal* (Chicago: University of Chicago Press, 2011), 229–34. Owens generally referred to his extraterrestrial contacts as Si's; following Mishlove's usage, I have normalized this to SIs, except in direct quotations.

17. Ted Owens, *How to Contact Space People* (Clarksburg, WV: Saucerian Books, 1969), 58.

18. Owens, *How to Contact Space People*, 59–60.

19. Mishlove, *PK Man*, 101.

20. Owens, *How to Contact Space People.*, 21.

21. Mishlove, *PK Man*, 60.

22. Mishlove, *PK Man*, 3.

23. Ted Owens to Gray Barker, February 27, 1968, Folder "Owens, Ted—Correspondence," GBC.

24. Ted Owens to Gray Barker, April 9, 1968, 1, Folder "Owens, Ted—Correspondence," GBC.

25. Gray Barker to Ted Owens, November 29, 1968, Folder "Owens, Ted—Correspondence," GBC; Ted Owens to Gray Barker, December 2, 1968, Folder "Owens, Ted—Correspondence," GBC.

26. Gray Barker, "Amazing New Book Describes: How to Contact Space People [Solicitation Letter for 'Timothy Green Beckley's Book of Space Brothers' and "How to Contact Space People"] (Saucerian Publications, September 1968), Folder "Promo—How to Contact Space People," GBC.

27. Ted Owens, "The SI's Want to Help," *Saucer News* 14, no. 4 (whole no. 70) (Winter 1967–Winter 1968): 9.

28. Gray Barker, "[Solicitation Letter for "How to Contact Space People ('Thank You for Requesting That Your Name Be Placed . . .')]" (Saucerian Publications, February 1969), 1, Folder "Promo—How to Contact Space People," GBC.

29. On charging, see Ted Owens to Gray Barker, [December 1969?], 1, Folder "Owens, Ted—Correspondence," GBC. The discs cost Barker about four cents apiece, assuming the figure 1,00 in the letter concerning their cost is a typo for 1,000. Gray Barker to Ted Owens, August 9, 1969, 1, Folder "Owens, Ted—Correspondence," GBC.

30. Ted Owens to Gray Barker, March 10, 1969, Folder "Owens, Ted—Correspondence," GBC.

31. "Use This Coupon to Request One of Ted Owens' SI Discs" (Saucerian Publications, May 1969).

32. Ted Owens to Gray Barker, [March 1–5, 1969?], 1, Folder "Owens, Ted—Correspondence," GBC.

33. Ted Owens to Gray Barker, July 30, 1969, Folder "Owens, Ted—Correspondence," GBC (emphasis original).

34. Barker to Owens, August 9, 1969, 2.

35. Gray Barker to Ted Owens, February 12, 1971, Folder "Owens, Ted—#3," GBC.

36. David Standish, *Hollow Earth: The Long and Curious History of Imagining Strange Lands, Fantastical Creatures, Advanced Civilizations, and Marvelous Machines below the Earth's Surface* (Cambridge, MA: Da Capo, 2006), 276.

37. For biographical material on Siegmeister/Bernard, see Brad Whitsel, "Walter Siegmeister's Inner-Earth Utopia," *Utopian Studies* 12, no. 2 (December 2001): 82–102, https://www.jstor .org/stable/20718317; Holly Folk, "Raymond W. Bernard, Hollow Earth, and UFOs," in *Handbook of UFO Religions*, ed. Ben Zeller (Leiden: Brill, 2021), 312–325; and Walter Jerome Gordon to Gray Barker, May 3, 1969, Folder "Bernard, Raymond—Correspondence," GBC.

38. Gray Barker to Raymond Bernard, December 9, 1963, Folder "Bernard, Raymond— Correspondence," GBC; Gray Barker to Raymond Bernard, December 30, 1963, Folder "Bernard, Raymond—Correspondence," GBC.

39. Gray Barker, "Did Dr. Bernard Vanish into the Inner Earth? [Solicitation Letter for 'The Hollow Earth' and "How to Contact Space People"] (Saucerian Publications, [March 1969?]), [4], Folder "Promo—Hollow Earth," GBC.

40. E.g., Michael X, *The Rainbow City and the Inner Earth People* (Clarksburg, WV: Saucerian Books, 1969), title page.

41. "Edwin John Dingle," Kook Science, July 24, 2022, https://hatch.kookscience.com/wiki /Edwin_John_Dingle.

42. Gray Barker, "Is Hitler Alive? [Solicitation Letter for 'We Want You' and Other Works by Michael X]" (Saucerian Publications, [September 1969?]), [1], Folder "Promo—Michael X," GBC. A second version of the solicitation letter issued after the books were published alters the claim to say that the request came from "emissaries from Michael X" rather than the author himself. Gray Barker, "Is Hitler Alive? [Solicitation Letter for 'We Want You' and Other Works by Michael X, Second State]." Saucerian Publications, [October–December 1969?], [1], Folder "Promo—Michael X," GBC.

43. Gorightly and Bishop, *"A" Is for Adamski*, 44.

44. Gorightly and Bishop, *"A" Is for Adamski*, 44.

45. Barker, "Solicitation Letter for 'We Want You' (First State)," [3].

46. Hoffman, *Questions and Answers about UFO's*, [7].

47. "John William Dean (1891–1970)," Family Search, 2017.

48. John W. Dean, *Flying Saucers and the Scriptures* (New York: Vantage, 1964). Dean was also the author of a book on leathercraft: John W. Dean, *Leathercraft Designs and Techniques* (Bloomington, IL: McKnight & McKnight, 1950).

49. Gray Barker, "Canadian Scientist Talks with Space People! [Solicitation Letter for 'Boys From Topside' and 'Flying Saucers Closeup']" (Saucerian Publications, [July 1969?]), [1], Folder "Promo—FS Closeup," GBC.

50. Dean, *Flying Saucers and the Scriptures*, figs. 65, 73, 81, 87–88.

51. John W. Dean, *Flying Saucers Closeup* (Clarksburg, WV: Gray Barker [Saucerian Books], 1969), 175.

52. Dean, *Flying Saucers Closeup*, 111.

53. Dean, *Flying Saucers and the Scriptures*, 52–54.

54. Dean, *Flying Saucers Closeup*, 2.

55. Dean, *Flying Saucers and the Scriptures*, 43.

56. Gray Barker to John W. Dean, October 19, 1968, 1, Folder "Dean, John W.," GBC.

57. Gray Barker to John W. Dean, February 11, 1969, 2, Folder "Dean, John W.," GBC.

58. Barker to Dean, February 11, 1969, 1.

59. John W. Dean to Gray Barker, June 16, 1969, Folder "Dean, John W.," GBC; John W. Dean to Gray Barker, July 9, 1970, Folder "Dean, John W.," GBC.

60. Barker to Dean, October 16, 1970, 2.

61. John W. Dean to Gray Barker, May 27, 1970, 1, Folder "Dean, John W.," GBC.

62. James L. Hill to Gray Barker, January 11, 1971, Folder "Dean, John W.," GBC.

63. Gray Barker to Arthur H. Snyder, December 21, 1970, Folder "Dean, John W.," GBC.

64. Gray Barker to John C. Sherwood, September 15, 1968, JCS.

65. Gray Barker to John C. Sherwood, July 12, 1968, JCS.

66. Barker to Sherwood, September 15, 1968.

67. Gray Barker to John A. Keel, June 1, 1970, 1, Folder "Keel, John—#2," GBC.

68. On Partridge, see Jeff Wamsley, *Mothman . . . : Behind the Red Eyes, the Complete Investigative Library* (Point Pleasant, WV: Mothman, 2005), 47.

69. Gray Barker, *The Silver Bridge* (Clarksburg, WV: Saucerian Books, 1970), 30.

70. Barker, *Silver Bridge*, 30–31 (emphasis original).

71. Barker, *Silver Bridge*, 31.

72. Gray Barker to Robert Sheaffer, July 19, 1980, 1, RS, https://www.debunker.com/historical/GrayBarkerPapers.pdf.

73. Agar's name comes from a threatening phone call that Moseley reported receiving, but it also appears in Keel's notes describing his bizarre experiences throughout 1967, at least some of which were pranks planned by Barker and Moseley. James W. Moseley, "Editorial," *Saucer News* 14, no. 4 (whole no. 70) (Winter 1967–Winter 1968): 4; John A. Keel, "Telephone Interview with Agar," July 10, 1967, DS, https://www.johnkeel.com/?p=3118.

74. Barker, *Silver Bridge*, 105 (emphasis original).

75. Barker, *Silver Bridge*, 107.

76. Barker, *Silver Bridge*, 81–82.

77. Barker, *Silver Bridge*, 82 (spelling error corrected).

78. Barker to Robert Sheaffer, July 19, 1980, 1.

79. On "ultraterrestrials," see John A. Keel, *Operation Trojan Horse: An Exhaustive Study of Unidentified Flying Objects—Revealing Their Source and the Forces That Control Them* (London: Souvenir, 1971), esp. 168; Jeffrey J. Kripal, "On the Mothman, God, and Other Monsters: The Demonology of John A. Keel," in *Histories of the Hidden God: Concealment and Revelation in Western Gnostic, Esoteric, and Mystical Traditions*, ed. April D. De Conick and Grant Adamson (Durham: Acumen, 2013), 234–258. Keel later described ultraterrestrials as "a literary device, not a theory." Quoted in David Clarke, "A New Demonology: John Keel and the Mothman Prophecies," in *Damned Facts: Fortean Essays on Religion, Folklore and the Paranormal*, ed. Jack Hunter (Paphos, Cyprus: Aporetic, 2016), 67.

80. Fort, *The Book of the Damned*, 156.

81. Keel, *Operation Trojan Horse*, 215ff.

82. Gray Barker, *A UFO Guide to Fate Magazine* (Clarksburg, WV: Saucerian Press, 1981), 84.

83. Barker, *The Silver Bridge*, 94 (emphasis original).

84. For further appearances of the preacher, see Barker, *At Giant Rock*, 55; Gray Barker, "Silenced! The Men in Black Are Back," *UFO Report* 7, no. 1 (February 1979): 49–50; Gray Barker, *M.I.B.: The Secret Terror among Us* (Jane Lew, WV: New Age, 1983), 18–19. The character may be related to Preacher Boone, a figure from Barker's childhood whom he describes as jumping on a table in the midst of an energetic sermon at the Perkins Fork School. Barker to Sanders, November 24, 1956, 4.

85. Barker, *Silver Bridge*, 60. Barker later told UFO skeptic Robert Sheaffer that Jamison was based on one of his nephews. Barker to Sheaffer, July 19, 1980, 1.

86. Barker, *Silver Bridge*, 62.

87. Barker, *Silver Bridge*., 63 (paragraph break removed).

88. Gray Barker to John C. Sherwood, October 12, 1968, 1, Folder "Sherwood, John," GBC.

89. Barker, *Silver Bridge*, 124. Barker recounted the same story about his childhood dog Old Ponto in Barker to Sanders, November 24, 1956, 5.

90. Barker, *Silver Bridge*, 117.

91. Barker, *Silver Bridge*, 118.

92. Barker, *Silver Bridge*, 120 (emphasis original).

93. Barker to Sheaffer, July 19, 1980, 2.

94. Barker, *Silver Bridge*, 142.

95. Barker, *Silver Bridge*, 145.

96. John A. Keel to Gray Barker, October 18, 1968, 1, Folder "Keel, John—#2," GBC.

97. John A. Keel to Gray Barker, October 19, 1968, 1, Folder "Keel, John—#2," GBC.

98. This is far less than is suggested by Eberhart, who simply says that Keel wrote the entire chapter. George M. Eberhart, *UFOs and the Extraterrestrial Contact Movement: A Bibliography* (Metuchen: Scarecrow, 1986), I:15).

99. Allen H. Greenfield to Gray Barker, March 4, 1970, Folder "Greenfield, Allen," GBC (typographical error corrected).

100. Compare Barker, *Silver Bridge*, 9–10; and Allen H. Greenfield, "An Introduction" (Original and photocopied typescript with manuscript additions, January 1, 1970), Folder "Mothman 1970," GBC.

101. Greenfield, "Introduction," 3.

102. Gene Duplantier, ed., *Outermost* (Willowdale, ON: privately printed by the author, 1970), 36–42.

103. James W. Moseley, "Dear Friend of Gray Barker [Solicitation Letter for 'The Silver Bridge']" (Saucerian Books, [1970?]), 2, Folder "Promo—Silver Bridge," GBC.

104. Moseley, "Dear Friend of Gray Barker."

105. Barker to Keel, June 1, 1970, 1.

106. Barker to Keel, June 1, 1970.

107. Gray Barker to Sandy L. Edison, May 2, 1971, Folder "E—Misc.," item E-89–1, GBC.

108. Moseley and Pflock, *Shockingly Close*, 218.

109. Philip Cestling [pseud.?], "The Death Throes of Ufology," *Caveat Emptor*, no. 1 (Fall 1971): 13, https://n2t.net/ark:/13960/t1nh2mj0h.

110. Barker to Dean, October 16, 1970, 1.

111. Barker, *At Giant Rock*, 40 (paragraph break removed).

112. Barker, *At Giant Rock*, 23.

113. Barker, *At Giant Rock*, 40.

114. Barker, *At Giant Rock*, 41 (paragraph breaks removed).

115. Moseley and Pflock, *Shockingly Close*, 218.

116. Gray Barker, "Return of the Crashed Saucers and Little Men," *Gray Barker's Newsletter*, no. 11 (January 1981): 2.

117. "Pittsburgh," *Boxoffice* 99, no. 7 (May 31, 1971): E7.

118. Gray Barker to Rose Hiett, [September 13, 1971?], 1, Folder "Hiett, Rose," GBC.

CHAPTER 11

1. Gray Barker to Laura Mundo, July 24, 1970, 1, Folder "Mundo, Laura #1," GBC.

2. Barker to Mundo, July 24, 1970.

3. Gray Barker to Ted Owens, August 16, 1970, Folder "Owens, Ted—Correspondence," GBC.

4. Gray Barker to John [Robinson?], September 26, 1971, Folder "Barker, Gray—Biography and chronology," GBC.

5. Gray Barker to Rose Hiett, February 10, 1972, Folder "Hiett, Rose," GBC; Rose Hiett to Gray Barker and Don Leigh McCulty, February 12, 1972, Folder "Hiett, Rose," GBC; Gray Barker to Rose Hiett, March 5, 1972, Folder "Hiett, Rose," GBC; the surgery is also mentioned in Gray Barker, "A L-o-n-g Letter from Gray Barker/Rare Book Sale," [January 1972?], Folder "Promo—Miscellaneous," GBC; Gray Barker, "[Solicitation Letter for 'Venusian Health Magic']" (Saucerian Publications, [March–May 1972?]), Folder "Promo—Michael X," GBC.

6. "Delbert Lovett Succumbs," E-7.

7. Gray Barker to Rose Hiett, January 9, 1972, Folder "Hiett, Rose," GBC; see also Gray Barker, "Gray Barker's Newsletter No. 2," July 1975.

8. "The Exhibitor Has His Say about Pictures," *Boxoffice* 102, no. 6 (November 20, 1972): a3.

9. Gray Barker to Trevor James Constable, June 28, 1976, Folder "James, Trevor," GBC.

10. "Pittsburgh," *Boxoffice* 103, no. 26 (October 8, 1973): E-6.

11. "Plan Ban on X-Rated Movies at Cinema V," *Boxoffice* 104, no. 3 (October 29, 1973): E-1.

12. "Pittsburgh," *Boxoffice* 104, no. 6 (November 19, 1973): E-6; "Pittsburgh," *Boxoffice* 105, no. 10 (June 17, 1974): E-6.

13. Gray Barker to Neville Spearman Armstrong, September 26, 1973, 1, Folder "Neville Spearman," GBC.

14. The location of the warehouse was given in Gray Barker, "Gray Barker's Newsletter No. 1," [January–March 1975?].

15. Steiger, "Fantastic Key."

16. Brad Steiger and Joan Whritenour, *The Allende Letters: Has the UFO Invasion Started?* (New York: Award Books, 1968).

17. Gray Barker to John A. Keel, March 24, 1968, Folder "Keel, John—#2," GBC.

18. John A. Keel to Gray Barker, March 26, 1968, Folder "Keel, John—#2," GBC. Keel did not identify the owner of this copy beyond saying that they were located in New York.

19. J. Ray Gilmer to Gray Barker, May 21, 1968, Folder "Varo (Jessup)," GBC.

20. Hal Crawford to Gray Barker, [January–March 1971?], 1, Folder "Crawford, Hal," GBC.

21. Hal Crawford, "Introduction to the Saucerian Edition" (Manuscript, [April 20, 1971?]), Folder "Crawford, Hal," GBC.

22. Allan J. Wilson to Gray Barker, April 28, 1971, Folder "Varo (Jessup)," GBC; Saucerian Press and Citadel Press, "Agreement [Contract for The Annotated Edition of The Case for the UFO]," December 20, 1972, Folder "Varo (Jessup)," GBC.

23. Barker, "The Enigma of M. K. Jessup," 9. For more documents from Barker's 1971 investigation of the Varo edition, see Doug Skinner, "Jessup-Allende (4)," *John Keel: Not an Authority on Anything* (blog), December 15, 2021, https://www.johnkeel.com/?p=4932.

24. "Resignations," *The U.F.O. Investigator* 1, no. 5 (September 1958): 2; Brewer, *Wayward Sons*, 60, 98.

25. Hiett had obtained the book from the mother of Michael Ann Dunn, the administrative assistant who had transcribed the book and its annotations. Riley Crabb to Rose Hiett, November 13, 1961, Folder "Crabb-Hiett correspondence," GBC.

26. Rose Hiett to Gray Barker, September 11, 1971, Folder "Hiett, Rose," GBC.

27. Hiett to Barker, November 17, 1971; Rose Hiett to Gray Barker, January 28, 1972, Folder "Hiett, Rose," GBC.

28. Saucerian Press and Citadel Press, "Agreement."

29. Ray Palmer to Gray Barker, February 14, 1972, Folder "Varo (Jessup)," GBC.

30. Moore and Berlitz, *Philadelphia Experiment*, 71.

31. Gray Barker, "[Solicitation Letter for the Annotated Edition of The Case for the UFO]" (Saucerian Press, Inc., [October 1973?]), (outer envelope), Folder "Varo (Jessup)," GBC.

32. Barker, "Solicitation Letter for the Annotated Edition of The Case for the UFO," [1].

33. Palmer had quoted production costs of $882.20 for five hundred copies or $1,227.60 for one thousand, indicating Barker's healthy margins for this publication. Palmer to Barker, February 14, 1972).

34. This number is indicated on a price quote for the letters from Tomorrow River. Palmer to Barker, February 14, 1972.

35. John A. Keel to Gray Barker, March 7, 1974, Folder "Keel, John A.," GBC.

36. Hal Crawford to Gray Barker, [October 10–20, 1973?], Folder "Crawford, Hal," GBC.

37. Jessup and Allen, *Case for the UFO*, 109.

38. Jessup and Allen, *Case for the UFO*, 34 (emphasis original).

39. Jessup and Allen, *Case for the UFO*, 8.

40. Jessup and Allen, *Case for the UFO*, 92.

41. Jessup and Allen, *Case for the UFO*, 39.

42. Gray Barker, "The Philadelphia Experiment and the Mystery of Dr. Jessup," *Gray Barker's Newsletter*, no. 9 (December 1979): [5–6]. Barker published the interview, and is it available, albeit misdated to 1967, in the Faded Discs Archive. Gray Barker, *Carlos Allende Speaks*, 1979, https://archive.org/details/HighStrangenessGuide/19.mp3.

43. Goerman, "Alias Carlos Allende" (emphasis original).

44. Andrew H. Hochheimer, "John A. Keel on the Philadelphia Experiment," *The Philadelphia Experiment from A-Z* (blog), [2016–2018?], https://www.de173.com/john-a-keel-letter.

45. Carlos M. Allende, "Annotated Reissue of *The Case for the U.F.O.* ([New Age Books], 1984)," n.d., "E," Gray Barker book collection, GBC (all spelling, punctuation, and underlining in original).

46. Allende, "Annotated Reissue of *The Case for the U.F.O.*"

47. Allende, "Annotated Reissue of *The Case for the U.F.O.*," 191.

48. Barker, "Gray Barker's Newsletter No. 1," 1.

49. "West Virginia," *Boxoffice* 107, no. 26 (October 6, 1975): E-7.

50. "Pittsburgh," *Boxoffice*. 106, no. 9 (December 9, 1974): E4; "Barker Ballys Boxoffice on Buckhannon Board," *Boxoffice* 108, no. 1 (October 13, 1975): E7.

51. "W. Va. Manager Finds Use For Stereo Sound System," *Boxoffice* 104, no. 19 (February 25, 1974): 22.

52. "West Virginia (10/6/1975)"; on the EPRAD SWORD system, see Haines, *The Moviegoing Experience, 1968–2001*, 96–97.

53. Gray Barker to John C. Sherwood, [November 1975?], JCS.

54. "West Virginia," *Boxoffice* 109, no. 18 (August 9, 1976): E-5.

55. Haines, *Moviegoing Experience*, 90.

56. The stated printing date of the reissue of *They Knew Too Much* is 1975, but it appears to have been delayed; the date of issue is inferred from Daniel Snyder to Gray Barker, February 20, 1976, 1, Folder "Bernard, Raymond—Correspondence," GBC.

57. Moseley is also credited with writing the book's introduction, but he stated that the attribution was false. James W. Moseley, "Inside 'Giant Crock,'" *New Saucers [Saucer Smear]* 23, no. 19 (April 1976): 1.

58. James W. Moseley, "A Letter from Jim Moseley about Gray Barker's New Book" (Saucerian Publications, 1975), [2], Folder "Promo—Gray Barker at Giant Rock," GBC.

59. Barker, "Letters (GBN No. 3)," 8.

60. Barker, "Letters (GBN No. 3),", 8–9.

61. Barker, "Letters (GBN No. 3),", 11.

62. Gray Barker to Albert K. Bender, [August 1979?], Folder "Bender, Albert K.—Roberts correspondence," GBC.

63. Bender's recording is available in the Faded Discs Archive of audio recordings, but the occasion of its recording is misidentified and the tape's title misspelled. Bender, *World of Kazik*.

64. Gray Barker to Timothy Green Beckley, March 28, 1976, Folder "Beckley, Timothy Green," GBC.

65. Timothy Green Beckley, "Global Communications," [1976?], Folder "Beckley, Timothy Green," GBC.

66. Timothy Green Beckley to Gray Barker, [1976?], Folder "Beckley, Timothy Green," GBC. Barker also wrote that he placed several later articles under pseudonyms; these have not been identified. Gray Barker, "Whatever Happend to Myron Fass?," *Hot Flash Bulletin!*, [October 1982?], [4].

67. Beckley to Barker, [1976?].

68. Gray Barker, "Chasing the Flying Saucers [New Series, No. 1]," *UFO Review* 1, no. 1 (1978): 10–12.

69. Gray Barker to Hal Crawford, [April 1982?], Folder "Newsletter orders #6 (Gray Barker's)," GBC.

70. J. Allen Hynek, *The UFO Experience: A Scientific Inquiry* (1972; repr., New York: Ballantine, 1974).

71. Mark O'Connell, *The Close Encounters Man: How One Man Made the World Believe in UFOs* (New York: Dey St. / William Morrow, 2017), 320.

72. David Clarke and Andy Roberts, *Flying Saucerers: A Social History of UFOlogy* (Loughborough: Alternative Albion, 2007), 203.

73. Moseley and Pflock, *Shockingly Close*, 121.

74. Gray Barker, "[Solicitation Letter for 'Secrets of the UFO']" (Saucerian Publications, 1977), [1], Folder "Promo—Secrets of UFO," GBC.

75. Gray Barker, "Chasing the Flying Saucers [New Series, No. 4]," *UFO Review* 1, no. 4 (June 1979): 16; Barker to Bender, [August 1979?].

76. Gray Barker to John A. Keel, May 9, 1974, Folder "Keel, John A.," GBC.

77. "'UFO: Target Earth' Given Boost Via TV Campaign," *Boxoffice*. 106, no. 8 (December 2, 1974): E8.

78. Cinema V, "[Handbill for 'Jack and the Beanstalk']," [June 1974?], Folder "Lovett & Co.," GBC.

79. Barker, "Gray Barker's Newsletter No. 2," [2]. Neither film appears to have survived.

80. Gray Barker, "Chasing the Flying Saucers [New Series, No. 9]," *UFO Review*, no. 9 (1980): 15; Gray Barker, "Movies: 'Hangar 18,'" *Gray Barker's Newsletter*, no. 10 (October 1980): 18.

81. James W. Moseley, "Misc. Ravings," *Saucer Wit Rides Again [Saucer Smear]* 26, no. 6 (May 30, 1979): 1. Barker also published a script excerpt and storyboard images by Duplantier. Gray Barker, "Chasing the Flying Saucers [New Series, No. 8]," *UFO Review*, no. 8 (1980): 17–21, 23.

82. Moore and Berlitz, *Philadelphia Experiment*.

83. See, e.g., Larry Kusche, review of *The Philadelphia Experiment: Project Invisibility*, by William L. Moore and Charles Berlitz, *Skeptical Inquirer* 4, no. 1 (Fall 1979), 58, https:// skepticalinquirer.org/1979/10/the-philadelphia-experiment-project-invisibility.

84. Gray Barker, "A Conversation with William L. Moore," *Gray Barker's Newsletter*, no. 9 (December 1979): [7].

85. Moseley and Pflock, *Shockingly Close*, 277.

86. Anna Lykins Genzlinger, *The Jessup Dimension* (Clarksburg, WV: Saucerian Press, 1981), 54.

87. Genzlinger's manuscript is in the Gray Barker Collection. Anna Lykins Genzlinger, "The Jessup Dimension" (Typescript, [1980?]), GBC.

88. On the development and marketing of the TRS-80, also known as the Radio Shack Model I, see Boisy G. Pitre, *CoCo: The Colorful History of Tandy's Underdog Computer* (Boca Raton, FL: CRC, 2014), 15–18.

89. Gray Barker, "Chasing the Flying Saucers [New Series, No. 12]," *UFO Review*, no. 12 (1982): 19.

90. Anna Lykins Genzlinger, "An Open Letter to the M.I.B.," *Gray Barker's Newsletter*, no. 14 (March 1982): [5].

91. The scholarly literature on alien abduction narratives is voluminous. Particularly useful sources include Erik A. W. Östling, "'I Figured that in My Dreams, I Remembered What Actually Happened': On Abduction Narratives as Emergent Folklore," in *Handbook of UFO Religions*, ed. Ben Zeller (Leiden: Brill, 2021), 197–232, https://brill.com/view/title/57043; Lepselter, *Resonance of Unseen Things*, 46–79; Brown, *They Know Us Better*; Scott R. Scribner, "Alien Abduction Narratives and Religious Contexts," in *Alien Worlds: Social and Religious Dimensions of Extraterrestrial Contact*, ed. Diana G. Tumminia (Syracuse, NY: Syracuse University Press, 2007), 138–152; Georg M. Rønnevig, "Toward an Explanation of the 'Abduction Epidemic': The Ritualization of Alien Abduction Mythology in Therapeutic Settings," in *Alien Worlds: Social and Religious Dimensions of Extraterrestrial Contact*, ed. Diana G. Tumminia (Syracuse, NY: Syracuse University Press, 2007), 99–127; Stephanie Kelley-Romano, "Mythmaking in Alien Abduction Narratives," *Communication Quarterly* 54, no. 3 (August 2006): 383–406, https://doi.org/10.1080/01463370600878545; Battaglia, "Insiders' Voices in Outerspaces"; Christopher H. Partridge, "Understanding UFO Religions and Abduction

Spiritualities," in *UFO Religions*, ed. Christopher H. Partridge (New York: Routledge, 2003), 3–42; Dean, *Aliens in America*, 98–152; Thomas E. Bullard, "UFO Abduction Reports: The Supernatural Kidnap Narrative Returns in Technological Guise," *Journal of American Folklore* 102, no. 404 (1989): 147–170, https://doi.org/10.2307/540677.

92. John G. Fuller, *The Interrupted Journey: Two Lost Hours "Aboard a Flying Saucer"* (New York: Dial, 1966). For a detailed look at the Hill case and its historical context, see Matthew Bowman, *The Abduction of Betty and Barney Hill: Alien Encounters, Civil Rights, and the New Age in America* (New Haven, CT: Yale University Press, 2023).

93. John G. Fuller, "Aboard a Flying Saucer, Part I," *Look* 30, no. 20 (October 4, 1966): 44–56; John G. Fuller, "Aboard a Flying Saucer, Part II," *Look* 30, no. 21 (October 18, 1966): 111–121; see also Featherstone, *Knowledge and the Production of Nonknowledge*, 38.

94. Budd Hopkins, *Missing Time: A Documented Study of UFO Abductions* (New York: Richard Marek, 1981), 23–24.

95. Gray Barker, "Catalog No. 13 ["You May Have Been Abducted without Knowing It!"]," *Gray Barker's Newsletter*, no. 13 (December 1981): [9].

96. Gray Barker, *Gray Barker's UFO Annual 1981* (New York: Global Communications, 1982), 61; see also Bader, "UFO Contact Movement," 85–87.

97. Scribner, "Alien Abduction Narratives," 2007, 139.

98. Saler, Ziegler, and Moore, *UFO Crash at Roswell*, 14.

99. Gray Barker, "Chasing the Flying Saucers [No. 17]," *Flying Saucers*, no. FS-17 (November 1960): 17; Gray Barker, "America's Captured Flying Saucers: Cover-up of the Century," *UFO Report* 4, no. 1 (May 1977): 32–35, 64–73; Barker, "Return of the Crashed Saucers"; Timothy Green Beckley, *Riddle of Hangar 18* (New York: Global Communications, 1981), 33–39. This material is adapted from Barker's correspondence on the topic: Nicholas E. von Poppen to Gray Barker, September 29, 1954, Folder "Von Poppen," GBC; Jacqueline Sanders to Gray Barker, January 24, 1955, Folder "Sanders, Jacqueline—1955," GBC.

100. The cases are numbered I–XXII, but four of them are marked "deleted in revision." Leonard H. Stringfield, "Retrievals of the Third Kind," *MUFON UFO Journal*, no. 128 (July 1978): 8–11; Leonard H. Stringfield, "Retrievals of the Third Kind, Part 2," *MUFON UFO Journal*, no. 129 (August 1978): 8–14.

101. Stringfield, "Retrievals of the Third Kind, Part 2," 11.

102. Among the narratives that Moore and Berlitz incorporate into their Roswell story are the Aztec crash narrative, publicized in Scully's *Behind the Flying Saucers*; Barker's account of the George Tyler/Nicholas von Poppen story, in the most expansively falsified version, from his 1976 article for *UFO Report*; and Gerald Light's account of a meeting between President Dwight D. Eisenhower and alien beings at Muroc Air Force Base in 1954, previously published by the BSRA. Though these narratives specified crashes occurring years and miles away from the supposed 1947 saucer crash in New Mexico, Moore and Berlitz present them as

being related to that single event alone. Charles Berlitz and William L. Moore, *The Roswell Incident* (New York: Grosset & Dunlap, 1980), 47–50, 94–96, 116–20; on subsequent developments of the Roswell metanarrative, see Saler, Ziegler, and Moore, *UFO Crash at Roswell.*

103. Gray Barker, "Expert Believes Govt. Holding Crashed Craft and Little Men: A Conversation with Leonard H. Stringfield," *Gray Barker's Newsletter*, no. 8 (June 1979): [1].

104. Gray Barker, "Barker, Gray R[oscoe]," in *The Encyclopedia of UFOs*, ed. Ronald D. Story (Garden City, NY: Dolphin Books / Doubleday, 1980), 41.

105. Barker, "Barker, Gray R[oscoe]."

106. Gray Barker to Robert Sheaffer, September 12, 1980, RS, https://www.debunker.com /historical/GrayBarkerPapers.pdf.

107. Barker to Sheaffer, July 19, 1980, 1.

108. Gray Barker, "Navy Admits Reality of the Philadelphia Experiment," *Gray Barker's Newsletter*, no. 10 (October 1980): [2].

109. Barker knew a significant amount about his audience's tastes thanks to a survey of his mailing list conducted by sociologists David Stupple (whom Barker pseudonymized as Dr. Bernard Benign) and Abdollah Dashti in 1977. The survey found that Barker's audience primarily consisted of older readers who had become interested in the contactee phenomenon in the 1950s, with a smaller subset of "scientific" ufologists and Middle Ufologists. David Stupple and Abdollah Dashti, "Flying Saucers and Multiple Realities: A Case Study in Phenomenological Theory," *Journal of Popular Culture* 11, no. 2 (Fall 1977): 479–493; Gray Barker and Bernard Benign, "The Saucerian Press Survey Research Report No. One," *Gray Barker's Newsletter*, no. 7 (March 1977): 6–7; see also Mckee, "A Contactee Canon: Gray Barker's Saucerian Books," 283–284; Saliba, "UFO Contactee Phenomena," 224; Stupple, "Mahatmas and Space Brothers".

110. Gray Barker, "A Conversation with Maj Colman VonKeviczky," *Gray Barker's Newsletter*, no. 12 (July 1981): [4].

111. Gray Barker, "Publisher's Editorial: The Great Iranian UFO Battle," *Gray Barker's Newsletter*, no. 12 (July 1981): [6].

112. James W. Moseley, "Missives from the Masses," *Saucer Smear* 28, no. 4 (December 15, 1981): 4; James W. Moseley, "Re-Hash of the 1982 National UFO Conference," *Saucer Smear* 29, no. 5 (June 15, 1982): 1.

113. *Shades of Gray*, 1:09:00; the same quote, with slightly different wording, appears in Moseley, "Re-Hash of the 1982 National UFO Conference," 1.

CHAPTER 12

1. Gray Barker, "Press Time Items," *Gray Barker's Newsletter*, no. 13 (December 1981): [8]; James W. Moseley, "Misc. Ravings," *Saucer Smear* 28, no. 12 (December 1981): 2.

2. *Whispers from Space*, 9:00.

3. Sharon Barker Stump, personal communication, February 28, 2024.

4. Timothy Green Beckley et al., "A Tribute to Gray Barker," *UFO Review*, no. 21 (1984): 12.

5. Gray Barker, "Secret Weapons & the Hitler/Hollow Earth Connection," [*Gray Barker's*] *Catalog*, no. 17-B ([May 1983?]): 1.

6. Gray Barker, "Varo Edition Available!," [*Gray Barker's*] *Catalog*, no. 17-B ([May 1983?]): 12. The exact model of copier is not known, but Richard Wilt, a technician who worked on Barker's printing equipment shortly before this period, speculates that it may have been a liquid toner photocopier like those manufactured by Savin. Richard Wilt, interview by author, October 10, 2023.

7. Gray Barker, "Catalog No. 17 ["Gray Barker's MIB Book and Varo Edition Available!"]," *Gray Barker's Newsletter*, no. 17 (December 1982): [10].

8. See, e.g., Gray Barker, *Year of the Saucer: Gray Barker's UFO Annual—1983: A Review of the Year 1982* (Jane Lew, WV: New Age Press, 1983), 9; Mckee, "Office Copying Technology."

9. James W. Moseley, "Miscellaneous Ravings," *Saucer Smear* 30, no. 1 (January 20, 1984): 2.

10. Gray Barker, "Catalog No. 18 ["Scientists and Seers Alike Predict Polar Flip"]," *Gray Barker's Newsletter*, no. 18 (October 1983): c1.

11. Years after compiling this bibliographical work, Walton became a well-known internet figure under the pseudonym Branton. His internet postings wove Shaver's experiences and the work of 1980s crashed-saucer theorists John Lear and Paul Bennewitz into a complex narrative web of subterranean conspiracy. On this later phase of Walton's career, see Barkun, *A Culture of Conspiracy*, 122–124, 134, 138–143, 162–163.

12. Richard Toronto, *Rokfogo: The Mysterious Pre-Deluge Art of Richard S. Shaver*, 2 vols. (San Francisco, CA: Shavertron, 2014); Toronto, *War over Lemuria*, 218ff.; Ray Palmer and Richard S. Shaver, *The Secret World: The Diary of a Lifetime of Questioning the Facts* (Amherst, WI: Amherst Press, 1977), 47ff.

13. Dominick C. Lucchesi, *Flying Saucers from Khabarah Khoom* (Jane Lew, WV: New Age Books, 1983), 70.

14. Barker, "Chasing the Flying Saucers [No. 10]," 42.

15. Gray Barker, "Chasing the Flying Saucers [No. 21]," *Flying Saucers*, no. FS-22 (November 1961): 27–39; Gray Barker, "Chasing the Flying Saucers [No. 22]," *Flying Saucers*, no. FS-23 (January 1962): 43–56.

16. Bender, *Flying Saucers*, 52.

17. James W. Moseley, "Book (?) Review," *Saucer Smear* 31, no. 6 (August 15, 1984): 5–6.

18. Gray Barker to Richard Toronto, May 1, 1984, Folder "Shavertron," GBC; James W. Moseley, "News Briefies," *Saucer Smear* 31, no. 8 (November 5, 1984): 8.

19. Duplantier, "I Remember Gray Barker," 3. The "book on Blavatsky" was probably the theo-sophically themed appendix of *After the Philadelphia Experiment*.

20. An early draft of the screenplay was written by John Carpenter, who is credited as an executive producer on the finished film. Justin Beahm, "On John Carpenter + Career Retrospective Interview," *Justin Beahm's Reverend Entertainment* (blog), June 23, 2016, https://www.justinbeahm.com/on-john-carpenter-career-retrospective-interview/.

21. "The Philadelphia Experiment," Box Office Mojo, accessed October 7, 2022, https://www.boxofficemojo.com/release/rl1164477953/weekend/; American Film Institute, "The Philadelphia Experiment," AFI Catalog of Feature Films, 2019, https://catalog.afi.com/Catalog/moviedetails/57165.

22. Gray Barker, "Chasing the Flying Saucers [New Series, No. 19]," *UFO Review*, no. 20 (1984): 8.

23. Moseley, "News Briefies."

24. "Wanted: Get Well Wishes for: Gray Barker & Orville Beckley," *UFO Review*, no. 20 (1984): 6.

25. James W. Moseley, "Miscellaneous Ravings," *Saucer Smear* 31, no. 9 (December 1984): 1; *Whispers from Space*, 1:18:00.

26. *Whispers from Space*, 1:17:00.

27. *Whispers from Space*, 1:16:00.

28. *Whispers from Space*, 1:19:00.

29. *Shades of Gray*, 1:06:00.

30. *Whispers from Space*, 1:19:00.

31. Sharon Barker Stump, personal communication, February 25, 2024.

32. Stump, personal communication, February 28, 2024.

33. Moseley, "Miscellaneous Ravings," *Saucer Smear* 31, no. 9: 1.

CONCLUSION

1. Richard Hall, "Richard Hall's Reality Check," *UFO Magazine and Phenomena Report* 11, no. 6 (December 1996): 9; see also James W. Moseley, "Miscellaneous Ravings," *Saucer Smear* 44, no. 1 (January 10, 1997): 4.

2. "These jobs keep body and soul together, but his consuming interest is saucermania"; another profile from the same month specifies that "those jobs pay the bills." "Man's Tales out of This World," *Grit* 97, no. 32 (July 1979): 13; "Flying Saucer Lore Fascinates U.S. Writer," *Winnipeg Tribune*, July 5, 1979, 22, http://hdl.handle.net/10719/2807912.

3. James R. Lewis, *UFOs and Popular Culture: An Encyclopedia of Contemporary Myth* (Santa Barbara, CA: ABC-CLIO, 2000), 50.

4. Robert T. Leach, "Men in Black," *UFO Magazine and Phenomena Report* 11, no. 6 (December 1996): 18–24.

5. Barker, *They Knew Too Much*, 246.

6. Barker, *M.I.B.*, 159.

7. *Whispers from Space*, 24:00.

8. *Hangar 18*, directed by James L. Conway, Sunn Classic Pictures, 1980.

9. *The Brother from Another Planet*, directed by John Sayles, Cinecom Pictures, 1984; Robbie Graham, *Silver Screen Saucers: Sorting Fact from Fantasy in Hollywood's UFO Movies* (Hove: White Crow Books, 2015), 251.

10. "Jose Chung's 'From Outer Space,'" *The X-Files*, directed by Rob Bowman, aired April 12, 1996, on Fox.

11. Aircel Comics, "The Men in Black: An Interview with Lowell Cunningham," *Men in Black* 1, no. 1 (January 1990): 25.

12. Peter M. Rojcewicz, "The 'Men in Black' Experience and Tradition: Analogues with the Traditional Devil Hypothesis," *Journal of American Folklore* 100, no. 396 (April 1987): 148–160, https://doi.org/10.2307/540919; Peter M. Rojcewicz, "The Folklore of the 'Men in Black': A Challenge to the Prevailing Paradigm," *ReVision* 11, no. 4 (Spring 1989): 5–16; Halperin, *Intimate Alien*, 158–161.

13. See, e.g., Timothy Green Beckley, *The UFO Silencers* (New Brunswick, NJ: Inner Light, 1990), 89–98.

14. *Dan Aykroyd Unplugged on UFOs*, Documentary (Graviton Entertainment, 2005).

15. Nick Redfern, *The Real Men in Black: Evidence, Famous Cases, and True Stories of These Mysterious Men and Their Connection to UFO Phenomena* (Pompton Plains, NJ: New Page, 2011), 164.

16. William M. Clements, "The Interstitial Ogre: The Structure of Horror in Expressive Culture," *South Atlantic Quarterly* 86 (January 1987): 39.

17. Sherwood, "Barker's Book of Bunk," 39.

18. Marshall Barnes, Fred Houpt, and Gerold Schelm, "Al Bielek Debunked," June 18, 2003, https://web.archive.org/web/20180907022649/http://www.bielek-debunked.com/index .html; on the incorporation of aspects of the film into the "non-fictional" metanarrative, see May, *Pseudoscience and Science Fiction*, 30.

19. Riley Crabb to Rose Hiett, May 21, 1962, Folder "Crabb-Hiett correspondence," GBC; Riley Crabb to Rose Hiett, July 29, 1962, Folder "Crabb-Hiett correspondence," GBC.

20. Preston B. Nichols and Peter Moon, *The Montauk Project: Experiments in Time* (New York: Sky Books, 1992).

21. See Joseph P. Laycock, "Mothman: Monster, Disaster, and Community," *Fieldwork in Religion* 3, no. 1 (2008): 70–86, https://doi.org/10.1558/firn.v3i1.70; Sara Brooke Christian, "The Cryptid Tourist Gaze: Cryptid Tourism and the Performance of Monster-Hunting" (PhD diss., Louisiana State University, 2021); Hasken, "The Migration of a Local Legend"; Lisa Troshinsky, "The Flatwoods Monster Comes Alive Again," WV Independent Observer, October 24, 2018, https://wearetheobserver.com/the-flatwoods-monster-comes-alive-again.

22. Robert Wood Lynn, *Mothman Apologia* (New Haven, CT: Yale University Press, 2022), https://doi.org/10.12987/9780300264975.

23. *The Mothman Prophecies*, directed by Mark Pellington, Screen Gems, 2002.

24. Jan Harold Brunvand, *The Vanishing Hitchhiker: American Urban Legends and Their Meanings* (New York: W. W. Norton, 1981), 10.

25. Ashley Lister, "Telling True Ghost Stories," *Short Fiction in Theory & Practice* 10, no. 1 (April 2020): 75, https://doi.org/10.1386/fict_00015_1. Lister speaks specifically of memorates (first-person oral accounts), but the strategies he discusses apply equally to published paranormal narratives.

26. Lister, "Telling True Ghost Stories," 76.

27. Susan Lepselter, "The License: Poetics, Power, and the Uncanny," in *E. T. Culture: Anthropology in Outerspaces*, ed. Debbora Battaglia (Durham, NC: Duke University Press, 2006), 148, https://doi.org/10.1515/9780822387015-005.

28. Barker, "Early Poems of Gray Barker," [16].

29. Ellis, *Aliens, Ghosts, and Cults*, 44–45 (emphasis original).

30. Boyle, *Fortean Influence on Science Fiction*, 22. Kripal defines a similar mode, which he calls "science mysticism." Jeffrey J. Kripal, *Authors of the Impossible: The Paranormal and the Sacred* (Chicago: University of Chicago Press, 2010), 123.

31. James W. Moseley, "Missives from the Masses," *Saucer Smear* 32, no. 3 (April 1985): 4.

32. For a telling case study involving several of the major authors in the field of ufology, including Keyhoe and Keel, see Davies, "Piri-Reis Map."

33. Keel, *Operation Trojan Horse*, 18–19.

34. Ted Phillips, *Physical Traces Associated with UFO Sightings: A Preliminary Catalog*, ed. Mimi Hynek (Evanston, IL: Center for UFO Studies, 1975), http://www.cufos.org/books/Physical_Traces.pdf; David F. Webb, *1973—Year of the Humanoids: An Analysis of the Fall, 1973 UFO/Humanoid Wave* (Evanston, IL: Center for UFO Studies, 1976), http://www.cufos.org/books/1973-Year_of_the_Humanoids.pdf.

35. He summed up his database project by cautioning that "the 'Flying Saucer' Mystery cannot be actually solved this way." Gray Barker, "Chasing the Flying Saucers [New Series, No. 6]," *UFO Review* 1, no. 6 (November 1979): 21.

36. On kayfabe, see Brian Jansen, "'It's Still Real to Me': Contemporary Professional Wrestling, Neo-Liberalism, and the Problems of Performed/Real Violence," *Canadian Review of American Studies* 50, no. 2 (July 2020): 302–330, https://doi.org/10.3138/cras.2018.024; Carrie-Lynn D. Reinhard, "Kayfabe as Convergence: Content Interactivity and Prosumption in the Squared Circle," in *Convergent Wrestling: Participatory Culture, Transmedia Storytelling, and Intertextuality in the Squared Circle*, ed. CarrieLynn D. Reinhard and Christopher J. Olson (London: Routledge, 2019), 31–44, https://doi.org/10.4324/9781351233989; Brian Jansen, "'Yes! No! . . . Maybe?': Reading the Real in Professional Wrestling's Unreality," *Journal of Popular Culture* 51, no. 3 (2018): 635–656, https://doi.org/10.1111/jpcu.12688; Sharon Mazer, "'Real' Wrestling/'Real' Life," in *Steel Chair to the Head: The Pleasure and Pain of Professional Wrestling*, ed. Nicholas Sammond (Durham, NC,: Duke University Press, 2005), 67–87, https://doi.org/10.2307/j.ctv11smpbc.

37. On hedging language in first-person ghost stories, see Lister, "Telling True Ghost Stories," 77–80.

38. Barker, "Did Dr. Bernard Vanish into the Inner Earth? [Solicitation Letter for 'The Hollow Earth' and "How to Contact Space People]," [4]; Gray Barker, "'Longevity Plants'/'Another Free Offer'" (Saucerian Publications, [September 1970?]), [1], Folder "Promo—Seeds," GBC; Science Research, "Have Space People Communicated with Earth? [Advertisement]," *Saucer News* 13, no. 3 (whole no. 65) (Fall 1966): 33.

39. Harris, *Humbug*, 23; see also Kembrew McLeod, *Pranksters: Making Mischief in the Modern World* (New York: New York University Press, 2014), 63–64.

40. Kevin Young, *Bunk: The Rise of Hoaxes, Humbug, Plagiarists, Phonies, Post-Facts, and Fake News* (Minneapolis: Graywolf, 2017), 10 (emphasis original).

Bibliography

ABBREVIATIONS

DS   Collection of Doug Skinner (johnkeel.com)
GBC   Gray Barker UFO Collection, Clarksburg-Harrison Public Library
JCS   Collection of John C. Sherwood
RS   Collection of Robert Sheaffer/debunker.com
TBP   Ted Bloecher Papers, 1950–2000 (MssCol 5984); New York Public Library Manuscripts
        & Archives

I have endeavored to provide stable URLs to open-access online resources wherever possible, but several periodicals that I have frequently cited do not provide stable URLs. In order to prevent repetition of long strings in the bibliography and notes, I am providing here URLs for individual directory pages for several of these. Similarly, I have included detailed citations of most letters and other archival sources held in the collections above in the endnotes, but have excluded them from the bibliography.

SOURCES

Civilian Saucer Intelligence of New York publications (*CSI News Letter*, *CSI-NY*): https://files.afu.se /Downloads/?dir=Magazines%2FUnited%20States%2FCivilian%20Saucer%20Intelligence%20 %28CSI%20New%20York%29

Flying Saucer Review: http://www.ignaciodarnaude.com/ufologia/

Glenville Mercury: https://www.glenville.edu/library/archives/mercury

Nexus: https://files.afu.se/Downloads/?dir=Magazines%2FUnited%20States%2FNexus%20 %28James%20Moseley%29

Saucer News: https://files.afu.se/Downloads/?dir=Magazines%2FUnited%20States%2FSaucer %20News%20%28James%20Moseley%29

Saucer Smear: https://files.afu.se/Downloads/?dir=Magazines%2FUnited%20States%2FSaucer %20Smear%20%28Jim%20Moseley%29

The Saucerian: https://files.afu.se/Downloads/?dir=Magazines%2FUnited%20States%2FSaucerian

The Saucerian Bulletin: https://files.afu.se/Downloads/?dir=Magazines%2FUnited%20States%2FSaucerian%20Bulletin

*

1966 Batman Pages. "Killer Moth," May 20, 2020. https://www.66batmania.com/bios/villains/killer-moth.

Adamski, George. "I Photographed Space Ships." *Fate* 4, no. 5 (July 1951): 64–74. http://www.adamskifoundation.com/gafhtml/News8Fate.htm.

Aircel Comics. "The Men in Black: An Interview with Lowell Cunningham." *Men in Black* 1, no. 1 (January 1990): 25–26.

"Alma M. Corder," November 24, 1962. New York State, Marriage Index, 1881–1967. https://search.ancestrylibrary.com/cgi-bin/sse.dll?db=NYStateMarriageIndex&indiv=try&h=3876424.

American Film Institute. "Bell Book and Candle (1959)." AFI Catalog of Feature Films, 2019. https://catalog.afi.com/Catalog/moviedetails/52477.

American Film Institute. "The Philadelphia Experiment." AFI Catalog of Feature Films, 2019. https://catalog.afi.com/Catalog/moviedetails/57165.

". . . And Now Back to Earth?" *Psychic News*, no. 1328 (November 16, 1957): 4. http://hdl.handle.net/10719/2953345.

Angelucci, Orfeo, and Paul M. Vest. "I Traveled in a Flying Saucer." *Mystic*, no. 1 (November 1953): 52–68. https://n2t.net/ark:/13960/t9481zr03.

"Anniversary Tribute to Gray Barker." Saucerian Publications, [April–June 1961?].

Arnold, Gordon B. *Flying Saucers over America: The UFO Craze of 1947*. Jefferson, NC: McFarland, 2022.

Arnold, Kenneth. "I *Did* See the Flying Disks!" *Fate* 1, no. 1 (Spring 1948): 4–10. https://s3.us-west-1.wasabisys.com/luminist/OC/FATE_1948_1.pdf.

Arnold, Kenneth, and Ray Palmer. *The Coming of the Saucers: A Documentary Report on Sky Objects That Have Mystified the World*. Boise, ID and Amherst, WI: privately printed by the authors, 1952.

Ashley, Mike. *Transformations: The Story of the Science-Fiction Magazines from 1950 to 1970*. Liverpool: Liverpool University Press, 2005.

Bader, Christopher. "The UFO Contact Movement from the 1950's to the Present." *Studies in Popular Culture* 17, no. 2 (1995): 73–90. https://digitalcommons.chapman.edu/sociology_articles/3.

Bailey, H. "On the Campus." *Glenville Mercury*, January 22, 1946.

Bain, Donald. *Long John Nebel: Radio Talk King, Master Salesman, and Magnificent Charlatan*. New York: Macmillan, 1974.

Bainbridge, William Sims. *The Sociology of Religious Movements*. New York: Routledge, 1997.

"Barker Ballys Boxoffice on Buckhannon Board." *Boxoffice* 108, no. 1 (October 13, 1975): E7.

Barker, Gray. "A Conversation with Maj Colman VonKeviczky." *Gray Barker's Newsletter*, no. 12 (July 1981): 1, 3–4.

Barker, Gray. "A Conversation with William L. Moore." *Gray Barker's Newsletter*, no. 9 (December 1979): 1, 3, 5, 7.

Barker, Gray. *A Note from the Desk of Gray Barker*. Clarksburg, WV: Saucerian Book Club, [1958?].

Barker, Gray. "A Ride in a Flying Saucer." *The Saucerian* 1, no. 2 (November 1953): 30–31.

Barker, Gray. *A UFO Guide to Fate Magazine*. Clarksburg, WV: Saucerian Press, 1981.

Barker, Gray. "About This Publication." *Saucerian Bulletin* 1, no. 1 (whole no. 7) (March 1, 1956): 1–2.

Barker, Gray, ed. *The Adamski Documents, Part One*. Clarksburg, WV: Saucerian Press, 1980.

Barker, Gray. "America's Captured Flying Saucers: Cover-Up of the Century." *UFO Report* 4, no. 1 (May 1977): 32–35, 64–73.

Barker, Gray. "And the Inevitable Would Come—Accounts of Having Met the Space People Themselves." *Saucerian Bulletin* 2, no. 4 (whole no. 15) (November 18, 1957): 3–4.

Barker, Gray. "Atomic Projection Made Easy in Ten Simple Lessons (Lesson I)." *Boxoffice/The Modern Theatre* 52, no. 13 (January 31, 1948): A44, A47. https://www.yumpu.com/en/document/view/26564360/boxoffice-january311948.

Barker, Gray. "Barker, Gray R[oscoe]." In *The Encyclopedia of UFOs*, edited by Ronald D. Story. Garden City, NY: Dolphin Books, 1980.

Barker, Gray. "Believes in Flying Saucers." *Nicholas County News Leader*, September 15, 1954.

Barker, Gray, ed. *Bender Mystery Confirmed: Consisting of Comments by Readers of "Flying Saucers and the Three Men."* Clarksburg, WV: Saucerian Books, 1962.

Barker, Gray. "The Big Flap of '66." *Spacecraft News*, [new series] no. 2 (Fall 1966): 3–5.

Barker, Gray. "Blindness Isn't Keeping This College Soph from Working toward Goal." *Glenville Mercury*, November 17, 1942.

Barker, Gray. "The Campus at Night: A Description." *Glenville Mercury*, February 15, 1944: 3.

Barker, Gray. *Carlos Allende Speaks*. Audio recording. 1979. https://archive.org/details/HighStrangenessGuide/19.mp3.

Barker, Gray. "Catalog No. 13 ["You May Have Been Abducted without Knowing It!"]." *Gray Barker's Newsletter*, no. 13 (December 1981): [9–16].

Barker, Gray. "Catalog No. 17 ["Gray Barker's MIB Book and Varo Edition Available!"]." *Gray Barker's Newsletter*, no. 17 (December 1982): [9–16].

Barker, Gray. "Catalog No. 18 ["Scientists and Seers Alike Predict Polar Flip"]." *Gray Barker's Newsletter*, no. 18 (October 1983): c1–16.

Barker, Gray. "Chasing the Flying Saucers [No. 2]." *Flying Saucers from Other Worlds*, no. 25 (August 1957): 30–40.

Barker, Gray. "Chasing the Flying Saucers [No. 6]." *Flying Saucers*, no. 30 [FS-6] (August 1958): 20–35.

Barker, Gray. "Chasing the Flying Saucers [No. 8]." *Flying Saucers*, no. 32 [FS-8] (December 1958): 43–56.

Barker, Gray. "Chasing the Flying Saucers [No. 10]." *Flying Saucers*, no. 34 [FS-10] (May 1959): 19–43. https://n2t.net/ark:/13960/t7jr1b887.

Barker, Gray. "Chasing the Flying Saucers [No. 14]." *Flying Saucers*, no. 28 [FS-14] (February 1960): 15–24.

Barker, Gray. "Chasing the Flying Saucers [No. 17]." *Flying Saucers*, no. FS-17 (November 1960): 22–28.

Barker, Gray. "Chasing the Flying Saucers [No. 21]." *Flying Saucers*, no. FS-22 (November 1961): 27–39.

Barker, Gray. "Chasing the Flying Saucers [No. 22]." *Flying Saucers*, no. FS-23 (January 1962): 43–56.

Barker, Gray. "Chasing the Flying Saucers [No. 23]." *Flying Saucers*, no. FS-25 (May 1962): 40–54.

Barker, Gray. "Chasing the Flying Saucers [No. 24]." *Flying Saucers*, no. FS-26 (July 1962): 24–34.

Barker, Gray. "Chasing the Flying Saucers [New Series, No. 1]." *UFO Review* 1, no. 1 (1978): 10–12. https://n2t.net/ark:/13960/t7xm68z7t.

Barker, Gray. "Chasing the Flying Saucers [New Series, No. 4]." *UFO Review* 1, no. 4 (June 1979): 16–17. https://n2t.net/ark:/13960/t41s4s52c.

Barker, Gray. "Chasing the Flying Saucers [New Series, No. 6]." *UFO Review* 1, no. 6 (November 1979): 18–21. https://n2t.net/ark:/13960/t1fk0f879.

Barker, Gray. "Chasing the Flying Saucers [New Series, No. 8]." *UFO Review*, no. 8 (1980): 17–21, 23. https://n2t.net/ark:/13960/t8wb3500q.

Barker, Gray. "Chasing the Flying Saucers [New Series, No. 9]." *UFO Review*, no. 9 (1980): 15–17. https://n2t.net/ark:/13960/t3pw4g694.

Barker, Gray. "Chasing the Flying Saucers [New Series, No. 12]." *UFO Review*, no. 12 (1982): 17–19. https://n2t.net/ark:/13960/t13p04b5f.

Barker, Gray. "Chasing the Flying Saucers [New Series, No. 19]." *UFO Review*, no. 20 (1984): 8, 15. https://n2t.net/ark:/13960/t6wx5c58c.

Barker, Gray. "Dear _____." In *Youranus*, [43–48]. [Clarksburg, WV]: [Gray Barker], 1957.

Barker, Gray. "Dear Book Club Member." *Saucerian Book Club News* 2, no. 1 ([July–September 1959?]): 2–3.

Barker, Gray. "Dear Saucerian Book Club Member." *Saucerian Book Club News* 1, no. 1 ([September–October 1958?]): 2.

Barker, Gray. "Editorial." *The Saucerian* 1, no. 1 (September 1953): 1–2.

Barker, Gray. "Editorial." *Saucerian Bulletin* 4, no. 1 (whole no. [20]) (May 15, 1959): 1–5.

Barker, Gray. "Editorial Notes." *Saucer News* 15, no. 3 (whole no. 73) (Autumn–Winter 1969): 0–2, 45–47.

Barker, Gray. "Editorial Notes: A Lively Corpse." *Saucer News* 16, no. 4 (whole no. 74) (Spring–Summer 1969): 0–2, 54.

Barker, Gray. "Editorial: The End of the World." *The Saucerian* 3, no. 2 (whole no. 6) (Spring 1955): 4–7, 55–60.

Barker, Gray. "Editorial: The I.F.S.B. Closing." *The Saucerian* 2, no. 1 (whole no. 3) (February 1954): 1–10.

Barker, Gray. "The Enigma of M. K. Jessup." *Flying Saucers*, no. 74 (September 1971): 8–12. https://www.debunker.com/historical/GrayBarkerPapers.pdf.

Barker, Gray. "The Exhibitor Has His Say about Pictures: Snow White and the Three Stooges." *Boxoffice* 80, no. 2 (October 30, 1961): 182. https://n2t.net/ark:/13960/t9b606z8b.

Barker, Gray. "Expert Believes Govt. Holding Crashed Craft and Little Men: A Conversation with Leonard H. Stringfield." *Gray Barker's Newsletter*, no. 8 (June 1979): 1–3.

Barker, Gray. *Gray Barker at Giant Rock*. Clarksburg, WV: Saucerian Publications, 1976.

Barker, Gray, ed. *Gray Barker's Book of Adamski*. Clarksburg, WV: Saucerian Books, 1966.

Barker, Gray. *Gray Barker's Book of Saucers*. Clarksburg, WV: Saucerian Books, 1965.

Barker, Gray. "Gray Barker's Newsletter No. 1," [January–March 1975?].

Barker, Gray. "Gray Barker's Newsletter No. 2," July 1975.

Barker, Gray. *Gray Barker's UFO Annual 1981*. New York: Global Communications, 1982.

Barker, Gray. "The Great Green God." In *Youranus*, [4–6]. [Clarksburg, WV]: [Gray Barker], 1957.

Barker, Gray. "Guest Editorial." *Flying Saucers*, no. 73 (June 1971): 2–3.

Barker, Gray. *Hoaxoffice*. [Clarksburg, WV]: [privately printed by the author], 1952.

Barker, Gray. "In and out of Zines." *Gray Barker's Newsletter*, no. 5 (March 1976): 2–6.

Barker, Gray. "The Inside of the 'London Story.'" *Saucerian Bulletin* 1, no. 4 (whole no. 10) (October 1956): 1–2.

Barker, Gray. "The Inside on Why 'Cosmic News.'" *Saucerian Bulletin* 1, no. 5 (whole no. 11) (November 1956): 4.

Barker, Gray. "The International Bankers." In *Youranus*, [28–35]. [Clarksburg, WV]: [Gray Barker], 1957.

Barker, Gray. "The International Bankers." *Saucerian Bulletin* 7, no. 1 (whole no. 25) (October 1962): 16–18.

Barker, Gray. "James Moseley." *Saucerian Bulletin* 2, no. 2 (whole no. 13) (May 1957): 2–3.

Barker, Gray. "Kollector's Korner." *Gray Barker's Newsletter*, no. 7 (March 1977): 16–17.

Barker, Gray. "The Lama's Story." *Saucerian Bulletin* 3, no. 4 (whole no. 19) (October 1958): 13–19.

Barker, Gray. "[Letter to the Editor]." *Saucer News* 6, no. 4 (whole no. 37) (September 1959): 2–3.

Barker, Gray. "Letters." *Gray Barker's Newsletter*, no. 3 (January 1976): 7–12.

Barker, Gray, ed. "Letters to the Editor." *Saucer News* 16, no. 4 (whole no. 74) (Spring–Summer 1969): 40–52.

Barker, Gray. "Mercury Musings." *Glenville Mercury*, February 6, 1945: 1.

Barker, Gray. *M.I.B.: The Secret Terror among Us.* Jane Lew, WV: New Age Press, 1983.

Barker, Gray. "The Monster and the Saucer." *Fate* 6, no. 1 (January 1953): 12–17.

Barker, Gray. "More on the Controversial State Department Letter." *Saucerian Bulletin* 3, no. 3 (whole no. 18) (June 1958): 10–13.

Barker, Gray. "Mountain Poet." *Echoes of West Virginia* 4, no. 3 (Winter 1953): 13.

Barker, Gray. "Movies: 'Hangar 18.'" *Gray Barker's Newsletter*, no. 10 (October 1980): [3].

Barker, Gray. "Navy Admits Reality of the Philadelphia Experiment." *Gray Barker's Newsletter*, no. 10 (October 1980): 1–2.

Barker, Gray. "Necrology." *Saucer News* 16, no. 4 (whole no. 74) (Spring–Summer 1969): 55.

Barker, Gray. "New Saucer Books." *The Saucerian* 2, no. 1 (whole no. 3) (February 1954): 51–60.

Barker, Gray. "The New Saucer Books." *The Saucerian* 2, no. 2 (whole no. 4) (September 1954): 32–39.

Barker, Gray. "Newest 'Contact' Story." *Saucerian Bulletin* 1, no. 5 (whole no. 11) (November 1956): 5.

Barker, Gray. "Nexus." *The Saucerian* 2, no. 1 (whole no. 3) (February 1954): 40.

Barker, Gray. "Now Let's Beat the Deadline." *Saucerian Bulletin* 4, no. 2 (whole no. 21) (September 1959): 20–22.

Barker, Gray. "On Cue: Easy Ways for Projectionists to End It All." *Boxoffice/The Modern Theatre* 53, no. 23 (October 9, 1948): A34. https://www.proquest.com/docview/1505808086/citation /2D3186FD0C864C42PQ/11.

Barker, Gray. "The Philadelphia Experiment and the Mystery of Dr. Jessup." *Gray Barker's Newsletter*, no. 9 (December 1979): 1–6.

Barker, Gray. "Press Time Items." *Gray Barker's Newsletter*, no. 13 (December 1981): [8].

Barker, Gray. "Publisher's Editorial: The Great Iranian UFO Battle." *Gray Barker's Newsletter*, no. 12 (July 1981): 5–6.

Barker, Gray. "Publisher's Introduction." In *Flying Saucers and the Three Men*, by Albert K. Bender, 9–12. Edited by Gray Barker. Clarksburg, WV: Saucerian Books, 1962.

Barker, Gray. "Recent News." *Saucer News* 15, no. 1 (whole no. 71) (Spring 1968): 10–20.

Barker, Gray. "Reflection: About the Author." *The Saucerian* 2, no. 1 (whole no. 3) (February 1954): 28.

Barker, Gray. "Return of the Crashed Saucers and Little Men." *Gray Barker's Newsletter*, no. 11 (January 1981): 1–4.

Barker, Gray. *The Saucerian: December, 1953 Bulletin*. Clarksburg, WV: Gray Barker, 1953.

Barker, Gray, ed. *The Saucerian Review*. Clarksburg, WV: Gray Barker, 1956.

Barker, Gray. "Saucernews: What's Doin' with the Saucers." *The Saucerian* 2, no. 2 (whole no. 4) (September 1954): 2–11.

Barker, Gray. "Secret Weapons & the Hitler/Hollow Earth Connection." [*Gray Barker's*] *Catalog*, no. 17-B ([May 1983?]): 1–3.

Barker, Gray. "Serious Doubt Has Been Cast on the 'Contact' Story." *Saucerian Bulletin* 2, no. 1 (whole no. 12) (January 1957): 2.

Barker, Gray. "Silenced! The Men in Black Are Back." *UFO Report* 7, no. 1 (February 1979): 48–56.

Barker, Gray. *The Silver Bridge*. Clarksburg, WV: Saucerian Books, 1970.

Barker, Gray. "Some Ills of Film Instruction." *West Virginia School Journal* 74, no. 10 (May 1946): 5–6.

Barker, Gray, ed. *The Strange Case of Dr. M. K. Jessup*. Clarksburg, WV: Saucerian Books, 1963.

Barker, Gray. "The Strange Case of R. E. Straith." In *Gray Barker's Book of Adamski*, edited by Gray Barker, 61–78. Clarksburg, WV: Saucerian Books, 1966.

Barker, Gray. *The Trip to the Moon: A Story*. [Clarksburg, WV]: [privately printed by the author], 1951.

Barker, Gray. *They Knew Too Much about Flying Saucers*. New York: University Books, 1956.

Barker, Gray. "To Eliminate the Many Wild Rumors . . ." *Saucerian Bulletin* 4, no. 2 (whole no. 21) (September 1959): 24.

Barker, Gray, ed. *UFO 96*. Clarksburg, WV: International Bankers, 1963. https://www.davidhalperin.net/ufo-96-the-ufo-world-of-50-years-ago.

Barker, Gray. "Varo Edition Available!" [*Gray Barker's*] *Catalog*, no. 17-B ([May 1983?]): 12.

Barker, Gray. "Whatever Happend to Myron Fass?" *Hot Flash Bulletin!*, [October 1982?], [3–6].

Barker, Gray. "Who Knows." Typescript, 1946. P8921. West Virginia and Regional History Center, University of West Virginia at Morgantown, Printed Ephemera Collection.

Barker, Gray. "Why the Bender Book Has Been Delayed." *Saucer News* 9, no. 2 (whole no. 48) (June 1962): 6–7.

Barker, Gray. "W.V.A. 'Monster': A Full Report." *The Saucerian* 1, no. 1 (September 1953): 8–21.

Barker, Gray. *Year of the Saucer: Gray Barker's UFO Annual—1983: A Review of the Year 1982*. Jane Lew, WV: New Age, 1983.

Barker, Gray. "You Have Just Read a Letter from George Adamski." *Saucerian Bulletin* 3, no. 2 (whole no. 17) (May 1958): 6.

Barker, Gray. "Your Editor Expelled from N.I.C.A.P." *Spacecraft News*, [new series] no. 2 (Fall 1966): 14.

Barker, Gray, and Bernard Benign. "The Saucerian Press Survey Research Report No. One." *Gray Barker's Newsletter*, no. 7 (March 1977): 6–7.

Barker, Gray, and Gene Duplantier. "They Knew Too Little about Flying Saucers." In *Youranus*, [53–54]. [Clarksburg, WV]: [Gray Barker], 1957.

Barker, Gray, and Jacqueline Sanders. "'Mon-Ka' Doesn't Come Through." *The Saucerian Bulletin* 1, no. 5 (whole no. 11) (November 1956): 1–3.

"Barker, Gray." *Who's Who among Students in American Universities and Colleges* 12 (1945–1946): 30. https://graybarker.wordpress.com/2017/03/30/gray-barker-in-whos-who-among-students.

Barker, Rose [Gray Barker]. "The Lady in White." *Fate* 9, no. 7 (whole no. 76) (July 1956): 103–104.

Barkun, Michael. *A Culture of Conspiracy: Apocalyptic Visions in Contemporary America*. Comparative Studies in Religion and Society. Berkeley: University of California Press, 2003.

Barnes, Marshall, Fred Houpt, and Gerold Schelm. "Al Bielek Debunked," June 18, 2003. https://web.archive.org/web/20180907022649/http://www.bielek-debunked.com/index.html.

Battaglia, Debbora. "Insiders' Voices in Outerspaces." In *E. T. Culture: Anthropology in Outerspaces*, edited by Debbora Battaglia, 1–37. Durham, NC: Duke University Press, 2006. https://doi.org/10.1515/9780822387015-002.

Batterham, Ian. *The Office Copying Revolution: History, Identification and Preservation*. Canberra: National Archives of Australia, 2008.

Beahm, Justin. "On John Carpenter + Career Retrospective Interview." *Justin Beahm's Reverend Entertainment* (blog), June 23, 2016. https://www.justinbeahm.com/on-john-carpenter-career-retrospective-interview.

Beasley, H. P., and A. V. Sampsel. "The Bender Mystery: Still a Mystery?" *Flying Saucers*, no. FS-30 (May 1963): 20–27.

Beckley, Timothy Green. "Gray Barker: The Man Who Knew Too Much about Flying Saucers." Exploring the Bizarre, January 31, 2016. YouTube video, 1:40:07. https://youtu.be/0m8weYukun4.

Beckley, Timothy Green. *Riddle of Hangar 18*. New York: Global Communications, 1981.

Beckley, Timothy Green. *The UFO Silencers*. New Brunswick, NJ: Inner Light, 1990.

Beckley, Timothy Green, John Keel, James W. Moseley, and Gene Duplantier. "A Tribute to Gray Barker." *UFO Review* 21 (1984): 8, 12. https://n2t.net/ark:/13960/t5m98677w.

Behdad, Ali. "Orientalism and Middle East Travel Writing." In *Orientalism and Literature*, edited by Geoffrey P. Nash, 185–201. Cambridge: Cambridge University Press, 2019. https://doi.org/10.1017/9781108614672.011.

Bender, Albert K. *Flying Saucers and the Three Men*. Edited by Gray Barker. Clarksburg, WV: Saucerian Books, 1962.

Bender, Albert K. "The International Flying Saucer Bureau." *Other Worlds*, no. 24 (December 1952): 156. https://n2t.net/ark:/13960/s2xwgpsqvtn.

Bender, Albert K. *The World of Kazik*. Audio recording. 1970. https://archive.org/details/HighStrangenessGuide/02.mp3. [Note: Title, date, and venue misidentified in metadata.]

Bennett, Colin. *Looking for Orthon: The Story of George Adamski, the First Flying Saucer Contactee, and How He Changed the World*. New York: Cosimo Books, 2008.

Bennett, Gillian. "Legend: Performance and Truth." In *Monsters with Iron Teeth*, edited by Gillian Bennett and Paul Smith, 13–36. Sheffield: Sheffield Academic Press, 1988. https://collections.mun.ca/digital/collection/clegend/id/360.

Berlitz, Charles, and William L. Moore. *The Roswell Incident*. New York: Grosset & Dunlap, 1980.

Bharati, Agehananda. "The Origin and Persistence of Rampaism." The Life and Career of Prem Rawat aka Maharaji. Accessed June 7, 2022. http://prem-rawat-bio.org/nrms/info/rampaism.htm.

Bishop, Greg. "Interview with J. Moseley." The Excluded Middle, 1994. https://web.archive.org/web/20110610232500/http://www.excludedmiddle.com/J.%20Moseley.html.

Blake, Joseph A. "Ufology: The Intellectual Development and Social Context of the Study of Unidentified Flying Objects." In *On the Margins of Science: The Social Construction of Rejected Knowledge*, edited by Roy Wallis, 315–337. Keele: University of Keele, 1979.

Bloecher, Ted. *Report on the UFO Wave of 1947*. Updated version. N.p.: Jean Waskiewicz and Francis Ridge, 2005. http://kirkmcd.princeton.edu/JEMcDonald/bloecher_67.pdf.

"Booker's Flying Saucer Hobby Makes Him Author and Film Aide." *Boxoffice* 69, no. 17 (August 18, 1956): 27. https://www.yumpu.com/en/document/view/27055393/boxoffice-august181956.

"Books Published Today." *New York Times*, May 17, 1956.

Bowman, Matthew. *The Abduction of Betty and Barney Hill: Alien Encounters, Civil Rights, and the New Age in America*. New Haven, CT: Yale University Press, 2023.

Boyle, Tanner F. *The Fortean Influence on Science Fiction: Charles Fort and the Evolution of the Genre*. Jefferson, NC: McFarland, 2021.

"Braxton Students Organize Club Here." *Glenville Mercury*, October 27, 1942.

Brewer, Jack. *Wayward Sons: NICAP and the IC*. N.p.: Published by the author, 2021.

The Brother from Another Planet. Directed by John Sayles. Cinecom Pictures, 1984.

Brown, Bridget. *They Know Us Better than We Know Ourselves: The History and Politics of Alien Abduction*. New York: New York University Press, 2007. https://doi.org/10.18574/nyu/9780814739174 .001.0001.

Brown, Stephen W., and Otis K. Rice. *West Virginia: A History*. 2nd ed. Lexington: University Press of Kentucky, 1993. https://muse.jhu.edu/book/671.

Brunvand, Jan Harold. *The Vanishing Hitchhiker: American Urban Legends and Their Meanings*. New York: W. W. Norton, 1981.

Buhler, W. "The A.V.B. Contact Case." *SBEDV Boletim*, no. 26–27 (April–July 1962): 1, 7–9, 14. https://files.afu.se/Downloads/Magazines/Brazil/SBEDV/SBEDV%20-%20No%20026-27 %20-%201962.pdf.

Bullard, Thomas E. *The Myth and Mystery of UFOs*. Lawrence: University Press of Kansas, 2010. https://doi.org/10.1353/book48323.

Bullard, Thomas E. "UFO Abduction Reports: The Supernatural Kidnap Narrative Returns in Technological Guise." *Journal of American Folklore* 102, no. 404 (1989): 147–170. https://doi.org /10.2307/540677.

Burden, Brian. "MIBs and the Intelligence Community." *Awareness* 9, no. 1 (Spring 1980): 6–13. https://files.afu.se/Downloads/Magazines/United%20Kingdom/Awareness%20(Contact %20UK)/Awareness%20-%201980%20-%20Vol%2009%20No%201%20-%20Spring.pdf

Burns, Adam. "Elk River Railroad." American-Rails.com, January 12, 2024. https://www.american -rails.com/elk.html.

Byford, Jovan. *Conspiracy Theories: A Critical Introduction*. New York: St. Martin's, 2011. https:// doi.org/10.1057/9780230349216.

"Campus Capers." *Glenville Mercury*, February 16, 1943.

"Canterbury Club Has Four New Members." *Glenville Mercury*, February 23, 1943.

Case, Justin [pseud.]. Review of *Space, Gravity and the Flying Saucer*, by Leonard G. Cramp. *Saucer News* 2, no. 7 (whole no. 13) (September 1955): 6–8.

Cattien, Jana. "Against 'Transracialism': Revisiting the Debate." *Hypatia* 34, no. 4 (Fall 2019): 713–735. https://doi.org/10.1111/hypa.12499.

Cestling, Philip [pseud.?]. "The Death Throes of Ufology." *Caveat Emptor*, no. 1 (Fall 1971): 13–14, 26. https://n2t.net/ark:/13960/t1nh2mj0h.

Chauncey, George. *Gay New York: Gender, Urban Culture, and the Makings of the Gay Male World, 1890–1940*. New York: Basic, 1994.

Chess, Shira, and Eric Newsom. *Folklore, Horror Stories, and the Slender Man: The Development of an Internet Mythology*. New York: Palgrave Macmillan, 2014. https://doi.org/10.1057 /9781137491138.

Christian, Sara Brooke. "The Cryptid Tourist Gaze: Cryptid Tourism and the Performance of Monster-Hunting." PhD diss., Louisiana State University, 2021.

Chryssides, George D. "Defining the New Age." In *Handbook of New Age*, edited by Daren Kemp and James R. Lewis, 5–24. Leiden: Brill, 2007.

Ciseri, Lorenzo Montemagno. "Can Failing to Check Sources Give Rise to Monsters? The Iconographical History of a Paradigmatic Case." *Preternature: Critical and Historical Studies on the Preternatural* 2, no. 2 (2013): 139. https://doi.org/10.5325/preternature.2.2.0139.

Civilian Saucer Intelligence. "Shapes in the Sky [No. 1]." *Fantastic Universe* 7, no. 3 (March 1957): 82–87. https://n2t.net/ark:/13960/t4wh6g190.

Civilian Saucer Intelligence. "The Straith Letter." *CSI Publication* no. 25 (CSI News Letter 11) (July 15, 1959): 2.

Civilian Saucer Intelligence. "'Very Sincere Fellow' Howard Menger Returns to Long John Nebel Program." *CSI Publication* 21 (CSI News Letter 9) (November 1, 1957): 14–16.

Civilian Saucer Intelligence of New York. "Reported Intimidation of UFO Researchers." *CSI-NY*, no. 15 (May 1956): 1–4.

Clark, Jerome. "The Odyssey of Sister Thedra." In *Alien Worlds: Social and Religious Dimensions of Extraterrestrial Contact*, edited by Diana G. Tumminia, 25–41. Syracuse, NY: Syracuse University Press, 2007.

Clark, Jerome. *The UFO Encyclopedia: The Phenomenon from the Beginning*. 3rd ed. 2 vols. Detroit, MI: Omnigraphics, 2018.

Clark, Jerome. *Unexplained!: Strange Sightings, Incredible Occurrences, and Puzzling Physical Phenomena*. 3rd ed. Detroit: Visible Ink, 2013.

Clarke, David. "A New Demonology: John Keel and the Mothman Prophecies." In *Damned Facts: Fortean Essays on Religion, Folklore and the Paranormal*, edited by Jack Hunter, 54–67. Paphos: Aporetic, 2016.

Clarke, David. *How UFOs Conquered the World: The History of a Modern Myth*. London: Aurum, 2015.

Clarke, David, and Andy Roberts. *Flying Saucerers: A Social History of UFOlogy*. Loughborough: Alternative Albion, 2007.

Clements, William M. "The Interstitial Ogre: The Structure of Horror in Expressive Culture." *South Atlantic Quarterly* 86 (January 1987): 34–43.

Cleves, Rachel Hope. "The Problem of Modern Pederasty in Queer History: A Case Study of Norman Douglas." *Historical Reflections* 46, no. 1 (Spring 2020): 47–61. https://doi.org/10.3167/hrrh.2020.460104.

Condon, Edward Uhler. *Final Report of the Scientific Study of Unidentified Flying Objects Conducted by the University of Colorado*, edited by Daniel S. Gillmor. New York: Bantam, 1969.

Condon, Edward Uhler. *Final Report of the Scientific Study of Unidentified Flying Objects Conducted by the University of Colorado*, edited by Daniel S. Gillmor. Internet edition. Washington, DC: National Capital Area Skeptics, 1999. https://files.ncas.org/condon.

Corrington, Robert S. *Wilhelm Reich: Psychoanalyst and Radical Naturalist*. New York: Farrar, Straus and Giroux, 2003.

Crabb, Riley, ed. *M. K. Jessup and the Allende Letters*. Vista, CA: Borderland Sciences Research Associates Foundation, 1962.

Craigo, Nina. "Screen Sketches." *Glenville Mercury*, May 13, 1947, 2.

Creighton, Gordon. "The Most Amazing Case of All: Part 1—A Brazilian Farmer's Story." *Flying Saucer Review* 11, no. 1 (January–February 1965): 13–17.

Crisman, Fred [as "ex-Capt. A.C."]. "Encounter in the Caves." *Amazing Stories* 20, no. 3 (June 1946): 178. https://n2t.net/ark:/13960/t0sr1jk1m.

Crisman, Fred L. "Report from Alaska." *Amazing Stories* 21, no. 5 (May 1947): 168. https://n2t .net/ark:/13960/t0jt51b57.

Curran, Douglas. *In Advance of the Landing: Folk Concepts of Outer Space*. New York: Abbeville, 1985.

Dahl, Gordon B. "Early Teen Marriage and Future Poverty." *Demography* 47, no. 3 (August 2010): 689–718. https://doi.org/10.1353/dem.0.0120.

Daley, Michael P. "Concerning the Discovery, Taxonomic Implications, & Initial Impressions of a Whispering Mold." In *Echoes of a Natural World: Tales of the Strange & Estranged*, edited by Michael P. Daley, 31–54. Chicago, IL: First to Knock, 2020.

Dan Aykroyd Unplugged on UFOs. Documentary. Directed by David Sereda. Graviton Entertainment, 2005.

Darnton, Robert. "What Is the History of Books?" In *The Book History Reader*, edited by David Finkelstein and Alistair McCleery, 9–26. 1982. Reprint, London: Routledge, 2002.

Darrach, H.B., Jr., and Robert Ginna. "Have We Visitors from Space?" *Life*, April 7, 1952, 80–96.

Davidson, Leon. *Flying Saucers: An Analysis of the Air Force Project Blue Book Special Report No. 14*. 4th ed. Clarksburg, WV: Saucerian Publications, 1971.

Davies, Paul C. W. "The Piri-Reis Map: Fact and Fiction." *Flying Saucer Review* 18, no. 2 (April 1972): 21–23.

Davis, [Isabel L.?], and Gene Duplantier. "Cartoon." *Saucer News* 5, no. 3 (whole no. 30) (April– May 1958): 17.

Davis, Isabel L. "Meet the Extraterrestrial." *Fantastic Universe* 8, no. 5 (November 1957): 31–59. https://n2t.net/ark:/13960/t3906127c.

Dawkins, Richard. *The Selfish Gene*. 40th anniversary ed. Oxford Landmark Science. Oxford: Oxford University Press, 2016.

Dean, Jodi. *Aliens in America: Conspiracy Cultures from Outerspace to Cyberspace.* Ithaca, NY: Cornell University Press, 1998.

Dean, John W. *Flying Saucers and the Scriptures.* New York: Vantage, 1964.

Dean, John W. *Flying Saucers Closeup.* Clarksburg, WV: Gray Barker [Saucerian Books], 1969.

Dean, John W. *Leathercraft Designs and Techniques.* Bloomington, IL: McKnight & McKnight, 1950.

Dégh, Linda. *American Folklore and the Mass Media.* Bloomington: Indiana University Press, 1994.

Dégh, Linda. *Legend and Belief: Dialectics of a Folklore Genre.* Bloomington: Indiana University Press, 2001. https://hdl.handle.net/2027/heb09308.0001.001.

Dégh, Linda. "UFO's and How Folklorists Should Look at Them." *Fabula* 18 (1977): 242–248. https://doi.org/10.1515/fabl.1977.18.1.242.

Dégh, Linda, and Andrew Vázsonyi. "Does the Word 'Dog' Bite? Ostensive Action: A Means of Legend Telling." *Journal of Folklore Research* 20, no. 1 (January 1983): 5–34. https://www.jstor.org/stable/3814298.

Delany, Samuel R. *Times Square Red, Times Square Blue.* New York: New York University Press, 1999.

"Delbert Lovett Succumbs; Projection-Airer Veteran." *Boxoffice* 102, no. 25 (April 2, 1973): E-7. https://www.yumpu.com/en/document/view/31854970/boxoffice-april021973.

D'Emilio, John. *Sexual Politics, Sexual Communities: The Making of a Homosexual Minority in the United States, 1940–1970.* 2nd ed. Chicago: University of Chicago Press, 1998.

Denzler, Brenda. *The Lure of the Edge: Scientific Passions, Religious Beliefs, and the Pursuit of UFOs.* Berkeley: University of California Press, 2001. https://doi.org/10.1525/9780520930278.

Dewan, William J. "'A Saucerful of Secrets': An Interdisciplinary Analysis of UFO Experiences." *Journal of American Folklore* 119, no. 472 (2006): 184–202. http://www.jstor.org/stable/4137923.

Dewan, William J. "Occam's Beard: Belief, Disbelief, and Contested Meanings in American Ufology." PhD diss., University of New Mexico, 2010. https://digitalrepository.unm.edu/amst_etds/10.

Dickey, Colin. *The Unidentified: Mythical Monsters, Alien Encounters, and Our Obsession with the Unexplained.* New York: Viking, 2020.

Dixon, Deborah. "A Benevolent and Sceptical Inquiry: Exploring 'Fortean Geographies' with the Mothman." *Cultural Geographies* 14, no. 2 (2007): 189–210. https://www.jstor.org/stable/44251140.

Dove, Lonzo. "Gray Barker's 'Three Men in Black.'" *Saucer News* 6, no. 3 (whole no. 36) (June 1959): 6–13.

Dove, Lonzo. Review of *Inside the Space Ships*, by George Adamski. *Saucer News* 2, no. 8 (whole no. 14) (November 1955): 14–17.

Dove, Lonzo. "Menger's Adamski-Type Saucers." *Saucer News* 4, no. 2 (whole no. 22) (March 1957): 6–7.

Dove, Lonzo. *The "Straith" State Department Fraud*. Broadway, VA: privately printed by the author, 1959.

Dowers, P. J. *Hoax: The Philadelphia Experiment Unraveled*. N.p: Pandora's, 2012.

"Drive-in Film Stampedes Cattle in Nearby Field." *Boxoffice* 55, no. 4 (May 28, 1949): 69. https://www.yumpu.com/en/document/read/26756123/mpaa.

"Drive-in Patrons View Extra Horror Picture." *Boxoffice* 58, no. 1 (November 4, 1950): 32. https://www.yumpu.com/en/document/read/26759859/boxoffice-11041950.

Dunbar-Ortiz, Roxanne. *An Indigenous Peoples' History of the United States*. Boston: Beacon Press, 2014.

Duncombe, Stephen. *Notes from Underground: Zines and the Politics of Alternative Culture*. London: Verso, 1997.

Duplantier, Gene. "Gray Days at Clarksburg." *Ufolk*, no. 1 (1978): 12–13. https://n2t.net/ark:/13960/t38132h7h.

Duplantier, Gene. "A Look at Books." *Saucers, Space and Science*, no. 52 (Summer 1968): 17. https://n2t.net/ark:/13960/t6q035q4h.

Duplantier, Gene, ed. *Outermost*. Willowdale, ON: privately printed by the editor, 1970.

Eberhart, George M. *UFOs and the Extraterrestrial Contact Movement: A Bibliography*. 2 vols. Metuchen: Scarecrow, 1986.

"Edwin John Dingle." Kook Science, July 24, 2022. https://hatch.kookscience.com/wiki/Edwin_John_Dingle.

"Eight-Page Moviews Being Published at Clarksburg." *Boxoffice* 78, no. 10 (December 26, 1960): 206. https://www.yumpu.com/en/document/read/27225475/boxoffice-december261960.

Eisenstein, Elizabeth L. *The Printing Press as an Agent of Change: Communications and Cultural Transformations in Early-Modern Europe*. Cambridge: Cambridge University Press, 1980.

Ellis, Bill. *Aliens, Ghosts, and Cults: Legends We Live*. Jackson: University Press of Mississippi, 2003.

Evans, Hilary. *Visions, Apparitions, Alien Visitors*. Wellingborough: Aquarian, 1984.

"Evelyn Finster . . ." *Glenville Mercury*, May 30, 1944, 4.

"Exhibitor Has His Say about Pictures, The." *Boxoffice* 102, no. 6 (November 20, 1972): a3.

"Exhibitor Turned Outdoors Sets Up 16mm Drive-In." *Boxoffice* 51, no. 8 (June 28, 1947): 88. https://www.yumpu.com/en/document/read/26762945/ponders-taft-hartley-wal.

Falzone, Carmella. "Letter to the Editor." *Saucer News* 11, no. 1 (whole no. 55) (March 1964): 4.

Family Search. "George E. Barker (10 November 1871–1 April 1950)," 2022. https://www.familysearch.org/tree/pedigree/landscape/9WP5-K8Y.

Family Search. "John William Dean (1891–1970)," 2017. https://www.familysearch.org/tree/person/details/MMB6-VYS.

Family Search. "Rosa Lee Frame," January 26, 2022. https://www.familysearch.org/tree/person/details/LD1D-TJ5.

Fancyclopedia 3. "Plane Trip," July 24, 2020. https://fancyclopedia.org/Plane_Trip.

Fancyclopedia 3. "Serious Constructive." Accessed January 10, 2023. https://fancyclopedia.org/Serious_Constructive.

FBI Records: The Vault. "UFOs," 2013. https://vault.fbi.gov/UFO.

Featherstone, Mark. *Knowledge and the Production of Nonknowledge: An Exploration of Alien Mythology in Postwar America*. Cresskill, NJ: Hampton, 2002.

Feschino, Frank C., Jr. *The Braxton County Monster: The Cover-Up of the Flatwoods Monster Revealed*. Charleston, WV: Quarrier, 2004.

Festinger, Leon, Henry W. Riecken, and Stanley Schachter. *When Prophecy Fails*. Minneapolis: University of Minnesota Press, 1956. https://catalog.hathitrust.org/Record/000818353.

"Flying Saucer Lore Fascinates U.S. Writer." *Winnipeg Tribune*, July 5, 1979. http://hdl.handle.net/10719/2807912.

"Flying Saucers Placed in Autos for 'Collide.'" *Boxoffice* 61, no. 20 (September 13, 1952): 213.

Folk, Holly. "Raymond W. Bernard, Hollow Earth, and UFOs." In *Handbook of UFO Religions*, edited by Ben Zeller, 312–325. Leiden: Brill, 2021.

Fort, Charles. *The Book of the Damned*. New York: Boni and Liveright, 1919. https://n2t.net/ark:/13960/t3125rm6k.

"Franklin Thomas (California, County Birth and Death Records, 1800–1994)." Accessed June 5, 2022. https://familysearch.org/ark:/61903/1:1:QGLN-3FLN.

"Freshmen Get into 'Swing of Things' and Start Careers in Higher Education." *Glenville Mercury*, September 26, 1944, 1.

Fuller, John G. "Aboard a Flying Saucer, Part I." *Look* 30, no. 20 (October 1966): 44–56.

Fuller, John G. "Aboard a Flying Saucer, Part II." *Look* 30, no. 21 (October 18, 1966): 111–121.

Fuller, John G. *The Interrupted Journey: Two Lost Hours "Aboard a Flying Saucer."* New York: Dial, 1966.

Genette, Gérard. *Paratexts: Thresholds of Interpretation*. Translated by Jane E. Lewin. Cambridge: Cambridge University Press, 1997.

Genzlinger, Anna Lykins. "The Jessup Dimension." Typescript, [1980?]. GBC.

Genzlinger, Anna Lykins. *The Jessup Dimension*. Clarksburg, WV: Saucerian Press, 1981.

Genzlinger, Anna Lykins. "An Open Letter to the M.I.B." *Gray Barker's Newsletter*, no. 14 (March 1982): [5].

Georges, Robert A. "The General Concept of Legend: Some Assumptions to Be Reexamined and Reassessed." In *American Folk Legend: A Symposium*, edited by Wayland D. Hand, 1–20. Berkeley: University of California Press, 1971.

Gerassi, John. *The Boys of Boise: Furor, Vice, and Folly in an American City*. New York: Macmillan, 1966.

Gilchrist, Neil. "[Letter to the Editor]." *Saucer News* 15, no. 2 (whole no. 72) (Summer 1968): 26.

"'Glenville Smirkury' Makes Debut at April Fools' Day Party Held Saturday." *Glenville Mercury*, April 4, 1944, 1.

Goerman, Robert A. "Alias Carlos Allende." *Fate* 33, no. 10 (October 1980). http://windmill-slayer .tripod.com/aliascarlosallende.

Goerman, Robert A. "Michael Ann Dunn: In Memoriam." Carlos Allende and His Philadelphia Experiment, 2007. https://windmill-slayer.tripod.com/aliascarlosallende/id12.html.

Goerman, Robert A. "The True Story of Mothman." [2021?]. https://robertgoerman.wixsite.com /mothman.

Gorightly, Adam. "Barbara Hudson & Those Sexy Saucer People." *Chasing UFOs* (blog), February 3, 2019. https://chasingufosblog.com/2019/02/03/barbara-hudson-those-sexy-saucer-people.

Gorightly, Adam. "Dick Miller's Favorite Martian." *Chasing UFOs* (blog), January 15, 2020. https://chasingufosblog.com/2020/01/15/dick-millers-favorite-martian.

Gorightly, Adam, and Greg Bishop. *"A" Is for Adamski: The Golden Age of the UFO Contactees*. Color ed. N.p.: Gorightly, 2018.

Graham, Robbie. *Silver Screen Saucers: Sorting Fact from Fantasy in Hollywood's UFO Movies*. Hove: White Crow Books, 2015.

Gray, Jonathan. "Afterword: Studying Media with and without Paratexts." In *Popular Media Cultures: Fans, Audiences and Paratexts*, edited by Lincoln Geraghty, 230–237. Houndmills: Palgrave Macmillan, 2015. https://doi.org/10.1057/9781137350374_12.

"Gray Roscoe Barker," May 2, 1943. U.S., World War II Draft Cards Young Men, 1940–1947. https://www.ancestrylibrary.com/discoveryui-content/view/13025286:2238?tid=&pid=&queryId =7ecf66066ce742308230276a26b8ebd3.

Gross, Loren E. *The Fifth Horseman of the Apocalypse: UFOs: A History, 1953 August-December, Supplemental Notes*. Fremont, CA: privately printed by the author, 2002. https://sohp.us/collections /ufos-a-history/doc/1953-Aug-Dec-SN.php.

Gross, Loren E. *UFOs: A History, 1953 August-December*. Fremont, CA: privately printed by the author, 1990. https://sohp.us/collections/ufos-a-history/doc/1953-Aug-Dec.php.

Gross, Loren E. "UFOs: A History/The Fifth Horseman of the Apocalypse." Sign Oral History Project, 2022. https://sohp.us/collections/ufos-a-history.

Gulyas, Aaron John. "And Then the Feds Showed Up . . ." *The Saucer Life*, November 26, 2017. Podcast, 28:06. https://saucerlife.com/2017/11/26/encounter-206-and-then-the-feds-showed-up.

Gulyas, Aaron John. *Extraterrestrials and the American Zeitgeist: Alien Contact Tales since the 1950s*. Jefferson, NC: McFarland, 2013.

Gulyas, Aaron John. "Storm Hangar 18!" *The Saucer Life*. September 18, 2019. Podcast, 41:58. https://saucerlife.com/2019/09/18/storm-hangar-18.

Haines, Richard W. *The Moviegoing Experience, 1968–2001*. Jefferson, NC: McFarland, 2003.

Halberstam, Jack. *In a Queer Time and Place: Transgender Bodies, Subcultural Lives*. New York: New York University Press, 2005. https://doi.org/10.18574/nyu/9780814790892.001.0001.

Hall, Richard. "Richard Hall's Reality Check." *UFO Magazine and Phenomena Report* 11, no. 6 (December 1996): 9, 38.

"Halloween Party in Science Hall Is a Major Highlight of Social Season." *Glenville Mercury*, November 7, 1944, 1, 4.

Halperin, David J. *Intimate Alien: The Hidden Story of the UFO*. Stanford, CA: Stanford University Press, 2020. https://doi.org/10.1515/9781503612129.

Halpert, Herbert. "Definition and Variation in Folk Legend." In *American Folk Legend: A Symposium*, edited by Wayland D. Hand, 47–54. Berkeley: University of California Press, 1971.

Hancock, Peter A. *Hoax Springs Eternal: The Psychology of Cognitive Deception*. Cambridge: Cambridge University Press, 2014.

Hangar 18. Directed by James L. Conway. Sunn Classic Pictures, 1980.

Hansen, George P. *The Trickster and the Paranormal*. Philadelphia: Xlibris Corp, 2001.

Harris, Neil. *Humbug: The Art of P. T. Barnum*. Boston: Little, Brown, 1973.

Hasken, Eleanor Ann. "The Migration of a Local Legend: The Case of Mothman." PhD diss., Indiana University, 2022. https://www.proquest.com/pqdtglobal/docview/2626020349.

Haymond, Henry. *History of Harrison County, West Virginia: From the Early Days of Northwestern Virginia to the Present*. Morgantown, WV: Acme, 1910. https://n2t.net/ark:/13960/t8gf12020.

"Heckert Heads 'YM' Chapter on Campus." *Glenville Mercury*, October 17, 1944, 1.

"Henry Graceland Barker," November 8, 1922. West Virginia Deaths, 1804–1999. https://www.familysearch.org/ark:/61903/1:1:NM86-MG8.

"History of GSC." Glenville State College. Accessed July 10, 2024. https://www.glenville.edu/about-us/history-gsc.

Hitchcock, John. "More Reviews." *Umbra*, no. 14 ([June 1956?]): 13–14. https://www.fanac.org/fanzines/Umbra/Umbra14.pdf.

Hochheimer, Andrew H. "John A. Keel on the Philadelphia Experiment." *The Philadelphia Experiment From A-Z* (blog), [2016–2018?]. https://www.de173.com/john-a-keel-letter.

Hoffman, Fannie, ed. *Gray Barker's Questions and Answers about UFO's*. [Clarksburg, WV]: [Saucerian Books], 1969.

Honko, Lauri. "Memorates and the Study of Folk Beliefs." *Journal of the Folklore Institute* 1, no. 1 (1964): 5–19. https://doi.org/10.2307/3814027.

Hopkins, Budd. *Missing Time: A Documented Study of UFO Abductions*. New York: Richard Marek, 1981.

Houchin, David. "Gray Barker: Notes from City Directories." [2001?]. Folder "Barker, Gray— Biography and chronology." GBC.

Howard, John. *Men Like That: A Southern Queer History*. Paperback ed. 1999. Reprint, Chicago: University of Chicago Press, 2001.

"Howard Menger Contact, The." *Proceedings of the College of Universal Wisdom* 5, no. 2 (November 1956): 1, 3–10. https://integratron.com/wp-content/uploads/2018/12/NOV-1956.pdf.

Hubbard, Gary. "Lettercolumn." *Trap Door*, no. 4 (May 1985): 25–26. https://fanac.org/fanzines /Trap_Door/Trap_Door04.pdf.

Hudson, Jan. *Those Sexy Saucer People*. San Diego: Greenleaf Classics, 1967. Reprint, n.p., 2019.

Hufford, David J. *The Terror that Comes in the Night: An Experience-Centered Study of Supernatural Assault Traditions*. Philadelphia: University of Pennsylvania Press, 1982.

Hynek, J. Allen. *The UFO Experience: A Scientific Inquiry*. 1972. Reprint, New York: Ballantine, 1974.

Hynek, J. Allen. "The UFO Gap." *Playboy* 14, no. 12 (December 1967): 143–146, 267–271. https://n2t.net/ark:/13960/t1fj5hr6g.

I Know What I Saw. Directed by James Fox. History Channel, 2009.

"An Inner Space Convention in Outer Jersey." *New York Post*, September 15, 1958.

International Flying Saucer Bureau. "A Special Announcement." *Space Review* 2, no. 4 (October 1953): 7. https://n2t.net/ark:/13960/t01054q9d.

International Flying Saucer Bureau. "Directory of Representatives." *Space Review* 2, no. 1 (January 1953): 8. https://n2t.net/ark:/13960/t47q6zg7t.

International Flying Saucer Bureau. "Late Bulletin." *Space Review* 2, no. 4 (October 1953): 1. https://n2t.net/ark:/13960/t01054q9d.

International Flying Saucer Bureau. "Statement of Importance." *Space Review* 2, no. 4 (October 1953): 1. https://n2t.net/ark:/13960/t01054q9d.

Jacobs, David Michael. *The UFO Controversy in America*. Bloomington: Indiana University Press, 1975.

Jansen, Brian. "'It's Still Real to Me': Contemporary Professional Wrestling, Neo-Liberalism, and the Problems of Performed/Real Violence." *Canadian Review of American Studies* 50, no. 2 (July 2020): 302–330. https://doi.org/10.3138/cras.2018.024.

Jansen, Brian. "'Yes! No! . . . Maybe?': Reading the Real in Professional Wrestling's Unreality." *Journal of Popular Culture* 51, no. 3 (2018): 635–656. https://doi.org/10.1111/jpcu.12688.

Jessup, Morris K. "A Report on Washington D.C.'s NICAP (National Investigations Committee on Aerial Phenomena)." *Saucer News* 4, no. 2 (whole no. 22) (March 1957): 5, 16.

Jessup, Morris K., [and Carl M. Allen]. *The Case for the UFO: Unidentified Flying Objects.* Annotated edition. Clarksburg, WV: Saucerian Press, 1973.

Johnson, Charlotte. "George Elliott Barker." Find a Grave, March 26, 2017. https://www.findagrave.com/memorial/177786130/george-elliott-barker.

Johnson, Colin R. *Just Queer Folks: Gender and Sexuality in Rural America.* Philadelphia: Temple University Press, 2013.

"Jose Chung's 'From Outer Space.'" *The X-Files.* Directed by Rob Bowman. Fox, April 12, 1996.

"Jury to Resume Studies; Barker Trial in Progress." *Clarksburg Exponent*, December 6, 1962.

"Justice Dept. Hunting 'Straith' Hoaxer." *NICAP Special Bulletin*, November 1958, 4. https://retroufo58.tumblr.com/post/633938260867072000/nicap-special-bulletin-november-1958.

Keel, John A. "Another 'Man in Black' Case." *Saucer News* 14, no. 3 (whole no. 69) (Fall 1967): 14–15.

Keel, John A. *Jadoo.* New York: Julian Messner, 1957.

Keel, John A. *Operation Trojan Horse: An Exhaustive Study of Unidentified Flying Objects—Revealing Their Source and the Forces that Control Them.* London: Souvenir, 1971.

Keel, John A. *Searching for the String: Selected Writings of John A. Keel,* edited by Andrew Colvin. Seattle, WA & Point Pleasant, WV: Metadisc Productions / New Saucerian Books, 2014.

Keel, John A. *The Mothman Prophecies.* 1975. Reprint, New York: Signet, 1976.

Keel, John A. "Three Letters of Undetermined Origin." *Anomaly,* no. 3 (December 1967): 45–49. https://n2t.net/ark:/13960/t2r57m367.

Keel, John A. "UFO 'Agents of Terror.'" *Saga* 35, no. 1 (October 1967): 28–31. https://files.afu.se/Downloads/Magazines/0%20-%20Articles/United%20States/SAGA/1967%2010%2000_SAGA%20-%20John%20Keel%20-%20UFO%20Agents%20of%20Terror.pdf.

Keel, John A. "UFO Kidnappers!" *Saga* 33, no. 5 (February 1967), 11–15, 50–62.

Keel, John A. "UFO Report: The Sinister Men in Black." *Fate* 21, no. 4 (April 1968): 32–39.

Keith, Michael C. *Sounds in the Dark: All-Night Radio in American Life.* Ames: Iowa State University Press, 2001.

Keller, Raymond A. "Lessons Learned from A Contactee: Woodrow W. Derenberger (1916–1990), Part II." *Phantoms & Monsters* (blog), July 21, 2020. https://www.phantomsandmonsters.com/2020/07/lessons-learned-from-contactee-woodrow_21.html.

Kelley-Romano, Stephanie. "Mythmaking in Alien Abduction Narratives." *Communication Quarterly* 54, no. 3 (August 2006): 383–406. https://doi.org/10.1080/01463370600878545.

Kemp, Earl. "Bye Bye Bellevue." *Nite Cry,* no. 1 (December 1953): 3–10. https://www.fanac.org/fanzines/Nite_Cry/Nite_Cry01.pdf.

Keyhoe, Donald. "Flying Saucers Are Real." *True Magazine*, January 1950, 11–13, 83–87. https://www.saturdaynightuforia.com/library/fsartm/truemagazinetheflyingsaucersarereal1950.html.

Keyhoe, Donald. *The Flying Saucer Conspiracy*. New York: Henry Holt, 1955.

Keyhoe, Donald. *The Flying Saucers Are Real*. New York: Fawcett Publications, 1950.

Keyhoe, Donald. *Flying Saucers from Outer Space*. New York: Henry Holt, 1953.

Klein, Larry. "The Fallen Angels." *Saucer News* 15, no. 2 (whole no. 72) (Summer 1968): 6–8.

Knipfel, Jim. "Midnight Spook Shows: A Brief History." Den of Geek, October 29, 2014. https://www.denofgeek.com/movies/midnight-spook-shows-a-brief-history.

Kripal, Jeffrey J. *Authors of the Impossible: The Paranormal and the Sacred*. Chicago: University of Chicago Press, 2010.

Kripal, Jeffrey J. *Mutants & Mystics: Science Fiction, Superhero Comics, and the Paranormal*. Chicago: University of Chicago Press, 2011.

Kripal, Jeffrey J. "On the Mothman, God, and Other Monsters: The Demonology of John A. Keel." In *Histories of the Hidden God: Concealment and Revelation in Western Gnostic, Esoteric, and Mystical Traditions*, edited by April D. De Conick and Grant Adamson, 234–258. Durham: Acumen, 2013.

Kugelberg, Johan, Jack Womack, and Michael P. Daley, eds. *The Tattooed Dragon Meets the Wolfman: Lenny Kaye's Science Fiction Fanzines 1941–1970*. New York: Boo-Hooray, 2014.

Kuper, Adam. "If Memes Are the Answer, What Is the Question?" In *Darwinizing Culture: The Status of Memetics as a Science*, edited by Robert Aunger, 174–188. Oxford: Oxford University Press, 2000. https://doi.org/10.1093/acprof:oso/9780192632449.003.0009.

Kusche, Larry. Review of *The Philadelphia Experiment: Project Invisibility*, by William L. Moore and Charles Berlitz. *Skeptical Inquirer* 4, no. 1 (Fall 1979): 58–63. https://skepticalinquirer.org/1979/10/the-philadelphia-experiment-project-invisibility.

Lachman, Gary. *Turn Off Your Mind: The Mystic Sixties and the Dark Side of the Age of Aquarius*. London: Sidgwick & Jackson, 2001.

Lagrange, Pierre. "Avant-propos: Gray Barker et l'invention des Men in Black." In Gray Barker, *Ils en savaient trop sur les soucoupes volantes*, translated by Vincent Carénini, 7–46. Bibliothèque des prodiges. Paris: Presses du Châtelet, 2002.

Lagrange, Pierre. "Close Encounters of the French Kind: The Saucerian Construction of 'Contacts' and the Controversy over Its Reality in France." In *Alien Worlds: Social and Religious Dimensions of Extraterrestrial Contact*, edited by Diana G. Tumminia, 153–190. Syracuse, NY: Syracuse University Press, 2007.

Lantern, The. Directed by Andrew Smith. YouTube video, 22:19. 2020. https://www.youtube.com/watch?v=C2PeOMIwk8Y.

Laycock, Joseph P. "Mothman: Monster, Disaster, and Community." *Fieldwork in Religion* 3, no. 1 (2008): 70–86. https://doi.org/10.1558/firn.v3i1.70.

Layne, Meade. "Welcome? Kareeta!" *Round Robin* 2, no. 10 (October 1946): 3–7. https://borderlandsciences.org/journal/vol/02/n10/Welcome_Kareeta.html.

Lazarus, Lillian. "Cincinnati Realart Celebrates 40 Years." *Boxoffice* 67, no. 4 (May 21, 1955): 70–79. https://www.yumpu.com/en/document/read/27024793/boxoffice-may211955.

Leach, Robert T. "Men in Black." *UFO Magazine and Phenomena Report* 11, no. 6 (December 1996): 18–24.

Lepselter, Susan. "The License: Poetics, Power, and the Uncanny." In *E. T. Culture: Anthropology in Outerspaces*, edited by Debbora Battaglia, 130–148. Durham, NC: Duke University Press, 2006. https://doi.org/10.1515/9780822387015-005.

Lepselter, Susan. *The Resonance of Unseen Things: Poetics, Power, Captivity, and UFOs in the American Uncanny*. Ann Arbor: University of Michigan Press, 2016. https://doi.org/10.3998/mpub.7172850.

Leslie, Desmond. "Leslie Strikes Back (Part One)." *Nexus* 2, no. 5 (whole no. 11) (May 1955): 7–8.

Leslie, Desmond, and George Adamski. *Flying Saucers Have Landed*. London: Werner Laurie, 1953.

"Letters to the Editor." *Spacecraft News*, [new series] no. 3 (June 1967): 26–28.

Leurs, Laurens. "The History of Prepress & Publishing: 1950–1959." *Prepressure* (blog), [2010?]. https://www.prepressure.com/prepress/history/events-1950-1959.

Lewis, James R. *UFOs and Popular Culture: An Encyclopedia of Contemporary Myth*. Santa Barbara, CA: ABC-CLIO, 2000. http://link.library.utoronto.ca/eir/EIRdetail.cfm?Resources__ID=890561&T=F.

Lind, Tom. *The Catalogue of UFO Periodicals*. Said of Saucers Research Publications. Hobe Sound, FL: privately printed by the author, 1982.

Lister, Ashley. "Telling True Ghost Stories." *Short Fiction in Theory & Practice* 10, no. 1 (April 2020): 73–87. https://doi.org/10.1386/fict_00015_1.

Long, Antoinette. "Rosa Lee Barker (Frame)." Geni, May 24, 2018. https://www.geni.com/people/Rosa-Barker/6000000076892853875.

Lopez, Donald S., Jr. *Prisoners of Shangri-La: Tibetan Buddhism and the West*. 20th anniversary ed. Chicago: University of Chicago Press, 2018.

Lorenzen, Coral E. "Quotes and Comments." *APRO Bulletin*, March 1957, 2–3. https://n2t.net/ark:/13960/t8dg4qp54.

Lorenzen, Coral E. "The Bender-IFSB Affair." *APRO Bulletin* January 15, 1954, 4–5. https://n2t.net/ark:/13960/t2p63jn1c.

Lorenzen, Coral E. "The Editorial." *APRO Bulletin* November 15, 1953, 2, 5–6. https://n2t.net/ark:/13960/t6j181k19.

Lorenzen, Coral, and Jim Lorenzen. *Flying Saucer Occupants*. New York: Signet, 1967.

Lowe, Virginia A. P. "A Brief Look at Some UFO Legends." *Indiana Folklore* 12, no. 1 (1979): 67–79.

Lucchesi, Dominick C. *Flying Saucers from Khabarah Khoom*. Jane Lew, WV: New Age Books, 1983.

Lynn, Robert Wood. *Mothman Apologia*. New Haven, CT: Yale University Press, 2022. https://doi.org/10.12987/9780300264975.

Mann, Jeff. *Loving Mountains, Loving Men*. Athens: Ohio University Press, 2005.

"Man's Tales Out of This World." *Grit* 97, no. 32 (July 22, 1979): 13.

"Marie Barker," September 12, 1922. West Virginia Deaths, 1804–1999. https://familysearch.org/ark:/61903/1:1:F1RR-54Y.

May, Andrew. *Pseudoscience and Science Fiction*. Cham: Springer International, 2017. https://doi.org/10.1007/978-3-319-42605-1.

Mazer, Sharon. "'Real' Wrestling/'Real' Life." In *Steel Chair to the Head: The Pleasure and Pain of Professional Wrestling*, edited by Nicholas Sammond, 67–87. Durham, NC: Duke University Press, 2005. https://doi.org/10.2307/j.ctv11smpbc.

McCann, Marcus. *Park Cruising: What Happens When We Wander off the Path*. Toronto: Anansi, 2023.

McGann, Jerome J. *The Textual Condition*. Princeton, NJ: Princeton University Press, 1991. https://doi.org/10.1515/9780691217758.

Mckee, Gabriel. "A Contactee Canon: Gray Barker's Saucerian Books." In *The Paranormal and Popular Culture: A Postmodern Religious Landscape*, edited by Darryl V. Caterine and John W. Morehead, 275–288. New York: Routledge, 2019. https://doi.org/10.4324/9781315184661.

Mckee, Gabriel. "Office Copying Technology in the Flying Saucer Subculture: Gray Barker's Saucerian Books." *Book History* 27, no. 2 (Fall 2024): 375–404.

Mckee, Gabriel. "'Reality—Is It a Horror?': Richard Shaver's Subterranean World and the Displaced Self." *Journal of Gods and Monsters* 1 (Summer 2020): 1–17. https://doi.org/10.58997/jgm.v1i1.1.

McLeod, Kembrew. *Pranksters: Making Mischief in the Modern World*. New York: New York University Press, 2014.

McLuhan, Marshall. *The Gutenberg Galaxy: The Making of Typographic Man*. 1962. Reprint, Toronto: University of Toronto Press, 2011.

M'Collum, Lem. "Mystery Visitors Halt Research, Saucerers Here Ordered to Quit." *Sunday Herald*, November 22, 1953.

Melton, J. Gordon. "The Contactees: A Survey." In *The Spectrum of UFO Research: Proceedings of the Second CUFOs Conference*, edited by Mimi Hynek, 99–108. Chicago: J. Hynek Center for UFO Studies, 1988. http://www.cufos.org/books/The_Spectrum_of_UFO_Research.pdf.

Melton, J. Gordon. "UFO Contactees: A Report on Work in Progress." In *Proceedings of the First International UFO Congress*, edited by Curtis G. Fuller, 378–395. New York: Warner Books, 1980.

Menger, Howard. *From Outer Space to You*. Clarksburg, WV: Saucerian Books, 1959.

Meyers, Bill. "Spreading the Fertilizer." *Cry of the Nameless*, no. 108 (October 1957): 20–22. https://fanac.org/fanzines/Cry_of_the_Nameless/Cry108.pdf.

Miller, Christopher L. *Impostors: Literary Hoaxes and Cultural Authenticity*. Chicago: University of Chicago Press, 2018.

Miller, Max B. "That State Department Letter." *Saucers* 6, no. 2 (Summer 1958): 8–12. https://n2t.net/ark:/13960/t3hx99q7h.

Miller, Neil. *Sex-Crime Panic: A Journey to the Paranoid Heart of the 1950s*. Los Angeles: Alyson Books, 2002.

"Minstrel, Fashion Show, Play, Songs, b'shop Quartet, Etc., in Big Variety Show to Be Presented Tomorrow at 8 PM." *Glenville Mercury*, April 30, 1946, 4.

Mishlove, Jeffrey. *The PK Man: A True Story of Mind over Matter*. Charlottesville, VA: Hampton Roads, 2000.

Monger, R. [pseud.] "The Wild Rumor Column." *The Saucerian* 2, no. 2 (whole no. 4) (September 1954): 25–26.

Montgomery, Ruth. *Strangers among Us: Enlightened Beings from a World to Come*. New York: Coward, McCann & Geoghegan, 1979.

Moore, William L., and Charles Berlitz. *The Philadelphia Experiment: Project Invisibility*. New York: Grosset & Dunlap, 1979.

Moreno, Richard. *Myths and Mysteries of Illinois: True Stories of the Unsolved and Unexplained*. Guilford, CT: Globe Pequot, 2013.

"Morris Jessup." *U.F.O. Investigator* 1, no. 8 (June 1959): 8. https://n2t.net/ark:/13960/t0xq71j4k.

Moseley, James W. "Book (?) Review." *Saucer Smear* 31, no. 6 (August 1984): 5–6.

Moseley, James W. "Editorial." *Saucer News* 14, no. 4 (whole no. 70) (Winter 1967–Winter 1968): 3–4.

Moseley, James W. "Editorial." *Saucer Smear* 58, no. 5 (May 2011): 1–3.

Moseley, James W. "Editorial: Saucer News Combines with 'The Saucerian Bulletin.'" *Saucer News* 10, no. 2 (whole no. 52) (June 1963): 2.

Moseley, James W. "Gossip Column." *Nexus* 1, no. 2 (August 1954): 4–5.

Moseley, James W. "In Which We Attempt to Take Another Look at the Famous 'Lost Creek' Saucer Case." *Saucer Smear* 33, no. 2 (March 1986): 2.

Moseley, James W. "Inside 'Giant Crock.'" *New Saucers* [*Saucer Smear*] 23, no. 19 (April 1976): 1.

Moseley, James W. "The Inside Story Regarding Our Feud with Gray Barker." *Saucer News* 11, no. 2 (whole no. 56) (June 1964): 2.

Moseley, James W. "Latest News about New York Lecture Series." *Saucer News* 11, no. 3 (whole no. 57) (September 1964): 4–5.

Moseley, James W. "Letters to U-No-Hu." *Saucer Clues* [*Saucer Smear*] 24, no. 3 (March 1977): 2–6.

Moseley, James W. "Misc. Ravings." *Saucer Wit Rides Again* [*Saucer Smear*] 26, no. 6 (May 1979): 1.

Moseley, James W. "Misc. Ravings." *Saucer Smear* 28, no. 12 (December 1981): 2–3.

Moseley, James W. "Miscellaneous Ravings." *Saucer Smear* 30, no. 1 (January 1984): 1–2.

Moseley, James W. "Miscellaneous Ravings." *Saucer Smear* 31, no. 9 (December 1984): 1–3.

Moseley, James W. "Miscellaneous Ravings." *Saucer Smear* 32, no. 3 (April 1985): 3.

Moseley, James W. "Miscellaneous Ravings." *Saucer Smear* 44, no. 1 (January 1997): 1–4.

Moseley, James W. "Missives from the Masses." *Saucer Wit* [*Saucer Smear*] 26, no. 3 (March 1979): 2–8.

Moseley, James W. "Missives from the Masses." *Saucer Smear* 28, no. 4 (December 1981): 4–8.

Moseley, James W. "Missives from the Masses." *Saucer Smear* 32, no. 3 (April 1985): 4–8.

Moseley, James W. "News Briefies." *Saucer Smear* 31, no. 8 (November 1984): 8.

Moseley, James W. "News Briefs." *Saucer News* 2, no. 8 (whole no. 14) (November 1955): 11.

Moseley, James W. "Publicity-Seeking Antics by Gray Barker." *Saucer News* 9, no. 2 (whole no. 48) (June 1962): 2.

Moseley, James W. "Recent News." *Saucer News* 11, no. 3 (whole no. 57) (September 1964): 8–23.

Moseley, James W. "Recent News." *Saucer News* 12, no. 4 (whole no. 62) (December 1965): 15–27.

Moseley, James W. "Recent News Stories." *Saucer News* 7, no. 2 (whole no. 40) (June 1960): 15–18.

Moseley, James W. "Recent News Stories." *Saucer News* 8, no. 1 (whole no. 43) (March 1961): 10–16.

Moseley, James W. "Recent News Stories." *Saucer News* 8, no. 4 (whole no. 46) (December 1961): 8, 11–16.

Moseley, James W. "Recent News Stories." *Saucer News* 9, no. 3 (whole no. 49) (September 1962): 20–24.

Moseley, James W. "Recent UFO Sightings." *Saucer News* 13, no. 4 (whole no. 66) (Winter 1966–Winter 1967): 28–33.

Moseley, James W. "Re-Hash of the 1982 National UFO Conference." *Saucer Smear* 29, no. 5 (June 1982): 1–2.

Moseley, James W. "Report on the Giant Rock Convention." *Saucer News* 7, no. 3 (whole no. 41) (September 1960): 3–9.

Moseley, James W. "Saucer News Non-Scheduled Newsletter #11," September 10, 1960. https://n2t.net/ark:/13960/t6r006x4s.

Moseley, James W. "Saucer News Non-Scheduled Newsletter #16," May 15, 1963. https://n2t.net/ark:/13960/t0wq7z64z.

Moseley, James W, ed. *Saucer News: Special Convention Issue*. Fort Lee, NJ: S.A.U.C.E.R.S., 1967.

Moseley, James W. "Some New Facts about 'Flying Saucers Have Landed.'" *Nexus* 2, no. 1 (whole no. 7) (January 1955): 7–17.

Moseley, James W. "Who's Lying? The Wright Field Story." *The Saucerian* 3, no. 1 (whole no. 5) (January 1955): 32–36.

Moseley, James W. "Ye Olde Mail Bag." *Son of Saucer Wit* [*Saucer Smear*] 26, no. 5 (April 1979): 2–5.

Moseley, James W. "Ye Olde Misc. Ravings." *Saucer Wit* [*Saucer Smear*] 26, no. 3 (March 1979): 1.

Moseley, James W., and Karl T. Pflock. *Shockingly Close to the Truth! Confessions of a Grave-Robbing Ufologist*. Amherst, NY: Prometheus Books, 2002.

Moseley, James W., and August C. Roberts. "This Unusual Picture." *Saucer News* 3, no. 5 (whole no. 19) (September 1956): 6.

Moseley, Sandy. "What Gray Barker Is Really Like." *Saucer News* 10, no. 4 (whole no. 54) (December 1963): 14.

Moskowitz, Sam. *The Immortal Storm: A History of Science Fiction Fandom*. 1954. Reprint, Westport, CT: Hyperion Press, 1974.

The Mothman Prophecies. Directed by Mark Pellington. Screen Gems, 2002.

Mundo, Laura. *Flying Saucers and the Father's Plan*. Clarksburg, WV: Saucerian Books, 1963.

Mundo, Laura. *Flying-Saucers and the Father's Plan*. Dearborn, MI: Planetary Center, 1962.

Mundo, Laura. "[Letter to R. L. Andrews]." *The Open Letter*, April 1959, 14–17.

Mundo, Laura. *The Father's Plan (and Flying Saucers)*. Dearborn, MI: Planetary Space Center, 1964.

Mundo, Laura. *The Mundo UFO Report*. New York: Vantage, 1982.

Mutton, Karen. *Lobsang Rampa, New Age Trailblazer*. Frankston, TX: Hidden Mysteries / TGS Publishers, 2006.

Nadis, Fred. *The Man from Mars: Ray Palmer's Amazing Pulp Journey*. New York: Jeremy P. Tarcher, 2013.

Nebel, Long John. *Long John Nebel—WOR—11.16.1958*. AM FM Archives, 1958. https://www.bitchute.com/video/WiHVlB8R4EMZ.

Nebel, Long John. *The Way-out World*. Englewood Cliffs, NJ: Prentice-Hall, 1961.

"New Utica, N.Y. Group." *Saucer News* 16, no. 4 (whole no. 74) (Spring–Summer 1969): 37.

New-York Historical Society. "A Flying Saucer Sighting in the Time Inc. Records." *From the Stacks* (blog), September 4, 2019. https://blog.nyhistory.org/a-flying-saucer-sighting-in-the-time-inc -records.

Nichols, Preston B., and Peter Moon. *The Montauk Project: Experiments in Time*. New York: Sky Books, 1992.

"Nominated: King and Furr Typical G.S.C. 'Bouncers.'" *Glenville Mercury*, October 23, 1945, 3.

"Obituary: M. K. Jessup." *The Spacecrafter*, December 1959, 27. https://n2t.net/ark:/13960 /t8sc22841.

O'Connell, Mark. *The Close Encounters Man: How One Man Made the World Believe in UFOs*. New York: Dey St. / William Morrow, 2017.

"Ohnimgohows Initiate 12 Pledges Wednesday." *Glenville Mercury*, January 19, 1943, 4.

Oring, Elliott. "Memetics and Folkloristics: The Applications." *Western Folklore* 73, no. 4 (2014): 455–492. https://www.jstor.org/stable/24551137.

Oring, Elliott. "Memetics and Folkloristics: The Theory." *Western Folklore* 73, no. 4 (2014): 432– 454. https://www.jstor.org/stable/24551136.

Östling, Erik A. W. "'I Figured That in My Dreams, I Remembered What Actually Happened': On Abduction Narratives as Emergent Folklore." In *Handbook of UFO Religions*, edited by Ben Zeller, 197–232. Leiden: Brill, 2021. https://brill.com/view/title/57043.

Östling, Erik A. W. "Yonah Fortner and the 'Historical Doctrine' of 'Extraterrestrialism.'" Presentation at the American Academy of Religion Annual Meeting, Denver, CO, November 2018.

Otto, John. "Come In, Outer Space." *The Saucerian* 3, no. 2 (whole no. 6) (Spring 1955): 37–40.

Owens, Ted. *How to Contact Space People*. Clarksburg, WV: Saucerian Books, 1969.

Owens, Ted. "The SI's Want to Help." *Saucer News* 14, no. 4 (whole no. 70) (Winter 1967–Winter 1968): 8–9.

Palmer, Ray. "Saucer Club News." *Flying Saucers*, no. 63 (April 1969): 35–37, 46.

Palmer, Ray, and Richard S. Shaver. *The Secret World: The Diary of a Lifetime of Questioning the Facts*. Amherst, WI: Amherst Press, 1977.

Parks, Randy. "Gray Barker Is Happy to Announce . . ." *Spacecraft News*, [new series] no. 3 (June 1967): 10.

Partridge, Christopher H. "Understanding UFO Religions and Abduction Spiritualities." In *UFO Religions*, edited by Christopher H. Partridge, 3–42. London: Routledge, 2003.

Pasulka, Diana Walsh. *American Cosmic: UFOs, Religions, Technology*. Oxford: Oxford University Press, 2019.

Pautz, Michelle. "The Decline in Average Weekly Cinema Attendance: 1930–2000." *Issues in Political Economy* 11 (2002): 18.

Peebles, Curtis. *Watch the Skies! A Chronicle of the Flying Saucer Myth*. Washington, DC: Smithsonian Institution, 1994.

"Philadelphia Experiment, The." Box Office Mojo. Accessed October 7, 2022. https://www.boxofficemojo.com/release/rl1164477953/weekend.

Phillips, Ted. *Physical Traces Associated with UFO Sightings: A Preliminary Catalog*, edited by Mimi Hynek. Evanston, IL: Center for UFO Studies, 1975. http://www.cufos.org/books/Physical_Traces.pdf.

"Pictureland Theater [Advertisement]." *Glenville Mercury*, May 6, 1947, 3.

Pierce, Roger. "Barker Speaks in Cleveland." *Cosmic News* ([1956?]): 7–8. https://files.afu.se/Downloads/Magazines/United%20States/Cosmic%20News%20(Pierce%20and%20Neuberger)/Cosmic%20News%20-%201956a.pdf.

Pitre, Boisy G. *CoCo: The Colorful History of Tandy's Underdog Computer*. Boca Raton, FL: CRC, 2014.

"Pittsburgh." *Boxoffice* 81, no. 8 (June 12, 1962): E-6. https://www.yumpu.com/en/document/read/27247609/boxoffice-june111962.

"Pittsburgh." *Boxoffice* 82, no. 4 (November 12, 1962): E-6. https://www.yumpu.com/en/document/view/27394589/boxoffice-november121962.

"Pittsburgh." *Boxoffice* 83, no. 11 (July 8, 1963): E-6. https://www.yumpu.com/en/document/read/27461130.

"Pittsburgh." *Boxoffice* 87, no. 14 (July 28, 1965): E-8. https://www.yumpu.com/en/document/view/27565126/boxoffice-july261965.

"Pittsburgh." *Boxoffice* 99, no. 7 (May 31, 1971): E7. https://www.proquest.com/docview/1476084225/citation/8DC9051BF8AD4645PQ/61.

"Pittsburgh." *Boxoffice* 103, no. 26 (October 8, 1973): E-6. https://www.yumpu.com/en/document/view/31901665/boxoffice-october081973.

"Pittsburgh." *Boxoffice* 104, no. 6 (November 19, 1973): E-6. https://www.yumpu.com/en/document/view/31902367/boxoffice-november191973.

"Pittsburgh." *Boxoffice* 105, no. 10 (June 17, 1974): E-6. https://www.proquest.com/docview/1476121715.

"Pittsburgh." *Boxoffice*. 106, no. 9 (December 9, 1974): E4. http://www.proquest.com/docview/1476127715/citation/2A86EF11FD3C4B5APQ/1.

"Plan Ban on X-Rated Movies at Cinema V." *Boxoffice* 104, no. 3 (October 29, 1973): E-1. https://www.yumpu.com/en/document/view/31902363/boxoffice-291973.

Polk's Clarksburg (Harrison County, W. Va.) City Directory, Vol. 30, 1957–58. Pittsburgh, PA: R. L. Polk, 1958. https://www.ancestrylibrary.com/imageviewer/collections/2469/images/14936005.

Pratt, Richard H. [pseudonym of John C. Sherwood]. "Flying Saucers: Time Machines?" *Saucer News* 16, no. 4 (whole no. 74) (Spring–Summer 1969): 3, [57].

Pratt, Richard H. "The Strange B.I.C.R. Affair." *Saucer News* 17, no. 1 (whole no. 75) (Spring 1970): 10–12.

Rampa, T. Lobsang. *As It Was!* London: Corgi / Transworld, 1976.

Rampa, T. Lobsang. "Saucers over Tibet." *Flying Saucer Review* 3, no. 2 (April 1957): 10–12.

Rampa, T. Lobsang. *The Third Eye: The Autobiography of a Tibetan Lama.* London: Secker & Warburg, 1956.

Redfern, Nick. *Contactees: A History of Alien-Human Interaction.* Franklin Lakes, NJ: New Page Books, 2010.

Redfern, Nick. *The FBI Files: The FBI's UFO Top Secrets Exposed.* London: Pocket Books, 1998.

Redfern, Nick. *The Real Men in Black: Evidence, Famous Cases, and True Stories of These Mysterious Men and Their Connection to UFO Phenomena.* Pompton Plains, NJ: New Page Books, 2011.

Reich, James. *Wilhelm Reich versus the Flying Saucers: An American Tragedy.* Santa Barbara, CA: Punctum Books, 2024.

Reich, Wilhelm. *Contact with Space: Oranur Second Report, 1951–1956.* 1957. Reprint, Haverhill, MA: Haverhill House, 2018.

Reich, Wilhelm. *Where's the Truth?: Letters and Journals, 1948–1957,* edited by Mary Boyd Higgins. New York: Farrar, Straus and Giroux, 2012.

Reinhard, CarrieLynn D. "Kayfabe as Convergence: Content Interactivity and Prosumption in the Squared Circle." In *Convergent Wrestling: Participatory Culture, Transmedia Storytelling, and Intertextuality in the Squared Circle,* edited by CarrieLynn D. Reinhard and Christopher J. Olson, 31–44. London: Routledge, 2019. https://doi.org/10.4324/9781351233989.

"Resignations." *The U.F.O. Investigator* 1, no. 5 (September 1958): 2. https://n2t.net/ark:/13960 /t9872jg4r.

Robinson, John J. "The Three-Faced Idol, or, The Identity of Brother Philip Hidden in the Secret of the Andes." *Saucer News* 9, no. 2 (whole no. 48) (June 1962): 10–13.

Rojcewicz, Peter M. "The Folklore of the 'Men in Black': A Challenge to the Prevailing Paradigm." *ReVision* 11, no. 4 (Spring 1989): 5–16.

Rojcewicz, Peter M. "The 'Men in Black' Experience and Tradition: Analogues with the Traditional Devil Hypothesis." *Journal of American Folklore* 100, no. 396 (April 1987): 148–160. https://doi .org/10.2307/540919.

Rønnevig, Georg M. "Toward an Explanation of the 'Abduction Epidemic': The Ritualization of Alien Abduction Mythology in Therapeutic Settings." In *Alien Worlds: Social and Religious Dimensions of Extraterrestrial Contact,* edited by Diana G. Tumminia, 99–127. Syracuse, NY: Syracuse University Press, 2007.

Roth, Christopher F. "Ufology as Anthropology: Race, Extraterrestrials, and the Occult." In *E.T. Culture: Anthropology in Outerspaces*, edited by Debbora Battaglia, 38–93. Durham, NC: Duke University Press, 2005. https://doi.org/10.1515/9780822387015-003.

Rothstein, Mikael. "The Rise and Decline of the First-Generation UFO Contactees: A Cognitive Approach." In *Encyclopedic Sourcebook of UFO Religions*, edited by James R. Lewis, 63–76. Amherst, NY: Prometheus Books, 2003.

Rouse, Sheelagh. *Twenty-Five Years with T. Lobsang Rampa*. N.p.: Published by the author, 2006.

Ruppelt, Edward J. *The Report on Unidentified Flying Objects*. Garden City, NY: Doubleday, 1956.

Saler, Benson, Charles A. Ziegler, and Charles B. Moore. *UFO Crash at Roswell: The Genesis of a Modern Myth*. Washington, DC: Smithsonian Institution, 1997.

Saliba, John A. "UFO Contactee Phenomena from a Psychosociological Perspective: A Review." In *The Gods Have Landed: New Religions from Other Worlds*, edited by James R. Lewis, 207–250. Albany: State University of New York Press, 1995.

Sanders, Jacqueline. "The Van Tassel Saucer Meeting." *The Saucerian* 2, no. 2 (whole no. 4) (September 1954): 15–17.

Sanderson, Ivan T. *Uninvited Visitors: A Biologist Looks at UFO's*. New York: Cowles, 1967.

Saunders, David R., and R. Roger Harkins. *UFOs? Yes!: Where the Condon Committee Went Wrong*. New York: Signet, 1968.

Schwarz, Berthold Eric. *UFO-Dynamics: Psychiatric and Psychic Aspects of the UFO Syndrome*. 3rd ed. Moore Haven, FL: Rainbow Books, 1988.

Science Research. "Have Space People Communicated with Earth? [Advertisement]." *Saucer News* 13, no. 3 (whole no. 65) (Fall 1966): 33.

Scribner, Scott R. "Alien Abduction Narratives: A Proposed Model and Brief Case Study." In *The Supernatural in Society, Culture, and History*, edited by Dennis D. Waskul and Marc A. Eaton, 210–231. Philadelphia: Temple University Press, 2018.

Scribner, Scott R. "Alien Abduction Narratives and Religious Contexts." In *Alien Worlds: Social and Religious Dimensions of Extraterrestrial Contact*, edited by Diana G. Tumminia, 138–152. Syracuse, NY: Syracuse University Press, 2007.

Scully, Frank. *Behind the Flying Saucers*. New York: Henry Holt, 1950.

Segrave, Kerry. *Drive-in Theaters: A History from Their Inception in 1933*. Jefferson, NC: McFarland, 2006.

"Semester Enrollment Down; Night, Extension Students Will Boost Semester Total." *Glenville Mercury*, September 29, 1942, 1.

Sergent, Donnie, and Jeff Wamsley. *Mothman: The Facts behind the Legend*. Point Pleasant, WV: Mothman Lives, 2002.

Shades of Gray: A True Story. Directed by Bob Wilkinson. Seminal Films, 2010.

Shalett, Sidney. "What You Can Believe about Flying Saucers, Conclusion." *Saturday Evening Post* May 7, 1949. https://n2t.net/ark:/13960/t3wv17j74.

Shalett, Sidney. "What You Can Believe about Flying Saucers, Part One." *Saturday Evening Post*, April 30, 1949. https://n2t.net/ark:/13960/t7rp5qg66.

Sharaf, Myron R. *Fury on Earth: A Biography of Wilhelm Reich*. New York: Da Capo, 1994.

Sherwood, John C. "Gray Barker: My Friend, the Myth-Maker." *Skeptical Inquirer* 22, no. 3 (May–June 1998): 37–39. http://www.csicop.org/si/show/gray_barker_my_friend_the_myth-maker.

Sherwood, John C. "Gray Barker's Book of Bunk: Mothman, Saucers, and MIB." *Skeptical Inquirer* 26, no. 3 (June 2002): 39–44. https://skepticalinquirer.org/2002/05/gray-barkers-book-of-bunk.

"Shotgun Wedding: Taglines." IMDB, 2022. http://www.imdb.com/title/tt0057496/taglines.

Skinner, Doug. "Jessup-Allende (4)." *John Keel: Not an Authority on Anything* (blog), December 15, 2021. https://www.johnkeel.com/?p=4932.

Skinner, Doug. "John Keel and 'The International Bankers.'" *John Keel: Not an Authority on Anything* (blog), December 12, 2012. https://www.johnkeel.com/?p=1667.

Skinner, Doug. "That 'Playboy' Article." *John Keel: Not an Authority on Anything* (blog), February 11, 2015. http://www.johnkeel.com/?p=2482.

Snellgrove, David. Review of *The Third Eye: Autobiography of a Tibetan Lama*, by T. Lobsang Rampa. *Oriental Art* 3, no. 2 (Summer 1957): 75.

"Spacecraft News, Issue No. 1." Saucerian Publications, November 1965.

St. Germain, Jules. "Out of This World." *Argosy* 348, no. 1 (January 1959): 34–35, 100–101.

Standish, David. *Hollow Earth: The Long and Curious History of Imagining Strange Lands, Fantastical Creatures, Advanced Civilizations, and Marvelous Machines Below the Earth's Surface*. Cambridge, MA: Da Capo, 2006.

Stapel, Christopher J. "Dismantling Metrocentric and Metronormative Curricula: Toward a Critical Queer Pedagogy of Southern Rural Space and Place." In *Queer South Rising: Voices of a Contested Place*, edited by Reta Ugena Whitlock, 59–72. Charlotte, NC: Information Age Publishing, 2013.

Steiger, Brad. "Fantastic Key to the Flying Saucer Mystery." *Saga* 35, no. 2 (November 1967): 22–25, 60–66.

Steiger, Brad, and Joan Whritenour. *The Allende Letters: Has the UFO Invasion Started?* New York: Award Books, 1968.

Steiger, Brad, and Joan Whritenour. *New UFO Breakthrough*. New York: Award Books, 1968.

Steinmeyer, Jim. *Charles Fort: The Man Who Invented the Supernatural*. New York: J. P. Tarcher, 2008.

Strayer, Michael, ed. *UFO Is a Bucket of Shit: A Gray Barker Zine*. Mothboys Podcast / Strange Days Zine, 2023.

Stringfield, Leonard H. "Retrievals of the Third Kind." *MUFON UFO Journal*, no. 128 (July 1978): 8–11.

Stringfield, Leonard H. "Retrievals of the Third Kind—Part 2." *MUFON UFO Journal*, no. 129 (August 1978): 8–14.

Stuart, John E. *UFO Warning*. Clarksburg, WV: Saucerian Books, 1963.

Stupple, David. "Mahatmas and Space Brothers: The Ideologies of Alleged Contact with Extra-terrestrials." *Journal of American Culture* 7, no. 1/2 (Spring/Summer 1984): 131–139. https://doi.org/10.1111/j.1542-734X.1984.0701_131.x.

Stupple, David, and Abdollah Dashti. "Flying Saucers and Multiple Realities: A Case Study in Phenomenological Theory." *Journal of Popular Culture* 11, no. 2 (Fall 1977): 479–493.

Stupple, David, Berthold Eric Schwartz, Ted Bloecher, and J. Gordon Melton. "Visiting with Space People: A Symposium on the Contactee Phenomenon." In *Proceedings of the First International UFO Congress*, edited by Curtis G. Fuller, 305–321. New York: Warner Books, 1980.

Sutton, John Davison. *History of Braxton County and Central West Virginia*. Sutton, WV: privately printed by the author, 1919. https://n2t.net/ark:/13960/t44q8z189.

Swazey, Judith P. *Chlorpromazine in Psychiatry: A Study of Therapeutic Innovation*. Cambridge, MA: MIT Press, 1974.

Swords, Michael D., and Robert Powell. *UFOs and Government: A Historical Inquiry*. San Antonio, TX: Anomalist Books, 2012.

Sydow, Carl Wilhelm von. "The Categories of Prose Tradition." In *Selected Papers on Folklore: Published on the Occasion of His 70th Birthday*, edited by Laurits Bødker, 86–88. Copenhagen: Rosenkilde and Bagger, 1948.

Tanselle, G. Thomas. *Literature and Artifacts*. Charlottesville: Bibliographical Society of the University of Virginia, 1998.

"Theatres Need Voice Like TV Guide, so West Virginia Editor Offers Moviews." *Boxoffice* 80, no. 81 (March 12, 1962): 42. https://www.yumpu.com/en/document/view/27246107/boxoffice-march121962.

Thompson, Keith. *Angels and Aliens: UFOs and the Mythic Imagination*. Reading, MA: Addison-Wesley / William Patrick, 1991.

Toelken, Barre. *The Dynamics of Folklore*. Rev. and expanded ed. Logan: Utah State University Press, 1996.

Toronto, Richard. *Rokfogo: The Mysterious Pre-Deluge Art of Richard S. Shaver*. 2 vols. San Francisco, CA: Shavertron, 2014.

Toronto, Richard. *War over Lemuria: Richard Shaver, Ray Palmer and the Strangest Chapter of 1940s Science Fiction*. Jefferson, NC: McFarland, 2013.

Trench, Brinsley le Poer. "U.S. Govt. Has Evidence of Extra-Terrestrials." *Flying Saucer Review* 4, no. 2 (April 1958): 2–3.

Troshinsky, Lisa. "The Flatwoods Monster Comes Alive Again." *WV Independent Observer*, October 24, 2018. https://wearetheobserver.com/the-flatwoods-monster-comes-alive-again.

Tumminia, Diana G. "From Rumor to Postmodern Myth: A Sociological Study of the Transformation of Flying Saucer Rumor." In *Encyclopedic Sourcebook of UFO Religions*, edited by James R. Lewis, 103–119. Amherst, NY: Prometheus Books, 2003.

Tumminia, Diana G. *When Prophecy Never Fails: Myth and Reality in a Flying-Saucer Group*. Oxford: Oxford University Press, 2005. https://doi.org/10.1093/0195176758.001.0001.

Tuvel, Rebecca. "In Defense of Transracialism." *Hypatia* 32, no. 2 (Spring 2017): 263–278. https://doi.org/10.1111/hypa.12327.

"Two British Showmen Win Bonus Awards for October." *Boxoffice* 58, no. 2 (November 11, 1950): 35. https://www.yumpu.com/en/document/view/26759867/boxoffice-11111950.

UFO, episode 3. Directed by Paul Crowder. Showtime, August 22, 2021. https://www.sho.com/ufo/season/1/episode/3/103.

"U.F.O. and New Age Books from Saucerian Publications." Saucerian Publications, [1962?].

"'UFO: Target Earth' Given Boost via TV Campaign." *Boxoffice*. 106, no. 8 (December 2, 1974): E8. https://www.proquest.com/docview/1476158678/citation/8DC66378CF564EAEPQ/1.

"Use This Coupon to Request One of Ted Owens' SI Discs." Saucerian Publications, May 1969.

U.S. Department of Health, Education, and Welfare, Anthony J. Celebrezze, and Luther L. Terry. *Vital Statistics of the United States, 1960*. Vol. 3, *Marriage and Divorce*. Washington, DC, 1964. https://www.cdc.gov/nchs/data/vsus/mgdv60_3.pdf.

Vallee, Jacques. "Anatomy of a Hoax: The Philadelphia Experiment Fifty Years Later." *Journal of Scientific Exploration* 8, no. 1 (1994): 47–71.

Villard, James D. "The 'R. E. Straith' Case." *Saucers* 6, no. 4 (Winter 1958–Winter 1959): 2–6. https://n2t.net/ark:/13960/t9b64jj55.

"W. Va. Manager Finds Use for Stereo Sound System." *Boxoffice* 104, no. 19 (February 25, 1974): 22.

Wald, Alan M. *The New York Intellectuals: The Rise and Decline of the Anti-Stalinist Left from the 1930s to the 1980s*. 30th anniversary ed. Chapel Hill: University of North Carolina Press, 2017.

Walker, Jesse. *The United States of Paranoia: A Conspiracy Theory*. New York: Harper Perennial, 2014.

Wallace, Richard E. Review of *Gray Barker's Book of Saucers*, by Gray Barker. *Saucer News* 13, no. 1 (whole no. 63) (March 1966): 15.

Wamsley, Jeff. *Mothman . . . : Behind the Red Eyes, the Complete Investigative Library*. Point Pleasant, WV: Mothman Press, 2005.

"Wanted: Get Well Wishes for: Gray Barker & Orville Beckley." *UFO Review*, no. 20 (1984): 6. https://n2t.net/ark:/13960/t6wx5c58c.

Warburg, Fredric. *All Authors Are Equal: The Publishing Life of Frederic Warburg, 1936–1971*. New York: St. Martin's, 1974.

Warner, Harry. *All Our Yesterdays: An Informal History of Science Fiction Fandom in the 1940s*, edited by Joe D. Siclari. Framingham, MA: NESFA, 2004.

Warner, Harry. *A Wealth of Fable: An Informal History of Science Fiction Fandom in the 1950s*. 2nd ed. Van Nuys, CA: Scifi Press, 1992.

Weatherspark. "Elkins 1963 Past Weather (West Virginia, United States)," n.d. https://weatherspark .com/h/y/19634/1963/Historical-Weather-during-1963-in-Elkins-West-Virginia-United-States.

Weaver, Bob. "'Exchange' Faded from Glory: Braxton Ghost Town." Hur Herald, February 23, 2024. https://www.hurherald.com/obits.php?id=74926.

Webb, David F. *1973—Year of the Humanoids: An Analysis of the Fall, 1973 UFO/Humanoid Wave*. Evanston, IL: Center for UFO Studies, 1976. http://www.cufos.org/books/1973-Year_of _the_Humanoids.pdf.

"West Virginia." *Boxoffice* 107, no. 26 (October 6, 1975): E-7. http://www.proquest.com/docview /1476157195/citation/CBA9EF9A873F4737PQ/1.

"West Virginia." *Boxoffice* 109, no. 18 (August 9, 1976): E-5. https://www.yumpu.com/en /document/view/31907487/boxoffice-august091976.

Weston, Kath. *Long Slow Burn: Sexuality and Social Science*. New York: Routledge, 1998.

Whispers from Space. Directed by Ralph Coon. [West Virginia?]: The Last Prom, 1995.

White, C. Todd. "Drama, Power and Politics: ONE Magazine, Mattachine Review and The Ladder in the Era of Homophile Activism." In *Gay Press, Gay Power: The Growth of LGBT Community Newspapers in America*, edited by Tracy Baim, 141–152. Chicago: Prairie Avenue Productions / Windy City Media Group, 2012.

"White Masters Ceremonies for Show Featuring Vocals, Minstrel, Style." *Glenville Mercury*, May 7, 1946, 1.

Whitsel, Brad. "Walter Siegmeister's Inner-Earth Utopia." *Utopian Studies* 12, no. 2 (December 2001): 82–102. https://www.jstor.org/stable/20718317.

Wilfong, Eunice. "Freshman Ohnimgohow Pledge Scores with Parody on 'Man with the Hoe.'" *Glenville Mercury*, January 19, 1943, 4.

Wilkins, Harold T. "Is Mr. Scully a Cynic?" *Saucer News* 2, no. 6 (whole no. 12) (July 1955): 14–17.

Williamson, George Hunt. "The Silence Group." *Saucerian Bulletin* 1, no. 5 (whole no. 11) (November 1956): 6.

Williamson, George Hunt, and John McCoy. *UFOs Confidential!* [Corpus Christi, TX]: Essene, 1958.

Willis, Walt. "The Harp that Once or Twice." *Oopsla*, no. 23 (November 1957): 10–13. https:// fanac.org/fanzines/Oopsla/Oopsla23.pdf.

Withers, Alexander Scott. *Chronicles of Border Warfare, or, A History of the Settlement by the Whites, of North-Western Virginia; and of the Indian Wars and Massacres, in That Section of the State; with Reflections, Anecdotes, &c.* Clarksburg, WV: Joseph Israel, 1831. https://n2t.net/ark:/13960/t2q59506z.

Womack, Jack. *Flying Saucers Are Real!: The UFO Library of Jack Womack*, edited by Michael P. Daley, Johan Kugelberg, and Gabriel Mckee. New York: Anthology Editions, 2016.

X, Elizabeth. "Laura Charlotte (Mundo) Marxer (1913–1989)." Wikitree, May 30, 2022. https://www.wikitree.com/wiki/Mundo-10.

X, Michael. *The Rainbow City and the Inner Earth People.* Clarksburg, WV: Saucerian Books, 1969.

Young, Kevin. *Bunk: The Rise of Hoaxes, Humbug, Plagiarists, Phonies, Post-Facts, and Fake News.* Minneapolis: Graywolf, 2017.

Yurevich, Liavon. "Ted Bloecher Papers, 1950–2000." New York Public Library Archives & Manuscripts, 2013. https://archives.nypl.org/mss/5984.

Zarkon 2. "Ray Stanford Uncensored." *The Truth Uncensored* (blog), November 21, 2009. http://the-truth-uncensored.blogspot.com/2009/11/ray-stanford-is-researcher-of-things.html.

Zinsstag, Lou, and Timothy Good. *George Adamski: The Untold Story; the Latest and Most Complete Evidence on the First Man to Claim That Extraterrestrials Live among Us.* Beckenham: Ceti, 1983.

Zirger, Michel, and Maurizio Martinelli. *The Incredible Life of George Hunt Williamson: Mystical Journey, Itinerary of a Privileged UFO Witness*, edited by Warren P. Aston. Baiso: Verdechiaro Edizioni, 2016.

Index

140, 154, 172, 177, 200, 205, 222, 226, 253n27, 254n40, 256n85, 291n56

Trip to the Moon, 20, 240n63

UFO Annual 1981, 208

UFO 96, 81, 138–139, 184

Who Knows, 15–17, 32, 239n40

Youranus, 74, 87–89, 138–139, 260nn51–52

writing by, 13–20, 28–33, 36–37, 49–52, 55–56, 62–63, 67–71, 74, 88–89, 98–99, 103, 116–118, 142–144, 160–161, 172–186, 193, 200–201, 217, 222–223

Barker, Henry, 10

Barker, Jimmy, 223

Barker, Joe, 213, 223

Barker, Lela, 10, 237n17

Barker, Marie, 10

Barker, Rosa, 10, 12, 55

Barker, Walter, 10, 12, 130, 237n17

Barkun, Michael, 8, 70, 236n30

Barnum, P. T., 229, 266n13

Barton, Michael X. *See* Michael X

Batman (TV program), 151, 279n24

Batterham, Ian, 235n24

Baxter, Marla. *See* Menger, Connie

Beasley, H. P., 45, 116

Beckley, Timothy Green, 144, 154, 158–160, 167, 201–202, 209, 219

Bell, Book and Candle (film), 97

Bender, Albert, 28, 33–44, 51, 54–55, 58, 69–71, 83, 86, 89, 111, 113–116, 121–123, 126, 154, 177–178, 200–201, 218, 242n29, 245n40, 246n45, 247n66, 269n1, 270n7, 270n12, 292n63

Bender Mystery. *See* Men in Black

Benign, Bernard. *See* Stupple, David

Bennett, Gillian, 234n13

Bennewitz, Paul, 296n11

Bensen, Donald, 154

Berlitz, Charles, 193, 205, 209, 219, 294n102

Bernard, Raymond, 166–167, 190–191, 285n37

Bethurum, Truman, 48–50, 99–100, 115, 135, 152, 163, 207, 228

B.I.C.R. hoax, 161–162, 283n12

Bielek, Al, 225

Binder, Otto, 147

Birth of a Nation (film), 135

Blake, Joseph, 233n4

Blavatsky, Helena, 218, 297n19

Blodgett, Charlotte, 63

Bloecher, Ted, 53–54, 72–73, 120, 241n1, 250n37, 254n43, 261n69, 261n73

Bob & Kay Show (radio program), 73

Boxoffice (magazine), 18–20, 32–33, 111, 119, 131, 242n24

Branton. *See* Walton, Bruce

Brasington, Virginia, 136, 155, 277n136

Braxton County, WV, 9–10, 13. *See also* Exchange, WV; Flatwoods, WV; Sutton, WV

Braxton County Chamber of Commerce, 155

Brazil, 167

Brewer, Jack, 257n6

Bridgeport, CT, 28, 44

British Book Centre, 63

Britton, Mae, 272n49

Brother from Another Planet (film), 223

Brother Philip. *See* Williamson, George Hunt

Brown, Bridget, 235n19

Brown, Hugh, 70

Brown, Marmel, 12

Brown, T. Townsend, 79

Brunvand, Jan Harold, 226

Brush Creek, CA, 69, 114

Brynner, Yul, 110

BSRA (Borderland Sciences Research Associates), 28, 44, 48–49, 242n23, 294n102

Buckhannon, WV, 190, 196

Buckley, Jennings "Red," 180–181

Bullard, Thomas, 4, 233n8, 235n13

Burden, Brian, 45

Weber, Connie. *See* Menger, Connie

Webster, Robert. *See* Palmer, Ray

Wentworth, Frank, 181

Wentworth, Ida, 181

Werner Laurie (publisher), 86, 97

West, Ota, 190

Weston State Hospital, 118–119

When Worlds Collide (film), 28, 56

Whispers From Space (film), 7, 256n76, 279n20

Whiting, Hunter, 17, 36

WHK (radio station), 73

Whritenour, Joan, 191, 218

Wilkins, Harold, 57

Wilkinson, Bob, 7

Wilkinson, Doreen, 55, 64, 69, 125–130

Williams, Tennessee, 110

Williamson, Betty Jane, 269n61

Williamson, George Hunt, 45, 48–49, 64, 87, 111, 247n67, 260n51, 269n61

Willis, Walt, 259n43

Wilson, John C. *See* Morrow, Felix

Wilt, Richard, 296n6

WNYC (radio station), 77

Womack, Jack, 2, 30

Wonderama (TV program), 72

WOR-TV, 107

Worldcon (World Science Fiction Convention), 37–38, 84–86, 90, 244n24, 259nn40–41

World Contact Day, 113–114, 269n5

World War II, 13, 24, 26, 104, 238n23

WPDX (radio station), 36

Wrestling, professional, 229, 300n36

Xerography, 6, 213, 296n6

X-Files, 223

X, Michael, 167–168, 191, 285n42

Yankee, Stephen, 191

Young, Kevin, 229

Zagga of the Galactic Tribunal, 168

Zamora, Lonnie, 145, 147

Zayron, 155

Ziegler, Charles, 5, 208, 233n7

Ziegler, Robert, 140

Zirger, Michel, 269n61

Zodiac (planet), 172